A WET ASS AND A HUNGRY GUT

Half a Century of Stories from the White River Valley

BY DANNY W. CAMPBELL

Danny, age sixteen, along with his dad, 1964.
PHOTO BY BETTY CAMPBELL

LIFETIME CHRONICLE PRESS/dba
LONDON PUBLISHING
Montrose, CO

The names of persons mentioned in this book may or may not have been changed to protect their identities.

© 2012 Danny W. Campbell
All rights reserved in whole or in part.

First Edition
Printed in the United States of America
ISBN: 978-0-9834423-3-2
Library of Congress Control Number: 2011937562

Cover and book design by Laurie Goralka Design

Front cover: Danny's dad fishing at Trappers Lake, fifty miles east of Meeker, Colorado.
Back cover: The White River as viewed from Circle Park bridge, Meeker, Colorado, on an early fall morning.
Photos by Danny W. Campbell

Lifetime Chronicle Press/dba
London Publishing
10614 Bostwick Park Rd.
Montrose, CO 81401
970-240-1153
chronicle@montrose.net
www.londonpublishing.net

DEDICATION

*I dedicate this book to Mary M. Hartwig,
my best friend, lover, and soul mate.*

ACKNOWLEDGMENTS

I extend a special thanks to Carole London, owner of Lifetime Chronicle Press, and to the editor, Bonnie Beach. Without their encouragement, *A Wet Ass and a Hungry Gut* would've taken years longer to come to fruition.

And a very special thanks goes to Mary Hartwig, who helped me brainstorm through many years of working and reworking this book, which we nicknamed "The Project." Her advice, patience, and love were priceless, and I wouldn't have done it without her. What a ride!

—Danny W. Campbell

TABLE OF CONTENTS

Chapter One
A Boy and His Hero 1

Chapter Two
Memorable Times 15

Chapter Three
A Family Crisis 38

Chapter Four
A Room with a View. 51

Chapter Five
Life Goes On 60

Chapter Six
Tragedy Strikes 70

Chapter Seven
The Letter 87

Chapter Eight
A Casualty of War 111

Chapter Nine
Anchors Away! 133

Chapter Ten
Home At Last 156

Chapter Eleven
A Chance Encounter 165

Chapter Twelve
The Temptress 175

Chapter Thirteen
The Chickens Come Home to Roost 187

Chapter Fourteen
The Transfer to Hell 216

Chapter Fifteen
An Angel Named Mary 228

Chapter Sixteen
Riding the Rails 257

Chapter Seventeen
Passages 270

CHAPTER ONE

A Boy and His Hero

"GET DOWN!" WE ALL DROPPED TO OUR KNEES, and Dad quietly worked the lever on his rifle, putting a live round into the chamber. He then put the rifle to his shoulder and took aim. I slid over to my right to see what he would be shooting. Oh, God! There was a big buck not far away, walking directly towards us, his large antlers glistening in the bright sunlight. *Boom*! I jumped when Dad pulled the trigger on his .300 Savage, a sound so loud that it shattered the morning's silence and echoed across the valley below us.

Dad yanked the lever down on the rifle to kick out the empty and put a live round in the chamber, then he put the safety on. The deer was no longer in sight. We all got to our feet and I said, "Did you get him, Dad?" He said, "Well, I'm sure that I hit him." We cautiously walked up the trail and soon spotted where the buck had been when Dad fired. There was a lot of blood on the snow, and the tracks headed towards a grove of aspen. We only walked a few feet when Dad said, "There he is." I could see a large, dark-gray body lying on its side about twenty yards away, an antler sticking up. Dad told us to stay where we were until he made sure the deer was dead.

I was just eight years old, and Mom wasn't happy about my hunting trip with Dad. I'd heard her say, "Don, I think Danny's too young to go with you." "Ah, Betty," he said, "don't worry. I'll take care of him." The four of us—Dad, Mom, my four-year-old sister, Donna, and I—had just moved to Meeker, population 1,500, in May from Yuma, Colorado. And I was so excited! This was my first time to go with Dad, and after all the stories I'd heard, I couldn't wait to get out in the forest and see the elk, deer, and whatever else we might encounter. Uncle Cal's son—my cousin,

Larry—was twelve, and he had come along with us. He hadn't been hunting yet, either, and in the days before opening day of big game season, we'd enjoyed guessing about what we thought might happen. It was mid-October 1956, and we had driven to the eastern branch of Big Beaver Creek, about thirty miles east of Meeker, at four this morning.

Minutes later, Dad called, "Come on, boys." Larry and I walked over to the deer, watching Dad remove the live shell from his gun and lean the rifle against a tree. I walked to the buck's head and stared at his huge antlers, four large points on each side. The horns had a dark-brown color except for the very tips of the points, which were white. Larry said, "Boy, Don, the buck is a *monster*!" Dad said, "Yeah, it's the biggest I've ever gotten." I'd only seen deer at a distance in the hayfields near Meeker, and I didn't realize how big they were. This animal had a huge body! I walked over to Dad and patted him on the arm, saying, "You did it, Dad!" He was my hero, and I was so proud of him.

Dad pulled his hunting knife from the leather sheath on his belt and cut the deer's throat, the snow turning crimson with blood. He handed me the knife to hold, then he took the deer's front leg and repositioned him to where he was laying on his back. He then had me hold the front leg to keep the deer in that position, and Larry held one of the hind legs as Dad knelt down between the buck's back legs. I handed Dad his knife, and he began to remove the genitals. I watched as he carefully poked the knife through the skin near the pelvic area. He told us, "You don't want the knife to go too deep. If it does, you'll cut into the guts and have a hell of a mess." He applied some pressure to the knife and started working his way towards the chest. When he got to that area, he told me to lean out of the way but to continue holding the front leg. He gripped the knife with both hands and, after several strong pulls, he managed to cut through the tough brisket. Laying the knife down, he straddled the deer, reached up and grabbed the windpipe, and started pulling. A few minutes later, the guts were laying on the ground. Dad dragged them several feet away and commented, "The coyotes will probably be dining on these by the time darkness sets in." Then he once again knelt by the deer's hind legs: with his left hand, he pushed his hunting knife straight down to the center of the pelvic bone then pounded the top of the knife's handle until it passed through the bone. He would pull the knife out, barely move it, then repeat the process. *Snap!* The bone finally split wide open and allowed the remainder of the blood in the cavity

Chapter One: A Boy and His Hero

to drain out. The three of us then dragged the deer a few feet so it'd be in the shade.

Dad washed his hands in the snow, trying to get the blood off them. Larry and I did the same, although we had very little blood on us. I think it made us feel like we were big game hunters!

It was about 10:00 a.m. by now, so we decided to sit down on a log and have some snacks. While we were eating, I spotted a hunter walking towards us, and I alerted Dad and Larry. A few moments later, he walked up to us and said, "Good morning. Looks like you had some luck." Dad stood up and said, "We sure did." The guy then introduced himself—his name was Bob—and Dad did the same, then added, "And this is my son, Danny, and my nephew, Larry." Bob walked over to the buck and said, "I've done a lot of hunting over the years, but that mule deer has the biggest body I've ever seen." Then he looked at the antlers. "What a big, beautiful rack!" He asked Dad if that was his flat-bed Chevy parked above the beaver ponds, and Dad told him it was. He said that he'd parked his Jeep there, too, and that he'd be glad to go get it and help us haul out our deer. Hearing this, Dad smiled and said, "Boy, we'd really appreciate your help. I was going to have to drive back to town to have one of my friends bring their Jeep. I knew that I couldn't get my two-wheel-drive truck back to this area." Bob said, "I'll go get my Jeep and be back."

While we waited, the forest was filled with our laughter. We were all so happy about the hunt! About an hour later, Bob returned with his half-cab Willys Jeep and, lucky for us, he was able to drive within fifty yards of the deer. Bob got hold of one side of the deer's antlers, Dad grabbed the other side, and Larry had one of the hind legs as they guided the deer down the snow-covered trail. A few minutes later, after some grunts and groans, we managed to get the buck loaded into the back of the Jeep. Bob used his rope to tie the deer's head up so it wouldn't drag on the ground. Dad got into the cab with his gear, and Larry and I crawled up on the deer and found a sitting place.

Bob started the Jeep and said, "Hold on, boys, we're headin' out." The snow was now starting to melt and the Jeep was sliding around in the mud. A few minutes later, we drove into a large stand of huge pine trees. When we came out into an open area, I could see some beaver ponds below us, then I spotted Dad's old pickup sitting on the knoll where we'd parked. Bob shifted gears, and soon we were driving down a very steep hill. Once we got to the bottom, we crossed above the beaver ponds and, a moment later, parked near the pickup. After loading the deer onto its bed, Dad and Bob used the rope to make sure the buck was tied down.

Soon, Bob left to resume his hunt and we headed for town. At home, Dad pulled into the alley and backed up to our old barn, which was located next door to Uncle Cal's house. Uncle Cal was Mom's uncle, and it was just him and Larry now, as Uncle Cal's wife had passed away when Larry was a very young boy. Cal heard the noise and came over to see what was going on. He smiled and said, "Looks like you guys did really well!" I ran to the house to tell Mom and Donna, and they followed me back to the barn to see the deer. Mom was happy that we'd gotten him, since it cut down on the grocery bill, and we always needed the meat. She worked hard each summer, washing and ironing other people's laundry, in order to make extra money for groceries and other needs. The venison was always welcome.

Once we got the deer off the truck, Dad cut the legs off at the knee joints. We dragged the animal to the barn, where he attached a meat hook to each leg and hoisted it into the air with a chain and come-along. Next, the deer was skinned to the neck, then Dad used a hand-held meat saw to cut off its head. Cal helped hold the buck steady while Dad used the saw to split the deer in half, going down the middle of the backbone. After all this was done, Mom brought a bucket of cold water, rags, a couple of sheets, and safety pins so she and Cal could clean both halves of the deer and wrap and secure them in the sheets.

Dad got a tape measure to see how wide the buck's antlers were. He put the end of the tape on the outside edge of one antler and stretched it across to the far edge of the other one. Twenty-eight inches! The four points on each side were all about the same, measuring eleven inches in length. Cal asked me if I wanted to save the horns, and I said, "Yeah!" He knelt down by the deer's head with the meat saw and carefully cut off the antlers, handing them to me.

I was glad Cal had asked about giving me the horns. It was a big rack, and I thought maybe I could have them mounted someday with a nice board as the background. Even at eight years old, I knew that finances were always an issue in our family; Dad couldn't afford to mount the antlers right now, but maybe I could when I got older.

After we all walked out of the barn, Dad placed a padlock on the door. As Cal and Larry walked back to their house, Larry called to us that he'd come over early the next morning to go hunting again.

Chapter One: A Boy and His Hero

At the supper table, Mom asked, "Are you tired, Son?" I hadn't thought about it—I'd been so excited from the whole day—but I *was* tired. She told me to take a bath when I finished eating, as she wanted me in bed no later than nine. I smiled and said, "You don't have to worry about that, Mom." As I crawled into bed, I reflected on my day, the most exciting of my life! My hero—my dad—had given me a wonderful memory that I would cherish forever.

The next morning, I felt Dad's hand on my shoulder, gently shaking me. He whispered, "Are you ready to go elk hunting?" I stretched and said, "Yeah, Dad!"

I quickly got up and dressed, then went to the kitchen for my cup of hot chocolate that Dad had fixed for me. He was sitting in the living room, drinking his coffee and smoking a Roi-Tan cigar. I heard Mom call from the bedroom, telling me that our lunch was on the bottom shelf in the refrigerator. I went to the bedroom door to say good morning to her. Even at my age, I knew Mom as my best confidante, and I told her secrets I could never tell Dad. But Dad was the one who I enjoyed doing things with outdoors—especially hunting!

I soon heard a knock at the front door. Looking out, I saw it was Larry and let him in. After we all finished our drinks, we got on our jackets, loaded all of the hunting gear and lunch things into the truck, then headed for Big Beaver again. The headlights on Dad's '49 Chevy pierced the darkness of the cold black morning; when we got to the turnoff to East Big Beaver, we put the chains on the rear tires once again, as it had snowed another four inches overnight. About an hour later, we arrived at the knoll where we had parked the morning before.

The early-morning air was so refreshing—crisp and cold—and the sky was filled with thousands of twinkling stars. We poured ourselves cups of hot chocolate from our thermos bottles and Dad poured himself a cup of coffee. Moments later, the flame on his Zippo lighter danced in the darkness as he lit one of his cigars.

Bang! I jumped at a loud noise, almost spilling my hot chocolate. I asked Dad what it was, and he said that it was just a beaver in the ponds below us, slapping his tail in warning on the water.

Soon, the eastern sky started to lighten: it was nearly dawn. Dad said softly, "Let's go, boys." I grabbed our lunch sack and binoculars and Larry and I got out of the pickup. Dad loaded his rifle, putting some extra shells into the pocket of his red-and-black wool coat, then we took off down the steep hillside toward the valley below. I hadn't really noticed the beaver ponds the morning before; a storm had just ended and they were hidden under the snow, and even now, they were still partially covered with snow and ice. Where the creek ran in was a lot of open water—probably where Mr. Beaver had made the loud bang. Across the valley, the pine trees towered, their boughs heavy with snow, and a few minutes later, we crossed a beaver dam over wet, slippery logs. On the other side, we reached a game trail that led us uphill into the aspens.

The sun's rays now edged their way over the distant peaks, the bright sunlight on the powdery snow making the tiny crystals sparkle like diamonds. After we'd walked about a mile and a half, we came to a place of sheer beauty: far below was the White River Valley, stretches of its river visible as it wound its way down the canyon. Towards the northeast, there were some high peaks, and I asked Dad if they had names. He pointed out Sleepy Cat, Sand Peak, and Pagoda Peak. Directly below us were large stands of pines and aspen. On the other side of the trees was a snow-covered meadow. What a wonderful place!

We spent a long day hunting, walking several miles without seeing any elk. We did find some tracks where a herd had crossed during the night. The hoofprints were huge, so much bigger than those of the buck's. As the sun neared the western horizon, Dad said that we'd better start walking back to the pickup. By the time we got there, it was nearly dark, and the temperature had dropped sharply. After loading our things, Dad started the engine and lit himself a new cigar, and we headed up the road. We hadn't traveled far when he turned on the headlights and the heater...the heat felt so good! After a stop at the highway to take the chains off, we traveled the twenty-mile stretch of paved road towards Meeker in silence. We were all tired from getting up so early and walking several miles.

Monday morning, Larry and I returned to school and Dad went back to work at Harp Transportation, a small trucking company that received freight from Denver. Dad and his coworkers would sort the freight at the dock and deliver it to local businesses in Meeker and the surrounding towns, including Craig, Rifle, and Rangely. The company also hauled sheep and cattle in the spring and fall. Larry's dad—Cal—worked for Kennedy Chevrolet as a mechanic.

When I got to school, I quickly found some of my friends and told them the story about the big buck. By the time the afternoon school bell

Chapter One: *A Boy and His Hero*

rang, I'd probably told it at least six times. A few days later, when I got home from school, I found Cal and Mom in the kitchen, cutting up the deer. Mom explained to me that we couldn't afford to take it to the locker plant and have it processed, so we had to do it at home ourselves. Cal had one of the hindquarters laying on a big wooden cutting board that was on the kitchen table. He told me that he'd just taken it out of the deep freeze, where he'd placed it a few hours earlier to freeze slightly. That way, the meat wasn't soft and he could get a straight cut. I watched him carefully cut the meat away from the large leg bone, creating a very large boneless slab.

Cal said it was very important to have a sharp knife when cutting meat, so he got out what he called a "steel" to put an edge on the knife. The ten-inch-long steel was fluted, tapered from handle to tip. He wiped the knife down with a damp rag then rapidly slid the blade full length from handle to tip down one side of the steel then the other. Besides the steel, he also used a small gray-colored, rectangular-shaped brick called a "whetstone" to sharpen the knives.

After Cal finished sharpening the knife, I watched him cut steaks. It was amazing, because with one gentle stroke, he'd have a perfect steak that was about a half-inch thick. It wasn't long before he had carved up the entire hindquarter. Mom placed the big pile of beautiful steaks on the other end of the table and started wrapping them in freezer paper. She told me that they'd already cut the rest of the deer into half-inch-thick chops using the hand-held meat saw, and they'd also cut some nice roasts. Mom had a big dishpan full of scrap meat that she was going to take down to the local butcher shop to have ground into hamburger.

Later that evening, I watched Mom place some steak on the cutting board and use a small hand-held device with points on it to pound the meat, tenderizing it. She prepared a great meal with very tender-fried deer steak, mashed potatoes and gravy, cream-style corn, salad, and homemade rolls. *Mmmm!* This became one of my favorite meals that I would enjoy in the years to come.

By late November, the snow and cold had arrived in the White River Valley and, in December, it started to get down to twenty and thirty below zero. Mom prepared many a great meal with the deer meat, and another new favorite of mine was Swiss steak. She would tenderize the steak, dip it in flour, then brown both sides in a skillet of hot grease. The meat was then placed in a roaster and covered with canned tomatoes, sliced onions, and bell peppers. With the lid on, the roaster was put into the oven for an hour or so. Along with the steak, we'd have boiled potatoes, salad, and another vegetable. What a meal to have on a cold winter night!

The first week of September 1957, the school bells rang across the small town of Meeker. I was now a fourth grader, and my routine quickly settled into going to and from school, doing my studies, and visiting with Cal and Larry next door. Sometimes, when I'd get home in the afternoon, Mom would be drinking beer from a plastic glass and her speech would be a little slurred. There were also some nights when, after my sister and I went to bed, I'd hear Dad telling Mom that he wanted her to slow down on her drinking. This often led to big arguments that always made me feel confused and sad. Mom was a beautiful black-haired, brown-eyed, twenty-eight-year-old woman, and I loved her with all my heart. But it really bothered me to see her drunk. Dad drank beer, too, but he usually just had a few on the weekends. There were times that I wished I had someone to talk to about Mom's drinking and the arguments, but my sister was too young, and I was ashamed to say anything to any adult, including my schoolteachers.

But it was time for hunting season again, and my attention quickly became focused on that. Mom had saved up enough money to buy Dad and me new hunting boots, which we really needed. The days seemed to drag, but—finally—the last Sunday in September arrived, and we got up early to drive up the White River Valley to scout our hunting country.

We got to our parking place about 9:00 a.m., and I jumped out of the pickup to run over to the edge of the knoll and look at the beaver ponds. The hillsides across from me looked as though they were painted with beautiful fall colors, the aspens dipped in brilliant orange, yellow, and gold. A few minutes later, we had packed our lunch stuff and begun the hike back into our hunting country. Down the hillside and across the beaver dam we went, where I noticed the animals had chewed down several aspens. A stiff gust of wind greeted us as we crested the game trail, sending thousands of leaves showering to the ground. What a beautiful day!

Chapter One: A Boy and His Hero

We arrived at the big meadow just minutes later, then turned south to walk to another beaver pond to see if the elk were watering there. We came across some droppings that were quite fresh, so we knew they were nearby. After checking around the pond, we headed northeast toward what we called "the big valley." The White River wound its way down the canyon there, and we could see quite a distance.

After about an hour, we arrived at the big valley and decided to sit down, rest, and enjoy the spectacular view. I got a Pepsi out from the lunch bag and Dad lit his cigar, its smoke trailing off with a slight breeze. *Ooooeeee, uh-uh-uh!* I sat up with a start when I heard these sounds break the silence. I asked Dad what it was, and he said that it was a bull elk bugling. "It's mating season—called 'rut'—for the elk, and the bulls bugle to call cows and to challenge other bulls," he said. "Sometimes the bulls fight each other in order to control an entire herd of cows, and sometimes one big bull might have as many as twenty-five in his 'harem,' what you call their herd of gals. Many bulls lose weight during rut because of having to defend their territories," he continued. He also said that as the bulls age, they get more points on their antlers. When a bull is three or four years old, he'll usually have six points on each side, and if they live long enough, some of them may even have seven points per side. Older bulls could have even more mass on their antlers, such as the huge bull that a friend of his had gotten a few years ago. Dad was a good teacher, and I enjoyed learning about game, elk in particular. Within minutes, the bull elk let another bugle rip—*ooooeeee, uh-uh-uh!*—and it echoed across the canyon.

I kept watching the valley below us where the sound was coming from, hoping and praying that we'd get to see the bull elk. After watching for about thirty minutes, Dad said, "Look in the meadow, by the dark timber." I quickly picked up the binoculars and started glassing the meadow. I spotted a herd of elk—all cows—and looked hard for the bull. I told Dad there were seven cows, but the bull was missing. He reminded me to be patient—to just keep watching. And all of a sudden, a large blond-colored elk—a big bull elk—walked out into the meadow! He was too far away to count the points, but he had a big rack. My heart was about to pound out of my chest; my first bull elk! He followed the cows across the meadow and they all disappeared into the dark timber. I laid the binoculars down and said, "Oh, Dad—that was quite a sight!" "Yes it was, Son," he smiled. We sat there at that breathtakingly beautiful spot, talking till late afternoon.

When I returned to school on Monday, I told my friends about seeing and hearing the big bull elk. Each day as I rode my bike to school, there were more leaves that had fallen on the sidewalks; every night, when I went to bed, I'd think about that bull elk, and I was counting the days until hunting season began.

Finally, on a Saturday morning, I felt Dad's hand on my shoulder. I rose up on my elbow and he whispered, "Are you ready to go elk hunting?" I said, "You bet, Dad." I got out of bed and glanced at my clock: it was 3:00 a.m. After getting dressed, I went to the living room, where Dad was enjoying his coffee and cigar. As he greeted me, I said, "I really had a hard time getting to sleep, Dad." "I didn't get much sleep myself," he responded. I guess we were both excited! I went on into the kitchen, poured a cup of hot chocolate, then went back to the living room. We sat at the table, talking in hushed voices while we both enjoyed the early morning. About thirty minutes later, Larry came to the door. It was time to go! We gathered our hunting gear and lunch stuff, then—as I was walking across the living room with our thermos bottles—I heard Mom's voice from the bedroom: "Good luck!" I said back to her, still in a hushed voice, "Thanks, Mom."

At about six, we arrived at our parking place on Big Beaver. Larry and I had some hot chocolate while Dad poured himself a cup of coffee and lit a new cigar. We sat in the darkness and talked in low voices; outside, it was stone quiet. A short time later the eastern sky started to lighten, so we got out. Dad loaded his rifle, putting extra shells in his coat pocket, and I got the binoculars; Larry grabbed our canvas lunch sack. We headed down the trail beyond the beaver ponds and towards our hunting country.

Just moments later, a herd of elk walked out on the hillside about a hundred yards from us. With the bright morning sun shining on them, they really stood out. I looked through the binoculars and counted seven cows. As they started walking into the nearby aspens, another elk appeared. I whispered to Dad, "It's a *bull!*" I watched him click off the rifle's safety and take careful aim. *Boom!* He shot and the elk went down.

I was so excited that my hands shook and I could hear my heart pound in my ears. Dad pulled the lever down on his .300 Savage, kicked out the empty, and put another live round in. Larry whispered, "Good shot, Don." Then I yelled, "Let's go, Dad!" He said that we needed to wait to make sure the elk stayed down. I kept watching it in the binoculars, praying that it didn't get up. We waited about ten minutes then started walking towards it. I got to him first and was really surprised at the size of the body: it was so much bigger than the buck Dad got last fall. Its legs were longer, the hooves much larger than I imagined, and the hindquarters were *huge*! Although it was just a spike bull, with only one large point on each side, it could've just as well been a seven-point bull to me.

Dad took the live round from the chamber of his rifle and leaned it against a tree. Larry gave him a pat on the back and congratulated him, and I gave him a big hug. "Thanks, boys," he said, "but it was just shithouse luck." We all started laughing! Then it was time to get serious. Dad pulled out his hunting knife and cut the animal's throat, and we helped slide the bull around so the hindquarters were on the downhill side. Because the elk was so much larger than the buck, it took more time to gut it, and everything in general was more difficult. Once Dad was finished, he showed us where the bullet had hit—just behind the right shoulder, where it had passed through the lungs.

It'd taken about thirty minutes to complete the gutting process, and it was now 8:30. We dragged the elk a short distance down the hillside to a shady spot in a small grove of pine trees. Dad told us that the elk needed to be kept in a cool place, and this was perfect.

We gathered up our things and started walking down the trail towards the pickup. We stopped at a nearby pond to wash our hands. *Brrrr!* The water was cold! We got to the pickup about 9:30 and headed to town so Dad could get his friends who owned a Jeep to come back and help load the elk. When we got home, it was decided that it would be best to take the elk to Purkey's Processing Plant, because it would be too much work for Mom and Cal to cut it up. It was about noon now, and Dad's friends came to pick him up. They returned at five, stopping at the house to show Mom and Cal the elk before taking it to Purkey's outside of Meeker.

We continued hunting every weekend, and Dad also got a nice three-point buck. It had been a great hunting season for us, and after Mom and Cal cut and wrapped the buck, our deep freeze was nearly full.

Within a few weeks, the White River Valley was covered with snow and it was very cold. It was definitely wintertime! Many evenings, while I was doing homework, the house would be filled with the smells of Mom's cooking. I now had a new favorite meal—chicken-fried elk steak—along with the side dishes I liked best: mashed potatoes and gravy, cream-style corn, salad, and Mom's delicious homemade rolls—all so very good!

I had asked Mom several times if she'd get me a BB gun for Christmas. It was what I wanted more than anything. You know…my friends already had theirs and talked about shooting them all the time. I figured I was overdue, and I'd been really patient. I even did chores around the house when Mom asked me to!

As Christmas got closer, Mom put up the tree and spent lots of time decorating it. This year, she put all blue lights on it, and when we plugged them in at night, it was so beautiful! On Christmas Eve, I snooped through all the presents beneath the tree, but I couldn't find a long box that I thought might have my BB gun in it.

When I woke up the next morning, I could still smell the cinnamon rolls Mom had baked the night before. It was 5:00 a.m., and the house was dark and completely quiet. I got out of bed, dressed, then quietly walked into the living room where the Christmas tree stood. As I plugged in the tree lights, I could see there were lots of presents—more than there'd been the night before! Some were long, too, but they didn't have my name on them. Finally, I spotted a box leaning up against the wall and scrambled over to get it. It had my name on it, and I tore the wrapping paper off. Oh, God! The writing on the box said, "Daisy BB gun"!

My heart was racing as I opened the end of the box and pulled out the rifle. It was a beauty! I put it to my shoulder—it was so light and easy to handle—and pointed it towards the big picture window. What a thrill!

Then I heard Mom say, "Merry Christmas!" I turned around—she was just a few feet away—and I ran over and gave her a big hug, then smiled and said, "Thanks so much, Mom!" She beamed at me in return. A few minutes later, Dad and my sister walked into the living room. Excitedly, I showed Dad the BB gun and thanked him, too. Donna was less interested; she was still too young to understand how important it was to me. We all started opening our presents then, and Donna got the doll she wanted. All I remember about it is that it had brown curly hair.

Although it was still very cold outside at 9:00 a.m., I couldn't wait any longer to go shoot my new BB gun. I got a tube of BBs and loaded it, then put on my hooded winter coat, got an empty milk carton from the trash to use as a target, and went out the back door. I waded through the snow to the coal shed and decided to place the carton near it. Then I heard Dad say, "Make sure you're careful, Son." I turned around and he was standing just a few feet from me. I'd shot some of my friends' BB guns, so I was familiar with this model. I placed the butt of the gun between my legs, clamping them tightly around the stock, pulled the lever of the rifle out and then back down, and the gun was ready to shoot.

I brought the butt of the rifle up to my left shoulder and aimed down the iron sights at the milk carton. I pulled the trigger and—*pop*. I heard the BB hit the milk carton, which was about twenty feet from me. Dad and I walked over to see where I'd hit it. Right in the middle! I was happy with that, because it was where I'd been aiming. Dad said, "I didn't know you shot left-handed!" "It just feels better than shooting right-handed," I said. It was rather strange, because I wrote, threw a ball, and ate with my right hand. Dad watched me shoot a few more times then said, "I'm going back to the house now. Make sure you're careful!" I assured him I would be. I probably shot nearly a hundred times before I gave it up. Boy, were my hands cold!

A few hours later, we had Christmas dinner, and that night, when I crawled into bed, I quietly thanked God for such a wonderful day.

It was now 1958. The long cold winter had passed and, at the end of May, another school year was over. During the days of summer, Uncle Jake—one of Mom's many brothers who was just a year older than me—and I would go down by the river where we'd hunt frogs with my BB gun. Other days, we'd hike up to China Walls, a mountain just north of Meeker, and spend all day hunting lizards. I had learned to fish last year, and Dad and I went nearly every Sunday on the White River, catching many beautiful rainbow trout.

In August, Dad and I hiked into Lake of the Woods, a place where I'd never been before. As we walked down the trail, the mountain air was filled with the smell of pine and the sounds of bees visiting the wildflowers. After a mile, I could hear the roar of the north fork of the river, and within minutes, we crossed an old rickety, narrow-boarded bridge that spanned its waters. I was leery of the bridge, but we finally reached the bank on the other side and, after about half a mile, we arrived at the lake. Dad and I found a good-looking spot, rigged up our fishing rods, threaded the hooks with juicy night crawlers, and cast our lines as far as we could into the crystal-clear lake. As we talked, I saw my line jerk, so I jumped up, grabbed the rod, reeled up the slack, and felt the weight of a fish on the other end.

I yanked and set the hook. A couple minutes later, I landed a brook trout about twelve inches long. It was very pretty with light pink and orange spots on it. "Way to go, Son!" Dad yelled. I got our steel stringer from the tackle box, attached the fish to it, and put it in the water so it would stay cool and fresh. A few minutes later, Dad got a bite and landed another brookie about the same size. "Well, I'm glad you caught one, Dad," I teased. He smiled back at me, saying, "It sure makes a person feel good when you land the first one. That way, you know you're not going to get skunked!" We both laughed and, over the next few hours, continued to catch some nice brookies. By noon, we had a total of sixteen and decided that was enough, so we cleaned all the fish and then had our lunch.

At about 2:00 p.m., we decided it was time to go. I dreaded crossing the river on that old bridge again, and I made it across as quickly as I could, so happy to step off onto the trail. It sure scared me, but I'd spent a great day sitting on the shoreline of a high-mountain lake, visiting with my dad and taking in the beauty of the forest that surrounded us.

CHAPTER TWO

Memorable Times

IN LATE MARCH 1959, during our noon recess, a bunch of us boys were playing on some big snowbanks that'd been created when the school janitors plowed snow away from the schoolyard over the winter. I noticed that one of the sixth graders, a boy named Tommy, was playing really rough with some of the smaller boys, knocking them down. I walked over and told him that he should pick on someone his own size. We started to argue, and Tommy told me to meet him on the courthouse lawn after school, that he was going to whip my ass. The bell rang, ending recess, and when I returned to my classroom, I told a friend, Ken, what had happened. He said that I'd better be ready for one hell of a fight, because Tommy was probably the toughest boy in grade school.

When the afternoon bell rang, I spent a few minutes talking to my girlfriend, Cindy, then I walked out of school, got on my bike, and rode home. As soon as I walked through the front door, I remembered: I was supposed to meet Tommy on the courthouse lawn! I ran outside and jumped on my bike, because I knew if I didn't meet him, it'd get around school that I was a chickenshit.

I only rode a block when I spotted Tommy and two of his classmates walking towards my house. Tommy saw me and turned my direction. I slammed the brakes hard on the bike, jumped off, and let it fall onto the graveled road. As Tommy got closer, I put up my guard. No words were spoken and fists started flying. Knuckles cracked, joints popped, and for the next couple of minutes, we both landed some good blows all around the face and head.

We both gave it everything we had. Finally, we stopped and took a step back from each other, panting hard. Tommy looked at me and said, "Do you want to call it a draw?" I only thought for a moment. "Yeah," I said.

He went over to his friends, turned, and walked back the way he'd come. I noticed him shaking his right arm and hand and rubbing his head. I picked up my bike and rode towards the house. The cool spring breeze felt so good on my hot face!

When I got home, I walked into the bathroom to look in the mirror. There was some swelling above my right eye and a red spot on my left cheek, but no blood. My right hand was starting to swell and hurt like hell. I felt good, though: I hadn't backed down, and I knew that I'd gotten in some good shots on Tommy.

At the supper table, I told everyone about the fight. With a smile on his face and a gleam in his eye, Dad said, "I'm so glad you didn't back down, Son." Mom said, "I'm proud of you, Son!" They looked at each other, and I could swear that not only their lips were smiling, but their eyes, too! It was Friday night, so I said I was going to the movie to meet my girlfriend.

When I walked into the lobby at the Rio Theatre, there stood Tommy. He walked over to me and said, "That was a damn good fight, Danny." "Yeah, it was," I said. We showed each other our bumps and bruises, then Tommy extended his right hand and, as we shook hands, said, "No hard feelings?" "No hard feelings," I smiled. A few minutes later, Cindy walked in and we took our seats in the theater. When I put my arm around her and she laid her head on my shoulder, I was in heaven!

On April 16, 1959, I turned eleven years old, and by the end of June, the White River had cleared and it was time to start fishing. I asked Cal if he'd water his garden spot so I could catch some night crawlers. He said he would, so that night I caught as many as I could, keeping them in a coffee can filled with moist dirt. I told Mom and Dad that I was going to walk down to the river the next day and do some fishing on Dave Smith's property, which was about two miles from our house.

The next morning I got up around seven, got my gear organized, and walked down along the riverbank to find a fishing spot where a few large cottonwood trees had fallen into the river. Just above the trees was deep swirling water, and I knew there had to be trout in this beautiful hole. I gently cast my night crawler in and, a few minutes later—*thump, thump*—I felt the line tug: I knew I was getting a bite. I patiently waited. *Thump,*

Chapter Two: MEMORABLE TIMES 17

thump, thump. I yanked the rod and all hell broke loose! A huge trout boiled the water's surface. *Zzzzzz!* My drag started screaming as the big trout headed for the swift water in the middle of the river.

For the next few minutes, I played the big fish. But then I suddenly remembered that I hadn't brought our fishing net. Damn! Gradually, the fish played down, and I decided to jump onto one of the big cottonwood logs near the hole to try to ease the trout up onto another log closest to the river, next to the one I was standing on. The cottonwood was almost submerged, so I'd only have to pull him up a few inches to where a large branch had broken off.

I very carefully tugged the fish from the water onto the log: my plan had worked! I stepped over onto the log where the trout was laying. As I walked towards the fish, I reeled up the slack in my line.

Oh, shit! I could see the big trout's rainbow glistening in the sun as I got near him. But then he started flopping. Damn! As I saw the hook come out of his mouth, I threw my pole to the side so I could run down the log. Just before I got to him, he made another big flop…then sploosh! He flipped off the log, landed in the river, and was gone. Tears welled up in my eyes as I screamed, "Son of a bitch!"

I picked up my pole, reeled in the line, and hopped from one log to another. After I got to the bank, I walked back to where my tackle box and lunch were sitting. I sat down in the shade for the next hour, my entire body feeling numb. I just stared at the river. I estimated that the big rainbow was about twenty-four inches long and probably weighed around six pounds. Damn it! If only I'd brought the net!

It was the first week of September: time to go back to school and start sixth grade! That first week, my friend Ken told me that I needed to go with him to his house: he had something to show me.

When the afternoon bell rang, we jumped on our bikes and headed out. On the way, I kept asking him what it was. Ken would only laugh, telling me that it was going to be one hell of a surprise. When we got to his house, we went down into the basement. He whispered, "Keep an eye on the top of the stairs—tell me if you see anybody." He walked over to a dresser, opened the bottom drawer, and pulled out several magazines. He handed me one and said, "Check this out." I flipped back the cover and... oh, shit! There on the page was a beautiful woman, totally naked with great big tits and a black pussy. Oh, oh, oh... My hands started shaking and my groin throbbed as I flipped through more of the pages and looked at those beautiful, naked women.

We heard the floor above us creak and we scrambled around, putting the magazines back in the drawer and quickly closing it. My heart was pounding! I was so scared of getting caught—by his parents or anyone else—looking at the dirty pictures. We decided we'd better go upstairs; we'd look at them again when no one was home.

In December, Dad started taking me rabbit hunting and taught me how to shoot his .22 rifle. He told me to be sure to shoot them in the head so no meat would be wasted. Before long, I was shooting rabbits and supplying the family with more food. After we cleaned them, Mom cut each into about six pieces then wrapped two rabbits per package to freeze them. When she prepared them, she would dip all the pieces in a mix of flour, salt, and pepper; brown them in a skillet of hot grease; then put them in the oven in a roaster with a small amount of water, cooking them slowly. The rabbit was always very tender and had great flavor.

Our freezer was usually stocked with a variety of wild game and trout, and I loved the way that Mom prepared the fish, too. She dipped them in flour, salt, pepper, and cornmeal, and fried them in a skillet. When they were done, the skin was always a golden brown. Even though you had to be careful to pick out the bones, it was well worth it—they were delicious!

After the holidays, we started playing basketball in PE, and I found that I loved playing! Although we didn't get to play other schools, our instructor had different teams within the grade school, and the tournament was very competitive. I loved the sport more and more and practiced and played as hard as I could. I was really looking forward to junior high next year, as we'd be able to play teams from other schools.

It was now 1960 and officially the start of summer, and Cal was busy planting his garden. I was constantly running around, playing with my friends. Our sports were football, kickball, baseball, and basketball. Before long, some of the neighborhood girls wanted to join in when we played

Chapter Two: MEMORABLE TIMES 19

sports, especially kickball. We guys didn't object; most of the girls were pretty athletic, especially a fourteen year old named Beverley who had moved to Meeker from Texas. She had a very cute figure and long brown hair, brown eyes, and a great tan. I liked talking to her, and we always had fun during kickball. We'd often play until dark and, after the games, I'd walk partway home with her, since she didn't live too far from me. Before long, Beverley and I were kissing and fooling around. One night, she allowed me to unbutton her blouse, and I slipped my hand inside her bra and rubbed her tits. They felt so good—soft and warm—and my dick got really hard.

The next day, I told Jake about feeling Beverley's tits, and he smiled and said, "Maybe she'll let you go all the way." I'd wondered about sex, but I didn't know very much. Some of the guys would say things about girls now and then, but it was really hard to believe that my dick was supposed to go in *there*! I'd get these little tickling sensations, too, when it would start to stiffen; it happened most often when Beverley and I were kissing. And now and then, I'd wake up from a deep sleep with my dick really hard, almost throbbing… Still, I was pretty naïve.

One afternoon in late July, Beverley and I were walking home after a kickball game. We always passed the same vacant lot, but today, we decided to go "hide" in its tall weeds and fool around. We lay down and started kissing. After several minutes, Beverley stuck her tongue in my mouth. *Whoa!* She'd never done that before. I decided to stick mine in hers, and we continued this back and forth—sort of "meeting in the middle" and kissing the whole time—for a while longer. Soon, my dick got really hard, and when Beverley began making moaning sounds, I started to wonder if she was alright. Then, out of nowhere, she stopped and reached down to take her shoes off…then her shorts and panties! When I saw those light-blue panties come off, and Beverley's white crotch area around her dark pubic hair with a tan line above and below, my dick got even harder! She said, "Take your clothes off!" Oh, shit! I was shaking…I didn't know what to do except what she told me. I pulled everything off as fast as I could. Beverley put the clothes over the weeds then lay down on them, and I could see this perfect triangle of black hair between her legs. Oh, shit! This was a real live pussy, not a picture in a magazine!

In one hell of a hurry, I got on my knees to lie on top of her. My heart was beating hard as we started kissing again, then she grabbed my dick and guided it between her legs. Oh, God! She was so warm and wet! I slid all the way in; she gasped and so did I! Then she told me to start going up and down, and I continued to do it without her coaching me, because it felt so good. *Harder and faster, harder and faster.* "Yes, yes—just like that!" she purred.

All of a sudden, I felt a flash of deep heat in my ass and my legs tightened up. My dick started to get a strange sensation in it, different from how it'd ever felt before. I pulled out of her and jumped to my feet, grabbing my dick. "What's *wrong*?!" she yelled. *"I...don't...know!"* was all I could get out. I was standing on my tiptoes with sperm shooting out onto the weeds. I thought I was going to pass out!

Finally, the strange feeling was gone and I told her we should go home. After we got our clothes on, we awkwardly told each other goodbye. As I was walking down the street towards home, it finally dawned on me what had just happened: I'd just had my first orgasm! Shit, what a feeling!

When I got home, I jumped on my bike and rode up to Jake's house to tell him the story. He said, "You lucky bastard," then started laughing about me jumping to my feet, shooting sperm all over the weeds.

The next day, we had another kickball game. When Beverley said hi to me, I could feel my face turning red; I was embarrassed about what had happened. But as the day went on, I got back to my normal self, and I walked her home.

In mid-September, Dad found out we wouldn't be able to use the road we used to take to get to Big Beaver. For some reason, the landowner was no longer allowing people to access the national forest through his property. Dad said we'd have to drive about eight miles on the highway and use Fawn Creek Road instead. Now we'd need a four-wheel drive, because Dad felt that our two-wheel-drive pickup couldn't negotiate Fawn Creek when it was wet or snowy. So in late September, he bought an old green 1949 Willys Jeep that we took for a test drive on some of the dirt roads north of Meeker. It had a full canvas top with plastic windows on the doors that you couldn't see through because they were so stained and scratched.

Chapter Two: MEMORABLE TIMES

Dad soon found out that the Jeep's transmission had some problems. Whenever we drove up a steep hill and he tried to downshift, it was nearly impossible. He'd have to come to a complete stop and wiggle the gearshift around to get it into first. When we came downhill, the Jeep would usually jump out of second gear and Dad would quickly engage the clutch, then force it back in.

When we were going back to Meeker from the test drive, Dad said, "What do you think of the Jeep?" I said, "Boy...I don't know, Dad." I didn't want to disappoint him by saying what I honestly thought. He was puffing on a cigar and replied, "Ah hell, Son—we'll get by." A few days later, he had a friend build a hitch on the pickup and install a tow bar on the Jeep so we could pull it to the Fawn Creek turnoff.

In mid-October, the day before hunting season started, I helped Dad get the Jeep hooked up behind the pickup. Later that evening, we had fried chicken for supper, and Mom told us that she'd fixed extra so we could have some to take with us.

I went to bed around ten and, before I knew it, Dad's hand was on my shoulder, shaking me. He whispered, "Are you ready to go get an elk?" I opened my eyes and smiled. "Yes, I am, Dad!" I looked at my clock and it showed 3:00 a.m.

He reminded me to put on warm clothes because the Jeep had big cracks around its doors and the heater barely worked. After I dressed, I told him that I wanted to have coffee instead of hot chocolate. He smiled and said he didn't care one way or the other. I poured myself a cup and took a sip. It was bitter! I doctored it with a couple spoons of sugar and a little milk, which made it taste pretty good. I decided to fill my thermos with coffee, adding a lot of sugar and some milk to make it a special treat.

About thirty minutes later, we headed up the road pulling the Jeep behind us. It was just Dad and me now, as Larry had turned fourteen and could hunt on his own. Thirty miles later, we came to the Fawn Creek turnoff and got out to unhook the Jeep, transferring all our stuff into it, and Dad started it. Shit, it was cold! He asked me to get the flashlight and shine it on the floorboard; he reached down and moved the two shifting levers, putting the Jeep into four-wheel drive. We pulled across the highway onto an old dirt road and started up a steep hillside.

After we'd traveled a few miles, Dad downshifted to first gear as we started down a steep hill. We passed by a few hunting camps, and I could see the lanterns burning in the tents. When we got to the bottom of the hill, the Jeep's headlights cast a beam on the ice that had formed on Fawn Creek during the night. We were the first vehicle to cross the creek, so the ice made loud cracking and snapping noises as the Jeep's front tires made contact.

After a short distance, the road leveled out and Dad shifted to second gear. Before long, we began climbing another steep hill, and partway up, the Jeep started to lose power. Dad engaged the clutch and tried to shift from second to first, but it wouldn't go into gear. He pushed the brake pedal in hard, and I heard it slam on the floorboard with a bang: we had no brakes! The Jeep started rolling backward down the mountain road. As it picked up speed, my heart went to my throat, fear shooting through me. Dad yanked down the latch on his canvas door, threw it back, and leaned out to see where to guide the Jeep so we wouldn't go off the road. He aimed it towards the uphill side of the road on our right, and it started up the steep bank. Then, as if in slow motion, it began to turn over. *Bang!* It landed on the driver's side—lunch stuff, thermos bottles, chains, and Dad's gun flew everywhere, and I landed on top of him. The Jeep's engine had died, but the headlights were still on, shining into the darkness. Now it was stone quiet.

I pushed against Dad's bucket seat to try to get off him. "Dad!" I yelled. There was no reply. I thought, "Oh no, God—not my dad!" I yelled again. "Dad!" He answered, "What?" I said, "Are you alright?" He said he was fine, then asked me if I was okay. I was, and he calmly said, "We need to find our flashlight, Son." I quickly felt around and found it, turning the switch on. Luckily, it still worked.

The Jeep had hit so hard that it split the canvas roof, so we crawled through the split. My legs were weak and trembling when I stood up. Dad noticed the headlights were still on, so he took the flashlight and crawled back inside to turn them off. We sat down on the bank in front of the Jeep; Dad fired up a cigar and said we'd wait till daybreak, then try to find his cable come-along. We'd see if we could hook it up to one of the aspens nearby and maybe right the Jeep on its wheels. Dad said, "Thank God we didn't get hurt, at least." I nodded in agreement then said, "It was a close call, Dad." I told him I was going to crawl into the Jeep and try to find our thermos bottles. After a few minutes, I found them and also got hold of Dad's rifle. We were both amazed that our thermoses hadn't broken.

Chapter Two: *Memorable Times* 23

The hot coffee tasted really good, maybe in part because it was so very cold out. Dad and I were surprised that no other hunters showed up and, at daybreak, we walked over to the edge of the road and stared down at the hillside towards Fawn Creek. Oh, God—if the Jeep had plunged that way, there is no doubt that both of us would've been killed or, at the least, badly injured. My dad's—my hero's—quick reaction and good driving skills had saved our lives.

Once again, I crawled through the split on the canvas top of the Jeep and handed Dad the remainder of our things and the cable come-along. I took the binoculars from the case and looked through them: they weren't broken! Dad hooked the come-along to a big aspen and pulled out some cable, then found a solid place to hook onto the frame of the Jeep. He had me stand on the road, several feet above the Jeep, so I'd be out of harm's way. He started to ratchet the handle on the come-along; when the cable tightened, the old Jeep made a creaking sound. A few minutes later, it landed on the passenger side's tires. Yes, Dad had managed to get the Jeep sitting upright, on all four wheels! Then he placed a rock behind each rear tire to keep it from rolling.

The sun was now starting to rise in the east over the distant mountains. *Boom! Boom!* Now and then, we could hear hunters shooting far across the river valley. Dad said, "Let's have another cup of coffee to give all the fluids in the Jeep some time to level out, then I'll try starting it."

After about ten minutes, Dad raised the Jeep's hood to look things over. He said that there was no brake fluid; evidently it had leaked out somewhere. He then checked the oil and added a quart, then crawled inside and pumped the foot feed several times. After a few tries, the old thing started up, but it took several minutes of wrestling with the gearshift to get it into first. Then Dad shut the engine off.

After he disconnected the come-along and put it back into the Jeep, Dad said, "Well, Son, I guess we'll leave the Jeep here for now and walk up the road towards Big Beaver to see if we can find some elk. We'll worry about getting out to the highway later." He loaded his rifle, I picked up the binoculars and our lunch bag, and we headed out. By now it was about eight o'clock and there were still no hunters on the road. The sky was a cloudless blue and the frost on the tall grass glistened from the sunshine.

After a few miles, Dad decided to leave the road, so we headed south cross-country towards Big Beaver. We hadn't gone far when Dad spotted a herd of elk on a distant hillside, not within shooting range. I put the binoculars on them and counted seventeen, but there were no bulls in the herd. This year, Dad could only shoot a bull, as he hadn't drawn a cow elk license.

It was now noon, so we decided to sit down and have lunch. The cold chicken really hit the spot, and after we finished, Dad decided we'd better go ahead and try to get the Jeep to the highway. We went back to the road and, while walking down it, three hunters showed up in a new-looking four-wheel-drive pickup. Dad put his hand up to stop them, telling them about our accident, and they said they'd be glad to help us get the Jeep down the mountain road.

We got into the back of their pickup and arrived at the Jeep in just a few minutes. The driver of the pickup pulled within a few feet of the Jeep's front bumper, nose to nose, and turned off his engine. Dad and I got out while they pulled a big log chain from the back of the truck, hooking one end to the Jeep's front bumper and the other end to the truck's front bumper.

Dad got in the Jeep and started it, and the driver of the pickup backed up slowly till the chain was tight. Then one of the other hunters removed the rocks from behind Dad's rear tires. Dad put the Jeep in reverse, and the pickup followed him down the mountain road, keeping the chain tight. The other two hunters and I walked after them. It only took a few minutes for the road to level out, and the Jeep soon came to a stop. The driver unhooked the chain and, as they talked and shook hands, Dad told them that he thought we could make it now by driving in first gear, low range.

The hunters stayed nearby while Dad got the Jeep turned around, then we waved goodbye. We headed down the old road at about five miles per hour, and it took us nearly an hour to make it to the highway. After we hooked the Jeep onto the pickup, I broke out a Pepsi and Dad lit a Roi-Tan as we started the drive back to town. It'd been one hell of a day!

The school year seemed to slip away, and it was amazing to me that I was now thirteen years old. Dad said that a friend of his had a .300 Savage rifle that he no longer wanted, and he told Dad that if I would mow his lawn once a week for the entire summer, he'd give me the rifle, which was in perfect condition. I told Dad that I'd be glad to make that deal!

Chapter Two: MEMORABLE TIMES

Summertime seemed to bring on old habits more strongly, and once again, I heard Dad arguing with Mom about her drinking. Now Dad was finding bottles of vodka and whiskey that she'd been hiding. Everything was getting worse, and lately I noticed that she was actually drunk by evening and I smelled whiskey on her breath. I always hoped it wouldn't lead to another fight.

Regardless of what was going on at home, I always had fun over the summer, and one of the things I really enjoyed this year was learning to play poker from my uncle Fenton, one of Mom's brothers. He came to visit for a few weeks and taught me how to play five-card stud, seven-card stud, and five-card draw. I really enjoyed the different games, and poker became one of my recreational stand-bys in later years.

In mid-August, Dad got rid of the old green Jeep and got a 1950 red Jeep that was in good condition. It had a full canvas top, and you could even see through the plastic door windows. And—by golly—it had a good transmission! I was so happy that we could go hunting in a reliable four-wheel vehicle and the old green Jeep was gone!

I had been practicing basketball every day over the summer and was looking forward to playing for Coach Holmes. I was determined to be on the starting five of the A team next fall. Then, at the end of August, I finished mowing Dad's friend's lawn and he told me that I could have the gun. I raced home on my bike to wait for Dad so we could pick it up. About six, he pulled up in front of the house, and we left to go get my .300 Savage.

When the guy handed me the rifle, I actually had goose bumps. I thanked him at least three times before we finished talking. He also gave me a box of shells, saying that he'd made sure the gun wasn't loaded. It was so hard to believe that I now had my very own hunting rifle! Dad told me that he'd take me to the shooting range so I could sight it in and do some practicing. On Sunday morning, we drove to the range; I set up a target at twenty-five yards, got my rifle, and set it on the shooting bench. We didn't have any sand bags to use as a gun rest, so I rolled up a pair of Dad's coveralls and placed them on the bench. I carefully loaded the rifle and sat down, moving around on the bench to get a comfortable rest on the coveralls. I peered through the 4x Weaver scope that had a small dot in the center of the cross hairs, put the dot on the target's white bull's-eye, took a deep breath, and squeezed the trigger. *Boom!* The gun went off and rocked my shoulder. I regained sight of the target and could see that I'd shot a little high and to the right. Dad told me to try two more shots to see if I hit the same place. After two more rounds, we made some adjustments on the scope, then I settled in and fired another round. I looked through the scope to see where I'd hit and saw a bullet hole in the center of the bull's-eye. God! I was so happy! We moved the target out to 100 yards and Dad found a flat rock to create a new rest for my rifle. He said, "Now that you're shooting at a hundred yards, you'll need a good rest."

It took a while to adjust the rest, but I was finally satisfied and fired a couple of rounds. We walked to the target to see where I'd hit: both holes were just above the bull's-eye. Dad said, "That's some darn good shooting, Son." We marked the holes on the target and then walked back to the bench. After four more rounds, we checked the target. I'd hit the top of the bull's-eye with one shot and the other three rounds were all within one inch. Dad said, "I'm really proud of you, Son—you're doing really well!" By now, my shoulder was hurting and I decided I was ready to give it a rest. I made sure the rifle was unloaded and we got in the truck to drive home. All of this practice made me think even more about hunting season and, in my mind, I was hoping and praying that someday I'd get a bull elk!

Summer came to an end and school started once again. Then, at the end of September, Dad decided we were going to take the Jeep up into the high country to scout for deer and elk. On Sunday morning, we got up around 5:30 and were soon driving up the river valley, the new Jeep in tow behind the pickup. About forty-five minutes later, we arrived at Fawn Creek Road and unhooked the Jeep, loading our things into it. Lighting a new Roi-Tan, Dad started the Jeep and put it into four-wheel drive, then we headed up the old dirt road.

The beauty of the forest always awed me: it was just beyond description. The trees were adorned in their fall colors—lush dark to pale green, bright red and gold, burnt orange, brown, and pale yellow greeted us everywhere we looked. After driving several miles, we crossed Fawn Creek and headed up the steep mountain on the other side. We were both talking like a couple of magpies until we came to the exact spot where we'd rolled the green Jeep. Neither one of us said a word as we passed by, and goose bumps ran up my spine when I thought about that dark October morning.

Chapter Two: MEMORABLE TIMES

A few miles down the road, we drove over a small bridge that crossed a crystal-clear mountain stream. "Stop! Stop!" I yelled. I'd seen a fish rise to the surface and wanted to check it out. We got out and walked over to the edge of the creek where I could see a large school of brook trout, darting one way and another. We hadn't brought our fishing poles, so...what to do?

The stream was shallow, so I decided to see if I could catch the trout with my bare hands. I waded into the creek and the brookies spooked, going in every direction. I pulled a log from the bank and laid it across the creek, confining the trout to a small area between it and the beaver dam located a short distance upstream. With water flying everywhere, I began chasing the fish up and down the creek, falling to my knees to grab at the lightning-fast brookies! I finally got lucky and nailed one, only to have the slimy seven incher slide out of my hands and splash back into the water. Dad started laughing so hard he was about to cry!

"Come on, Dad—help me!" I pleaded. He waded into the creek and started chasing the fish, too, and for the next few minutes, the two of us ran up and down the stream, yelling and laughing. When all was said and done, we were both soaked head to toe, but we'd managed to catch six small trout. What a show! We spent the next hour talking, laughing, and drying our socks on logs and bushes before continuing the drive to our hunting country.

A short time later, we pulled onto our parking place above the beaver ponds. I'd named it "Beaver Knob" the year before with Dad's approval. *Ooooeeeee-uh!* The sound of a bull elk bugle echoed across the valley. "Did you hear him, Dad?" I asked. "Yeah, Son, I did. It sounded like it came from the big meadow area." *Ooooeeeee-uh-uh-uh!* The bull let another bugle go, and Dad and I smiled at each other.

We quickly gathered our lunch stuff and the binoculars, walked down the knob, crossed the beaver dam, and made our way up the game trail that led into the timber. Then we thought we heard another bull answering the first one, and we began to move very slowly as we walked down the trail, making sure that we didn't step on any twigs. About a hundred yards from the big meadow, a bull bugled again.

My heart started pounding hard. I'd never been this close to a bull elk when he was bugling. There was a stiff breeze coming out of the north, so we decided to head south to make sure that when we got to the meadow, the elk wouldn't smell us. Dad whispered, "Stay low and watch your step. We don't want to make any noise." We made it to a small stand of pine trees, which gave us some good cover. A few seconds later, we got to the edge of the timber and peered out through the trees.

There they were, a big herd of elk, grazing in the meadow. Where was the bull? *Ooooeeee, uh-uh-uh!* He let another bugle rip. Dad whispered, "There he is," and pointed to the far side of the large meadow that was surrounded with aspens. The big bull had his antlers laid back over his shoulders and was trotting towards the main herd of cows and calves.

I quietly took the binoculars out of the case and put them to my eyes. Oh, what a sight! The bull had a big, dark-colored rack—I counted six points on each side—and the snow-white tips on each point glistened in the sun. By now, he was only about seventy-five yards from us. Dad and I got down on our knees and slowly moved behind a small pine tree, trying to make sure we weren't spotted by any of the elk.

All of a sudden we heard another bull bugle close by—it sounded like he was about a hundred yards towards the east. The big six point stretched out his neck and answered him. Shit! I glassed the far side of the meadow and spotted the other bull coming through the aspens. When he walked into the clearing, I could see his rack and counted five points on each side—not nearly as big as the herd bull. The five point started walking toward the six point. When he was about thirty yards from the big bull, he stopped. For a few seconds, they just stared at each other. All of a sudden, the big bull charged the smaller one. *Crack!* Their racks collided. They twisted their heads back and forth, the antlers entangled. The big bull started pushing the smaller one down, and the smaller bull yanked his rack free, trotting off into the thick timber. As quickly as the fight had started, it ended. I watched the big bull stretch his neck out—*ooooeeeee, uh-uh-uh!* He let out a long, loud bugle, as if to say, "Yes, I'm king of the mountain!" Dad and I looked at each other and smiled: what a sight!

I noticed one of the cow elk in the herd appeared to be nervous, smelling the air. In just a few seconds, she started walking towards the north, and the entire herd lined up in single file and started following her, the big bull at the end of the lineup. I watched them in the binoculars and counted a total of twenty-one elk. A couple minutes later, they completely disappeared into thick, dark timber.

Chapter Two: *Memorable Times*

Dad and I gathered up our things and headed for our favorite spot at the big valley to have lunch. As we walked through the tall yellow grass in the meadow where the elk had been, I could still hear the bull elk bugling in my mind. After we arrived at our spot, we sat down to enjoy the cold fried chicken that Mom had packed and a Pepsi. We continued to discuss what we had just seen, saying to each other, "Wasn't that something?"

As we talked and I sipped on my Pepsi, I stared at the unbelievable beauty all around us: the red leaves on the oak brush, the mountainsides covered with yellow, gold, and pink aspens, and the towering dark-green pine trees below. By now, after spending five different fall seasons with Dad at Big Beaver, it had become a sacred place to me. This is where we'd built a special bond with one another that I truly cherished. There were no arguments to be heard, no school bells or tests, no pressure of any kind. When Dad and I weren't talking, elk weren't bugling, or pine squirrels chattering, there was nothing but stone silence and sheer beauty everywhere I looked.

For the next few hours, we talked about school, hunting, fishing, and the upcoming big game season. I finally decided to throw a question to him, asking if I could buy a deer license this year. He replied, "I don't think so, Son. You're only thirteen years old and, legally, you have to be fourteen." I told him that two of my classmates said they were going to get theirs—that their uncles had done it over the past several years and had gotten away with it. Dad reminded me that he couldn't afford to pay a fine if I got caught. I said, "Dad, I want to at least be able to go deer hunting, now that I have my own gun, but if you say I can't do it, I'll understand." Dad paused for a few seconds then said, "Okay, Son. Give me a little more time to think about it." He took a new cigar out of his shirt pocket and fired it up. After a few more minutes, he said, "Son, if you don't say anything to anyone, you can buy a deer license, but let's keep it on the hush-hush." I said, "That sounds great, Dad! Thank you!"

He told me we'd be going to Big Beaver on the opening weekend of hunting season to try to get a bull elk, and if we saw a buck, I could shoot it. He said, "If you don't get a deer, I'll take you up Strawberry Creek on the second weekend where there are a lot of deer, and you should be able to get a buck." I said, "Okay—that sounds like a great plan, Dad."

By now it was about four o'clock, and Dad decided we'd better gather up our things and start for home. The Jeep had performed perfectly, and

Dad and I were both proud to now have a dependable four-wheel drive. By the time we got home it was eight, and Mom warmed up some leftovers for supper. We told Mom and Donna about our day's adventures—the elk we'd seen, the bulls bugling, and our fishing adventure. Mom smiled and said, "I hope one of those bulls is in my deep freeze in a few weeks." We all started laughing; we loved watching these magnificent animals in their natural surroundings, but we also enjoyed their tasty, nutritious meat and the good health that it brought us. Of course, Mom and Donna both got a kick out of Dad and me fishing for brookies bare-handed.

On Monday morning, the school bells rang, and when the recess break came, I told my friends about seeing the bull elk fight. We all came from hunting families, and they were interested in the story. When I got home from school, Mom said that she had a surprise for me. She went into her bedroom and brought out a box that had a picture of boots on the outside. I opened it, and there was a very nice pair of rubber snow packs inside. My eyes teared up, because I knew she'd worked hard over the ironing board in order to get the money to buy them. I gave her a long hug and said, "Thanks, Mom. I really appreciate these." I laced up the boots and tried them on—they fit perfectly! She said, "I don't ever want you to freeze your feet again."

The year before, after we'd rolled the green Jeep, we tagged along with Uncle Jimmy and Larry on a hunt, riding in the back of Jimmy's 1948 half-cab Jeep. It was unusually cold then, and after a very wet day of tromping through the snow, my old boots were soaked and I'd gotten a fairly serious case of frostbite on the toes of my right foot. New skin was grafted on, and they were fine now, but these new boots would keep the cold and wet from ever being a problem again!

I told her what Dad had said about me buying a deer license. She smiled and said, "Do you have enough money to buy one?" "No," I said, "but if you have seven dollars and fifty cents, I'll pay you back next summer when I mow some lawns." She laughed, walked over to her purse, and handed me eight dollars. I took the money and, as I was running out the front door, yelled, "Thanks! Thanks, Mom!" I jumped on my bike and headed for Gambles Hardware Store to apply for the license. My heart was racing as I pumped my bike down main street. I kept saying to myself, "Just act normal. They don't know if you're thirteen or fourteen years old. Make sure you tell them you were born in 1947, not 1948." A few minutes

Chapter Two: MEMORABLE TIMES

later, I parked my bike on the sidewalk outside of Gambles and walked into the store. I heard a voice say, "May I help you?" I looked over and saw that it was the owner, Mr. Harris. Oh, shit! I was hoping someone else would be waiting on me. My heart started pounding! I steadied myself and said, "Yes, I need to buy a deer license." He said, "Alright," and pulled out a booklet from one of the drawers. "I need your full name, address, and birth date." I gave him the information, making sure I used 1947 for my year of birth. He then asked me for my height and weight and filled in that information. After I signed the license, he tore it from the booklet, folded it very neatly, put it in a small folder, and handed it to me. "That'll be seven dollars and fifty cents." I gave him the eight dollars and he handed me my change. I headed for the front door when he suddenly said, "Danny." Oh, shit! I stopped and turned around. He said, "Good luck on your deer hunt." I said, "Thank you, Mr. Harris." Whoa! For a minute there, I'd nearly jumped out of my skin!

When I got on my bike, I truly thought I was a big-time stud. *Yea!* I had a deer license in my billfold! When I got off the sidewalk onto main street, I started pumping my bike as hard as I could. The cool breeze was blowing across my face, and it felt like I was going at least thirty miles per hour. A couple minutes later, I rode onto our front lawn, dropped my bike, and ran into the house to show Mom my license. She got quite a kick out of it and said, "Now you *have* to get a deer." I said, "I'm going to get a buck, Mom. I won't shoot a doe." Then I ran out the back door and went over to Cal's house to show him my license. "So, now you're a big game hunter?" he smiled. I started laughing and said, "Yeah!"

I could hardly wait to show Dad my license when he got home from work. When he opened the front door, I was leaning across the top of the Stokermatic, our coal heater, trying to be Mr. Cool. I said, "I got my deer license, Dad." "Did you really?" "Yip," I responded, "I'll show it to you." I pulled out my billfold, removed the license from the small folder, and showed it to him. He said, "I'm glad you got it, Son, but you know the deal: let's keep it on the hush-hush." I thanked my parents again for letting me get the license. What a great day it had been—a new pair of snow packs *and* a deer license!

The weekend before hunting season, Dad and I got the Jeep ready to go and organized all of our hunting gear: we were now ready for opening day. During the school week, I prayed that Dad wouldn't have to work on

Saturday. When the afternoon bell rang on Friday, I ran out the front door and jumped on my bike. I was so excited, because if Dad didn't have to work, I'd be able to carry my very own rifle on a hunt for the first time! A few minutes later, I arrived at home and parked my bike in the shed.

When Dad pulled up, I ran to his pickup and asked him if he had to work. He said, "A-hunting we will go, my boy!" I started laughing and said, "Thank God!" A few minutes later, he pulled around to the back yard and I helped him hook the Jeep onto the pickup, then he pulled around to the front: we were ready to go.

Mom had fixed a beef roast for supper and told us that we'd better get some game, because buying beef was too expensive. We laughed and said, almost in unison, "We're going to fill the deep freeze!" She laughed, saying, "We'll see." After we finished eating, she packed us a nice lunch for the next day—roast beef sandwiches.

When I went to bed, I had a hard time going to sleep. When I glanced at my clock and it showed 3:00 a.m., I got out of bed and dressed. Dad was already in the kitchen, brewing coffee.

I put my snow packs on and—boy—were they nice and warm! About thirty minutes later, we were driving up the White River Valley. It'd rained in Meeker during the night, so we were sure there'd be snow in the high country. By the time we got to the Fawn Creek turnoff, there were about two inches on the ground. We unhooked the Jeep, put chains on the front tires and started it so the engine could warm up, then loaded our things and headed up the mountain.

We got to Beaver Knob about 6:15. The Jeep had a great heater, and it was a good thing, as it was very cold outside. After drinking more coffee, we could see the dark, star-filled eastern sky beginning to lighten. Within a few minutes, it was daybreak, so we quietly got out of the Jeep. Dad loaded his rifle and I loaded mine, then he reminded me to make sure I didn't have a shell in the chamber. We got our lunch sack and binoculars then headed down Beaver Knob toward the dams. We walked slowly, as there were about four inches of snow on the ground and it was slick going down the hillside. As I followed him across the slippery snow-covered logs, memories started rushing through my mind. It seemed as though it was only a year or so since I'd first walked behind him across this dam—when I was eight years old. Now I was thirteen and carrying my own rifle. God! How could the years pass by so quickly?

Chapter Two: MEMORABLE TIMES

A few minutes later, we were getting close to the big meadow where we'd watched the bull elk fight in September. We walked slowly, looking in every direction. It was really cold, and even though I was comfortable in my new snow packs, I was glad to see the sun starting to rise over the distant snow-covered peaks. When we got to the middle of the meadow, we came across some fresh elk tracks. Dad whispered, "Watch real good, Son. I'm sure the elk have just been through here." We followed the tracks, heading east. Not five minutes later, I spotted a herd on a brush-covered hillside about a hundred yards away. I tapped Dad on the shoulder and pointed towards them. He pulled the lever down on his .300 Savage and put a shell into the chamber, slowly walked a few feet, and rested his rifle on a tree limb. I stood nearby, resting my rifle in much the same way, and watched the elk through my 4x scope. I whispered, "All I see is cows, Dad." The elk slowly started walking up the hillside. As they passed through a clearing, I quietly identified them, "Cow, cow, calf, cow," until there were no more elk.

Dad asked, "Are you sure there are no bulls, Son?" I said, "Positive, Dad. I got a good look at all of them." He whispered, "Damn—I wish I'd drawn a cow license this year!" We waited a few minutes then started walking towards our big valley. *Crack! Crack!* The timber was snapping on our right. My reflexes took over and I slammed a shell into the chamber of my rifle. I put the gun to my shoulder, waiting. In a few seconds, a doe and two fawns came bouncing out of the woods. Dad and I looked at each other, smiled, then took the shells out of the chambers and continued walking. Once we got to the big valley, we stayed for a while. *Boom! Boom!* We could hear other hunters shooting at game far across the White River Valley.

At 10:00 a.m., we decided to have a sandwich and then walk to our other favorite spots. We hiked several miles that day, but we didn't see any more deer or elk.

Later that evening, we got back to the Jeep and drove out of the high country. A few miles from where we always hunted, we passed by some hunting camps that had deer and elk hanging in the trees. By now it was almost dark, and it'd been a long day. When we got home, Mom noticed we didn't have any blood on our clothes. She didn't tease us about it but just said that maybe we'd do better tomorrow, then she warmed some supper for us.

We went to bed early that night and tried again the next day, but it was still disappointing. To make me feel better, Dad said he'd take me deer hunting the next Saturday. The week seemed to drag by but, finally, the afternoon bell rang on Friday and I hauled ass on my bike. I wanted to get home and get my hunting gear ready for the next day.

Once I got into bed that night, I tossed and turned: I kept imagining what I'd do if I saw a big buck. It seemed like I'd just fallen asleep when I felt Dad's hand on my shoulder. Time to get up! I could smell the coffee brewing in the kitchen, and when I walked into the living room, I softly said, "Mornin', Dad." He asked if I was ready to get a big buck—as though I needed pumping up! I told him, "You'd better believe it!" He teased me about whether or not I thought I could hit one. I started laughing and said, "Just give me the chance!" After a couple cups of coffee, we headed for Strawberry Creek, twenty minutes from town.

Since this was going to be the first time I'd hunt alone, Dad reviewed some safety tips with me: always treat every gun as if it's loaded; never point a gun at anyone, even if you're sure it's unloaded; never totally rely on the safety of a gun; always be sure of your target and make sure there's a backstop behind the animal you're shooting at. If you should miss your shot—on top of a ridge, for example—the bullet from a big game rifle can continue traveling for nearly a mile. He also advised me not to cross through or over a fence with a shell in the rifle's chamber, and to make sure to take the shell out of the chamber before getting into a vehicle. While walking by yourself, it's alright to have a shell in the chamber—just make sure that you have the safety on. If you're not going to hold your rifle while sitting, make sure to lean it against something so it can't fall over. Always make safety come first! I told him he could count on that.

A few minutes later, we arrived at our hunting area, and we had more coffee as we waited for daybreak. When it was light enough to see, we got out of the pickup and loaded our rifles. Dad pointed towards a large patch of cedar and piñon about a half mile east of us. It reminded me of an island in shape, as the trees ran in a north-south direction, probably about a quarter-mile wide and a half mile in length, and were surrounded by hundreds of acres of gray sagebrush. He told me to walk to the south end of the trees and find a good hiding spot, approximately fifty yards from the trees. At eight o'clock, he'd enter the trees and start walking towards me in hopes of spooking a buck my way.

Minutes later, I arrived at a perfect spot, a big fallen piñon that would give me cover and a place to rest my rifle. I quietly put a shell into the

Chapter Two: MEMORABLE TIMES

chamber then put the safety on. I was glad to see the sun peek over the distant mountains, because I was starting to shiver from just sitting and waiting. The grass and brush were covered in a thick layer of early-morning frost.

I spotted a herd of deer south of where I was sitting and put my scope on them. There was a two-point buck in the herd, but I really didn't want to shoot a small one. As 8:00 a.m. neared, I started watching towards the north; Dad should be walking through the large patch of cedar and piñon soon. *Thump! Thump!* I could hear a deer bouncing in the trees not far from me. Oh, shit! There he was! A huge buck came bouncing out into the sagebrush about seventy-five yards from me, headed east. I flipped the safety off and rested my rifle across a big limb. I pulled the trigger and *boom*! As the kick of the gun rocked my shoulder, I lost sight of the deer in my scope. I yanked the lever down, kicking out the empty, and slammed another live round into the chamber. Then I jumped to my feet, but I still couldn't see the buck. My heart was pounding hard. Shit! Where was he? I had my doubts that I'd even hit him, everything happened so fast. I kept looking towards the east at acres and acres of sagebrush where the buck would've run, but I couldn't see anything moving. I put the rifle on safety and started walking towards where I'd shot at him. When I got close, I took my gun off safety and walked very slowly. Suddenly, I came upon him: a huge buck lying on his side, motionless. Oh, shit! I'd gotten him after all! I approached him cautiously, ready to shoot if he got up. When I was within ten feet of him, I broke off a long piece of brush and touched his eye with it. He didn't blink or move at all, so I knew he was dead. At the top of my lungs, I yelled, "Dad! Dad!" There was no answer. Again, I yelled, "Dad!" *Sereeee!* I heard him let out one of his neat, shrill whistles, and I hollered, "I got a huge buck!"

I happened to remember about having a shell in the rifle's chamber, so I removed it. Hell, my hands were shaking so badly I could barely hold the rifle, let alone think! I stared at the big animal's dark-brown antlers: there were four large points on each side, and the rack had a big spread. I heard the brush cracking and looked up to see Dad walking towards me. When he got to where I was standing and saw the buck, he said, "That's a dandy, Son! I'm so proud of you!"

We both leaned our rifles against the brush and gave each other a long hug. My emotions took over then and tears started rolling down my cheeks. I was happy—and relieved! Dad let me gut the buck myself, and I took my time, as I wanted to do a perfect job. About thirty minutes later, I completed the process and felt good about it. Dad offered to go get the pickup, as it looked like he could drive within fifty yards of the deer.

I got my license from my billfold, punched out the date, signed it, and tied it to one side of the deer's horns. A few minutes later, Dad arrived and we loaded the deer. As we headed home, he fired up a new cigar and said, "Always remember—be proud of your accomplishments, but never brag." I told him I understood.

When we got home, we pulled into the alley and Dad backed the pickup close to the barn. I jumped out and ran to the house to get Mom so she could come look at the buck. While she was walking to the pickup, I ran over to tell Cal and asked him to please bring his tape measure; he smiled and nodded that he would. By the time I got back to the truck, Mom was looking at the buck and started questioning me. "Did *you* really shoot him? How far away was he when you shot?" I shared the whole experience with her. Then Cal brought the tape measure and said, "Gee, Danny, that's a hell of a nice buck!" Then he measured the horns: the outside spread was twenty-six inches, and each point measured about nine inches in length. Mom gave me a big hug and congratulated me.

I told Cal and Dad that I wanted to skin the buck by myself. I cut the front and back legs off at the knee joints, then skinned around the hind legs where Dad would be inserting the long bar to attach the hook of his trusty come-along. We then dragged the buck into the barn and, a few minutes later, we had it hoisted up off the ground. Cal and Dad coached me as I removed the hide. When I got the deer skinned and pulled the hide about halfway down its neck, I took Dad's knife, cut through the meat to the bone, then finished by using the meat saw to cut through the neck bone. While they stood on each side of the carcass to steady it, I used the meat saw to go down the center of the backbone. Boy! My right arm—the saw arm—got tired and I had to take a couple of breaks before I finally got the deer split in half.

I could see the bullet hole behind the buck's front shoulder: I'd hit him in the lungs. Cal took the saw and carefully removed the antlers. He handed me the rack and, with a big smile on his face, said, "I figured you might want to save them." I proudly took the horns.

Mom went to the house and returned with a bucket of water, rags to wipe the meat clean, and two old sheets to wrap around each half of the deer to protect it from flies. About thirty minutes later, we latched the padlock on the barn door. The buck would now hang for a few days before Mom and Cal would cut it up and put the meat in the freezer. I was certainly one very happy boy!

The next morning, Dad and I went elk hunting at Big Beaver, but luck wasn't with us. The week passed by quickly, then Dad and I were looking at the last weekend for him to get a bull elk. We hunted hard that Saturday but saw nothing. We were now down to Sunday, our very last day.

On the following morning, we had good fortune: Dad shot a two-point bull, and some guys from Meeker helped us load him into the back of the Jeep. About noon, we headed out of the high country and, after we got home, showed off the elk before taking it to be processed. It was a successful hunting season that filled the freezer!

CHAPTER THREE

A Family Crisis

HUNTING SEASON WAS OVER NOW, so I turned my focus to basketball. My teammates and I worked extremely hard: we all had the utmost respect for our great coach, Mr. Holmes. He had a special way of bringing out the very best in all of us. My dream came true when I was picked to be on the starting five of the A squad, along with my friend, Lawerence. We'd been buddies since the fourth grade, and he was a good player. We had a great season until we played Craig, and then we literally got our butts kicked. Craig had a powerhouse of a team, and the talk of the northwestern league was the great player they had—Brad Smith—who was averaging about twenty points per game. He was unbelievable!

Dad had started to work Saturdays again, so he wasn't able to attend the games. Mom was back to her old drinking habit, and I really didn't want her to show up at the home games when she was drunk: it would just be too embarrassing. I was having a hard time dealing with her alcoholism, so I'd decided to ignore it and put my entire focus on basketball. The game meant everything to me.

Before long, Christmas break came, and we wouldn't be returning to school until after the New Year. I'd sure miss playing basketball with my teammates! Christmas vacation came and went: I'd gotten a new hunting knife, which was exactly what I wanted. Finally, I was once again where I wanted to be—on the basketball court, giving it everything I had.

By mid-January, we'd only won about half our games, but Coach Holmes was happy because we were really starting to show improvement. On a cold evening around 5:30, I was walking home from practice. When I got about half a block from our house, I could see Dad's Jeep loaded on the back of a flatbed truck parked in front. I started running down the street as hard as I could go. The truck driver was putting chains around the Jeep's axles, booming it down. I yelled, "What're you doing?!" He replied, "Ask

Chapter Three: A Family Crisis

them," and pointed towards two guys dressed in suits walking towards a car parked in front of the truck. One of them was carrying some papers in his hand. I ran over and asked him why Dad's Jeep was being loaded onto the truck. He looked at me and said, "I'm sorry, son, but we're repossessing the Jeep." I asked why, and he said that there hadn't been a payment made on it for three months, even after they'd sent two different notices. I wanted to know why they didn't wait until Dad was home, and he said that they'd given the papers to my mom. They got into their car and drove off, and the truck driver followed them. I dropped to my knees and started screaming, "No! No!" Tears streamed down my cheeks. My dad's great hunting Jeep was gone, the only decent four-wheel drive that he'd ever owned. He didn't deserve this! His whole life revolved around hunting, and now the Jeep that he was so proud of was gone.

I finally composed myself and got to my feet; my knees were nearly numb from kneeling in the snow. Then it dawned on me why the Jeep payments hadn't been made: Mom was in charge of the finances, and instead of paying on the Jeep, she'd been spending the money on booze. I ran into the house and found her sitting on the couch. I didn't see my sister anywhere, so I said, "Why in the hell haven't you been making payments on Dad's Jeep?" Mom muttered, "I don't know what you're talking about..." Her eyes were glassy; she was so drunk she could barely talk. "You've been drinking something besides beer!" I accused. Her words were slurred as she said, "No, I haven't." "I'm going to find your damned booze." I started looking everywhere—under the bed, in the closet, in her dresser drawers, under the kitchen sink, in the oven, and I finally found a pint of vodka stuffed alongside the refrigerator. Mom yelled, "Give me that bottle!" I started towards the back door with it. She screamed, "You'd better give me that bottle!" I walked out and threw the bottle as hard as I could towards the alley. *Crack!* I heard it hit Dad's scrap iron pile and knew that it'd shattered into a thousand pieces.

The scene was horrible. Mom was madder than hell and staggered through the kitchen into the living room. The front door opened; thank God it was Dad! I told him about the Jeep and throwing out the bottle of vodka. I could see the deep hurt in his eyes. He wasn't exactly sure what to do. Mom was sitting on the couch in a stupor. Dad looked at me and said, "I think we'd better take your mom to the hospital." The door opened again. It was Donna, coming home from her friend's house. When she saw and heard what was going on, she broke down and started crying.

Everyone was in a lot of pain. It was as though a living hell had unfolded before my eyes. Dad said, "I'll go start the car and let it warm up for a few minutes." My sister started packing a suitcase for Mom so she'd have a housecoat, pajamas—all the things she'd need. A few minutes later, we arrived at the hospital and Dad checked her in. Donna and I waited in the lobby for what seemed like forever. Dad finally came back and told us that the reason it took so long was because he had to wait for the doctor, and once he arrived, they had a long talk. When we got to the car, Dad told us that it looked like Mom was going to be taken to the state hospital in Pueblo to be admitted to the rehab center for drug and alcohol abuse.

Donna broke down again. Dad put his arm around her and said, "It'll be alright, Punkin. Your mom has to get some help before something bad happens to her." As we headed home, the only sound inside the car was my sister, sobbing. I felt sorry for her, and my heart was bleeding for Dad. He worked so hard, and in the winter he had to make deliveries to either Rangely or Craig on dangerous, icy highways. And now, all of this had to happen! When we got home, Dad asked if we were alright. I said, "Yeah, Dad. Are you?" "Yeah, I'm okay." My sister started crying again, so he put his arms around her to comfort her. Donna was only nine, so this had to be especially hard on her.

I got some leftovers out of the refrigerator and warmed them up for supper. After we finished eating, I heard Dad make several phone calls. He told his boss about the situation and said he needed the rest of the week off. He also called several friends and relatives. He asked Donna if she'd see if she could stay with her best friend while Mom was gone. Donna called her friend, and the parents said that they'd be more than glad to have her stay with them as long as she wanted.

Dad asked me what I wanted to do, and I told him I wanted to stay with him. We all went to bed about ten, and once I got into bed, the tears started flowing. Besides dealing with a terrible situation, Dad's Jeep was gone! The next morning, he took us to school and told us he was going to go to the hospital to see how Mom was doing. He said he'd take us there to visit her when we got home from school.

That afternoon during practice, I told Coach Holmes what had happened, and he said that he'd help me in any way he could. I thanked him for being so considerate and understanding. Even though it was still

Chapter Three: *A Family Crisis*

embarrassing to talk about it, it was a relief that my mom's drinking was no longer a secret and that she was getting help.

When I got home that evening, Dad told me that the doctor had filled out all the necessary paperwork for Mom to be admitted to the state hospital, and that he had to sign the papers to admit her. Understandably, she was very upset that she'd have to be there for six weeks. He said that my sister was staying with a friend, and that we'd pick her up on the way to the hospital. Dad would take Mom to Pueblo the next day—a Thursday—and he would be back on Friday. He said that he'd talked to Cal and that I could stay with them while he was gone.

We drove to Donna's friend's house, picked her up, and went to the hospital. Mom was glad to see Donna and me, but she treated Dad very coldly. Everyone was feeling so badly. My sister started crying, and as Mom held her, she started crying, too. My heart was shattered. Oh, God—what a mess! I tried to be strong, but when I put my arms around Mom to tell her goodbye, tears started running down my face. I could barely get the words "Goodbye, Mom" out. I couldn't take it anymore and walked out of the room. All I could do was hope and pray that the rehab center would be able to get her off alcohol.

The next morning, Dad dropped me off at school. On the way, he reassured me that it was best that Mom get some help. I agreed with that, because I knew that she'd been getting worse. When we pulled up in front of the junior high, I patted him on the shoulder and said, "Please be careful, Dad. I love you so much." "I love you, too, Son," he said, "and I'll see you tomorrow."

When the afternoon bell rang, I stopped by my locker then went to suit up for basketball practice. I was tired because I hadn't gotten much sleep last night. We had a tough game scheduled at Rifle on Saturday, so I darn sure didn't want to miss practice tonight or tomorrow night. At about 5:30, we finished, and I took a shower and walked home. *Brrrr!* It was a cold January night. When I got home, I tried to make the evening routine. I filled the Stokermatic and fed our cat, Tom. The house had a haunted feeling to it with everyone gone, and knowing that Mom wouldn't be home for six weeks almost made me nauseous. I sat down in Dad's chair and stared out the picture window into the darkness. Oh, God—I was hurting!

I gathered up a few of my things and walked over to Cal's. When he asked me how I was getting along, I quietly said, "Okay." Cal said, "I thought it'd be a good night to have some steak from your buck." "Oh, Cal," I said, "that sounds great!" A few minutes later, we sat down to supper, and we had fried deer steak, potatoes and gravy, and green beans. It was a good meal, and it lifted my spirits to know how much Cal cared about me.

We went to bed around ten. I lay in the darkness, staring at the flames on Cal's gas heater, wondering how Mom was doing. I slept fitfully, but I must have drifted off, because I heard Cal get up the next morning, so I got up and had coffee with him. A few minutes later, he fixed breakfast for all of us.

The day passed at school and, after basketball practice, I hurried home to see if Dad was there yet. As I neared the house, I spotted the car parked in front. I was so glad to see that he'd made it back safely! When I got there, he asked me how things were going. Again, I said, "Okay," even though I didn't really feel that way. Then I asked how Mom had done. He said that she was very upset and madder than hell at him for having her committed to the state hospital. I just felt sorry for him. I knew that he was just trying to do the right thing. He said, "I stopped by and checked on your sister when I got to town, and she seemed to be doing alright." He suggested that we have bacon and eggs for supper. The eggs were burnt a little around the edges, but I didn't say anything; he was trying to do his best.

He called his boss and found out that he needed to work the next day, which was Saturday. I told him that I had a basketball game in Rifle and I wished he could be there. But he had missed work all week, so he had to go in.

The phone kept ringing—word had traveled fast around the small town, and people were calling to see if Mom was alright. The next-door neighbor called and said she'd do our laundry while Mom was away. Dad told her that we would take her up on the offer, and that he'd bring her our dirty clothes once a week.

I woke up early the next morning when I heard Dad talking to the cat, so I got up to have coffee with him before he left for work. We visited for a while and, after he left, I sat down on the couch to check my duffle bag, just to make sure everything was in it for the game. I got tears in my eyes when I looked at my perfectly ironed gold uniform that Mom had washed and pressed the previous Sunday. It was just so hard to believe that her drinking had led to such a tragedy for us as a family. I zipped the bag closed and headed for the junior high school to board the bus.

Chapter Three: *A Family Crisis*

At 11:30 we headed for Rifle and, after suiting up, we completed our warm-ups, then the buzzer sounded to start the game. Final instructions from Coach Holmes were given, and the five of us walked to the center of the gym for the tip-off. The ball was thrown up and we controlled the tip: the game was on!

Both teams played extremely hard and, at halftime, it was tied twenty-two to twenty-two. The second half was another hard-fought battle, and the score was tied time after time. With only fifteen seconds remaining in the game, Rifle's best player scored and was also fouled. He made the free throw and the score was now Rifle, forty; Meeker, thirty-seven. Our coach called a timeout: I knew that it would now take a miracle to win.

Coach Holmes drew up a play and we returned to the court. Lawerence and Allan quickly got the ball inbounds and the seconds started ticking. Lawerence passed me the ball—I was only about ten feet from the basket—but before I could go up for a shot, I was fouled. When I stepped to the free throw line, the referee handed me the ball and said, "You'll be shooting one and one."

I looked up at the clock—there were just seven seconds remaining. I dribbled the ball a couple of times, took a deep breath, exhaled, and took the shot. *Thwack!* The cords snapped on the net. Whew! The referee handed me the ball again and said, "One shot." I took a couple of dribbles, stared at the basket, and then took the shot. It seemed as though the ball traveled through the air in slow motion. *Thwack!* It snapped the net's cords again! The Meeker fans roared! Rifle's lead was now just one point, but they'd have the ball with only seven seconds remaining. The referee handed one of the Rifle players the ball on our end of the court and we all guarded our assigned players. Oh, shit! Allan stole the ball on the inbound pass, and I wheeled around and headed for our basket.

He dribbled towards the basket and threw up a shot, the ball banged on the rim, then rolled off the edge. As it was coming down, I jumped as high as I could and tipped the ball off the backboard. *Bzzzzzz!* Just as the ball went through the hoop, the game-ending buzzer sounded across the gym. We won the game, forty-one to forty! The Meeker fans and our cheerleaders let out a loud roar. My teammates stormed around me and kept yelling and slapping me on the back. What a thrilling ending! The coach shook my hand, slapped me on the shoulder, and said, "You played one hell of a good game, Danny!" I then made my way over to Allan, shook his hand, and said, "Great steal! If it hadn't been for you, we wouldn't have won the game!" We were all so happy!

The locker room was filled with electricity as we took our showers. We were still fired up when we got on the bus and headed back to Meeker. I was sure that this game had given all of us some great confidence—and it was needed, as we would soon be playing in the district tournament.

After about eighteen miles, the bus started up Rio Blanco Hill. I stared out the window at the snow-covered mountains and silently thanked God for a great day. I really needed something to lift my spirits.

At home, there was a note on the kitchen table from Cal, saying that there was an elk roast with potatoes and carrots in the refrigerator—all we had to do was warm them up. I put them on the stove to heat then watched for Dad out the picture window. I was really anxious to tell him about the ball game. When he got home at 6:30, I told him the story and he said, "I'm so proud of you, Son. I wish I could have been there!" After the great meal Cal had made for us, we turned in around ten. As I lay there, I noted that this particular day was filled with happiness.

On Sunday, Dad took our dirty clothes over to the neighbor lady who'd offered to wash them for us. The school week went by quickly, and each evening, Dad and I did the best we could for our meals. Cal prepared some elk steak one evening and elk hamburger another; sometimes Dad cooked our old faithful—bacon and eggs.

We received a long letter from Mom—gosh, it was good to hear from her. She wrote that she'd made a couple of good friends and was attending classes about alcoholism each day. I read the letter twice. God! I sure missed her! Dad said that he'd take the letter to my sister so she could read it, too.

The next couple weeks passed and we split on our last two basketball games of the season. It was now time for the district tournament that was going to be held at the high school in Craig. I was very excited—this would be my first big tournament! We'd be playing the Steamboat Sailors for our first game.

On Thursday afternoon, we loaded up on the bus and headed for Craig, arriving there about an hour later. As we were walking through the lobby, Lawrence said, "Come here—I want to show you something." I walked over to the trophy case and he pointed at ten small gold trophies. He said that when the tournament concluded on Saturday night, they'd be

Chapter Three: A Family Crisis

given to whomever the coaches felt were the ten best players in the northwestern league during the entire season and tournament. "I think you're going to get one," he said. I started laughing. "No way, Lawerence. Come on—let's go get ready for the game." We got suited up and, after Coach Holmes gave us a serious talk, we headed down the hallway that took us to the gym. I said to myself, "This is it. This is what you've been looking forward to since you were in fifth grade. Give it everything you've got! When we entered the gym, the stands were packed with people. The Meeker crowd stood up and gave us a booming cheer!

After our warm-ups, we took our positions and the referee threw the ball up. We controlled the tip and, within seconds, Lawerence put up a jump shot that ripped the cords and set the course of the game. We played hard and won, which meant that tomorrow afternoon, we'd play the powerhouse of the league—the Craig Bulldogs.

When I got home that evening, I gave Dad a detailed report then went to bed. I tossed and turned for hours, thinking about Mom and the next game. Up early the next morning, I talked to Dad for a while then grabbed my duffle bag and walked to school, where everyone was wound up about the game. On the bus to Craig, there was very little laughter; everyone was in a serious mood.

In Craig's locker room, Coach Holmes gave a long talk. He said that Craig did have a great team, but it didn't mean that they couldn't be beaten. He told us to try our best and to hit the boards hard. He closed with, "Come on, you guys—make me proud!"

As we walked down the hallway towards the gym, the electricity started building up in my body. We trotted out into the gymnasium and the room exploded with a loud roar. The place was packed, standing room only. As we warmed up, I couldn't help glancing towards the other end of the gym and watching their star player, Brad Smith, take some practice shots. I noticed that a lot of Craig's players were talented.

After receiving final instructions from the coach, we walked to the center circle. The referee threw the ball up, and in the first few minutes, there was a lot of action as we matched Craig basket for basket. Then suddenly—*crack!* I caught a wicked elbow just above my right eye while going up for a rebound. I put my hand to my eye to check for blood. The referee blew his whistle and Coach Holmes called time out. I walked over to the bench and he had me sit down while he inspected my eye, which had already begun swelling shut. He asked me if I could see out of it, and I said, "I'll be alright." With a gleam in his eyes, he said, "Go get 'em!"

The referee's whistle sounded to restart the game as I walked out onto the floor. For the next several minutes, the back and forth action continued, and when the buzzer sounded at halftime, the score was tied. In the locker room, excitement and confidence flowed as we chattered away. We were playing a great team and were even up at the half!

The second half wasn't any different: the game was tied, time after time. With less than thirty seconds to go in the fourth quarter, Craig called a time out: we were leading by one point. Everyone in the gym got to their feet and gave both teams a standing ovation. The sound was deafening and gave me goose bumps! It was so loud that it was hard to hear what Coach Holmes was saying.

The game restarted; Craig brought the ball down the court and we set up our defense. They worked the ball around and, with just seconds on the clock, one of their players took a long shot from the baseline. *Snap!* The ball ripped the cords, and Coach Holmes called time out. He drew up a plan and said, "There's still time to score—just don't make any mistakes!" Lawerence and Allan quickly brought the ball down the court as the seconds ticked away. A pass was tipped and a Craig player caught the ball. *Bzzzzz!* The game ended as the buzzer echoed across the gym. The scoreboard read Craig, forty-six; Meeker, forty-five. Damn! We'd come so close! I walked over and shook the Craig players' hands, and then it was a long walk to the locker room. The coach told us that he couldn't be any more proud of us, but it didn't really help with how disappointed we felt.

We'd be returning to Craig on Saturday to play for third place. As the bus wound its way down the highway in the darkness, there was no talking—and damn sure no laughing! It was about ten when I got home, and Dad was already in bed. I went into his bedroom, sat down on the bed, and told him about the game. He was supportive, of course, saying, "I'm really sorry you didn't win, Son, but I'm sure you boys all played as hard as you possibly could." I muttered, "Yeah, Dad—it was one hell of a game!" Once I got to bed, I kept replaying it over and over before finally dozing off.

The next morning, I took my uniform over to the neighbor lady, who said she'd be glad to wash and iron it for me. About eleven, I got my uniform from her and headed for school. As I was walking, I wondered how

Chapter Three: *A Family Crisis*

Mom was getting along. I missed her so much! What I'd give to see her and hear her voice.

A few minutes later, I met Lawerence at the bus and we both boarded, sitting in our usual seats. He slapped me on the leg and said, "Are you ready to play another game?" I laughed and said, "Yeah, I'm ready. How 'bout you?" "I'm *always* ready!" he smiled.

At the high school, I was putting on my uniform when I suddenly realized that this would be my last junior high game. It was hard to believe! And as we played our final game with Rifle, it was hard-fought but, in the end, we lost. I think losing to Craig the day before had drained us mentally. That evening, Lawerence and I watched the championship game, a real nail-biter all the way, with Craig defeating Glenwood Springs. They deserved the victory—they had a great team.

The announcer picked up a microphone and said they would now present trophies to the top three teams. When that was over, they'd present trophies to the ten players who had been selected to be on the northwestern league all-tournament team. After the team trophies were passed out, they started announcing names. After three names of different players came over the loudspeaker, the announcer said, "Lawerence Klinglesmith—Meeker Cowboys." I slapped Lawerence on the back and said, "Way to go!" He made his way down out of the packed bleachers and walked across the gym floor to receive his award. Then the next name that came over the loudspeaker was mine! A huge roar went up from the crowd—even fans from other towns were cheering. I thought, "Oh, my God!" I stood up and, as I was making my way to the gym floor, the Meeker fans clapped and cheered for me, just as they had for Lawerence.

Finally, I got across the gym floor to where the announcer was standing. What a thrill! A gentleman handed me a small gold trophy and congratulated me. Lawerence wrapped his arms around me, patted me on the back, and said, "I *told* you!" After all ten players had been selected, they had us line up for a picture. I shook the hands of everyone who had been picked and, as we walked off the floor, the entire crowd of about a thousand gave us a standing ovation. How I wished Mom and Dad were here! Coach Holmes ran up, shook our hands, then said that he was very proud of our accomplishment. That meant so much to me, because if it hadn't been for his great coaching, I wouldn't have been holding that trophy.

By the time everyone got on the bus, it was nearly 10:00 p.m. After we'd traveled about twenty-five miles, the bus became quiet. When I asked Lawerence a question, there was no reply; I glanced over and could tell that he'd fallen asleep. As I stared out the window into the dark night, my emotions ran wild; half of my heart was filled with happiness because of winning the award, the other half was filled with sadness, as my mom was hundreds of miles away in the state hospital. My poor dad was working his butt off for just enough pay to make ends meet, and I knew that he was also missing Mom. The past month had been such a mental strain on me—trying to focus on school, get good grades on tests, and stay sharp on the basketball court. There was no doubt in my mind that the game and Coach Holmes had been a blessing for me during these troubled times. And I couldn't help wondering if God had put a basketball in my hands in the fifth grade for a special reason.

The bus finally pulled up at the school. *Brrrr!* It was cold when I stepped out into the chilly nighttime air. I told Lawerence I would see him Monday, said goodbye to some of the other guys, and then headed home. I trotted several blocks to try to stay warm. Dad was in bed when I got there—he'd left the living room light on for me. I walked to his bedroom doorway and said, "Are you awake, Dad?" "Yeah—I heard you come in." "Get up!" I said enthusiastically. "I have something to show you." He slipped on his Levis and came into the living room. I got the trophy out of my duffle bag and showed it to him; I told him why the award was presented to me, and that we'd lost our bid for third place. He gave me a long hug. "I'm so proud of you, Son. I wish I could've taken the day off and driven to Craig to watch you!" Deep down, I really wanted him to be there, but I said, "That's okay, Dad. I know you need to work." We talked for a few more minutes, then he went back to bed. I put my trophy on top of the TV. I'd be so glad when Mom got home so I could show it to her! After having milk and cookies, I decided to go to bed. As I walked by Dad's bedroom, I said, "I love you, Dad," and he answered back, "I love you, too, Son." After I crawled into bed, I fell fast asleep.

The next morning, I got up around seven and went over to Cal's; I wanted to tell him and Larry about the tournament. I spent a few hours visiting with them, then Cal said that he was going to fix a big stew for supper and there'd be enough to make a few meals for Dad and me. I thought that sounded great, and I told him how much we appreciated all the meals that he'd prepared for us over the past month.

Chapter Three: *A Family Crisis*

Later that evening, while we were sitting at the supper table, I asked Dad when Mom was coming home. He said that we should hear something soon and that, hopefully, she'd be back the first week of March, which was about two weeks away.

On Tuesday afternoon, we got a letter from her. I was so excited that I opened it at the post office instead of waiting till I got home. Oh, God! It was the news we'd been waiting for: she would be discharged on the first Monday in March! I rushed home and went over to Cal's to let him read the letter. He said, "Boy, that's great news! I know it's been hard on you and your sister with your mom gone." I was really anxious, and I decided to go back to the house to wait for Dad. My hands shook as I sat in his chair, petting Tom and staring out the picture window. Finally, at six, I saw him drive up.

I ran out to his pickup and yelled, "Mom gets to come home in a couple of weeks!" His face broke into a smile. "That's great, Son!" I watched his eyes brighten as he read Mom's letter, and I could see a lot of happiness in them when he came to the part about her being released the first of March. He said, "Let's take the letter down to your sister so she can read it." We drove to Donna's friend's house, told her the good news, and let her read the letter. She was so happy that she started crying! Dad hugged her and said, "Just two more weeks, Punkin, and Mom will be home."

Over the next several days, I had a hard time staying focused. Every conscious hour, my mind was totally consumed with the thought of Mom coming home. Finally, it came time for Dad to drive to Pueblo to pick her up. He'd leave the next day—a Sunday—and they'd be back around five on Monday evening. I told him that I wanted to stay at the house by myself and, after some convincing, he agreed.

On Sunday morning around nine, I gave him a big hug goodbye and said, "I'll see you tomorrow. Please be careful!" I spent most of the day visiting with Cal and had supper with him and Larry. I went back to the house around seven that evening, turned on the TV, and sat down in Dad's chair. It wasn't long before Tom jumped up on my lap, so I gave him a good petting. I decided to go to bed at 10:30, but my mind was still racing, filled with anxiety for Mom and Dad and their return Monday evening. I tossed and turned for hours. Every time the Stokermatic shut off, I'd hear creaking and cracking sounds that I'd never heard before. It seemed like the harder I tried to go to sleep, the more awake I was. I looked at the clock. Shit!

It was 2:00 a.m.! I decided to get up and have some cookies and milk—maybe that would help me relax so I could go to sleep. But I still watched the hours slowly pass. At five, I decided to give up on trying to get any sleep. I sat and sipped my coffee, watching the sun come up. I fixed toast then got ready for school.

During the day, I really didn't hear a word the teachers said, and I didn't pay much attention to my friends. I was counting the minutes until the afternoon bell would ring—3:30 p.m. When it did, I rushed to my locker, threw my books in, and ran out the front door. I walked home as fast as I could, my heart pounding with excitement. I knew that within the next hour or two, I'd see my mom!

Once I got home, my eyes stayed glued on the picture window and what was happening outside. Finally, at 4:30, our car pulled up out front. I busted out the front door, and as soon as Mom got out, I wrapped my arms around her and she wrapped hers around me. Tears streamed down my cheeks. I muttered, "I love you, Mom! I'm so glad you're home!" She was crying, too, and said, "I love you, too, Son." For the next full minute, there were no words spoken—we just held each other. Dad and Donna, who they'd picked up on the way home, got out of the car, and we all walked into the house.

I waited a few minutes, then showed Mom and Donna my trophy and told them all about the tournament. Moments later, Cal and Larry showed up and gave Mom a big welcome home. Cal had brought a huge pot of ham and beans for our supper. What a guy!

We stayed up until eleven that evening visiting, and then everyone finally went to bed. The next day, when I got home from school, Mom said, "I'm fixing your favorite meal for supper." "Chicken-fried elk steak?" I asked excitedly. "Yes," she said, "just for you, Son." By five, the house was filled with the smell of fried elk and Mom was busy moving around in the kitchen, preparing the rest of the meal. Dad got home at 5:30 and, after washing up, sat down in his easy chair and lit a Roi-Tan. Tom quickly jumped up on his lap for his evening petting. Donna was in her bedroom, doing her homework. As I leaned across the Stokermatic and looked out the picture window, there was no way that I could really describe the happiness that I felt. Having our family back together went far, far beyond "special." While Mom had been gone, the house had been *just* a house; now that she was back, it was a home again.

CHAPTER FOUR

A Room with a View

ON APRIL 16, 1962, I TURNED FOURTEEN. By now, everything felt like it was back to normal. Dad was already starting to talk about hunting season, and he decided to apply for a cow elk license for the coming fall. I said I was going to purchase a bull license across the counter, because I wanted to try to get a six point. He laughed and said, "My main concern is to get some meat in the freezer!" I started laughing and asked, "You don't think I can get a big bull?" He smiled, saying, "We'll see, my boy." He told me that the landowner at Big Beaver had reached a deal with the forest service and that we'd be able to drive to Beaver Knob this fall, the way we used to. What good news! Now we could get there in the pickup because we wouldn't need a four-wheel drive.

The first part of May, a neighbor girl named Tina, who was eighteen, came over to our house and told Mom that they were having some plumbing problems. She wanted to know if she could borrow our bathroom so she could take a bath. Mom told her yes, of course she could use our bathroom any time she needed. I thought to myself, "Oh, shit! What I wouldn't give to be able to get into a tub with Tina!" I guessed she was about 5'7" and weighed around 130. Her breasts looked giant to me, and she was very good looking.

About forty-five minutes later, Tina came into the living room and thanked Mom for the use of the bathroom. I didn't have any idea what kind of lotion or perfume she was using, but what I *did* know was that its sweet smell drove me crazy as I sat staring at her beautiful butt, seen through a pair of very tight Levis. She told Mom that she didn't have any idea when they'd be able to get the plumbing fixed. Mom said, "Tina, you can use our tub whenever you want." As she walked out the door, my mind started racing: there *had* to be some way I could watch her take a bath!

A few days later, when I got home from school, everyone was gone. I inspected the bathroom door and found that the wood was only about a quarter-inch thick. I quickly got Mom's sewing box out and picked the biggest needle I could find. Then I got a piece of cardboard and poked a hole through it. When I put the hole to my eye, I discovered I had a very good view. I then cut a small square off a roll of white adhesive tape and put it on the white bathroom door to see if it would match the paint. Ah, yes—it was *perfect*.

Thunk! I thought heard a car door slam, so I scrambled around, putting everything back, then I walked to the picture window in the living room and looked out. Hell, it wasn't Mom that I'd heard—it was the neighbors across the street! I returned to my project, knowing that I didn't have much time. I got a pair of pliers and the big needle from Mom's sewing kit. Kneeling by the bathroom door, I tried to guess the right height to place the hole—picking what I thought would be the right spot—then clamped the needle in the pliers, closed the bathroom door, and put a lot of pressure on the needle to force it through the wood. Damn, that wood was hard! Finally, the needle went through and I opened the door, put the needle in the hole from the other side, and wiggled it around. I went back to the outside of the door, knelt down, and looked through the hole. Oh, shit! I'd gotten really lucky, as I had a perfect view of the tub.

I cut two tiny white squares of adhesive and placed one on each side of the door to cover the needle hole, then quickly put everything away. Within just a few minutes, Mom pulled up into the driveway.

The following Saturday, I was hanging out at home; Dad was at work and Donna had stayed overnight with one of her girlfriends. Around noon, Mom said that she was going to see one of her sisters nearby and then do her weekly grocery shopping. Shortly after she drove away, I couldn't believe what I saw: Tina was walking towards our house carrying some clean clothes and her makeup case!

Damn! I ran to the bathroom door and peeled off the tiny pieces of adhesive that were covering the hole. *Knock-knock-knock.* I went to open the front door for Tina, saying to myself, "Be cool! Be cool!" "Hi, Tina," I said. "Hi," she answered. "I was wondering if I could use your bathroom for about thirty minutes?" "Sure—come on in." But what I was thinking was, "You can stay in there all afternoon!"

Chapter Four: A Room with a View

She went into the bathroom and I heard her lock the door. I walked to the refrigerator and got myself a Pepsi. My hands were shaking as I opened it, and I was so damned excited that I missed my mouth when I went to take a sip! I listened to the water running in the bathtub, and when I heard her shut it off, I decided to make my move.

I tiptoed towards the door. *Creeeak!* Damn it! There was a spot in the floor that squeaked just before I got to my spot, and I prayed she didn't hear it. I knelt down on my knees and put my left eye to the tiny hole. I could only see to her waist, but as I watched, she took off her lacy pink panties. Oh...my...God. There it was—a beautiful, very hairy, coal-black pussy! Instantly, my dick got hard as a rock! Then she got into the tub and laid back. Oh, shit! I could now see her big beautiful tits; hell, they were the size of grapefruits! I started to breath hard then. I watched her lather up a washrag and start to wash those big, beautiful grapefruits. I couldn't take it any longer—I thought I was going to go off in my Levis!

I stood up stiffly, tiptoed very slowly across the floor, and went to my bedroom, shutting the door. Unbuttoning my Levis, I yanked them and my shorts down, grabbed a bunch of Kleenex in my left hand and my dick with my right hand. It was so hard! I started pumping: within seconds, I absolutely exploded into the Kleenex—hell, even my legs were trembling! I got cleaned up, pulled up my shorts and pants, then headed for the kitchen.

I thought to myself, "You may never get another chance. You'd better take one last look." I eased across the kitchen floor—*creeeak*! That same damned place in the floor made a squeaking sound. I knelt down and peered through the hole. She had one of her legs all lathered up and was shaving it. Shit! Was she ever built! Those long beautiful legs, that black pussy, and those gorgeous tits! A few minutes later, she finished shaving and I saw her lean forward to pull the plug. She stood up, stepped out of the tub, and began drying herself. When she started rubbing the towel back and forth across that black pussy, I got another hard on. Damn! But now I thought I heard someone pull up out front. I quickly got to my feet and slowly walked through the kitchen to the picture window. I couldn't see anybody, but I decided not to push my luck and sat down in Dad's chair. I was so exhausted!

About fifteen minutes later, I heard Tina unlock the bathroom door and walk into the living room. I got up and walked over to open the front door for her. When she got close to me, I could smell her sweet lotion and perfume. She said, "Thanks so much for letting me use your bathroom." I muttered, "You're welcome, Tina." I watched her till she was out of sight.

I went back to the bathroom door and covered the holes with the pieces of tape. You never know—I might get another opportunity to watch Tina take a bath!

It was fall 1962 and I was now a freshman in high school. I'd gone on many fishing trips over the summer, sometimes on private property along the White River. We'd had a great Fourth of July celebration at Trapper's Lake, where our family and Uncle Cal and Larry picnicked and spent the day fishing and relaxing. I'd continued to mow lawns during the summer and used some of my savings to buy my deer and elk licenses. Now I could *legally* go elk hunting!

I counted the hours till opening day of elk season. When the morning came, Dad and I loaded up and began the drive to our hunting country. We arrived at Beaver Knob and—in the dim light of daybreak—loaded our rifles and hiked down the trail. The morning's frost covered a heavy layer of fallen leaves, and our passage was silent. We split up at the big meadow and headed for our sitting spots.

Snap! Crack! Snap! Something in the timber was headed my way. Heart pounding, I put a shell in the chamber of my rifle. God, I was hoping that it was an elk! But a doe and her two fawns came bouncing by. Shit! Just a false alarm.

Boom! I heard a gunshot about a mile south of me, from the area where Dad was sitting. I listened for more shots, but the forest was eerily quiet. I watched a clearing about 100 yards down the ridge, hoping that Dad would appear, telling me he'd gotten an elk. A few minutes later, I spotted the familiar red-and-black plaid wool jacket that he always wore. He gave me a hand signal and I hustled down the ridge. Once I got closer, I could see him grinning, and he said, "I got my cow, Son." I slapped him on the shoulder. "Good for you, Dad!"

After walking a half mile, we came to the elk: she was huge! We gutted her then walked toward the pickup, running into some local hunters parked nearby who offered to haul the elk out for us. Dad and I were really

Chapter Four: *A Room with a View*

wound up as we headed to town, and by two o'clock, the elk was hanging on the rail at Purkey's Processing.

The next morning, we repeated our routine, and during the long drive to Big Beaver, my mind whirled: would today be the day that I'd get my first bull elk? Or would I have to wait till next weekend—or perhaps even next year?

Shortly after arriving at our parking spot, darkness gave way to the dim light of day and we headed down the trail. At the big meadow, we wished each other luck and went our separate ways. I quietly put a shell into the chamber of my rifle: I wanted to be ready.

I'd been at my sitting spot only a few minutes when I started to shiver. Damn, it sure was cold—probably around fifteen degrees! For the next few hours, my eyes strained as I scanned across the meadow below me, the distant mountainsides, and any opening near and far, searching for the illusive elk. The only thing I heard or saw was a pesky pine squirrel, chattering in a nearby tree.

Even though I was still young, I'd learned that there was a large degree of luck involved in bagging a bull elk, especially when hunting on public property that was accessible by anyone with a vehicle. Each year, there were more hunting camps around the area where we hunted. After the first few days of the season, many of the elk headed for private property, where there was less hunting activity. I was thankful that there *was* private property where they could find refuge.

At 10:30, I spotted Dad walking towards me. When he reached my sitting spot, we talked about the morning's hunt. He'd seen a small herd of elk, but there weren't any bulls in it. I said, "Well, Dad—at least you *saw* some elk. All I saw was one squirrel!"

We had some lunch and decided to stay together the rest of the day. Neither of us had ever been that enthused about hunting elk in the afternoon; not only were you less likely to see them, but if you did make a kill, it would take till after sundown to gut and transport the elk back home. We knew that the very best time to hunt was the first two hours after daybreak.

We did a good deal of walking over the next several hours. Soon, late afternoon shadows were cast by the tall trees and Dad thought we'd better head home. The crunching sound of the aspen leaves beneath our boots was all that could be heard in the quiet forest. When we entered the dark timber at the west end of the big meadow, I pulled up the hood on my sweatshirt. Without the sun's warmth, it was cooling down in a hurry. By the time we reached Beaver Knob, we could see our breath. Frigid cold was starting to grip the high country.

We drove toward home. Soon, the truck had warmed up and I could feel hot air blowing from the heater. It felt so good! My entire body was chilled, and even though my toes had been damaged from frostbite a few years ago, I was warming up all over. Dad's cigar smoke filled the cab of the truck as we drove through the darkening forest, the pickup's headlights illuminating the dirt road and reflecting off the towering trees.

It was late by the time we got home and unloaded our gear. Mom was disappointed that I hadn't had a chance at a bull, but she said, "Maybe next weekend?"

The following Wednesday, Dad told me that he had to work on Saturday. I was disappointed, but I knew there was no choice. When he got home from work the next evening, he said that he'd found a ride for me to Big Beaver on Saturday with a guy that we knew well named Tim. Tim was going up to meet with friends who were camping in the area where we hunted. He told Dad that I could camp with them on Saturday night, then Dad would drive up early Sunday morning to meet me. What a great solution! I'd be able to hunt on Saturday after all.

Saturday morning, Tim picked me up, along with everything I'd need for camping out. When we arrived at the campsite, the large canvas tents were glowing in the pitch-black morning with light cast from Coleman lanterns. When I stepped out of the truck, I heard a lot of chatter coming from one of the tents; the air was filled with the smell of frying bacon. Tim opened the tent flap and we greeted everyone. I knew all the guys, even though they were fifteen to twenty years my senior.

One of them offered me coffee and told me that breakfast would be ready in just a few minutes. After I ate with them, it was time to drive to Beaver Knob. We arrived there at daybreak, and I grabbed my rifle and snacks out of Tim's truck and told him I'd see him around eleven.

After crossing the beaver dam, I put a shell into the chamber of my rifle. It was a strange feeling, walking up the trail without Dad. The forest was quiet—*really* quiet. The leaves were again covered with heavy frost, and I was able to walk without making any noise. I stayed at my sitting spot at the big valley for about ten minutes, then I decided to walk to the beaver

Chapter Four: *A Room with a View*

pond south of me—the area where Dad had gotten his cow elk on opening day. As I walked by the pond, I couldn't help but notice the early morning sun glistening off the clear ice. What a pretty place.

Damn! I was extremely nervous, and I just couldn't stay at one spot for any length of time. I wanted to get a bull elk so badly! I walked up the hill through a thick patch of aspen to where Dad had shot the bull years ago, when I was nine. I didn't see anything there, so I decided to head for the big meadow and circle around to the valley.

I'd only walked a short distance down the hill when I froze: there they were, a large herd of elk, about 150 yards from me. I slowly stepped over to a nearby aspen and rested my gun up against it. Peering through my scope, I looked through the herd in search of a bull. They were in a thick patch of aspens, so it was hard to get a good look at all of them.

Suddenly, I saw the sun glistening off the tips of the antlers of one of the elk. Oh, shit! My heart felt like it skipped a beat! There was my bull, if I could only get a clear shot. The elk were grazing, and they slowly meandered out of sight. "Calm down," I kept telling myself. I quietly tiptoed down the trail and headed towards the area where I'd last seen them. As soon as I passed through the trees, all hell broke loose: *snap-crack-crack*! The timber exploded on both sides of me! I put my rifle to my shoulder, desperately trying to find the bull. Cows were running in both directions. *Boom!* I jumped as a hunter fired a shot from the direction of the big meadow. Damn it! I figured he'd probably gotten the bull. *Boom!* Another shot echoed through the timber. I kept watching in the direction of the shooting. Oh, shit! I spotted the bull, maybe seventy-five yards away, running right towards me.

My hands trembled and my legs felt weak. I didn't have time to find a rest for the rifle, and I was hesitant to shoot him in the chest. At about forty yards, he spotted me and turned to his right, crashing through the forest. *Boom!* I fired a round, trying to hit him behind the shoulder. I yanked the lever down and slammed another round in the chamber. *Boom!* I fired again, the rifle rocking my shoulder. I kicked out the empty and put another round in. I caught a glimpse of an elk's hindquarters disappearing into the timber.

Son of a bitch! I thought that I couldn't have missed him, but then I could see movement in the aspen, about sixty yards away. It was the bull! He was down, trying to get up. I ran as fast as I could; when I got closer, I stopped and shot him in the neck. He stretched out, then stopped moving. It was over: I'd gotten my first elk!

"Good morning." I jumped and turned around to see who'd spoken. There stood a towering, gangly red-headed giant of a man, probably at least 6'4". His name was Red Gulliford, a local about the same age as Dad. I returned the greeting, and he said, "It looks like you had some luck." "Yeah, it's my first bull elk." He smiled and then said that he was glad I got him, that he'd shot twice and missed. He asked me if I needed some help gutting him, but I replied that I didn't want to delay his morning's hunt—that I could take care of the bull myself. I watched as the red-haired giant disappeared into the timber.

My legs still trembling, I sat down on a log and stared at the spike bull. God, how I wished Dad was here! After sitting about fifteen minutes, I decided to get to work. It took almost thirty minutes, and my Levis were soaked with blood. I walked over to the nearby beaver pond, broke a hole in the ice, and washed my hands. Afterwards, I picked up my rifle and headed for where Tim would be waiting for me.

When I got to Beaver Knob, there were three vehicles parked just off the road and seven guys standing around. One of them asked if I'd seen anything. I tried to be calm and said, "Yeah, I got a spike bull!" There were some snickers, then one of them said, "I wouldn't laugh too hard—look at all the blood on his jeans! Looks like he got more than we did!"

A nice guy named Lon Maudlin spoke up. "I'd be glad to haul him out for you." I took him up on the offer, and Lon, his son, and I got into his Jeep and drove back to where the elk lay. We loaded it up, and when we got back to Beaver Knob, all the guys shook my hand, congratulating me. Lon said that they were going to Meeker later that afternoon, and I was welcome to ride back with them. Hell, it didn't take me long to say, "That sounds great!" I wanted to get the elk to town so I could show him off.

Later that afternoon, we pulled into the alley behind the house and unloaded the bull near the barn. After Lon drove away, I ran to the house to get Mom. She came out to look at the elk, congratulated me, and gave me a hug.

I put all my hunting and camping gear away then started watching for Dad. At about six, he pulled into the driveway. When he opened the front door, he asked, "What are you doing in town?" I said, "I got my bull elk!" "You're kidding!" he smiled. "Nope," I replied, "I'm serious. I got a spike

Chapter Four: A Room with a View

bull, and he's out by the barn!" Dad walked over and slapped me on the back, saying, "Good for you, Son! Let's grab a flashlight and go have a look at him." He was shocked that I'd gotten the elk. Larry and Cal helped us load it into the truck and we took it on to Purkey's for processing.

A couple weeks later, basketball season started. The longtime coach had left, and the new one, Dick Castle, was said to be very strict. He came with a winning record from the school he'd previously coached. Our freshman squad was missing two players, as Lawerence had moved to Paonia, Colorado, and Allan had moved to Steamboat Springs, so some of the guys on the team were new to me. Each night of practice, I felt as though the coach had no interest in me or my playing ability. I loved the game, but I was getting tired of being benched while other guys were on the court—guys that I knew I could outplay. Just before Christmas, I checked in my uniform and walked away from the sport: I just wasn't enjoying it anymore. As the holidays passed, there wasn't a day when I didn't think about my decision to quit basketball. Back in school after the holidays, I was glad to be able to play during PE classes.

CHAPTER FIVE

Life Goes On

OVER THE SUMMER AND FALL, I had gone on many more fishing trips and hikes with Dad, had several steamy sexual encounters with a local girl, started my sophomore year, and—along with everyone else—endured the mystery and heartache of the Kennedy assassination. We had had a successful hunting season, and I had again decided to forgo playing basketball.

I wasn't idle over the winter, though, as I had become good friends with another of Mom's brothers, Donnie, and he'd taught me more about the ins and outs of poker. Erika, Donnie's wife, loved playing, and we had many penny-ante games at their house. And it seemed ironic now that *both* Mom and Dad were drinking beer. I didn't say a word to them. I felt as long as it didn't cause problems between them, it was okay with me. Besides, I'd started smoking cigarettes, a habit that I knew Dad would disapprove of.

On a beautiful Sunday morning in late February 1964, Dad said, "Well, it's getting close to your sixteenth birthday. Do you want to learn how to drive the panel?" I jumped up from the couch and said, "Let's go!" Dad drove up Sulphur Creek on a gravel road that led to the city dump. When we came to a wide spot, he pulled over, turned off the engine, and we switched places. How exciting!

He told me to push the clutch in and put the gearshift into neutral. I did as he told me, wiggling the shifter back and forth. He said, "That's fine, Son. It's in neutral. Now start the engine." I turned the key to the on position then pushed the starter button. The starter was making a horrible sound. Dad yelled, "Let go of the starter button! The engine has started!" I quickly pulled my thumb off the button. He advised, "As soon as the engine starts, you must release the button; otherwise you'll burn up the starter." I was embarrassed and told Dad that I understood.

Chapter Five: LIFE GOES ON

He said to push the clutch all the way to the floor and pull the gearshift down towards me. I felt the shifter go into second gear. He said, "Now push down on the foot feed to give it a little gas, and at the same time, let out on the clutch." Shit! The panel wagon lunged forward—jumped and jerked—and the engine died. Dad laughed, "No no, Son—that isn't the way to do it. Let's try again." Once again, I put the gearshift into neutral and pushed in on the starter button. *Urrrr, urrrr...va-room!* The engine started and I released the button. I put the shifter into second gear and pushed down on the foot feed, gradually letting out the clutch. *Ooooooorrrrrrr!* The engine was roaring and gravel started flying out from behind the back tires. Dad yelled, "Let up on the gas!" *Vrooomhhh!* The panel jerked, throwing us forward, then the engine died. I thought, "Son of a bitch!"

Dad smiled, "Do you want me to show you how to do it?" I replied defiantly, "No! I can do it!" I was feeling frustrated, and my heart was really pounding. I told myself to just calm down and think about it. I started the engine, gave her a little gas and, at the same time, slowly released the clutch. Oh, shit! It was perfect! We were driving up the road! Dad told me to pick up a little more speed, then—in one motion—push the clutch in, let off the gas, shift to third gear, let the clutch out, and push on the foot feed to pick up speed. Then do the same thing when shifting to fourth gear. A couple minutes later, we were cruising at about thirty miles an hour. I'd done much better on my shifting than during "take-off"!

Over the next hour, Dad let me practice from a stopped position. I now had it figured out! I spent several hours studying and passed the test for my learner's permit. Dad went with me on several occasions, allowing me to practice in the family car. That one was easy: it had an automatic transmission! We also took the panel for several trips, and by that time, I really enjoyed driving it.

When I walked out of my bedroom on the morning of April 16—my birthday—Mom and Dad were sitting in the living room. Mom said, "I wonder whose car is parked behind mine?" I looked out the window and saw a light-blue 1956 Ford. I told her I'd never seen it before. Dad said with a big smile, "Here," handing me a set of keys, then he said, "happy birthday, Son!" Oh, shit! I grabbed the keys and ran out to get in the car. I could see that it had been well taken care of—there weren't any holes in the upholstery—and it had an automatic transmission and brand new floor mats. I started the engine and turned on the radio. Mom, Dad, and Donna were standing nearby, watching with big smiles on their faces. Oh God, it was a great car! I got out and gave each of them a big hug. Later, Dad informed me that I'd need to earn enough money over the summer to pay for half of the car, and that I'd be responsible for most of the gasoline. That was fine with me! I was so proud when I parked *my* car in the high school parking lot. By suppertime, I'd probably racked up fifty miles cruising the streets of Meeker. Yes, my little '56 Ford was a dandy!

On a beautiful spring day in late May, the school year came to an end. After hanging out with my friends at the pool hall for about an hour, we went our separate ways. I decided to drag main street a couple of times and then drive around town, listening to the radio. Meeker hadn't grown much: its population was still around 1,500, it didn't have one stoplight, and many of the streets weren't paved. The entire business district was about four square blocks, which consisted of a very old post office, the courthouse, a bank, two drugstores, two hardware stores, three cafes, and four bars. It also had one liquor store that did a booming business, a couple of grocery stores, the Rio Theatre, two motels, two car dealerships, four gas stations, and a few other businesses, including the old Meeker Hotel. I'd spent many hours over the years in that lobby, where there were huge mounted bull elk and massive bucks from the 1930s and 1940s. One other business, located two miles west of town, was the Stagecoach Inn.

Another unique business was a clothing store, A. Oland & Company. The building it was in, built in the early 1900s, had been well cared for. When I walked in to buy new Levis, the first thing I noticed was the smell of leather coming from their large assortment of cowboy boots and belts. The old hardwood floor would creak beneath my feet as I walked through the store.

As the years had gone by, Meeker attracted more and more hunters to the area, and many of the businesses relied on the four weeks of hunting season for a good percentage of their annual income. This was common

Chapter Five: LIFE GOES ON

in areas where hunting big game was such a huge attraction, and it wasn't unusual to see long lines at many businesses that time of year.

I decided to take a drive on a county road south of town. By now, the fields were starting to green up, and the cattle and sheep on the ranches were having their calves and lambs. The ranchers and their hands harvested thousands of tons of hay during the summer.

While driving back to town, I couldn't help thinking how glad I was that Dad had chosen this little town to live in. All of our neighbors were friendly, helping each other when needed. Everyone knew everyone—the gossip flew from one person to another, and the phone lines were burning with chatter. It was a place where the old-timers would often say, "You'd better have your groceries by 6:30 p.m. and your gasoline by nine, because after that, they roll up the sidewalks."

The first of June rolled around, and Dad was able to get me a part-time job at the trucking company. Literally speaking, it was a "shitty" job. I was required to clean out stock trailers that hauled sheep, their urine soaked into dried waste. The trailers had very little air circulation, so as I peeled the caked-on crap from the deck, the air was filled with the smell of ammonia. It was so strong that it made my eyes burn and water. It was hard, sweaty work, but I needed the money to help pay off the car.

By now, I had a serious girlfriend, Donna Cook, who I'd been seeing since early May. She was about 5'3" and weighed around a hundred pounds, had big brown eyes, auburn hair, and beautiful lips. She was truly gorgeous, very smart, and had a dynamite personality. There was just one big problem—her parents didn't want her to date me, so we were forced to sneak around. I told Mom about Donna and how her parents felt, and she advised me to be careful. She didn't think deceiving them was such a good idea.

While hanging out with Ken one day, he said, "How'd you like to make some extra money?" "Sure...but how're we going to do that?" I questioned. He laughed, "Rob the feed store!" I told him that I didn't want any part of a robbery, but he insisted, "Just listen to my plan—there's no way we'll get caught."

Ken had worked at the feed store, so he knew everyone went home at noon for an hour. He told me we could park his vehicle behind the

Conoco station, walk down the alley to the feed store, slide one of the big back doors open just enough to get in, and when we got to the office area, we'd crawl on our hands and knees to the register so no one would see us through the big front windows. He'd pop open the cash register, take out some cash, and then we'd haul ass. "Hell," he added, "we can have the entire job pulled off in less than ten minutes!" I told him that it sounded like it was something that *could* be pulled off, but that he'd better count me out. But after several minutes of arguing, he talked me into it.

A few days later, we put the plan into action, and it went off without a hitch. While walking back down the alley towards Ken's car, I felt as though someone was following us. I glanced over my shoulder twice, but I didn't see anyone. We got into Ken's car and went back to his house. After splitting up the cash—which only totaled $120—I headed home.

Feeling guilty for my part in the robbery, I decided to go for a drive to get my mind off it. It was mid-afternoon, and while cruising west on Park Street, I saw flashing lights in my rearview mirror. Shit! It was the town marshal. I pulled over, straight across the street from the back of the courthouse. The marshal walked up to the car and told me to get out. After obliging, I asked, "What's the problem?" He yelled, "Put your hands on the trunk of your car and spread your legs!" After frisking me, he said to start walking towards the courthouse. We went inside, down a set of stairs and a long hallway to the sheriff's office. I was taken to a small room and told to have a seat. The sheriff walked in and informed me that the Meeker Feed Store had been robbed and he had every reason to believe that Ken and I had done it. He said there was a witness who had seen us walking down the alley near the feed store around noon. I said, "I haven't been near the feed store." He yelled, "Don't lie to me!" "I'm not!" For the next hour, he questioned me and I lied to him. I'd made up my mind that I wasn't confessing to anything.

The sheriff left the room and came back about thirty minutes later. He slammed a piece of paper down on the desk in front of me. "Lie *now*, you son of a bitch!" I took my time and read every word. Damn it! Ken had handwritten a complete confession, giving them every single detail. I looked at the sheriff and said, "Looks like the game is over."

Reality quickly set in: they took my fingerprints and a picture for my mug shot, then the sheriff summoned the jailer. I said, "I need to make a phone call." He barked back, "I'm locking your ass up!" I thought quickly.

Chapter Five: LIFE GOES ON

"I don't claim to know everything about the justice system, but I *do* know that I have the right to make one phone call." He calmed down then and said, "Alright, but make it quick."

I picked up the phone, called Mom, and told her what had happened. She seemed surprised, but not shocked, and during our brief conversation, she remained cool and calm. She told me that she and Dad would do what was necessary to get me out of jail. Before hanging up, I said that I loved her and that I was sorry. She said, "I love you, too, Son. Please try not to worry."

I stood up then so the jailer could cuff me; at that moment, I felt as though I was being treated as a hard-core criminal. We walked to the elevator and went to the top floor where the jail was located. He removed my handcuffs and put me into the cell. *Bang!* The steel door slammed shut and I heard it being locked behind me.

On the other side of the cell and through the steel bars, I could see out a window located across the hallway—there was my car, parked across the street. By standing on my tiptoes, I could also see part of the parking lot below me.

Something Uncle Donnie said kept running through my mind: "Your first intuition is right 99 percent of the time." Dirty, rotten son of a bitch! Why hadn't I followed *mine*? I'd let my parents down, and this would be a huge strike against me, as far as winning over Donna's parents. It could also jeopardize the coach letting me go out for basketball next year, and on top of that, I would now have a criminal record. I could also be sent to Buena Vista, a state prison where juveniles are placed! A beautiful summer day had turned into one helluva nightmare!

At six that evening, the jailer slid the supper tray through a slot in the door. I couldn't bring myself to eat—not even one bite. Ken was a few cells away, totally out of sight. We had had a brief conversation, but I really didn't feel like talking to him. Besides, there could be someone listening in. I continued standing, staring out the window. Just before darkness set in, I spotted Mom and Dad across the street: they were taking my car home.

After a sleepless night, I got up at daybreak and stared out the window. At around seven, the jailer showed up with breakfast. It only took me a couple of minutes to wolf down the bacon, eggs, and toast, and the coffee sure did taste good! Now if only I had a cigarette to go with it!

Time crept by. Every so often, I'd stand on my tiptoes to see if Dad's green panel was in the parking lot. I'd convinced myself that he was going to be very pissed off. Finally, at ten, I saw him pull in. My heart started racing as I wondered what he was going to say.

Minutes later, I heard the jailer's keys rattling at my cell door. He said, "Come with me," and when we got in the sheriff's office, I spotted Dad standing inside the doorway. The sheriff told me my bond papers were taken care of and I could leave.

The walk down the hallway and across the parking lot to the panel seemed like a mile long. Dad didn't say one word. Once we got inside the vehicle, he lit a Roi-Tan and started the engine. The silence was deafening! I just knew that any minute, all hell was going to break loose. After about two blocks, he yelled, "I hope you've learned your goddamned lesson!" I struggled to speak, saying, "Yes, Dad, I have. I'm sorry I let you down." He told me I needed to thank Cal for signing the bond papers.

When we got to the house, Mom gave me a big hug. "Thank God you're home!" I managed to crack a smile and say, "Being locked up was hell, Mom." After a few minutes, I walked over to Cal's to thank him. He didn't ask any questions—he was just glad that I was back home.

That afternoon, I slipped off with Donna to tell her what had happened. I told her I was sorry to let her down and asked for her forgiveness. She put her arms around me and told me not to worry. Wow! She was amazing!

The first week of August was my preliminary hearing, and I had been appointed a public defender. After I met with him, we went over everything that had happened. He said that he thought we could probably have the case thrown out of court because the town marshal and county sheriff had never—not one time—read me my rights. "Legally, you didn't have to answer any of their questions before hiring an attorney." I told him that it was tempting to fight the case, but that I just wanted it over with. He said, "I understand that. Since this is your first offense, you'll probably just receive probation, but I want you to know there might be a chance that you have to do some jail time." I told him I understood.

The next day I went back to work at Harp Transportation, painting the outside of the stock trailers. August slowly passed, and the closer the trial date got, the more sleepless nights there were. What if the judge *did* send me to Buena Vista? Damn! I hope not!

Chapter Five: LIFE GOES ON

At the end of August, Ken and I walked into the courtroom at the Rio Blanco County courthouse. I was by myself because Mom and Dad had to work. It may sound strange but—for some reason—I was feeling very calm.

The court proceedings took less than an hour. We both pled guilty, and the judge sentenced us to two years probation and restitution. That meant we could no longer spend time together—we had to pay back the money we stole from the feed store and be home by eleven every night. *Pow!* The sound of the wooden gavel echoed throughout the courtroom as it pronounced the end of our trial. I shook hands with my attorney, said goodbye, and walked out of the courthouse. Thank God it was over!

The Saturday of Labor Day Weekend found Dad and me driving up the river highway at 6:00 a.m. We were going to hike into Swede Lake, elevation 8,700 feet. It would be a steep, four-and-a-half-mile long hike, starting at 7,000 feet.

By eight, we were up the trail into thin air, and we took frequent breaks to catch our breath. We hiked through groves of aspen where the forest floor was covered with tall ferns that were starting to turn brown. The grass in the meadows had yellowed with the fall temperatures, and the wildflowers had lost their color. It was obvious that the vegetation had already "tasted frost," and soon—very soon—Mother Nature would be breaking out her magical paintbrush, changing the tree leaves to their dazzling fall colors.

We reached Bailey Lake—the lower lake—by nine. Swede was located another three-quarters of a mile east of Bailey. Since there was no longer a trail, Dad and I wove our way through some very thick timber. A few minutes later, we broke out of the woods and were standing on the south end of Swede Lake.

Oh, my! What a sight! The lake was small—about 175 by 150 yards. On its west was a thick stand of pines, and some of them had toppled into the lake; their lifeless trunks, bleached nearly white and with no limbs, rose a few inches above water level.

At the place where we were standing, the surface of the lake was completely covered with something we hadn't seen before—a green algae.

It extended from the shoreline to about sixty feet out into the lake. The wide band of green ran all the way down the west side, but the rest of the lake was algae free. I dipped my hand into the water and discovered that the algae were made up of very tiny individual plants about the size of a very small nail head.

Looking towards the north, we could see a towering mountain—Buford Peak—which stood at nearly 10,000 feet. Against the dark-blue sky, the jagged cliff at its top seemed to be touching the puffy clouds that were floating by.

Dad and I decided to have lunch. While eating, we scanned the mountains around us. Towards the southeast was the majestic South Fork Rim; the massive flat-top mountain extended for miles in a north-south direction. Just below its summit were sheer, rocky cliffs, and the miles of steep terrain below them were covered with huge stands of pines and aspens, creating a sea of green.

As we looked towards the southwest, we could see Burro Mountain, 10,164 feet, in the distance. Far, far below, in the bottom of the enormous valley that separated the South Fork Rim and Burro Mountain, was the South Fork of the White River, slicing its way through the beautiful meadows where it would soon connect with the North Fork. We were surrounded by paralyzing beauty!

We rigged our fishing rods and got down to business. Over the next several hours, Dad caught six beautiful brookies and a twenty-one-inch rainbow; I caught a total of seven trout. After cleaning our catch and putting them in the canvas bag to stay cool, we talked, teased each other, and laughed a lot. We were in agreement: we had to return to this lake next summer. We soon gathered our things and started the long hike out. How lucky I was to have such a great companion in my dad, in surroundings that were beautiful beyond belief.

The weeks flew by and it was now fall, 1964. I was a junior and anxious to get back into basketball. But first: opening day! I got very lucky when, right before sunrise, I shot a huge four-point buck. Its dark-colored horns had an outside spread of twenty-seven inches, and its body was nearly the size of a spike bull elk.

Chapter Five: LIFE GOES ON

By early afternoon, we had the buck in the barn. I rushed to the house to get Mom, but she had a message for me: "Donna called—she wants you to call her as soon as you can." "Where'd she call from?" I asked. Mom said, "From her house." Shit! I didn't know what was going on: I was afraid her mom would answer the phone. I guess if she did, I could just hang up. I nervously dialed the number and was relieved to hear Donna's voice answer, "Hello?" then say, "I have some great news! Mom and Dad have given me permission to go to the movie with you!" Oh, God! I fumbled for words and finally asked, "Are you *serious?*" She laughed, "Yes." I told her how happy I was. "I'll pick you up at seven." Hell, I was so nervous and excited that I forgot to tell her about the buck!

I ran out the back door to the barn to tell Mom and Dad about the conversation, and they were as shocked as I was. We took care of the deer, then I took a long bath, shaved, and did some serious primping.

I pulled into Donna's driveway at 7:00 p.m. Shit! I was so nervous! She had me come in for a few minutes. I knew her parents and, of course, they knew me. Donna's dad told her to come straight home after the movie. I will never, ever forget the feeling I had while holding her hand when we walked through the front doors of the Rio Theatre. It truly was one of the happiest nights of my life. And yes, I did take Donna straight home after the movie. I didn't want to get on the wrong side of her parents!

The first of November, I talked with the basketball coach. He was concerned that I would quit again, as I'd done a few years before. I assured him that I wouldn't. He smiled and said, "Welcome aboard, then." Oh, what a relief! I wanted one last chance to prove to him that I could play the game.

A few days later, I walked onto the basketball court for the first night of practice. It felt so good! I had one hell of a lot of catching up to do, since I'd missed my freshman and sophomore years. My primary goal was to be on the starting five of the A team by the time the district tournament was played in my senior year. I wanted one more crack at the Craig Bulldogs after our heart-breaking one-point loss to them in junior high.

CHAPTER SIX

Tragedy Strikes

ON FRIDAY, NOVEMBER 13, I was sitting in class when an announcement came over the intercom for me to report to the principal's office. A buddy seated nearby said, "Ooooo—somebody's in trouble!" I left class and, as I rounded the corner to the office, I looked down the long hallway and saw my uncle Harold standing there. A wave of fear shot through me: I knew something had happened to Dad.

Harold said that Dad was in the hospital in Rifle. He and some other workers were using a winch truck to unload a thousand-pound piece of steel from Dad's work truck, and either the cable on the winch snapped or the hook somehow came loose, and the piece of steel fell several feet, landing on Dad's left foot. It had been crushed.

The news shocked me and tears started streaming down my cheeks. It was as if someone had driven a spear right through my heart. I managed to say, "I'll meet you at our house," and headed out the front door of the school. To make matters worse, it was snowing hard, so the road to Rifle would be slick and snow-packed, and visibility would be horrible.

I was so shook up that I could barely get the key in the ignition of my car. Minutes later, I got home to find both Mom and Donna crying. After they finally got a suitcase packed for Dad, we started our long drive. Normally, it would take about forty-five minutes to get to Rifle, but because of the snowstorm and slick roads, it took about an hour and a half. The shock of Dad being severely injured, plus the icy roadway, put our nerves on edge.

We found Dad in the intensive-care unit. Oh, God. It broke my heart to see him lying there in a hospital bed. I tried hard not to cry when I laid my hand on his arm. "How are you feeling, Dad?" I asked. I couldn't believe what he said: "Not too bad, Son. But the doctor told me they're going to have to amputate part of my foot."

Mom and Donna broke down, crying. Shit! I felt like I was going to pass out! I said, "No, Dad. They're not going to amputate one inch of your foot!" "There's no other choice, Son—it's too badly mangled." I told him I'd be back in a few minutes—that I needed to go to the restroom.

Once I got in the men's room, I started crying so hard that dry heaves set in. For several minutes, I hung my head over the sink, periodically reaching for Kleenex to wipe the tears away and blow my nose. I couldn't help thinking that Dad would probably never be able to hike or walk very well again, which meant he wouldn't be able to go fishing or hunting anymore. What a horrible thought! I finally calmed down enough to go back to Dad's room.

We spent the next few hours with him, and around four o'clock, we met separately with the doctor who would be doing the surgery. He explained that he'd have to remove a lot of Dad's foot and why. I asked, "Will he have to walk with a cane the rest of his life?" The doctor said, "No, I don't think so. I'll try to save as much as I can, but I won't know the extent of the damage until I do the surgery." We thanked him and said we'd see him the next day after Dad's surgery.

We returned to Dad's room and told him we were going to go get something to eat. When we came back to the hospital, Mom and Donna visited with him for a few hours, then they went to a motel for the night. I decided to spend the night with Dad.

As I sat near him, the mental pain—the anguish—was devastating. I felt nauseated, my head hurt, and my heart was heavy. I was having a hard time accepting the upcoming amputation. I thought, "There *has* to be some way they can reconstruct his foot and save it." "Dad," I said, "I want to look at your foot." His leg was propped up on a pillow, and I thought I could remove the bandages without disturbing the wounded area. "I don't think that's a good idea, Son," he said. "It's really in bad shape." I finally convinced him to let me take a look.

I unhooked the clips and slowly started removing the covering, wrap after wrap. The closer I got to the last wrap, the harder my heart pounded. Finally, I removed the final layer. Oh, God. Dad was right—I never should've talked him into letting me look at it. It was a mangled mess, and I couldn't even decipher where his toes were. It reminded me of looking at a two-pound package of hamburger. I carefully rewrapped the covering over his foot and placed my hands on his arm. "I'm so sorry, Dad." He looked up at me and said, "You can't cry over spilt milk, Son." Those words would be embedded in my memory forever.

A nurse came in and told Dad she was going to give him a shot to relieve the pain so he could get some sleep. He calmly said, "Oh, I don't think that's necessary." She said, "Yes, it is," and gave him the shot. "My hero," I thought, "the toughest guy I know. He has a crushed foot, and he didn't think he needed a shot for pain!" Moments later, he drifted off to sleep. I walked to the nurses' station and asked if I could have some coffee. She showed me where to go and, after fixing it with cream and sugar, I walked outside. I had a few cigarettes stashed in my coat pocket, so I lit one, hoping it would help calm me down.

It was the longest night of my life. I probably drank at least ten cups of coffee and went outside several times to smoke. Finally, daybreak showed its face: the sky was clear and the storm had moved out. I walked to Dad's room to see if he was awake, slowly pushing the door open. "Mornin', Son," he said. "Mornin', Dad. How're you feeling?" "Not too bad," he replied. We talked for a while and, a short time later, Mom and Donna walked into the room.

At about 7:30, the doctor came in. After greeting everyone, he explained a test he wanted to do, where he would use a sharp instrument to poke the top of Dad's foot. He wanted Dad to tell him when he could feel the sharp prick. The doctor unwrapped Dad's foot, took the instrument, and gently began touching it. It was gut wrenching to watch. There were times when Dad would say "yeah" when the doctor hadn't even touched him. Other times, there'd be a tiny spot of blood from the instrument's prick, and Dad wouldn't say anything or even flinch. He was fighting for every inch of his foot, while the doctor was trying to figure out the extent of the damage.

After a few minutes of this, the doctor took a black marker and drew a line across Dad's foot. Tears streamed down my cheeks: the mark was near Dad's heel, and I realized that this was where the doctor was going to cut. Dad would be losing two-thirds of his foot.

The doctor explained the situation to Dad, reassuring him that he'd try to save as much as possible. Dad said, "I understand, Doc." Mom and Donna each gave Dad a kiss and wished him luck; I squeezed his hand and

Chapter Six: TRAGEDY STRIKES

told him I loved him, then the nurses wheeled him out of the room and we were left alone.

By noon, the surgery was completed. The doctor talked with us and said things had gone reasonably well. I asked, "How much had to be amputated?" He said that Dad had a little more than his heel remaining, and that he'd probably be in the hospital eight to ten days. He told us that in the months to come, after the stub healed, there would be a prosthetic piece made that conformed to it and filled out the rest of Dad's shoe or boot. Finally, he said, "In time, Don should be able to walk without a cane. He'll have a distinct limp, and he will always be missing some of his balance."

About an hour later, a nurse came to let us know Dad was back in his room. She said we could only stay a few minutes, as the doctor wanted him to get some sleep. Mom and Donna stood on one side of the bed and I stood on the other. Softly, I said, "How do you feel, Dad?" He replied, "Not too bad." My hero, the tough guy! I knew he had to be feeling some pain. We talked for a few minutes, telling him how much we loved him and that he needed to sleep now. I said that we'd be back tomorrow morning around nine.

The drive back to Meeker was long. The kingpin of our family was down, and the pain for the three of us was nearly unbearable. When we got to town, I dropped Mom and Donna at home and told them I was going to see my girlfriend. When I got to Donna's house, I wasn't able to tell her the complete story without breaking down. She slid across the car seat, put her arms around me, and held me tight. She whispered, "I'm so sorry, Danny." She hadn't gotten to know Dad yet, but she knew how I felt about him.

As soon as I got home, I forced myself back into routine. I cleaned the Stokermatic and filled it with coal—a good thing, since the hopper was nearly empty. When we had supper, it was so strange sitting there without Dad at the end of the table. Afterwards, Mom was on the phone for almost three hours, talking to Dad's relatives, coworkers, and friends, who were all asking about him.

It was plain to see that Tom missed Dad, going from room to room, looking for him. I was mentally and physically exhausted and went to bed at ten. It seemed like it'd been forever since I put my head on a pillow.

When we got back to Rifle the next morning, we talked to a nurse before going to Dad's room, and she reported that he was doing pretty good. She smiled and said, "We've had a problem convincing him to take pain medication."

Dad was glad to see us and his spirits were high. It just blew my mind that he continued to have a great attitude. We visited off and on till noon and were glad when he took a nap from 12:30 to three. At around four o'clock, we told him goodbye. I said that I'd see him on Wednesday and he replied, "Oh, Son, that's not necessary. You need to go to school and basketball practice." I smiled, "I'll see you Wednesday morning at nine."

Later that evening, I spent a couple hours with Donna. I told her I was really worried that Dad wouldn't be able to hike and hunt anymore. "It will shatter him, and it'll be *devastating* to me!" She said, "I truly believe that, after your dad's foot heals and he completes therapy, the two of you will return to the mountains, doing what you love." The one thing that I admired most about Donna was how upbeat she was. Her positive outlook for Dad made me feel a lot better.

My friends sought me out the following day in school, telling me how sorry they were about Dad's accident. It was hard to focus in class, and I gave it my best in basketball practice.

On Wednesday, I drove to Rifle by myself and spent the entire day with Dad. He was glad to see me and his spirits were still high. He told me that the doctor would probably release him the following Tuesday or Wednesday. When I said goodbye later that afternoon, I told him that Mom, Donna, and I would see him the next Saturday. When I got home, Mom said that Dad's brother and his wife were flying in from California on Friday, and that they planned to stay until Monday. They would rent a car in Grand Junction and stay at a motel in Rifle to be close to Dad.

That weekend, we spent several hours visiting with Dad, his brother, and the brother's wife, and the following Wednesday, we drove to Rifle and brought Dad home. What a great day! He did very well walking with his crutches, but it was tricky getting him up the steps at home. Once he was seated in his easy chair, I slid the footstool over and he propped his legs up on it. *Plop!* Just that quick, Tom jumped up on his lap. "Boy, a cold beer would taste good right now!" he exclaimed. I rushed to the refrigerator and got him one. He fired up a Roi-Tan and said, "I'm so glad to be home!" At supper, it was good to see him sitting at the end of the kitchen table again.

Chapter Six: Tragedy Strikes

On Sunday, I brought Donna to the house to meet Dad and Mom. It filled my heart with joy to watch and listen to them talk. Heck, it was as though they'd known each other their entire lives.

The cold winter months passed slowly. During that time, Mom, the neighbors, and friends took Dad to his doctor appointments in Rifle and Grand Junction. The first of March, Dad was fitted with the prosthetic piece that the doctor had talked about, and Dad started walking with a cane. He amazed everyone with how quickly he progressed.

In school, basketball season had gone very well, and the coach allowed me to start on the B team the last two games. I was playing a forward position and had become extremely accurate when shooting long shots from the baseline; I even shot 80 percent from the free-throw line! I just knew that I would be on the starting five of the A team by district tournament time next year.

The cane soon left Dad's hand and he started walking on his own, a transition we were excited and happy to see. He did have a distinct limp, but he showed very good balance, and by mid-April, he had returned to work. Through the past five months, I never heard him complain, nor had he felt sorry for himself. God, I hoped when I grew up that I'd be as brave as he was!

On April 16, 1965, I turned seventeen. A couple days later, Donna's parents invited me to supper. Oh, shit! Prior to going to her house, I put on a new pair of Levis and a shirt that Mom and Dad had gotten me for my birthday. I primped and primped in front of the mirror before leaving, making sure that there wasn't one hair out of place. I knocked on the door—I was so anxious!—and Donna answered it, inviting me in. I greeted her mom and dad—Patty and Jim—and then I met her sisters—Barbara, Jaime, and Marty—and her little brother, Kenny, the youngest. I had seen them all around town but hadn't talked to them very much.

After supper, Donna walked me to my car, where she teased me mercilessly about being so nervous. We both laughed! By now, we had found some secluded parking places where we'd love one another while listening to songs such as the "House of the Rising Sun," "You've Lost that Lovin' Feelin'," "Don't Let the Sun Catch You Cryin'," and many new hits from the Beatles. Yes, we were two teenagers, falling in love.

But far away, bombs and bullets were flying. The United States military had escalated the war with North Vietnam, and it had now become a major talking point at dinner tables throughout the country. There were more questions than answers as to why we had become involved in Vietnam, and the fear of being drafted was common for high school boys. Many of them were rushing to the altar to marry so they would be put in a different classification; others were doing whatever was possible to obtain a deferment. I was starting to worry, because Uncle Donnie, who had been in the army, told me that the war would probably get worse and last for years.

The school year soon ended. For me, there wouldn't be much of a summer vacation—I'd agreed to work for Donna's dad, who was a fencing contractor. The site for the barbed-wire fence we'd be building was about forty-five miles southwest of Meeker in the Piceance Creek area.

Because it was such a long drive, Jim decided to park his thirty-foot trailer house near where we'd be working. Donna and her mom cleaned and stocked the trailer with supplies, and on June 3, 1965, our little caravan headed for Piceance Creek. Jim and Kenny, Donna's little brother, were in Jim's old Willys Jeep station wagon towing the trailer, and Donna—the "chief cook and bottle washer"—and I followed them in my car.

In about thirty miles, we arrived at Pat Johnson's ranch on Piceance, where I left my car so we could all ride in it to Meeker on the weekends. Pat was a well-liked, highly respected cattleman, and he was the guy we were building the fence for. He came out to greet us, then Donna and I got in the Jeep to continue on to PL Ranch, owned by Si Berthelson, another cattleman. His son, Wiley, and I were classmates and teammates on the basketball squad. We headed straight west beyond the ranch up Willow Creek and, after another eight-or-so miles, finally arrived at our campsite. Jim had cut thousands of cedar posts over the winter and they were stacked nearby, along with many new rolls of barbed wire and boxes of fence staples.

After unhooking the trailer and leveling it, we took several loads of wire and boxes of staples in the Jeep to where the fence would be built

Chapter Six: TRAGEDY STRIKES

and unloaded them near the fence right-of-way. Back at the campsite, we loaded seven- and eight-foot posts. The seven footers would be used for line posts; the eight footers would be used where braces were needed and for corner posts. By now it was nearly five o'clock, so Jim said we'd shut it down for the day.

Around six, we sat down to a supper that Donna had prepared, and when darkness set in, we all went to bed. I stepped out of the trailer while Donna got undressed and into bed. She had the top bunk above a larger bed where Jim and Kenny slept, and I bedded down on a couch.

Early the next morning, around 5:30, I heard Jim get up and put the coffee on, then I heard the trailer door open and shut, so I figured he was going out to use the latrine that he'd made. While I was slipping on my Levis, I heard, "Pssst." I looked over at the top bunk and saw Donna motioning to me to come over. I glanced down and saw that Kenny was sound asleep, so I tiptoed over. She was laying on top of the covers, wearing short, silky, sexy PJs. I gave her a long, passionate kiss then pulled away, fearing that her dad might open the door and catch us. Oh, shit! I wished we were alone and I could crawl into bed with her!

By seven, we'd finished breakfast and Jim, Kenny, and I got into the Jeep and headed up the mountain to the fence right-of-way, where we'd string out the load of posts. Donna stayed at the trailer to continue to get things organized. We spent the entire day hauling load after load, only stopping for a short thirty-minute lunch break. By evening, I was exhausted after handling what must have been hundreds of cedar posts, and shortly after supper—at dark—we turned in. During the night, we were all awakened by a pack of yipping coyotes that came very close to the trailer.

The next morning, we started building fence. Using a spade, Jim and I dug all the postholes by hand to a depth of about twenty inches. After placing a seven-foot post in a hole, we partially filled each one then used the handle end of the shovel to tamp the dirt. More dirt and more tamping followed till the hole was completely packed and full, with the post standing perfectly straight and solid. We'd dig the next posthole about sixteen feet away, making sure that it lined up with the previous one. Jim was very particular and wanted a straight fence line.

After putting several line posts in place, we set three or four eight-foot posts just a few feet apart to construct what was called a "brace," which acted as an anchor system to hold the stress of the long, tight spans of barbed wire. After we set sixty or seventy posts, we wound the wire, one strand at a time, around a brace post and made sure it was well-secured. Placing a six-foot steel bar through the hole in the center of the spool of wire, we walked it down the fence line—Jim on one side and me on the other—unspooling the wire as we went along until we came to the next brace. Here, the wire was cut and attached to a stretcher, which was hooked onto a brace post, and the wire was tightened and secured to the post with staples. This process was repeated until four strands were evenly spaced and stapled to every post. Damn! It was sure hard work, but I needed the money and Jim paid me a fair wage.

After a few days, we had developed a system of getting undressed at night, dressed in the morning, and using the outdoor bathroom. Some days, Donna and Kenny would stay at the trailer, but most of the time, they came on the job with us. We would work until noon on Saturday, then drive to Pat Johnson's ranch, get in my car, and drive to Meeker. Sunday was our day off. Back at home, it felt so good to get into the tub, take a long bath, and shave a five-day growth of whiskers. On Monday morning, we'd load my trunk with groceries, drinking and washing water, and a couple cases of soda, then head back to the trailer. Jim told me that we'd be working this schedule during the entire summer.

Donna and I looked forward to the weekends because every Saturday night, we went to the movie. Her parents still insisted that I bring her straight home afterwards, so we usually left the theater in the middle of the show and went to our favorite parking place. It was the only time we could really be alone together, so these nights were always passionate.

The last Sunday in June, Dad and I decided to go fishing at Lake of the Woods, our first outing since his accident. We left early, arrived at the trailhead about an hour later, and hiked in. God, it felt good to be in the high country! The sweet smell of pine filled the cool mountain air and wildflowers were just beginning to bloom on the hillsides. We walked slowly, because Dad's stride had shortened and, with his limp, he couldn't walk as fast as he used to.

After a half mile, we could hear the roar of the river, and in a few minutes, we came to our crossing spot. Damn! The rickety bridge was gone! The forest service had dropped a massive pine tree across the river to act as a bridge, and even though it was probably forty inches wide, I was concerned about Dad walking across because of the rounded surface.

Chapter Six: TRAGEDY STRIKES

The sound of the raging river was so loud, pounding the boulders below us, that I had to get close to Dad's ear to yell, "What do you think!?" He yelled back, "I'll crawl across." "Are you sure?" He smiled, "I want to catch some fish!"

I made two trips across the log, taking all of our things, and then walked back to the middle, waiting for Dad to crawl on his hands and knees. Just six feet below, the swift water slammed into boulders with such force that it was kicking a mist into the air, and I could feel the moisture on my face. "If a person was to fall here," I thought, "they probably wouldn't get out alive."

As I watched Dad crawl, chills ran up my spine. My forty-year-old dad—my hero—was showing gutsy, gritty determination beyond belief. As he got near me, I turned and walked down the tree, staying close by in case something went wrong. Minutes later, he'd made the crossing. He got near my ear and yelled, "Hell, Son—that wasn't *too* bad!" We both laughed as I said, "Let's go catch some fish!"

We ended up catching our limit of nice brookies, and after I cleaned our catch, we kicked back to enjoy lunch. This was one of several moments spent with my dad in the high country, and they were all priceless. But on this occasion, the picture of him crawling on his hands and knees down the middle of the huge pine tree, just to catch some trout and be in the high country, was inspiring.

At five the next morning, I had coffee with Dad then drove to Donna's to pick everyone up, and we headed for Piceance Creek. Time to start digging postholes again! It was hot, dirty work, and by that week's end, we'd built close to a mile of fence. The sweat was pouring!

Over that summer, Jim and I spent hundreds of hours building miles of fence. Donna worked her tail off, helping on the fence line, keeping the trailer spotless, and cooking meals for us. Kenny did his best to keep himself busy as he played in the dirt, threw rocks, chased lizards, and read comic books.

Sometimes after supper, Jim took us for long drives in the high country of Willow Creek. The summer scenery was beautiful, and we saw a lot of wildlife—especially deer with the bucks' antlers in velvet. At night, the four of us would lie in bed and listen to the coyotes yipping. Many times there would be powerful thunderstorms with loud cracks of thunder. Lightning illuminated the trailer, followed by the sound of rain pounding on the metal roof.

On Saturday, the last day of July, we rolled into town around two. By now my face, arms, and neck were cocoa brown from all the exposure to the sun. I was 6' tall, a lean 165 pounds, and my biceps were as hard as a rock because of all the hard work. I headed home to clean up and get ready for our date at the movies, and on Sunday, I went to Donna's in the evening and had supper with the entire family. It was Kenny's eighth birthday.

On Monday morning, Jim and I drove alone back to Piceance. Donna was in 4-H and needed to stay home to work on a dress for the fair, and Kenny had really gotten bored the past couple of weeks and was going to stay in town to play with his friends. So, early in the morning, we headed back to Piceance with a big batch of stew and goulash that Patty, Jim's wife, had made, so all we had to do was heat up food for our suppers.

By now, the temperature was boiling hot in mid-afternoon. The days seemed to creep by, and I missed Donna and Kenny, who really broke up the boredom of constant work. Jim and I often fenced till almost dark, as he wanted to complete the project before I went back to school. At the end of this particular week, Jim had business to take care of, so we took off Friday and Saturday instead of the usual Saturday and Sunday.

On Sunday, August 22, I went to pick up Jim, and Kenny decided to go with us. While transferring supplies from my car into Jim's Jeep at Johnson's ranch house, Pat came out and talked to us. He said that the new right-of-way had been bulldozed by Torrence, his hired hand, a couple miles from our campsite and was ready to have new fencing built on it. He also said that we'd have to roll up the old barbed wire fence before starting the new one. Jim said that we'd take care of it; then we left.

At the trailer, we unloaded our supplies then loaded the back of the Jeep with as many seven-foot posts as we could, clear to the roof. About thirty minutes later, we arrived at the freshly dozed area. Jim decided the best way to take care of the old barbed wire was to tie the four strands to the grill guard of the Jeep, walk down about 200 feet, cut the wire, and pull it out onto the hard-packed roadway with the Jeep. Then we'd be able to roll up each strand individually. His plan worked, and we started making good progress.

By about two o'clock, we'd reached an area at the top of a steep hill where there had been a lot of dirt bulldozed on top of the wire. When Jim backed up to pull the wire, it was snapping just a few feet from the Jeep because of the weight on top of it. He decided to pull up to the old fencing

Chapter Six: TRAGEDY STRIKES

on the crest of the hill and park the Jeep with its front tires resting against a big post that was lying on the ground. The Jeep's emergency brake didn't work, and he figured that the post would keep it from rolling. He left the Jeep idling, otherwise it would often vapor lock after it had been running for a while, especially when it was as hot out as it was now. Kenny stayed in the Jeep, sitting on the passenger side.

Jim and I tied the four strands of barbed wire to the grill guard, then he told me to go down the hill about sixty yards, cut the wire, and start pulling sections of it up out of the dirt that was covering it. I would work my way up the hill and he'd do the same down the hill. Once we got all of it uncovered, it would pull out easily without breaking.

Damn! It was backbreaking work, bending over and pulling on the wire. Sometimes the barbs would act like fishhooks and get hung up in my heavy leather gloves. With the August sun beating down, the sweat was rolling.

Then out of the corner of my eye, I thought I saw the Jeep move. I stared at it for a few seconds. I decided the heat must be getting to me, because I didn't see it moving again. Just as I bent over to get hold of a strand of wire, I saw it move again—then I saw it rolling. I yelled, "Jim! The Jeep is rolling!" At the same time, I took off running up the steep hill as fast as I could go. Jim was much closer than I was, and I saw him start running towards the Jeep, too.

Suddenly, the Jeep swerved to our left, disappearing from view over the hill. Within seconds, I cleared the hilltop, following the Jeep down the other side. I ran by Jim, who was lying in the sagebrush, holding his stomach. I knew that the barbed wire tied to the Jeep's grill must have caught him when he was trying to get to it.

It was now a downhill grade, and I could run much easier. I flew down the mountainside, jumping and dodging sagebrush. Because the Jeep kept running into the sagebrush bushes, I was starting to gain on it. Shit! I felt like my lungs were about to blow up! But I had to get to the Jeep—Kenny was still in it!

I finally got within thirty feet of it, and I could hear the sagebrush popping and snapping as the Jeep ran over them. Then the hill became even steeper and the Jeep picked up speed—I was losing ground now. I screamed, "Kenny, jump! Jump out the window!" The door handle on the inside didn't work. I stopped running when the Jeep veered more to the right. The last thing I saw was the load of cedar posts in the back of it.

Seconds later, I heard a loud boom. It sounded like a game rifle had gone off, and it echoed across the valley. Oh, my God! I bent over with my hands on my hips. I felt sick and I thought I might pass out. I heard some brush snap and turned to see Jim coming towards me, holding his stomach. His light-colored shirt was soaked with blood where the barbed wire had sliced him.

We made our way quickly down the steep hillside towards the Jeep. It took a few minutes to reach the top of the deep gully where it had gone over, coming to rest at the bottom. I could finally see what made the loud booming sound: it had become airborne for nearly forty feet, slamming into a rock ledge on the other side of the gully.

Jim and I slid down the steep dirt bank. I was scared—*really* scared—about Kenny. When we walked around the Jeep, we found him hanging halfway out of a hole in the windshield on the passenger side. His head, chest, and arms were resting on the buckled-up hood. I was terrified as we gently pulled him the rest of the way out of the hole in the windshield. Jim cradled him in his arms, and I saw that Kenny's head flopped all the way back. I *knew* that his neck was broken, but I didn't want to believe it, and I couldn't say it to Jim. After walking a few feet, Jim sat down in the shade of a cedar tree, holding Kenny across his lap.

"Jim," I said, "I'm going to get help!" "Hurry!" he yelled. I clawed my way back up the steep bank and took off running up the hill. Oh, God! Adrenalin was pumping through my veins. I was so afraid that Kenny was dead.

By the time I got to the top of the hill where the Jeep had been parked, I had to stop for a minute. I had run a long way uphill and I was gasping for air. I looked at my watch and saw it was a little past three, then took off running down the hill, sweat pouring off my forehead.

Whack! Whack! Whack! The only sound to be heard was that of my work boots hitting the old dirt road. I still felt scared, and I knew I was a long, long way from any ranch house. I slowed down to a trot, my mouth so dry that I couldn't swallow. I desperately needed to make it to the trailer, which was another mile, so I could get some water.

Finally, I made it to the trailer. My face was burning up, and my hair and shirt were soaking wet with sweat. I grabbed a gallon jug full of water

Chapter Six: TRAGEDY STRIKES

and dumped the entire thing on my head. I opened the fridge and got a plastic jug filled with cold water. To start with, I just took small sips: I knew if I chugged it, I'd get sick to my stomach. Oh, God! Did that water ever taste good!

I took the plastic jug of water with me and headed down the road. There was a cabin about two miles away where Pat's hired hand, Torrence, stayed, and I could only hope and pray that he was there, or that there was a telephone.

I started thinking of Jim. He was waiting there with Kenny, and I just *had* to get help as quickly as possible. I started trotting again, but it didn't last long. After a quarter of a mile, I had to slow down. I'd literally run myself out, so I settled on walking as fast as I could. By 4:30 p.m., I arrived at the cabin. No one was there, and I ran around in it like a wild man, searching for a telephone. I just kept looking—I wanted to make sure I wasn't overlooking it. If there was no phone, I'd have to walk to the PL Ranch, about seven miles away.

Convinced there wasn't a phone, I started walking to the ranch. I felt depressed now, because I hadn't found any kind of help and I knew Jim was depending on me. I'd walked about a mile when I stopped, thinking I'd heard the distant sound of a vehicle. I listened and listened, but I couldn't hear it anymore. Damn it! Just a false alarm. Again, I started walking as fast as I could, then—*there*—I *knew* I had heard a vehicle! I stopped and turned around.

Oh, God! I could see dust in the distance. It *was* a vehicle, headed my way. Moments later, a white Ford pickup pulled up. It was Elige Joslin, the owner of an excavating company, with his wife. I hurriedly told them what had happened and he told me to jump in. We headed for the PL Ranch.

Once there, I jumped out of the pickup, running for the house. A lady met me at the door and I told her what had happened—to call for an ambulance. It was now about 5:30 and they were preparing supper for their ranch hands. Within a few minutes, the lady came to the back porch where I was sitting and said that she had contacted Pat Johnson. He was on his way, and so was the ambulance.

It seemed to take an eternity for Pat to show up with his hand, Torrence. When he did, Wiley, my classmate, came roaring up in his truck at the same time. I quickly told Pat what had happened, and he had Wiley and me jump in the back of his pickup. "We're not waiting for the ambulance," he said. Pat and Torrence got in the cab and we headed up the road, dirt flying.

The sun had gone down and darkness was beginning to set in; Pat had even turned on his headlights. Oh, God…I couldn't even imagine Jim sitting up there in the dark with his little boy. There was no sign of him at the trailer, so we continued up the road. We'd gone just a short distance when we saw him walking towards us, carrying Kenny in his arms. He'd carried him for nearly two miles, up that steep mountain to here.

We all got out of the pickup and ran to Jim. He said, "He's gone." Pat took Kenny from Jim's arms and had Torrence get some blankets from the truck, putting one in the back of the pickup. Pat laid Kenny on it and covered him with the other blanket.

There were no more words spoken. Torrence shut the tailgate and Wiley and I got in the back. Jim got in the front with Pat and Torrence, and we headed back down the valley. In the darkness, I could see Kenny's body move whenever we hit a bump. Like turning on a faucet, tears started gushing from my eyes. It was so hard to believe he was *dead*!

A few miles down the road, we met Meeker's ambulance. The paramedics loaded Kenny in their unit, and once we got to Pat's ranch, he took Jim and me to get my car. As we followed the ambulance back to Meeker, Jim spoke for the first time when we neared the city limits, asking me to stop at his parents' home so he could change clothes before going to his house. I knew it was going to be horrible for him to tell Patty and his daughters what had happened. I stood quietly by his side as he related the afternoon's events. Shock, agony, and sadness ripped through their home. I was on the verge of crying, but I tried to be strong and comfort everyone the best I could, especially Donna and her mom. Jim gathered around his other daughters and hugged and comforted them as terrible pain filled the room.

I stayed for nearly two hours, much of the time holding Donna in my arms while we sat in my car. Around midnight, I kissed her goodnight and told her I'd do anything for her, or for the family, that I possibly could.

When I got home, everyone got out of bed and I told them the complete story. We visited till nearly two. Everyone felt horrible—it was just so hard to accept.

After everyone else went back to bed, I took a bath and then turned in, but I stayed wide awake. Everytime I closed my eyes, I could hear the loud crunching of the brush snapping and popping when I was running near the Jeep. I could see Kenny hanging out of the windshield when we found him and—oh, God—the sight of Jim in the headlights, carrying his little boy. I couldn't get any sleep, so I got up when Dad did at 5:30. We drank coffee and talked, and Mom joined us around six. They both tried to comfort me; they knew I'd been through hell.

Dad left for work at 7:30 and, at eight, the phone rang. It was the Rio Blanco County sheriff, Russell Harp. He wanted me to ride with them to the site of the accident and explain what had happened.

Damn it! I wanted to hang up on him. He never asked how I was feeling or if I *felt* like going. Hell, no, I didn't want to go down to that ghostly site and look at the mangled Jeep! But I agreed to do it so Jim wouldn't have to.

Minutes later, Russell and a deputy sheriff picked me up and we headed for Piceance Creek. It was a long ride, and I was exhausted and still upset, frequently holding back tears. We arrived at the site around ten and they both looked it over. After listening to my description of events, they concluded that there was a slight downhill grade where the Jeep's tires had been resting against the big post. Evidently, due to the heavy load of posts in the Jeep, the constant weight and pressure had caused the post the Jeep was braced against to start sliding across the loose dirt. We figured it probably moved a few feet, then stopped for a minute or so. That would explain why I thought I saw it moving the first time. Then the Jeep had started nudging the post across the dirt to a steeper grade. Once there, gravity took over and it picked up speed. We could see where the right front tire had hit a rut, causing the Jeep to turn sharply to the right.

We followed the Jeep's path down the slope through the sagebrush. A few minutes later, we came to the gully where it was sitting. Son of a bitch! It was hard for me to walk up to that Jeep again! After looking at it for a few minutes, I told Russell that I had to walk away. He understood. He wrote down a few more things on his clipboard and we climbed back up the slope to their vehicle to head back to town.

Once they dropped me at home, I drove to Donna's. Over the next couple days, I spent every spare minute with her, trying to be a comfort. Her only brother was gone. At night, I was plagued with horrible nightmares, and it was nearly impossible to get any sleep. The day of the funeral, the small church was filled with family and friends. It was the first funeral I'd ever attended, and I found it to be a profoundly sad experience, especially at the graveside in Highland Cemetery. I stared at the small casket that held Kenny, tears streaming down my cheeks.

CHAPTER SEVEN

The Letter

IN SEPTEMBER, IT WAS TIME TO START my senior year, and Donna and I walked through the front door of Meeker High School holding hands. Opening day of elk season quickly followed in October, and Mom yelled from her bedroom, "What the hell is going on out there?" Dad hollered back, "I forgot to pull the stem on the goddamned alarm clock!" It was 5:30 a.m., and we were running around in the kitchen and living room and running to and from the truck, loading thermoses of coffee and hunting gear. Every couple minutes, one of us would say, "Son of a bitch! Son of a bitch!" Mom yelled, "You two need to settle down—you're acting like a couple of wild men. It's not the end of the world!" Dad shot back, "Don't worry about it, Betty Marie!" I busted out laughing, knowing Mom was right.

By the time we got to the turnoff twenty miles up the river, it was breaking day. Dad pulled over and we got out to load our rifles, just in case we saw some elk during the drive to Beaver Knob. Right before we got to our hunting country, at a place called "Windy Bill's," I yelled, "Stop, Dad—there they are!" He slammed on the brakes and we jumped out. About 150 yards away were seven elk, making their way up a steep hillside.

We ran to the edge of the road, lying down on our stomachs to get a rest for the rifles. I peered through my 4x scope and whispered, "The last one is a bull. On three, Dad: one, two, thr..." *Boom!* We both fired exactly at the same time and the elk went down. Lying just a few feet apart, we looked at each other and started laughing. "We did it! We did it!" The old saying "the right place at the right time" was so true.

We were able to drive down a road that took us within fifty yards of the two-point bull. After I finished the gutting, we dragged him down a steep hill and, with some grunting and groaning, loaded him into the truck. Dad did really well, even though his limp and slight off-balance walk slowed him down.

It was 8:45 a.m. when we pulled up in front of the house. Mom and Cal were in shock: they just couldn't believe we'd already gotten an elk! I drove to Donna's to show the bull off to her and her mom, then we took him to be processed. We spent the rest of the day relaxing, in high spirits.

A few weeks later, when I came home from school, Mom said, "I have a little surprise for you. It's sitting on your bed." It was a brand-new pair of Converse All Star tennis shoes! They were the best you could buy at Oland's Clothing store, and I knew Mom had spent many hours over her ironing board and doing other people's laundry in order to get enough money to buy them.

The next week, basketball practice started, and it sure felt good to be out on the court again. I was more excited than ever because Dad told me that he and Mom were planning to attend every game. Our first one was in December, and during warm-ups, I saw them walk into the gym. I was concerned about Dad walking on the bleacher's narrow wooden boards, but he did just fine. It meant the world to me that they were there, and it would be the first time they would see me play. I didn't get a lot of time on the court, but I made the best of what I did get and scored four points. After the game, Donna ran across the gym floor and congratulated me. I knew with God's help and me giving it 110 percent that I stood a good chance of making the starting five by district tournament time, the first of March.

Over the next couple of months, Mom and Dad traveled to our away games at Glenwood Springs, Rifle, Rangely, Craig, and Steamboat Springs, and I sure felt good when I saw them in the bleachers. I had worked hard on every phase of the game and, at practice one night, I made eighteen free throw shots in a row; our guard, Mike, held the record with nineteen.

By now, Coach Castle was showing some real interest in me; I'd moved up to the number six position and was participating in at least half of every game. In February, we played the Rifle Bears, who had a good team. With the score tied at halftime, the coach put me in. It was an action-packed game and, with only six seconds to go, the score was still tied. Under our basket, Mike stole the ball on an inbound pass, and I left the guy I was defending and broke towards the basket. I was about eight feet from the basket on the right-hand side when Mike sent a laser pass to me;

Chapter Seven: THE LETTER

I caught the ball and jumped high in the air to shoot over the Rifle guard. The ball kissed the glass on the backboard and, just as it went through the hoop—*bzzzzzzzz!*—the final buzzer sounded. The game was over and we'd won by two points!

The Meeker fans went wild and I was mobbed by my teammates. Donna ran up excitedly and gave me a big hug and kiss. After we found Mom and Dad in the huge crowd, Dad said that they'd had car trouble in Meeker and didn't get to the game till the last quarter. I smiled, "Thank God you got to see the *end* of the game!"

The regular season came to a close; next, we'd be going to the district tournament, held in Glenwood Springs. Our first game would be against the Rangely Panthers.

At Monday's practice, Coach Castle decided to change the line-up and put me with Mike, John, Jim, and Wiley. It appeared that my long hard-fought-for dream was about to come true and I'd be on the starting five at the tournament! I hoped my dream would become a true classic: if we beat Rangely, we'd play the Craig Bulldogs Friday night, and I'd get another chance to beat them in tournament play.

We got on the bus Thursday afternoon and had one of our best games of the season, handily beating Rangely. I played my heart out and scored sixteen points, the net snapping time after time with my accurate long-range shooting. When we got to the locker room, Coach Castle walked up to me and slapped me on the shoulder. "You played one *hell* of a good game!" And so the stage was set: tomorrow night we'd play the number one, AA-ranked team in the state—the Craig Bulldogs.

In Glenwood the next day, we suited up for the game and Coach gave us a long, serious talk. He told us to forget about the two season games when Craig had beaten us. He said, "You can't afford to make any mistakes tonight, so don't take any haphazard shots—and rebound, rebound, rebound!" He walked over and handed me a basketball. He said, "You've been selected as captain for tonight's game, so take the team out." Oh, shit! Chills ran up my spine. What a thrill!

Believe me, I was nervous when I led the team down the tunnel and out to the gym floor. Oh, my God! What a spectacle it was when I dribbled the ball towards the basket and put in a lay-up shot! The entire gym was packed to the rafters, and the Meeker fans gave us a standing ovation. Bands were playing, cheerleaders bouncing, and the entire gym was rocking! I'd never, ever been in such a loud arena before! I spotted Mom, Dad, and Donna in the packed crowd and gave them a wave.

I glanced down towards the other end of the gym and watched my old nemesis, Brad Smith, take a couple of long jump shots, and both snapped the cords. Many sports writers had picked him as one of the greatest high school players *ever*. The tall, 6'3" guard was averaging close to thirty points a game.

A few seconds later, the teams took their positions at center court, with Jim and Angelo, the player for the Bulldogs, inside the circle for the tip-off. The ref stepped between them and threw the ball up. Craig controlled the tip; Smith brought the ball down the court, pulled up, and snapped the cords on the basket with a long jump shot. It seemed to send a quick message to our team: "You'd better be ready to play some ball!"

We were jittery the first quarter, and Craig jumped out to an eight-point lead. In the huddle, Coach said, "Settle down—start playing the game you're capable of, or they're going to blow you off the court!" The second quarter went much better on our part, and beneath the baskets, elbows were flying, both teams fighting hard for the rebounds.

Oooooo-raaa! The buzzer sounded like a foghorn when it went off, ending the first half. It'd been a high-scoring, blisteringly paced game, with point totals at forty-two for Craig and forty for Meeker. The locker room was buzzing with confidence, and Coach was extremely pleased with our performance.

The third quarter was a barnburner: both teams were red hot, matching each other basket for basket. *Oooooo-raaa!* When the horn sounded to end the period, the scoreboard read Meeker, sixty-two; Craig, sixty-two.

By now, Coach had lost his voice. While in a tight huddle on the sidelines, the roar of the crowd made it almost impossible to hear his instructions. I looked at my teammates and said, "These guys *can* be beat. *Let's do it!*"

Jim stepped into the center circle and everyone took their positions. The ref tossed the ball up, and Jim tipped it to John. He and Mike brought it down the court and Mike rifled a pass to me on the baseline. I went up for a long jump shot. *Ker-snap!* The ball ripped the cords. For the first time, we'd taken the lead! Just seconds later, Craig's ace forward ripped the cords to tie the game. As the next few minutes ticked away with a constant roar from the fans, each team exchanged baskets time after time, and the score was still tied, now at eighty-eighty.

Chapter Seven: THE LETTER

With only thirty seconds remaining, Craig had the ball and called time-out. The entire crowd got to their feet and gave both teams a standing ovation. After the time-out, Craig started working the ball around at their end of the court, seconds ticking away. With only fifteen seconds remaining, Smith took a long jump shot and ripped the cords. Then Coach called a time-out and drew up a play. He told us if the shot was missed and Craig got the rebound, we should foul them immediately!

Mike and John brought the ball down the court to put Coach's plan into action, and—with only seven seconds remaining—the shot was taken. Damn it! The ball hit the heel of the basket, bounced around the rim, and fell out. Now down to four seconds, a Craig player was fouled. He'd have to miss his first shot of a one-and-one, then we'd have to rebound and hit a quick miracle shot. If he made both free throws, it was over.

The Craig player's first shot snapped the cords and my heart sank. The ref handed him the ball and he made the second shot. We took the ball but the inbound pass was tipped, and it rolled across the floor. *Oooooo-raaa!* The game was over. Craig Bulldogs, eighty-four; Meeker Cowboys, eighty.

I stood in the middle of the gym, trying to hold back the tears. Donna made her way through the crowd and put her arms around me. "I'm so sorry. I know how much this game meant to you." Like turning on a faucet, tears started gushing from my eyes. I'd waited four long years for a tournament rematch, and we came so close to winning. After regaining my composure, I walked over and shook hands with the Craig players and congratulated them. When I found Mom and Dad, they both said, "Son, that was one hell of a game!"

Once everyone got to the locker room, Coach said with just a whisper of a voice that he'd like to talk to everyone. The locker room became stone quiet. He said, "I don't know if you've ever seen a grown man cry," and the tears started streaming down his cheeks, "but I just want you to know that I'm so proud of you!" It was a very touching moment with very few dry eyes.

Losing to Craig seemed to have drained us, and the following night we lost third place to Rifle. Craig and Glenwood played for the championship and—as usual—Craig won. To no one's surprise, the Bulldogs later waltzed their way through the class AA state tournament in Denver. But the entire Western Slope was shocked when Craig lost the state title to a school named College High by a score of seventy-three to seventy.

I was sorry that my basketball career was over, but I was extremely thankful that my family and Donna had attended all of my games. Yes, even though sometimes the roads were icy and it was snowing like hell, Dad fulfilled his promise. I was grateful to the man upstairs for allowing my dream of making the starting five come true and for giving me a last crack at the Craig Bulldogs.

On April 16, 1966, I turned eighteen and had to register with the Selective Service board at the local courthouse. There were now over 300,000 soldiers in Vietnam. Thousands came back in body bags, and thousands more came home without arms or legs. The government had changed the rules for deferments so that even if you were married, you were still classified as 1A—the same as if you were single. That meant that for many of the guys my age, acquiring a deferment became the name of the game—or they packed their bags and headed for Canada.

Millions of citizens were against the Vietnam War, and hundreds of thousands of young men didn't feel that it was worth losing their lives over or becoming disabled. I was extremely nervous, as it appeared that the government was going to escalate the war even further. It weighed heavily on my mind.

The school year was winding down. On the night of graduation, my heart was filled with pride when I received my diploma. I suddenly remembered what Dad had told me at the end of my sophomore year, when I said that I wanted to quit high school and get a job. He'd said, "It'll be a cold day in hell when I allow you to quit. You may not realize it now, but your school years are some of the best you'll experience in your entire life." Leave it to my mom: she bought me a beautiful lever-action .22 rifle as a graduation present, its blonde stock engraved with acorns and leaves. It was just what I wanted.

I quickly learned that life was full of surprises. Just a few weeks later, on June 3, 1966, Donna and I were married in a small ceremony held at the Methodist Church. Standing at the altar, my eyes filled with tears as I watched her walk down the aisle towards me in her beautiful wedding

Chapter Seven: THE LETTER

dress, escorted by her dad. Once she got to me, I found her beauty stunning—those big brown eyes and sensuous lips. Her brilliantly white dress magnified her features.

In a few short minutes, the ceremony was over—we were pronounced husband and wife, and I kissed her. The reception was held at Mom and Dad's, where everyone enjoyed punch and wedding cake. We'd be living in a small trailer that both our moms had feverishly cleaned and gotten ready for us. They furnished it and put up curtains. It wasn't fancy, but it was *ours*. After the reception, everyone wished us luck and we drove a few blocks to our home. We were two very young teenagers starting a life together, so much in love.

I was extremely happy, but I felt a little disappointed: I couldn't take Donna on a honeymoon. Two days later, I started working at the Texaco gas station where Uncle Donnie had worked. He was now employed at the Rio Blanco County Road and Bridge Department, and he thought he could pull some strings and get me a job there, too.

In July, Dad and I bought a 1962 full cab 4x4 International Scout together. Finally, after all these years, we had a great four-wheel drive to take hunting and fishing! In mid-September, Dad, Donna, and I loaded up the Scout and went to Big Beaver. Even though Donna didn't fish, she enjoyed the outdoors and going with us to look at the beautiful scenery. We had a perfect day, saw lots of elk, and heard several big bulls bugling. It only took that one trip for Donna to be hooked on hearing the bull elk screaming across the mountain valleys. She loved it!

The next weekend, Dad had to work, so Donna and I took the Scout to Sand Peak, which included a scary drive up and down a steep mountainside. The scenery was worth it, though, because the brilliant fall colors were always captivating. About an hour later, when we were nearer Sand Peak, we pulled over and I shut the engine off. *Ooooeeee, uh-uh-uh!* Just that quick, we heard a bull bugle in the dark timber below us. We grabbed the binoculars and my homemade bugle, then slipped into the pine trees, hoping we could sneak up on the bull to see how big he was. As I called to him, he'd answer, and we'd quietly tiptoe towards him through the woods.

Ooooeeee, uh-uh-uh! Shit! We both jumped when the bull blasted a rip-roaring call about twenty yards from us. Suddenly, the timber started cracking; he'd picked up our scent and spooked. We whispered to each other that we wished we could've seen him, then we headed back to the

Scout and drove as close to Sand Peak as possible. We walked right out on top of the 10,000-foot peak and enjoyed its panoramic view, talking, laughing, and listening to the elk bugling in the distance. Later, we enjoyed lunch and, on the way out, spotted several elk in a distant meadow.

A few weeks later, hunting season arrived, and it felt good to have a dependable vehicle to use. Hell, now we had a radio to listen to and a good heater, to boot! We hunted hard for the whole season, trading off from Big Beaver to Sawmill Mountain. Donna went with us some of the time. The season ended with disappointment because we only got two bucks. Money was tight and Mom told me that the two deer wouldn't last long.

I decided to take care of the problem and, one week after hunting season closed, Donna and I drove to Nine-Mile Cutoff, private land located a few miles east of Meeker, where I shot a five-point bull. We drove back to town and a friend went with me after dark to get it. We hung the bull in our cellar, where we skinned him. A few days later, Mom, Donna, Cal, and I cut and wrapped the meat and put it in the freezer. Everyone could now breathe a little easier, as we had a good supply of winter meat.

Almost every Saturday or Sunday during the months of December and January, Donna and I would get up before daylight and drive the Scout up the river, where we'd look at the elk that had been driven down from the high country due to deep snow. Traveling the main roadways on the north and south forks of the White River, there were many mornings that we saw between 100 and 300 elk. We both loved looking at them and nearly wore out the binoculars!

A huge break for Donna and me came the first part of February. Donnie showed up at our house and said, "Are you ready to start driving a dump truck for the county?" I replied, "Hell, yes!" He smiled, "Be at the county shop at 7:00 a.m. on Monday."

God, it was so special! Now I'd have a job that had health insurance for the two of us, plus paid vacation and holidays! As the rest of February and the month of March passed, I found I really liked my job, and the pay was great!

At the beginning of April, Larry, Gerald—a friend of Donnie's—and I decided to drive east of Meeker to Ripple Creek, which is as far as the

Chapter Seven: THE LETTER

county plowed in the winter months. We were going to snowshoe in to one of the most private areas in the valley, the "101 Ranch," to fish in their lake.

On Sunday morning, we loaded up the Scout and, about an hour later, arrived at Ripple Creek. We gathered all our gear, strapped on the snowshoes, and headed up the road on our two-mile hike. In the shaded areas, the snow was nearly three feet deep. Once we got to the south-facing slope, the snow had melted and we were able to take off the snowshoes. Around eleven, we walked up to the edge of the lake. We were sure nobody was around, but we stared at the distant cabins, looking for any sign of people, such as smoke coming from a chimney. Convinced the coast was clear, we quickly rigged our rods with some big juicy worms and night crawlers.

I was the first to get rigged up. I reared back and made a long cast. *Ker-thunk!* My sinker and crawlers landed on the ice. I gently reeled in just enough so my rig would drop into the open water. *Thump, thump, thump!* I instantly had a bite! I yanked and said, "Got 'im!" Gerald yelled, "You son of a bitch!" We all started laughing as I eased a beautiful fourteen-inch brook trout onto the bank. Larry yelled, "Got 'im!" and reeled in another brook trout the same size as mine. I looked over at Gerald and said, "What's the problem?" "Fuck you!" Gerald yelled. Then he said, "Got 'im!" and reeled in a fifteen-inch brookie. Over the next few hours, we were yelling and laughing like grade school boys. Almost as fast as we could throw in, we caught a fish. I finally said, "Let's shut it down, you guys, and count the fish." Shit! The gunnysack was heavy when I picked it up and dumped out the trout—a total of fifty-six!

We broke down our rods and kicked back, then gathered our stuff and headed back to the Scout, taking turns carrying the gunnysack. I was sure it weighed well over sixty pounds.

We arrived at the Scout around four and, for some reason, I walked over to the creek and cut off a big willow branch. Gerald asked, "What are you going to do with that?" I told him I was going to string thirteen or fourteen trout on it and leave them out in the open in the back of the Scout. "I'm going to put the gunnysack with the remaining fish underneath my tire-chain sacks, just in case we get stopped." They both looked at me as if I was crazy. Larry said, "Shit, we're not going to get stopped." I smiled, "I'd rather be safe than sorry, Larry. We're way over our limit!"

A few miles down the road, we rounded a corner on the southeast side of Snell Creek. I said, "It's all over—they finally got us." Larry asked,

"Why do you say that?" I pointed across the canyon to a Colorado Fish and Game pickup that was parked on the same road we were on. "They're in a position to have watched our every move." Son of a bitch!

As we neared the pickup, there were no red lights flashing. When the distance narrowed to about fifty yards, we could see two wardens standing by the truck. I said, "They better step out in the middle of the road. Otherwise, hang on to your asses, because we're going to get rid of that sack of fish!" They stared at us as we went by, giving us a dirty look. A short time later, I shifted to second gear and slammed down the foot feed. Larry, who was in the middle, spun around, leaned over the seat, and got hold of the sack. After some confusion as to who was in the best position to toss the gunnysack, Larry handed it to Gerald. Son of a bitch! I knew the game wardens were going to come around the corner behind us any second to see what we were doing. I screamed, "Throw 'em, Gerald!" Larry reached over and tripped the door handle. The door flew open and Gerald muscled a throw, nearly falling out. Larry grabbed his left arm and pulled him back in, and Gerald slammed the door shut.

Ker-splat! The gunnysack full of fish hit the shallow barrow pit below the road. I looked in the rearview mirror. Damn! The fish exploded from the gunnysack! I saw several skidding across leaves and brush. I prayed the wardens wouldn't spot them.

Now I could see the wardens' pickup coming quickly behind us, dust flying and red lights flashing. I continued down the road until they got really close before I pulled over. We got out and the two wardens walked up to us. One was a tall fellow, the new guy who I just barely knew. The older one had been in the Meeker area for many years, and he knew me very well! There was no love lost between us.

I decided to give them a true western greeting. "Howdy," I said. The tall one responded with, "Have you guys been fishing?" I replied, "Yes, we have." He asked if we'd had any luck, and I told him we'd caught a few trout. "I'd like to check your fishing licenses and take a look at your fish," he said. After showing him our licenses, I opened up the back of the Scout and the two of them inspected and counted the trout.

The older warden said, "Where'd you catch these?" I told him we'd been at the Lake of the Woods. "I've never seen brook trout *that* big come out of Lake of the Woods," he said. I replied, "You have now!"

Chapter Seven: THE LETTER

The tall warden said, "We'd like to look around in your vehicle, if you don't mind." I said, "Oh, I don't think that's necessary. Besides, that'd require a search warrant." *Uh-oh!* He told me they could radio Meeker and have one delivered while detaining us, if I wanted to play games. I said, "Go ahead—look around—but you'll just be wasting your time." I didn't want to wait for who knows how long for a search warrant to get there.

What happened next was unbelievable! The two of them started combing my Scout like bloodhounds! They looked beneath the front seat, crawled on their hands and knees looking under the Scout, and had me open the hood so they could search around the engine. I had to turn my head and laugh when I saw one of them open the tiny glove compartment!

The tall one asked me what was in the gunnysacks behind the front seat. "Just some tire chains," I responded. He crawled up in the back and pulled the two sacks out. I said, "I'll tell you right now, if you remove those chains from the sacks, you'll put them back *exactly* the way you found them." I'll be a son of a bitch if he didn't go ahead and dump the chains out on the road!

By now, they'd virtually run out of places to look. The older warden said, "Well, I guess you guys can go now." But I was mad about the tire chains, and I stood my ground. "We're not going anywhere till you put those tire chains back in the sacks and put them behind the seat, exactly the way you found them." Reluctantly, they put the chains back. I closed up the back of the Scout and we headed out, laughing our asses off.

We hadn't even gone two miles when—lo and behold, coming right at us like a bat out of hell—there was *another* state Fish and Game pickup. A short distance from us, the truck moved towards the middle of the road and red lights started flashing. I said, "Shit, it looks like they deployed the entire cavalry!" As I braked to slow down, I quickly recognized the lone person in the pickup—the district supervisor. I got out and walked to his pickup as he rolled down his window. I said, "They already checked us out back up the road." There was no reply, just a deer-in-the-headlights look. I asked, "Did you hear what I said?" He said, "Really?" "Yeah! Call them on your radio! I'm tired of playing games here." I walked back to the Scout, hoping there'd be no more stops.

Just before we got to town, Larry and Gerald started talking about going back up the river after dark to retrieve the fish we threw out. I told them I didn't think it was worth taking a chance. They insisted and, later on that night, they came back to Meeker with the trout.

But the story doesn't end there! On my way to work Monday morning, I spotted the two wardens that had stopped us the day before parked at the Texaco station. They had a big trailer hooked up onto their pickup, and sitting on it was a large cleated Snow-Cat. I thought, "I'll bet money they're headed for Ripple Creek and they're going to load up in that Snow-Cat to follow our tracks!" Later that evening, I called Larry and Gerald to tell them what I'd seen and my thoughts about it. They both laughed and said they were sure the wardens were headed elsewhere.

But no! On Tuesday afternoon, while filling out my time card at the county shop, one of my coworkers tapped me on the shoulder and said, "Look who's parked by your Scout." Damn! I could see my two buddies, the wardens, sitting in the Fish and Game pickup, waiting for me.

I took an extra few minutes to fill out my time card. Hell, there wasn't any need to get in a hurry! I walked directly to the Scout, pretending I didn't see them. The tall one jumped out of the pickup and said, "I've got something for you," and handed me some papers. Not saying anything, I carefully read over the paperwork. It was a summons to appear in court at Rifle, Colorado, on April 17, 1967. Larry, Gerald, and I had been charged with fishing without permission at the 101 Ranch, located in Garfield County. I looked at the warden and said, "We'll see you in Rifle."

When I got home, I showed Donna the summons. Soon, Larry and Gerald called, telling me that they'd also gotten a summons to appear in court. I said, "I'm going to call a lawyer I know—Jerry Jones—and set up an appointment." Larry was reluctant, but Gerald yelled over the phone, "Hell, yes! Let's fight it!" The actual date we went fishing at the 101 was April 9; the wardens had been to the lake with the Snow-Cat on Monday, April 10, and they had given us our summons on Tuesday, April 11.

On Friday evening, the fourteenth, we met with the attorney and told him the entire story. He smiled and said, "It's hard to believe that Fish and Game is actually charging you guys. This entire case is based solely on circumstantial evidence. You weren't apprehended on private property, nor are there any eyewitnesses." Jerry agreed to take the case for a small fee.

He explained that on Monday, April 17, he would file a motion in court stating that we needed more time to consult with counsel. He said that he'd like us to drive up to Ripple Creek before the seventeenth to see if the wardens had taken the Snow-Cat to the 101 Ranch, and check to see

Chapter Seven: THE LETTER

if they had driven it up the road to Lake of the Woods. He said to give him a call when we got back.

On Sunday, April 16—my nineteenth birthday—we returned to Ripple Creek, strapped on our snowshoes, and headed up the road, following the cleated tracks left by the Snow-Cat. They turned off the main road at 101 Ranch, and there were absolutely no tracks of any kind on the main road that led to Lake of the Woods. When we got back to Meeker, I called Jerry and told him about the tracks. He said, "I figured as much. I'll see you guys tomorrow."

On Monday, the court proceedings lasted about ten minutes. The judge granted the motion, and the next trial date was set for May 1. During the week, we met with Jerry on two different occasions, and on Monday, May 1, we met him at the courthouse in Rifle, where the three of us entered a plea of Not Guilty. Jerry requested a three-man jury trial and the judge agreed; the next court date was set for May 8 at 9:30 a.m.

Dad was all wound up, saying that we were going to get our asses thrown in jail. Through everything that had taken place over the past three weeks, it hadn't bothered Donna or Mom. In fact, Mom had nicknamed Jerry "Perry Mason."

On Friday evening, May 5, we had our last talk with Jerry and the battle plans were drawn up. He said he wanted us to bring three sets of boots on Monday. "Put them in sacks so they can't be seen in the courtroom. I may use them as evidence."

Finally, after all the wrangling over the past month, we walked into the courtroom on Monday, May 8, 1967. The wardens and the prosecutor had several large pictures laid out on the table in front of them, and Gerald—ever the wild one—walked over and said, "Looks like you have some great pictures there. Can I look at them?" I nearly busted out laughing as they scrambled around, grabbing the pictures to turn them over. The prosecutor hissed at Gerald, "Get away from here!" Minutes later, the judge entered the room and said, "Order in the court!" Over the next hour, Jerry and the prosecutor questioned potential jurors. After going through nine of them, the three-man jury was selected and the trial started at about 10:45 a.m.

The first few minutes of the trial, the prosecutor gave the jury some details of the case and told them he'd prove that we did, in fact, sneak into the 101 Ranch lake and fish it without permission. He called the tall young warden as the first witness.

Over the next several minutes, the warden explained to the members of the jury how they had stopped us on Sunday, just a few miles below Ripple Creek, to search our vehicle and found fourteen eastern brook trout. He explained that they returned to Ripple Creek on Monday with a Snow-Cat and followed three sets of tracks that went directly to the lake at the 101 Ranch. He then said that they went up the road to Lake of the Woods and found no tracks. He claimed they even went to the lake and found no evidence of anyone being there.

After nearly thirty minutes, the prosecutor told the warden he had no further questions at this time, so the witness was turned over to Jerry. Jerry's first question to the warden was, "Did you see any of the three defendants fishing at the 101 Ranch lake?" The warden replied, "No." "Did you see any of the defendants walking on the road to or from the 101?" "No." "Then how do you know they were the ones who made the tracks?" The warden replied, "Because they were in the area." Jerry: "You stopped them five miles from the 101 Ranch lake. Couldn't someone else have made those tracks on Sunday? Or, as far as that goes, why not on Saturday?" The warden: "Because we *know* they were the ones that made the tracks." Jerry: "Did you get a good look at the tracks?" "Yes, I did." "What size boots made the tracks?" "I'm not sure." "Did you take any pictures of the tread design?" "No." "Could you give me a *description* of the tread design?" "No." "But yet, you've just told the jury that you got a good look at the tracks."

Jerry walked over to the desk where we were sitting and got the three pair of boots out that we'd brought in paper sacks, took them to the judge, and had them labeled and approved to be used as evidence. He showed the bottoms of one pair to the warden and asked, "Are these the boots that made the tracks?" The warden hesitated: he knew if he said yes that Jerry was going to say, "Prove it!" The warden answered, "No." Jerry showed the other two pairs of boots to him, asking the same question and getting the same answer. He ended with, "I have no further questions of this witness at this time."

It was now noon and the judge called for a recess; court would reconvene at 1:30. We headed for a restaurant to have lunch. Jerry was pleased with how things had gone and was happy that we'd now have over an hour to go over the warden's comments, then he'd have time to prep me before calling me to the stand.

Chapter Seven: THE LETTER

We quickly ate our lunch, talked about our tactics for testimony, and returned to the courthouse at 1:30. A few minutes later, I was sworn in and took the stand. Jerry began the questioning by asking me to please give a complete summary of the events on Sunday, April 9. I explained the route we'd taken to Lake of the Woods. We'd walked on the county road for a short distance, then left the roadway and walked on the south-facing slope where there wasn't any snow. Once we got to the lake, we found some open water and caught fourteen fish. Later, we were stopped by the wardens while driving down the county road. After checking our licenses, they counted our fish then insisted on searching my Scout, which included looking beneath the hood and even looking in the small glove compartment.

Jerry then brought the three pairs of boots to the stand. I testified that the one pair of boots were mine and that I'd worn them fishing on April 9. I testified that the other boots belonged to Larry and Gerald, and that they'd worn them on the same day. Jerry said, "I have no further questions."

The prosecutor then took his turn. Right out of the gate, he said, "You do understand that you are under oath?" I replied, "Yes, I do." He asked, "The warden testified that they didn't find any tracks or evidence of *anyone* being at Lake of the Woods. How can you explain that?" I said, "Evidently, they didn't look in the right places." For the next thirty minutes, he fired questions at me, desperately trying to get me to trip up or blow up. I remained calm and stuck to my story.

Finally, the prosecutor said, "I have no further questions." The judge asked if there were any more witnesses to be presented, and Jerry and the prosecutor both said no. "Very well," the judge said, "closing arguments can be given to the jury at this time."

Jerry walked over to the jurors and said, "It's so hard for me to believe that these three defendants are even *in* this courtroom. This entire case is based on nothing more than circumstantial evidence. The Colorado Fish and Game Department has absolutely no concrete proof of *any* kind. It's also troublesome that the wardens stopped the defendants on a county road, not even knowing what the defendants had been doing. Also, searching the Scout from top to bottom on a routine stop bothers me." He then concluded, saying, "*Anyone* could have made those tracks into the 101 Ranch lake." The prosecutor then gave his closing argument, insisting we were guilty of illegally fishing at the 101 private lake on April 9, 1967. The judge then gave the jury instructions, and they left the courtroom to reach a verdict.

We walked outside and I asked Jerry what he thought about the prosecutor not showing the pictures they had. He smiled and said, "I believe it was a cat-and-mouse game to get you guys nervous and maybe change your pleas." He was confident that we'd be acquitted.

About an hour later, we were summoned to the courtroom. The judge asked the jury if they'd reached a decision. The foreman said, "Yes, we have, Your Honor," and handed him some paperwork. The judge said, "Would everyone please rise?" One by one, the judge read our names and said, "Not guilty." Gerald yelled, "Yahoo!" and I started laughing. I looked over at the prosecutor and saw him slam the lid shut on his briefcase. He said, "Let's get the hell out of here!"

We shook Jerry's hand and congratulated him on a job well done. Once we were out of the courtroom, I felt someone's hand on my shoulder. I turned and saw it was the tall, young warden. He firmly squeezed my shoulder and said, "Looks like you out-fished us." "Yeah," I smiled, "maybe you'll have better luck next time."

We drove to a nearby ice cream parlor and celebrated by having malts, then we headed back to Meeker. When Gerald let me off at my house, Donna rushed out to greet me. I yelled, "We won!" She wrapped her arms around me and, after telling her the story, we drove to Mom and Dad's to share the news. Dad shrugged his shoulders. "That was just shithouse luck, my boy." But Mom said, "So, Perry Mason came through?" "Yes, Mom," I laughed, "he did."

The first of June, summer unfolded in the White River Valley. Donna decided to take a job at he Bright Spot Drive-in, a small hamburger stand, to make some extra money for Christmas. Nearly every weekend, Dad and I traveled to different lakes to go fishing.

Everything was going well until a late night in August. A friend and I had been fishing, and when we pulled into his driveway at about ten that evening, his coworkers were waiting to take him to an oil rig where they were employed. He said, "Darn, they're running early tonight." He ran into his house, grabbed lunch, and got into the waiting vehicle, driving away. I

Chapter Seven: THE LETTER

had loaded my things into the Scout and just gotten in when his twenty-six-year-old wife walked up to me and said, "What's your hurry?" I smiled and said, "I'm running late." She walked around to the passenger door, opened it, crawled in, and slid across the seat. She put her arms around me and planted a big kiss on my lips!

Within a few minutes, things were out of control. All she had on was a housecoat, and she took that off and was completely naked. I slid over to the middle of the seat and yanked down my Levis and shorts, and she straddled me. We had sex, right there in my fishing buddy's driveway! Just minutes later, she said goodnight, got out, and walked to her house. "Son of a bitch!" I thought. "What have I done?" During the drive home, I was a nervous wreck. Once I got there, I was relieved to find Donna in bed, so I tiptoed into the bathroom and washed up. Shit! The smell of this woman's perfume was all over me!

Once I was in bed, Donna stirred and said, "Did you catch any fish?" "No," I said, "we didn't have any luck." For the next several hours, I was wide awake with worry. I felt filthy for betraying both my wife and my friend. Why didn't I tell his wife *no*!? Around 4:30, I finally drifted off to sleep, and just an hour later, the alarm went off. Damn! Not only was I tired, but I also felt horrible.

That evening at supper, Donna asked what was wrong. "Nothing," I lied, "why?" She said, "You just seem different." I told her everything was fine—I was just tired. For the next three days I struggled. I got very little sleep, and guilt continued to eat away at me. I started to think that maybe it'd be best if I just told Donna what had happened, then I'd say to myself, "No, that'd only make matters worse."

After nearly a week, I felt so overwhelmed that I broke down and told Donna everything. It broke my heart to watch her cry, and I held her in my arms and said, "Please, *please* forgive me!" Our cute little home was now riddled with sadness, and we stayed up until 3:00 a.m. talking about it. I pleaded with her to please give me a second chance. Over the next few weeks, our relationship went through great difficulty. She was deeply hurt, and I continued to feel horrible about it. By the last part of September, things had finally improved. Dad, Donna, and I drove to Big Beaver to enjoy the beautiful fall colors and listen to the elk bugle. My heart was filled with joy to see her smiling and laughing again, and as more time passed, love and happiness returned to our home.

Opening day soon arrived, and on the weekend, Dad and I hunted hard on Big Beaver but didn't have any luck. We decided that we'd give Sawmill Mountain a try the following weekend. On Thursday my longtime friend, Gary Wright, called from Yuma, Colorado, and told me he'd like to come to Meeker to go elk hunting with us. I was glad to hear from him and told him he was more than welcome. He arrived late Friday afternoon, and Mom fixed chicken-fried elk steak for supper. Around eleven, Donna and I told everyone goodnight and headed home. Then, on the way there, I remembered that I needed to fill the Scout with gas. There had just been too much going on, and I'd forgotten to do it earlier in the day. The gauge was showing just a little over a quarter, and now the stations were closed; they wouldn't open till at least 5:30 a.m. I said, "I guess I'll roll the dice and go with what I've got; otherwise, we won't get to Sawmill Mountain till way after daybreak."

The next morning, I got up early and discovered it had snowed during the night. I quickly got my things loaded, kissed Donna goodbye, and drove to Dad's house to pick him and Gary up. By the time we got to our turnoff at the top of Yellow Jacket Pass, there were about six inches of snow on the ground, so we decided to chain up all four tires. I locked the hubs in, put the Scout in four wheel, and we headed up the steep mountain. We were all excited because of the snow. Usually, the hunting is very good the morning after a snowfall, as the elk are more active than they normally are.

After traveling a few miles, we neared what was called "Wilson Park," and in our headlights we could see a hunting camp that appeared to have two elk hanging in the trees. As we passed the large canvas tent, I noticed the glow of a lantern inside and saw the silhouettes of hunters scurrying around.

Just before daylight, we reached our destination. After a quick cup of coffee, we loaded our rifles and started walking down a canyon where I pointed out a good place for Dad to sit, then another one for Gary, and I walked nearly one mile further before finding a spot I liked. Before I sat down, I surveyed the area. God, it looked like there were at least forty elk in the meadow just below me. My heart started racing because surely, with that many, there'd be a big bull! Maybe my dream of killing a six-point was finally going to come true.

I knelt on my knees, brushed the snow off a boulder, then lay down on my stomach behind it, resting my rifle on the rock. I scanned the herd

Chapter Seven: THE LETTER

with my scope, hoping to find a big bull. To my surprise, there was only one: a two point.

I had to wait nearly ten minutes before I could shoot, because the bull was in the middle of the herd. Finally, he walked to the outside. *Boom!* I shot and he went down. The rest of the herd spooked and, after watching for a few minutes to make sure the bull didn't get up, I walked down to him to make sure he was dead. I went back up the canyon to get Gary and Dad, and we retrieved the Scout, driving within fifty yards of the bull. After cleaning and loading him, we had some snacks and coffee, then I said, "Well, I guess we'd better head back to Meeker and take the bull to the locker plant." Dad didn't want to give up hunting and insisted we drive to another place called "Martin Creek." I didn't have the heart to say no, but I did mention that we didn't have much gas in the tank.

By the time we got to Martin Creek, it was nearly 11:00 a.m. The temperatures had warmed, the snow was melting, and the Scout was sliding around in the mud. I told Dad we'd better turn back before conditions got worse. After turning around and starting up the steep road, all four tires began spinning and throwing mud. I looked down at the gas gauge. Because the Scout had worked so hard to get back up the hill, the needle had dropped like a rock. It now showed nearly empty.

We didn't travel much further when, all of a sudden, the engine died, as though I'd turned the key off. I tried restarting it, but—no luck. Gary and I raised the hood, removed the cover on the air breather, and Gary watched the carburetor as I pumped the foot feed. He said, "You might as well quit trying. You're out of gas!"

"Son of a bitch!" I thought to myself. We hadn't seen any other hunters all morning, so our only hope was the hunting camp we'd passed in the darkness earlier, and it was nearly three miles away. I told Dad and Gary that I'd see them later and started walking up the snowy, muddy road. In about an hour, I arrived at the camp, pleased to see a Jeep parked by the tent. I said, "Is anybody home?" A voice replied, "Yeah." A man about forty-five years old opened the tent flap and stepped out. I introduced myself, explained the problem, and told him where the Scout was located. He gave me a cold stare. "So, you ran out of gas." "Yes, sir. I was wondering if you happened to have any." He said that he did have some extra, so I pulled out my billfold and handed him a five-dollar bill. He said, "Ah, hell—gasoline is only thirty-two cents a gallon. A couple bucks is enough." I handed him two dollars and he walked over to a tarp, threw it back, and got out a five-gallon GI can, placing it in the back of his Jeep.

After a few minutes, we got into the Jeep and headed down the road. At the west end of Wilson Park, he braked and we came to a stop. "This is where we part ways," he said. I pointed to the road to the left. "But my Scout is about two miles down that way." Again, he gave me a cold stare. "Your gas is in the back. Do you want it or not?" I said, "Yes, of course!" and got out to remove the five-gallon metal can. He opened his door and said, "Make sure you leave my can at my camp," then drove away towards Sawmill Mountain.

I yelled after him, at the top of my lungs, "Kiss my fuckin' ass! Dirty rotten son of a bitch!" I started down the road with the heavy can of gasoline, slipping and sliding in the mud and snow. Before long, it got heavier and heavier, so I kept switching it from one hand to the other, stopping every few minutes to take a break. I kept saying, "Son of a bitch!" After about a mile, both my arms felt like they were going to fall off, and I still had another mile to go. Finally—*finally*—I arrived at the Scout.

After we got the Scout started, we headed up the road and stopped at the hunting camp, leaving the gas can near the tent. Later that evening, Donna and I ate supper at Mom and Dad's. While sitting at the table, Mom said to me, "I'll bet you don't run out of gas again." Everyone started laughing and I said, "I'll bet you're right, Mom."

The following morning, we headed back to Sawmill Mountain with a full tank of gas. Once again, we could see the lantern glowing in the hunters' tent where I'd gotten the gas. I thought, "You dirty rotten prick!" Then a different thought suddenly entered my mind. I could picture the guy giving me the cold stare and saying, "So, you ran out of gas." I now knew the reason he didn't take me to my Scout. It was to teach me a lesson that I'd never forget.

We still didn't have any luck hunting, and on Monday, Gary told us thanks for taking him along and headed back to Yuma. Before long, old man winter arrived in the valley; snow was piled high and it was bitter cold. Dad and I had each gotten a buck the last weekend of hunting season, so we had a good supply of winter meat for the freezer, and Donna and I had started going up the river on weekends to look at the elk—something that we both enjoyed.

On the national scene, the Vietnam War was raging and getting worse every day. In the evening, we watched Walter Cronkite on the news; we

Chapter Seven: THE LETTER

felt he told the truth of what was happening in the war. Thousands and thousands of soldiers continued losing their lives while more yet returned home without limbs. Women were suddenly faced with burying their husbands and many young kids no longer had their dads. The war was also taking a huge toll on marriages, as thousands ended in divorce. Every day, I became more worried and scared of being drafted.

But the holiday season was upon us, and clear up to Christmas Eve, I kept asking Donna what she'd gotten me. All she'd do was smile and say, "You'll just have to wait till tomorrow." The next morning, I got up as soon as I saw daybreak through the bedroom window. After slipping on my Levis, I quietly tiptoed to the living room and started snooping around under our Christmas tree. I spotted a long wrapped box with my name on it. When I picked it up, I couldn't help but think it might be a rifle. I quickly—and not so gently—ripped away the wrapping paper and removed the top half of the box. Oh...my...God! It was a beautiful big game rifle! I took it from the box and quickly noticed that it had a left-handed bolt and rollover cheek piece on the stock to accommodate a left-handed shooter. I then read the engraving on the barrel: it was a 7mm Magnum made by Savage. Ranked as being one of the best calibers in the world for hunting elk, it was exactly what I'd dreamed of owning. With a good scope and rest, I'd now be able to make 300-yard, or maybe even 400-yard, shots that I'd never even try with my little .300 Savage.

The light-colored wooden stock glistened in the light cast from the Christmas tree bulbs, and I found myself feeling overwhelmed. My eyes filled and tears ran down my cheeks. I knew that Donna had spent a small fortune on this rifle, working very hard at the drive-in to earn the money.

"Merry Christmas, honey!" I looked towards the bedroom doorway and saw her. I laid the rifle down and ran to her, putting my arms around her. "Oh, honey, thank you so much! Merry Christmas!" Over the next thirty minutes, I sat on the couch, rifle across my lap, and watched Donna open her presents. I felt guilty because I'd only gotten her some perfume and a coat.

Afterward, we drove to Mom and Dad's to wish them a Merry Christmas, and I brought my new rifle along to show off. "Mom, I can tell you for sure that your deep freeze will be full each year, now that I have this new rifle." She laughed and said, "You think so, huh?" I took it over to Cal and Larry's to show it to them, and after dinner, we drove to Donna's parents. Everyone was envious! I was so darned proud to have it and of my sweet, gorgeous wife, who had gone above and beyond to get me my ideal Christmas present! I knew I'd cherish it the rest of my life.

When April 1968 came, Donna and I decided to take a drive around town on a beautiful spring evening. I asked her if she had checked the mail, and she said she hadn't, so I stopped at the post office. When I opened our mailbox, my heart instantly went to my throat. There was only one piece of mail, and in the top left-hand corner, I could see the words "Selective Service Board." It was like spotting a diamondback rattlesnake at my feet, ready to strike! My hands started trembling as I ripped the envelope open. There it was: The Letter. It stated that I had sixty days to join a United States military branch of my choice or I would be inducted into the United States Army.

A huge wave of fear gripped me followed by rage. I squared up on a nearby metal trash can and kicked it as hard as I could, sending it flying across the room. *Bang!* It sounded like a gun going off when it hit the wall. I yelled, "Damn it!"

I walked to the Scout, opened the door, and handed Donna the letter. "They got me!" "What?" she said, eyes wide. "The fuckin' Vietnam War has caught up with me!" I yelled. "I've been drafted!" After reading the letter, she started crying and yelled, "No! No!" over and over. She slid across the seat, put her arms around me, and—for the next five minutes—we didn't say a word: we just cried. We drove to Mom and Dad's, and Mom and my sister cried their eyes out. Dad said, "You'd better join the navy, Son." I was so shook up I couldn't even think, but I replied, "Yeah, Dad, I guess that's the best option." About an hour later, we drove to Donna's parents and told them. Everyone felt badly about it, but there was nothing we could do.

We went home and stayed up till two, talking about what to do. Both our hearts had been shattered. Once I went to bed, all I did was toss and turn: so many questions raced through my mind. Would I be going to Vietnam? Would I be killed? Would our marriage survive? What a mess!

As soon as daybreak arrived, I got out of bed and fired up the coffeepot. After fixing myself a cup, I decided to go outside so I wouldn't disturb Donna. I leaned across the Scout's hood, lit a cigarette, and stared at the

Chapter Seven: THE LETTER 109

mountains north of town. It was so hard to believe that I'd be losing my freedom. Over the next hour, I drank a pot of coffee and chain-smoked, then I called in sick to the county shop. I was so tired, and my entire body felt numb and empty. When Donna got up, we talked for a while, then I called the navy recruiting office in Grand Junction to set up an appointment for the following week.

When I met with the recruiter, he had me fill out several forms, then scheduled tests for the next week that would determine acceptability. A few days later, I turned twenty, and just a few days after that, we returned to Grand Junction, where I spent several hours taking the tests. The recruiter told me that he'd grade them and give me a call to let me know the outcome.

Those next few days were anxious ones. Finally, the recruiter called and said that I'd been accepted—that the navy had just come out with a two-year program, and I qualified for it. Shit, that was *somewhat* good news; at least it wasn't going to be three or four years. He explained the pay rate and told me that I'd receive my orders in the mail in about two weeks.

Because of the rate of pay, Donna and I decided it'd be best if she moved in with her grandmother while I was gone. Our lives had literally been turned upside-down! Everyone was glad that I'd only have to serve two years and that it was in the navy. If I'd been inducted into the army, I probably would've automatically been sent to Vietnam, where I would be engaged in hand-to-hand combat in a jungle somewhere.

A couple weeks later, around the first part of May, I received my orders. I was to report to a military facility in Denver on June 3, 1968, to take a physical. I'd end up at the Great Lakes Naval Station in Chicago, Illinois, for eight weeks of basic training, usually referred to as "boot camp."

I decided to work till the last weekend of May, and on the twenty-ninth, I bid my coworkers goodbye. Over the weekend, Donna and I packed boxes and moved a lot of things to her grandmother's house. The clock was ticking, and in just two more days, I'd be giving up my freedom and leaving my beautiful wife, my parents and sister, Cal, Larry, my friends, and other relatives. It was a sickening thought! On my last evening, we had supper at Mom and Dad's then went home to spend the rest of the evening together.

By now, our house was nearly empty. For the past several months, it'd been filled with love and laughter; now, everything was different. The next morning, June 2, I got up at the crack of dawn. I hadn't gotten one minute of sleep and felt torn up, both physically and mentally. I slammed down my coffee and chain-smoked several cigarettes; at ten, we loaded my suitcase and headed for Mom and Dad's. We'd take Dad's car to Rifle, where I'd get on a Continental Trailways bus headed for Denver at one.

After arriving at Mom and Dad's, I walked to Cal's to tell him goodbye. I had a hard time keeping my composure when I said, "I'll see you, Cal." I hugged my sister goodbye and, at eleven, Mom, Dad, Donna, and I got in the car and headed out. As usual, Dad was puffing on a cigar while driving down the highway. He said, "Ah hell, Son—you'll be amazed how fast the two years will go by." Sitting behind him in the back seat, I fought back tears. "I guess so, Dad." He then told me that in June of 1970, we'd be going fishing at Trappers Lake. I knew he was trying hard to lift my spirits, but there wasn't anyone who could do that at that moment.

When we got to Rifle, we had lunch and stepped out of the restaurant to wait for the bus. A mere five minutes later, I said, "I can hear it coming." Sure enough, it pulled around the corner and stopped nearby, where a few people got off. This was the moment I'd been dreading. I hugged Mom for a solid minute and shook Dad's hand, then gave him a big hug. Now it was time to hold my beautiful wife. We wrapped our arms around each other and the tears started streaming. We kissed and said "I love you" one last time before I picked up my suitcase and boarded the bus.

I sat down near a window and looked out at the three of them standing on the sidewalk, waving at me. The driver put the bus in gear and we pulled away. It was so hard to grasp what was going on. All I could think was, "Dirty rotten son of a bitch!" Moments later, the bus headed east, diesel engine humming. Mile markers added up; the distance between me, my loved ones, and my hometown started growing.

CHAPTER EIGHT

A Casualty of War

IT TOOK SEVERAL HOURS FOR THE BUS to arrive at the depot in Denver, where I caught a cab to a cheap motel. At a nearby restaurant, I forced myself to eat something, then—to help pass the time—I decided to just sit in the booth, drink coffee, smoke, and listen to the jukebox.

Around ten, I went back to my room to go to bed. Even though I was extremely tired, I still couldn't sleep. Finally, around four, I dozed off. At daybreak, I walked to the restaurant to have some coffee, then checked out of the motel and took a cab to the military's medical facility. For the next several hours, I stood in long lines, filled out several forms, was poked and prodded, answered many questions, had blood drawn, and—by late afternoon—had completed the physical process. All of us were then bussed to Stapleton International Airport for our flight to Chicago.

Around six that evening, I boarded a commercial plane—my first time to fly on a jet. After everyone sat down and buckled up, it taxied to its take-off position and, moments later, raced down the runway to gently lift off. From my window seat, I looked down on thousands of rooftops, then lay my head back. I had never felt so alone and helpless.

I was so pissed off, and many thoughts started spinning through my mind. If I refused to serve in the military, I would be incarcerated. By now, it'd been several years since a handful of politicians had weaseled their way around, convincing those in the chain of command to invade North Vietnam. Those politicians weren't thousands of miles away from *their* loved ones in some steamy jungle or rice field, bullets flying around their heads or booby traps at their feet! Nor were they waking up in a hospital missing an arm or a leg, or in a body filled with shrapnel, or laying in a pool of blood, dead. No—hell, no! They were being chauffeured around in limousines, eating lavish meals, perhaps tipping expensive wine, and living in mansions.

One could also bet that the sound of clinking champagne glasses was echoing across many exquisite dining tables, as CEOs and other executives of large corporations celebrated the signing of yet another huge contract from the Pentagon, enabling them to build more guns, grenades, bombs, vehicles, helicopters, tanks, and jet fighters and manufacture millions of bullets. A select few individuals and large stockholders were getting filthy rich because of this war. Those ugly realities, along with other sickening thoughts, ran through my mind as the large jet sliced through the air.

Late that evening, on June 3, 1968, we touched down at O'Hare International Airport in Chicago. I damn sure hadn't planned on celebrating Donna's and my second wedding anniversary *this* way! Once inside the terminal, I was taken aback by the size of it—it was *huge*! When I got my suitcase, I found an airport employee and showed him my papers that gave a designated area for me to meet navy personnel for transportation to the training center. The gentleman gave me directions and, hell, it was so far away that I had to take a cab! Once there, I went into a small restaurant and grabbed a quick hamburger and Pepsi.

I waited, along with some other young guys, for the bus to pick us up. Minutes turned into hours and, finally, at 1:00 a.m., the bus arrived. About forty minutes later, we pulled through the front gate at the US Naval Training Center. I couldn't help but notice the extremely high chain link fence around the area, laced with barbed wire on the top.

Two guards checked out the bus then gave the driver permission to continue. A few minutes later, we came to a stop. Once we got off, two military men ordered us to hand over any pocket knives or bottles of cologne, which they took and threw into the trash, yelling, "You won't need this shit while you're in here!" I knew the game had now officially started. Hell, by the time I lay down in a temporary rack, it was three in the morning. I was so damned tired that I couldn't even think straight.

At 4:30 a.m., someone's boot struck the side of my rack near my head. A loud voice barked, "Reveille! Reveille! Get your ass up! Now!" For the next forty-eight hours, there were hundreds of us herded from one complex to another. We were issued a sea bag, footwear, socks, briefs, dungarees, shirts, snow-white sailor caps, and dress-white uniforms, along with a belt that had a shiny brass buckle. Everywhere we went, the person in charge yelled, "Tighten up those lines, nuts to butts!" All of us had our heads shaved. Shit, the barber was standing in mounds of hair, and the clippers he ran across my scalp nearly caused blisters, they were so hot! By the third day, I was assigned to a company and now had permanent barracks. The mess hall was about four blocks away, and the one positive was that the navy fed us very well.

The next couple of days involved classroom work and being shown around the base. Each evening, our company commander would walk into the barracks around 1830—6:30 p.m.—and say, "The smoking lamp is lit in all designated areas." Those who smoked would scramble to their lockers, grab lighters, matches, and cigarettes, and haul ass for the smoking lounge that had a pop machine. I really looked forward to this time, because it helped me relax. But after about twenty minutes, the commander would step into the lounge and say, "The smoking lamp is out!" And that's *exactly* what he meant: you'd better not take one more drag—just put the cigarette in the ash tray or get your ass ripped! On the fifth night, we smokers had just lit our first cigarette in the lounge when the commander walked in and yelled, "The smoking lamp is out until further notice!" He screamed, "That means *now*!" Son of a bitch! The one thing that I truly enjoyed and looked forward to had been taken away. After five long days and nights, our company commander "relit" the smoking lamp, thank God, so we could all get together again.

We were given rifles to march with each day, but they weren't loaded. In fact, they were very old, probably from World War II, and were used for marching purposes only. We'd been taught to make our beds military style, and they had to be perfect. Also, all of our clothes had to be folded to meet military specs. Every morning, we marched to an area called the "grinder," an asphalt section near a football field, where we were given a very close personal inspection. It was always held as the sun was just coming up, and we were told to face the east. I had a heavy beard and had to shave twice, otherwise the inspector would spot one or two small whiskers with the sun shining on my face. We were required to be completely squared away—from our beds to our clothing, including organized lockers—and we had to be clean-shaven, or we'd receive demerit marks. If there were too many marks, you'd be held back in boot camp.

Each night, "taps" sounded over the intercom at 2200 hours, instructing everyone to turn out all lights and remain silent throughout the berthing compartment. I seemed to be the last one to fall asleep, and I always woke up around 0500, thirty minutes before reveille sounded. I quickly learned that it was to my advantage to stash the items I'd need for my shower beneath my rack when going to bed. I could quietly grab everything when I woke up, tiptoe to the distant shower room, take my shower and shave—all before reveille—and avoid the huge crowd.

I managed a few minutes here and there to write to Donna and Mom and Dad, giving them my mailing address. We still didn't have any telephone privileges, so the mail was my only means of communication with them, and the days seemed really long. Usually, we were required to march in cadence for miles with a rifle leaning across our right shoulder. The squad leader following alongside us would yell, "Left, left, left!" to make sure everyone stayed in step. In between marching, we spent several hours in classrooms, being taught about ethics, personal hygiene, and the basic layouts of ships, including destroyers, battleships, tenders, submarines, and aircraft carriers. The navy instructors were extremely bright and did a really good job.

Every evening at 1900 hours, a third-class sailor came into our berthing compartment. He yelled, "Mail call!" then announced the last names of guys who had received mail. At the end of my second week, my name was finally announced. Oh, God! I had a letter from Donna and one from Mom. I sat on the edge of my rack and read the letters over and over, putting their voices to every word. Soon, my eyes would fill with tears—oh, how I missed them! I quickly got my tablet from my locker and wrote both of them a long letter—that I really missed them, how much I loved them, and that boot camp was rough, with each and every day a long seventeen hours.

The next day, the company commander approached me to tell me that I'd been chosen to be a squad leader. He handed me a sheet of paper that listed my duties. Basically, I was in charge of keeping members in my squad squared away—"on time to all classes, drills, marches"—and to inform them to make sure they kept a "tidy rack, a clean and organized locker, that they were well-dressed and clean shaven."

A few days later, I received two more letters, one each from Donna and Mom. They lifted my very low spirits, as I was really homesick. At the end of my third week, around June 25, the sailor yelled, "Mail call!" My name was announced and I quickly ran to the front of our berthing compartment. There was a letter from Mom, but nothing from Donna. Over the next three days, I counted the minutes until mail call, and each evening, my heart sank. I thought, "Doesn't Donna realize how important a letter from her is?" It was so hard to be a thousand miles away from home, putting up with all kinds of bullshit and marching in pounding rainstorms and humid heat! I couldn't help but fear the worst: was she seeing someone else?

Again, my name was announced at mail call, but I'll be a son of a bitch: there was a letter from Mom but nothing from Donna. I sat down on the edge of my rack and removed her letter from the envelope. I thought I was going to pass out when I read the second paragraph: "Son, I have some bad news to tell you. I've been informed by two reliable sources that Donna has been seen several times with another guy." Damn it! Those words ripped through my heart! Here I sat behind a guarded chain-link fence laced with barbed wire, my ass belonging to the US military. If I tried to escape, I'd be sent to federal prison, and now I hear Donna is sleeping with someone else? What a heartbreaking, tear-jerking mess!

I was unable to hold back the tears, so I moved around on my rack so nobody could see me crying. Moments later, I walked to the head and locked myself in a stall, where I spent several minutes having dry heaves. After I finally calmed down, I returned to my rack.

A couple hours later, the intercom sounded off. "Taps! Taps! All lights out! The smoking lamp is out in all designated areas. Now taps!" I laid my head back on my pillow and stared at the rack above me. After a few minutes, the nearby whispering subsided and, with the exception of a few snores, the barracks became quiet. Minutes turned into hours, and there was no way I'd be able to go to sleep with my mind still racing.

At 0500 I got up, took my shower, and shaved, and a few minutes later, reveille sounded. Once my new friend, Earl, was ready, we walked to the mess hall, where I pounded the coffee. I was damned tired and my nerves were shot. The day began to slowly drag by, and I was relieved when evening came. I cornered the company commander and told him my problem. He was very understanding and told me that because of the rules, I'd have to go through the chaplain to get phone privileges. When the smoking lamp was lit, I chain-smoked as many cigarettes as possible in twenty minutes. Later, I still had a hell of a time going to sleep, but I finally dozed off around 0300 and woke up at 0500. Late that afternoon, I met with our chaplain and got permission to use a phone.

I waited until after supper then walked to the building where the phones were located. There were long lines of guys waiting but, finally, my turn came and I called Donna's grandmother's house, praying she would be there and answer the phone. She did answer, and I said, "I've been informed that you're seeing another guy. Is that true?" There was nothing but silence on the other end. Finally, she softly said, "Yes." I screamed, "Are you *sleeping with him?!*" Silence, silence, and more silence, then, "Yes." I felt as though she'd just driven a dagger right through my heart! I yelled, "*Damn you, Donna!*" and slammed the phone down.

I was in shock when I walked out of the building, and the five blocks back to the barracks didn't help. My mind was spinning out of control. I felt nothing but pain, and I hadn't hurt this bad since Dad lost his foot! Fuck! I was looking at another month of boot camp and didn't know how I was going to make it.

That night, I didn't sleep again. I knew that when I got back to Meeker in August, I'd be filing for divorce. Over the next week, I averaged about three hours of sleep a night. Reality had finally hit: be it the Vietnam War or losing my wife, my worst fears were coming true.

"Left, left, left!" Day after day, the platoon leader's voice rang out as we marched for miles in near-perfect cadence. We were informed that we would be starting extensive fire training and swimming classes, and the navy instructors went all out for the fire training courses. Once we completed the classroom portion, we were taken to an area where we fought *real* fires. We had to put on self-breathing apparatuses and walk through smoke-filled metal buildings. We were given direct orders that no matter what, *do not* let go of the hand of the guy in front of you or the guy behind you. It was a terrifying experience: once inside the smoke-filled room, you couldn't see *anything*. God, was I ever glad when we got outside and I could see the clear-blue sky! The navy instructors were extremely professional and did a great job.

I was dreading the swimming classes, because I'd never been a very good swimmer. I just about shit my trunks when the instructor told me to climb a nearby ladder that led to a diving platform and jump into the pool, feet first. I'm not exactly sure how high the platform was above the pool, but I do know that when I walked to the edge and stared down, it was too damned far to be jumping! It may have been around thirty feet!

Chapter Eight: *A Casualty of War*

Fear raced through my body as I took a deep breath and stepped off the platform. *Ka-sploosh!* I hit the water feet first and went down, down, down! When I quit sinking, I scrambled to the surface and swam to the edge of the pool; I held on to the concrete and gasped for air. Shit! I was hoping that I never had to jump off *that* son of a bitch again!

Over the next few weeks, I really struggled with all the rigorous swimming exercises. In fact, I had to take a few extra classes but, finally, the main instructor told me that I'd passed. I was so damned happy! Many guys had breezed through the program, but it'd been a grueling experience for me, and I felt that getting very little sleep had also put me at a disadvantage.

The month of July moved by at a snail's pace. I crossed out July 31 on the small calendar Mom had sent me, and in just three more days, graduation ceremonies for us and other companies would be held. I was so glad the eight weeks of hell were nearly over. Through all of it, my dear mom had written two letters to me every week.

On Friday, August 2, 1968, our training exercises concluded and everyone was busy getting ready for graduation. I polished my dress shoes and brass belt buckle and made sure my sailor cap was spotless; my dress-white uniform was perfectly pressed. The next morning, everyone boarded a bus going to the stadium where graduation was to take place. Once we got off, we were given our rifles. Our company then grouped up in lines and marched into the stadium in perfect formation, following the other companies. In the distance, I could hear a military band playing in the stands. "Left, left, left," our platoon leader's voice barked out, and with our rifles resting across our shoulders, we marched towards the middle of the field. There were hundreds of graduating sailors, covering the green grass with a sea of white uniforms, and the brass horns from the military band glistened in the bright sunlight.

We marched past the dignitaries as the band played, then all the companies were ordered to stop. Our platoon leader yelled, "Parade rest!" With perfect timing, each of us quickly removed his rifle from his shoulder, stood the butt of the rifle on the grass, and held the barrel end, allowing the gun to stand straight up. I noticed there were many relatives and friends of graduating sailors seated in the stands.

A navy admiral gave a speech and congratulated all of us, and a few minutes later, the ceremony ended. Our platoon leader yelled, "Attention!

Right shoulder arms!" Simultaneously, we all picked up our rifles and placed them on our right shoulders. The platoon leader then barked, "Left face!" At the same exact time, everyone turned to their left. He then said, "Forward, march!" As we started marching, the navy band began to play "Anchors Away." I mean to tell you, the band members could flat-ass play.

Once out of the stadium, we handed over our rifles, boarded the bus, and returned to the barracks. A few minutes after we arrived, our company commander stood at the front of the room and congratulated everyone. He said, "The smoking lamp is now lit and will remain so until 2200 hours. It'll be lit tomorrow morning at reveille and remain lit until 2200 hours. On Monday morning, you will be given your travel tickets and orders. Make damn sure you don't lose or misplace the large manila envelope." It made me feel good when he walked up to me, shook my hand, and said, "I sure hope everything works out for you." I had a lot of respect for him: he'd always treated me fairly, and the draft was not his fault.

Earl and I spent the rest of the day in the smoking lounge drinking Pepsis and bullshitting. The next day, I cleaned out my locker and packed my sea bag. We now had phone privileges, so I called Mom and Dad to tell them I'd call the next day from the airport when I knew what time I would arrive in Grand Junction.

I woke up the next morning at 0400 and decided to get up. I was so damned excited knowing that, in just a few hours, I'd be headed home. At around 0600, Earl and I had breakfast and then returned to the barracks. A short time later, everyone was given their manila envelope. I quickly opened mine and saw that I was to report to the USS *Hugh Purvis*, stationed at Newport, Rhode Island, no later than 2400 hours on August 20, 1968.

We soon boarded a bus and headed out. When we pulled through the front gate, I let out a huge sigh of relief. The past eight weeks had been nothing but pure hell, especially the last four. While traveling to the airport, I looked over my plane tickets to make sure they were correct. I'd leave O'Hare at eleven, fly to Stapleton, then change planes and arrive at Walker Field in Grand Junction at five that evening. About forty-five minutes later, we arrived at the airport.

I told Earl goodbye, as he was headed back to New York. I lugged my sea bag through the terminal and checked in at my designated gate. I had some time to burn, so I called Mom and told her what time I'd be arriving in Grand Junction.

Chapter Eight: A Casualty of War

At 5:00 p.m. on August 5, the passenger jet I was on touched down at Walker Field in Grand Junction. There were many tears of happiness shed when I hugged Mom and Dad. I was so glad to see them and hear their voices! I retrieved my sea bag and we got on the road to Meeker. Mom opened a can of beer and poured it into her old faithful plastic glass. During the drive, she continually tried talking about upbeat things to lift my spirits, but Dad kept bringing up Donna. "You make damn sure you get divorce papers filed." "Yeah, Dad—I know that," I'd reply. Mom asked how long I'd be home, and I said until August 20. I then told them that I'd be going to Newport, Rhode Island, and gave them the name of the ship I'd be serving on.

Oh, God, when we pulled up to the house, I spotted the Scout. It was like seeing a long lost friend! I walked over, opened the door, and got in. It seemed as though I'd been gone for years. As soon as I walked into the house, I noticed our old white tomcat lying on the couch. I gave him a good petting.

After I finished unpacking my clothes, my sister showed up, and we had a good reunion. Mom fixed elk burgers for supper; it was great to taste some wild meat again. The evening passed, and around eleven, all of us turned in. It felt strange to be back in my old bed! Leave it to Mom—the sheets were fresh and smelled so good.

Early the next morning Mom, Dad, and I enjoyed coffee before Dad left for work. When the attorney's office opened, I called and set up an appointment with Jerry Jones for August 7 at 10:00 a.m. When my sister left, Mom and I had a long talk—I'd never held anything back from her. She told me she was really sorry about everything that had happened with Donna.

I walked over to Cal's and we gave each other a warm handshake and a hug. Boy, it was good to see him! We visited for a couple of hours, then I decided to go for a drive. I felt haunted as I cruised around town because Donna wasn't sitting on the passenger side of the Scout. Regardless of where I went, a memory came to mind pertaining to us as a couple.

That evening, I sat down at the supper table with Mom, Dad, and my sister, and we enjoyed my favorite meal. It tasted so good that I ate till I thought I was going to explode! Soon after, I drove over to Donnie and Erika's and visited with them till nearly midnight. Donnie was his usual self—all wound up about the upcoming hunting season. He was going to take three weeks' vacation and guide some out-of-state hunters to the private property he'd leased. He said, "I'm going to make a shit-pot full of money." I started laughing—yes, I was actually laughing!

The next morning, I met with Jerry Jones and filed the divorce papers. He told me that it'd be final in ninety days. Then he said, "Are you going to have any time to try some private fishing?" I smiled and said, "Not this time."

Later that afternoon, I met Donna's mom at her mother's house—Donna was still staying there—and loaded up my personal belongings. She had little to say, so I thanked her and drove to Mom and Dad's to unload everything. In the evening, I walked over to Cal's and spent a couple hours talking to Larry, who I'd missed earlier that morning.

Over the next several days, I spent a lot of time driving around, visiting with friends and relatives. I spent a couple evenings at the pool hall and had supper with Donnie and Erika on two occasions. And how quickly the days passed! The day before I was to leave, I was driving down Water Street and spotted Donna getting out of a vehicle at her grandmother's. I pulled over, got out, and asked her how she was doing. She said, "I guess okay. Why don't you come in?" Once inside the house, she told me to please sit down and stay awhile. She sat down on the couch across from me.

She didn't get five words out before she broke down and started crying. What happened next was unbelievable. I sat down next to her and held her in my arms. She said, "I'm so sorry!" For the next several minutes, we held each other tight while we both cried. We had a long talk and she asked for my forgiveness. She said she didn't want to get a divorce. How could I consider taking her back after all the hell she'd put me through? The answer was that I was still deeply in love with this drop-dead gorgeous gal who I'd spent so many happy times with over the past four years. Did I have doubts? Hell, yes! We decided to spend the night together, so I told her I would go home, pack everything for the trip the next day, and she could take me to the airport.

Now I found myself feeling guilty on the way to Mom and Dad's, as I was dreading telling them my plans. I knew Mom would be understanding, but Dad was going to hit *tilt*. Sure enough, when I told them, Dad yelled, "You're making one hell of a mistake!" "Maybe so, Dad," I defended, "but it's my life." He yelled, "You won't be gone one week before she goes back to the guy she's been seeing!" Mom said, "Don, you don't know what you'd

Chapter Eight: *A Casualty of War*

do if you were in the same shoes." He hollered, "Bullshit!" For the next ten minutes, Dad and I continued to argue. Finally, I couldn't take it anymore; it just hurt too much. I packed all my stuff and told them I'd stop by early the next morning to tell them goodbye. Dad yelled, "You make *damn* sure you park the Scout out front tomorrow! And I want *both* sets of keys!" As I walked out the front door, my heart was heavy. It'd been the worst argument that Dad and I had ever had, and I felt like I was betraying him.

Late that night, clothes were strewn across Donna's bedroom. It felt so good to taste her lips and touch her body. We made passionate love then fell asleep in each other's arms.

The next morning, we got up and loaded my things into the '56 Ford. Donna followed me to Mom and Dad's, where I parked the Scout. She stayed in the car while I went inside. I gave my sister a hug, then walked over to Mom. I wrapped my arms around her and said, "I love you so much, Mom, and I'll miss you!" She started crying and could barely talk. She murmured, "I was hoping *we* could take you to the airport." Guilt rushed through every vein in my body. "I know, Mom. I know." I shook Dad's hand and gave him a long hug. Tears were streaming down my cheeks and I could see his eyes watering. "I love you, Dad," I managed. "I'm so sorry about last night." "Yeah—me too, Son. But I still believe you're making a big mistake." After that, I walked out the door. It was so hard to say goodbye again.

Donna and I had a great talk during the drive to Grand Junction. After checking my luggage in, the dreaded moment arrived: it was time to go. Once again, we held each other tight, whispering "I love you," then the tears streamed down our cheeks as we kissed goodbye. When I got to the top of the steps of the ramp attached to the jet, I turned and waved to Donna. I took my seat then looked out the window: she was already gone. A few minutes later, the jet lifted off into the dark-blue Colorado sky. I'd decided I wasn't going to run for the door of denial, nor put my head in the sand and pretend everything was going to be okay. No, I wasn't going to call Jerry Jones and tell him to stop the divorce proceedings. Why? Because deep down, I knew it was over.

A short time later, the jet landed in Denver. Within an hour, I boarded a different plane and began my long flight to Providence, Rhode Island. During the trip, my mind was spinning—wondering what Donna was doing, if I'd ever hold her again, where the ship that I had been assigned to would be going… It was all so depressing.

After landing in Providence, I took a bus to Newport. Late that afternoon, I got off the bus, retrieved my sea bag, and asked the driver how to get to the navy's port. He gave me directions to the area where the shuttle buses took sailors to their ships. I thanked him and started up the sidewalk, the strap from the sea bag digging into my right shoulder.

I heard someone say, "Excuse me, sailor, do you need a ride?" I glanced over and saw a navy officer and a lady sitting in a car. I walked to the driver's side, smiled, and said, "Yes, sir. I would really appreciate a lift, because I have no idea where my ship is located." The lieutenant helped me load my bag in the trunk as he introduced me to his wife, then we headed out.

We soon arrived at the base. There were many government buildings scattered around and we finally came to the harbor, where there were several ships. After the lieutenant stopped at a guard shack, we were given directions and permission to drive down the pier to the USS *Hugh Purvis*. When we got to the ship, I retrieved my sea bag from the trunk, thanked him for the ride, and walked across the gangplank to show the duty officer my orders. He summoned a sailor to take me to the berthing quarters. I could see that the ship had many big gun barrels on the upper deck and figured it would fall into the category of being called a "destroyer."

After going through many hatches and down some steel stairs, we finally arrived at the berthing compartment. It was extremely tight quarters with small lockers, and it was a hot son of a bitch—probably close to ninety degrees with no air moving at all! I asked the sailor, "Where is this ship going?" He snapped back, "Where in the fuck do you think? Vietnam!" My heart went right to my throat and my legs nearly buckled. I said, "When?" He yelled, "Day after tomorrow!" Shit! I was devastated! The sailor walked away and I started unpacking my things. My hands were trembling as I placed my belongings into a small locker. Dirty rotten son of a bitch!

Later, I got directions to the mess hall, which was very small compared to the one at boot camp. I hadn't eaten anything for several hours, and after choking down some food, I found a secluded area on the fantail of the ship where I could smoke and watch the sun go down. I still had a hard time believing what had happened over the past two months and what was happening now. I stood on the fantail for several hours, staring across the harbor. I felt so alone and depressed, and I didn't feel like talking to anyone.

Chapter Eight: *A Casualty of War*

As 2200 hours neared, I decided I'd better get to my rack before taps sounded. Not saying anything to any of the sailors in the berthing compartment, I got undressed and lay down in my rack. "Taps, taps...lights out! The smoking lamp is out in all designated areas. Now taps!" sounded across the intercom. Only nightlights mounted on the walls kept the compartment from being totally dark. I remained wide awake, staring at the rack above me. All of a sudden, I started getting a throbbing ache in one of my teeth. Within an hour, it really hurt—like someone had driven an ice pick into the roof of my mouth.

Damn it! Now what?! I suffered—really suffered—the entire night, not getting one minute of sleep. When reveille sounded, I dressed quickly, went to the mess hall, and slammed down some coffee, not having one bite to eat. Then I headed for sick bay and explained that I was having pain in my jaw. They informed me that the ship didn't have a dentist and gave me permission and directions to the dental office on base.

Once I found the office, I checked in and, after waiting about thirty minutes, was seated in a chair. A few minutes later, a navy dentist with the rank of lieutenant entered the room and examined the problem area, then told his assistant that he wanted full mouth x-rays taken.

Before long, the lieutenant and a high-ranking officer entered the room and went over the x-rays. The officer talking to the lieutenant had a lot of gold braid across the brim of his cap: I wasn't sure if he was an admiral or a captain. I heard him ask the lieutenant what ship I was on. The officer told him and said it was being deployed to Vietnam tomorrow. I heard the high-ranking officer say, "There is *no* way he can make that tour with *these* problems," and the lieutenant voiced agreement.

The dentist then worked on the tooth that was really bothering me. I overheard the high-ranking officer talking on the phone in the next room. At one time, he raised his voice, nearly yelling. "He will *not* be going to Vietnam on your ship! Do I make myself clear?"

The dentist explained to me that he'd put in a temporary filling that might help with the pain. He said, "We're going to be working up some new orders for you, and hopefully you'll be put on a ship that has complete dental facilities." He then gave me some pain medication and told me that I had severe dental problems that would require many appointments. I thanked him and headed back to the ship. Oh, God! I wondered how long it would be before I received my new orders. Hell, the ship was going to be departing in less than twenty-four hours!

As soon as I got back to the ship, I took a couple of pain pills, and about an hour later, I was feeling much better. Oh, what a relief! I watched sailors scurrying around the ship, preparing for its long journey. I decided to clean out my locker and repack my sea bag. I wanted off the USS *Hugh Purvis* the second I got my new orders in hand!

As the afternoon disappeared, I had a light supper, then once again returned to the ship's fantail where I nervously smoked. I still hadn't received any orders. When taps sounded, I lay back in my rack: it was going to be a long, long night. I went to sleep about 0300 and woke up when reveille sounded at 0530. I jumped out of bed, dressed and shaved, and headed for the mess hall.

Oh, shit! By 0700, a large tugboat had pulled up on our starboard side. Huge lines were being attached to connect it to the ship, preparing to tow us from the harbor. Deployment time was 0900. By 0800, a large crowd had gathered on the pier—a lot of relatives and friends of the sailors on board. *Tick! Tick! Tick!* The clock was running as I stood on the bow of the ship, watching, waiting, and praying for someone to show up with my orders.

Finally, I spotted a sailor nearly fifty yards away, walking very fast with a large manila envelope. Oh, God, *please* let that be my orders! A few minutes later, my name was called over the intercom, saying to report to the quarterdeck. I ran like hell, grabbed my sea bag, and went to the quarterdeck. Once there, I gave them my name and service number. The officer pulled the orders from the envelope and said, "You are to report to the USS *Yosemite* no later than 1200 hours today." I saluted the officer and said, "Yes, sir!" I took the envelope, my sea bag, and walked down the gangplank to the pier. I walked away from the crowd towards some dumpsters, placed my sea bag on the concrete, sat down, and lit a cigarette. My hands were shaking.

Five minutes later, a navy band marched down the pier and took position. Sailors scampered around, removing the large lines from the chocks on the pier the ship was tied to. Once those sailors were back on board, the gangplank was removed. The massive tugboat's engine roared on the starboard side and the ship started moving away from the pier. Another tugboat pulled up on the port side parallel with the ship. Large lines were attached to it from the ship as the band started to play "Anchors Away." The crowd began to wave goodbye, and the sailors on the ship waved back. So much sadness.

Chapter Eight: A Casualty of War

The tugboat's huge prop boiled and churned the seawater as the lines tightened. Slowly, the ship was turned around and the tugboats pulled it towards the Atlantic Ocean. I watched till the ship was out of sight. I knew beyond a shadow of a doubt that I'd just been dealt what every poker player dreams about: a royal flush! I had barely—*just* barely—missed going to Vietnam!

One more time, I gathered up my sea bag and started walking down the pier in search of the USS *Yosemite*. When I found it, I was shocked by its size: it was monstrous! After checking in at the quarterdeck, a sailor with the rank of seaman escorted me to my assigned berthing compartment, which required going up several levels of steel stairs. I was impressed when we got there—it was quite spacious and had large gear lockers to stow clothes, uniforms, and work and dress shoes. Once I had all my gear unpacked and neatly stored, a second-class petty officer introduced himself and offered to give me a short tour of the ship. He took me to the head and showed me a large shower room, then we went to a machine shop, optical shop, and the electrical divisions. We went to the boat deck, where several twenty-six-foot vessels were sitting in racks. He told me we were in charge of their upkeep, and if we were shipped overseas, some of us would be operating them. He then took me to the mess hall. God, it was big—able to seat many sailors at one time. We only covered a small portion of the ship before returning to the berthing compartment.

I asked him how long the ship was, and he said, "From bow to stern, she's 540 feet." Then I was introduced to the first class who was directly in charge of the crew, then to the chief who ranked above him, and then to the division manager, whose rank was lieutenant junior grade. When talking to the chief, he asked me where I was from, and I told him Meeker, Colorado. "Welcome aboard, neighbor! I'm from Cody, Wyoming." He told me he'd been in the navy for nearly thirty years. I smiled, "That's about twenty-eight more than I plan on staying." I had a brief conversation with the Lt. JG, who was young and seemed to be a nice guy. He told me that the ship had been built in the mid-1940s and that there were several hundred sailors on board.

Later that evening, I went to the mess hall for supper, where they served meat loaf, mashed potatoes, corn, hot rolls, and salad—a pretty good meal. I could see many cooks scampering around in the kitchen area. What a huge operation! I asked the guy sitting next to me what classification the ship was. He said that it was called a "tender," and its main function was to repair and fabricate parts for other ships. The optical shop repaired any and all telescopic devices; there was also a large sick bay staffed by doctors and male nurses and a large dental office. I thanked him for all the information then headed back to the berthing compartment, getting lost on my way.

After taking a long shower, I asked the first class in charge where the nearest telephone was located. He gave me directions to the enlisted men's club and permission to leave the ship. I then asked another sailor for our mailing address and wrote it down so I could give it to Donna and Mom. It was a long walk to the club, but I finally made it. For nearly an hour, I tried to call Donna, but there was no answer, and the fear of her being with the guy she'd slept with started racing through my mind. I decided to call Mom instead, and as soon as she answered, she said, "Son, I'm so glad you finally called. I want you to know that Donna went back to the same guy she'd been seeing the day after you left." My heart sank and tears started running down my cheeks. "I'm so sorry, Son. I know how hurt you are. I wish there was something I could do for you, but I know I can't." It was hard for me to talk. Even though I knew when I left Grand Junction that the relationship was over, I was still hopeful things had changed. When I'd regained my composure enough to talk, I muttered the mailing address to her, talked to Dad for a couple of minutes, then said goodbye.

The walk back to the ship seemed to take twice as long. Every step of the way I thought about the draft, the upcoming divorce—hell, the thought even entered my mind that until the divorce was final, she'd continue to receive half my paycheck every single month! Damn it!

Before getting to the ship, I dried my tears and regained my composure. Just before taps sounded, I asked one of the sailors when our ship would be leaving. He started laughing and said, "Hell, who knows? She's been in port for so long that she's become anchored with coffee grounds! Rumors are that we might be going on a Mediterranean cruise in February—maybe to Naples, Italy—for seven or eight months." I thanked him for the information then got into my rack. Moments later, taps sounded and things became very quiet in the dimly lit compartment. There were red lights mounted on the walls to give people some light to find their way to the head. God, I was so tired, and I hurt inside...

Chapter Eight: A Casualty of War

Early the next morning, reveille sounded over the intercom. I dressed, went to the head, and shaved. Our job that morning was to sweep and swab large sections of the ship. After completing the designated areas, we went to breakfast, which was darn good—scrambled eggs and French toast! Afterward, I got permission to go to the dental office on board, where I was seen by a lieutenant. He replaced the temporary filling with a permanent one and examined my entire mouth and the x-rays. He smiled and said, "We're going to get to know each other very well!"

Over the next few weeks, I was trained to stand watch at the quarterdeck. A third-class petty officer taught me how to use a boatswain's whistle, which could be manipulated to create different tones for different occasions. At the time for reveille, the person on watch flipped a switch that activated the ship's intercom, put the whistle near a speaker, blew into it, then spoke: "Reveille, reveille—all hands heave out and trice up! The smoking lamp is lit in all designated areas. Now reveille!" The watches were required twenty-four hours a day, and each one was four hours long. During the day, you were required to log in any visitors. If a high-ranking officer arrived on the pier, you sounded off a bell with a certain number of gongs, depending on his rank; announced his rank, followed by his last name; then he boarded the ship. The same procedure was done when the high-ranking officer departed. If you were on the night watch from 2000 hours to 2400 hours, you would activate the intercom at 2200 hours, blow into the boatswain's pipe, and "trill"—vibrate your tongue on the roof of your mouth—to give the whistle a quavering sound. The procedure lasted a few seconds, then you spoke into the microphone: "Taps! Taps! Lights out! The smoking lamp is out in all designated areas. Now taps!" It took a few days of practice, but I got the hang of the trilling. I was then trained to stand watch at the guard shack on the pier, where you inspected incoming vehicles and logged the arrival and departure times. You were required to step out of the shack and salute all arriving officers, who always rode in a black car with flags on both ends. When not standing watch during the day, we removed covers from the twenty-six-foot liberty boats located on the very top deck of the ship and started sanding them down, prepping them for primer and new paint.

In early September, some of us were chosen to start boat-coxswain training. We spent several hours in a classroom, taught by a first-class petty officer. After completing some written tests, we were taken to a small lake on the base and taught how to operate a twenty-six-foot boat called a "liberty launch." By the end of the month, I'd passed all the requirements and was certified a boat-coxswain. If and when the ship went overseas, it'd be anchored in a port and a team of us would be operating the liberty launches to take sailors on liberty.

Through all the training, sweeping and swabbing of decks, sanding and painting of boats, and standing watch, there wasn't a conscious hour that went by that I didn't think about Donna, and I had many sleepless nights because of it. On weekends that I didn't have duty, I'd ride the bus uptown to Newport. Once there, I'd walk for miles around town, looking at huge estates with old mansions, and I'd sit on park benches, watching people—young mothers pushing babies in strollers, elderly couples holding hands, kids laughing and playing on the swings and merry-go-rounds. Lord knows I was lonely and depressed. I was thankful for my precious mom at mail call, because she wrote me two long letters every single week.

The first part of October, I called Jerry Jones and he informed me that the divorce hearing was scheduled for November 13. I went through the chain of command that ended up taking me to our division officer. After I explained what was going on, he was very understanding. He told me he'd personally cut through all the red tape that was required in order for me to get emergency leave. A few days later, he called me into his office and told me he'd successfully gotten my leave approved. I'd be allowed to go home on November 8 and return no later than 2400 hours on November 14, 1968. The following Saturday, I went to a travel agency and booked my reservations. I'd be leaving on an early bus to Providence on November 8, fly to JFK in New York, then connect to Denver and Grand Junction, Colorado.

By the end of October, I'd started to make some friends: Donn from Minnesota, Louie and his brother, Alan, from Mississippi, and Gary and Bruce from Georgia. It was nice to know people I could bullshit with during meals and at night when the daily routine shut down.

I called home to check up on Dad and see if he had gotten a deer or elk on opening day. Mom answered and said that he hadn't. I told her I'd be arriving in Grand Junction around 4:00 p.m. on November 8, and she was so excited. "Your dad and I will be there. I can hardly wait!" When I talked to Dad, he said, "Boy, Son, it just doesn't seem like hunting season without you here." "Yeah, Dad—I know," I replied. "I wish things were different." He asked me if I'd feel like going hunting with him on the ninth and tenth, the last weekend of the season. I had mixed feelings—the fight that we'd had over Donna when I was home on leave had left a bad taste in my mouth—but I didn't have the heart to tell him no, so I said, "Sure, Dad—we'll go hunting." He replied, "You don't know how good that makes me feel, Son!"

On Saturday, November 2, I went to town and bought a suitcase and started getting my things organized for the trip. The day before I was to leave, I had a four-hour watch at the guard shack on the pier from 1600 hours to 2000 hours. I was bent over, making a list of things that I hadn't yet packed in my suitcase, when I caught some movement from the corner of my eye. Oh, shit! A shiny black car with flags on it had driven by the shack. I saw the brake lights come on, then the backup lights. My heart went right to my throat as I rushed from the shack and walked up to the passenger side of the vehicle. The rear-tinted window rolled down. All I could see was a lot of gold: he was a captain. He said, "Is there something wrong with your arm?" I snapped my heels together, stood at attention, and saluted him. "No, sir!" He gave me a cold stare then said, "That's better." The window rolled back up and the car drove away. I quickly put the list in my shirt pocket and focused my attention back to what I was supposed to be doing.

The next morning, I got up early and a shipmate took me to the bus terminal. Wow—what a long day of travel, flying hundreds of miles! Finally, around four o'clock that afternoon, my jet touched down in Grand Junction. It was a happy reunion with Mom and Dad, and by the time we got to Rifle, it was nearly 5:30, so we decided to stop there and eat. That way, Mom wouldn't have to cook supper.

At home, I got our hunting gear ready for the next day. After making sure there was plenty of gas in the Scout, I went to bed. Damn, I was tired, and it seemed as though I'd just dozed off when I felt Dad's hand on my shoulder, waking me. About an hour later, we were headed to our hunting country. After getting to Beaver Knob, I quickly turned off the engine and the headlights. We poured ourselves some coffee and talked in low voices, Dad puffing away on his cigar as I enjoyed a cigarette. I loved being with him, and I'd always loved hunting. But today, I just didn't feel the normal electricity. The upcoming divorce was weighing heavily on my heart.

When the eastern sky began showing signs of light, we got out, loaded our rifles, and started down the trail. Son of a bitch, it was cold!

I whispered "good luck" to Dad when I left him at his sitting spot, and I continued on. I quietly placed a shell in the chamber of my new 7mm magnum: I wanted to be ready. I hadn't been standing at my place for more than five minutes when I spotted a herd of elk in the valley below me, winding their way through heavy oak brush. I quickly got a good rest on a tree limb, took the safety off, and watched them through my scope. I was glad to see the lead cow walk across a small meadow at about 300 yards. I figured the other elk would follow her, and they did. The last one in the herd was a spike bull. I held the dot at the top of his back, just behind the front shoulder, and squeezed the trigger. *Boom!* The sound of the magnum shattered the morning silence. I heard the bullet hit, and the young bull went down.

Later that evening, Mom fixed a delicious meal, then she asked if she could go with us the next day—that she would just sit in the Scout while we hunted. We both said, "Sure, you're more than welcome!" It was a little surprising that she asked—she hadn't before—but I knew she wanted to spend as much time with me as she could while I was home on leave. The next morning, we got up early and decided to try Sawmill Mountain. It was really nice to have Mom riding along—we talked a lot while I drove up the road.

Shortly after daybreak, Dad and I went for a long walk, leaving Mom behind in the Scout. We didn't see any elk or deer, so we returned around eleven. After lunch, we drove around on several roads but didn't see a thing. The woods were extremely quiet: we didn't even see any other hunters.

At around three o'clock, we decided to call it a day and head back to town. When we got to the graveled road called "Coal Creek," Dad asked, "Son, do you want to take a chance and drive up Nine-Mile Cutoff?" It was private property, but I said, "Hell, yes!" A few minutes later, I turned off and we headed up the dirt road. We hadn't driven even a mile when I slammed on the brakes and said, "There's a big buck, Dad!" He jumped out, slammed a shell into the chamber of his rifle, rested it in the V of the door, and—*boom!*—he dropped the deer just as it was crossing the road. Dad jumped back in and I pulled up alongside the four-point buck. We got out and I opened the back of the Scout; with some grunting and groaning, we loaded him, guts and all. I shut the back of the Scout, we both got back in, and I quickly turned it around. We hauled ass, taking the buck down Coal Creek to the spud cellar, where we had permission to hunt deer. We gutted the deer there, and the three of us were really laughing after we got it reloaded in the Scout. Once we got home, Dad and I hung the carcass in the barn and prepared it for cutting up.

After supper, Mom talked about how much she enjoyed going hunting with us. "Thanks so much for taking me with you—I had so much fun!" I gave her a big hug. "You're welcome, Mom." Around ten, we all went to bed. While lying there, I replayed the day in its entirety. It was so gratifying to spend quality time with Mom and Dad—and have a lot of laughs, too! But now I was dreading the divorce, and I would leave Meeker again in a few days to complete the remainder of my obligation to the navy. Shit! I really didn't have much to look forward to.

The days flew by and, the morning of the following Wednesday, November 13, I took a bath and put on some nice clothes, preparing for the divorce hearing that was scheduled for ten. I decided to walk the six blocks to the courthouse, and when I arrived in the lobby, Donna and her mom were sitting on a bench. Donna was all decked out—makeup, stylish slacks, and a pretty sweater. It was hard to avoid looking at her. A rather strained "hi" was shared amongst the three of us; moments later, we were called to the courtroom. The entire procedure only took thirty minutes.

As I walked down the sidewalk towards home, my heart felt broken. It was a sad day for me. The gorgeous little gal with the dynamite personality that I had laughed with, cried with, and held in my arms so many times over the past four years would no longer be a part of my life. My stomach ached just thinking about it. I'd be leaving tomorrow to go back to the navy, and I didn't know when I would return, or *if* I would return alive. The fucking Vietnam War had ruined my life!

Early the next morning, I hugged my sister goodbye and Dad, Mom, and I drove to Walker Field in Grand Junction, beginning my long journey back to Newport, Rhode Island. Deeply depressed, I was thankful that the trip came to an end when I walked across the gangplank of the USS *Yosemite* around 9:00 p.m. that night.

The following day, it was back to the dentist's office for my last appointment. After the lieutenant finished, I thanked him for all the great work he'd done over the past three months. Now it was back to the normal routine, with the day-to-day requirements on the ship much different from those of boot camp. Normally, we only had one personal inspection per week, and rarely did we have a locker inspection. We could only grow our hair to a certain length—no beards, but mustaches were allowed if they were kept well trimmed. Also, we had to keep our bunks neatly made with clean bedding.

On Thanksgiving day, the ship served turkey and all the trimmings. It was excellent! After I finished eating, I called Mom and Dad, and Mom told me that the meat from the spike bull was very tender and had great flavor. Dad asked if I wanted to go hunting at Nine-Mile Cutoff again next year. I started laughing and said, "Do you?" He replied, "Hell, yes—Columbus took a chance, didn't he?" The conversation helped lift my spirits, but only briefly. Memories of Donna haunted and taunted me day in and day out, and the thought that it would be many months before I'd touch Colorado soil again weighed heavily on me.

The first week of December, Louie asked me if I wanted to go in with him and his brother to rent an apartment. That way, we'd only have to stay on the ship on duty nights and duty weekends. I agreed, so we moved into a two-bedroom apartment and rode the shuttle bus to and from the ship, mornings and late afternoons. Within a couple of weeks, the refrigerator was filled with beer and there were bottles of rum and whiskey sitting on the counter. I quickly found that I loved beer, along with the euphoric feeling I got after drinking eight or ten bottles of it and a couple of mixed drinks. It seemed to help dull the emotional pain of the divorce and eased how trapped I felt, having to be in the military. Once I achieved a certain high, I'd just sip beer or booze, because I wanted to be able to carry on a conversation without slurred speech, and I didn't want to be so drunk that I staggered.

Louie knew a guy that made perfect IDs, so I got one, showing that I was born in 1947 instead of 1948. This allowed me to be served in the local bars and Club Binnacle, where there was a band on Friday and Saturday nights. We started bringing women to the apartment and having wild parties. On weekends, the parties sometimes lasted until sunup. We ate on the ship most of the time; otherwise, we had bologna sandwiches, hamburgers, or we ordered in pizza. By the first of January, I continued my daily recipe of drinking several beers, along with a couple of stiff mixed drinks every single night. On weekends I consumed even more alcohol, continually trying to dull the mental pain and erase the homesickness.

CHAPTER NINE

Anchors Away!

MID-JANUARY, WE WERE INFORMED that the ship would be deployed in the middle of February to Naples, Italy, for at least seven months, so on February 1, we moved back onto the ship. It'd been a wild son of a bitch at our apartment over the past two months! Over the next few weeks, we were busy preparing the ship for the cruise. We made sure all the boat covers on the liberty boats, officer's gig, and captain's gig were lashed down securely and inspected all of the rigging that'd be used to lift the boats off the ship when we got to Naples.

Time ticked away. Groceries and other supplies had been loaded onto the ship, and in just two more days, we would be leaving. I walked to the enlisted men's club and called Mom and Dad to tell them I wouldn't see them till October, and Mom and I broke down crying. Dad stayed calm, though. "Good luck, Son. Keep your chin up." I told them goodbye then, 'cause it was too hard to talk without crying.

On the morning of February 17, 1969, Donn and I got up before reveille sounded, went to the mess hall for breakfast, then reported to the starboard side of the ship, where we'd be helping feed the huge lines to the tugboats. Around 0700, the two tugboats arrived, and several of us worked to get the ship tied off. On the port side, a large crowd had gathered—close to a thousand people—and a navy band marched down the pier and took its position, their brass horns gleaming in the sun.

Sailors scrambled on the pier to disconnect the ropes from the tie-downs, and we hoisted the lines onto the ship. The gangplank was removed and engines on the tugboats revved up, their props causing the water's surface to churn and boil. The lines tightened and the ship slowly started to move away from the pier. When there was enough room, two more tugboats pulled up on the port side where lines were attached to them. As they started pulling the ship from the harbor, the band played "Anchors Away" and sailors waved to their loved ones on the pier. Once out of the port, the lines were disconnected from the tugboats and the huge ship started moving under its own power. We traveled along the coastline of the United States, around New York's Long Island and the Statue of Liberty, until we arrived at Earl, New Jersey, where we pulled into a port. During the night, we loaded more supplies, ammunition, and fuel.

The next morning, we pulled out of port. I had a pair of binoculars that a friend from the optical department had loaned me, and as I peered through them, I watched the coastline of the United States until it disappeared. Now there was nothing to see but the Atlantic Ocean. Donn and I walked to the bow, looked over the side, and watched the massive ship slice through the ocean's water. Within a matter of hours, several guys started getting seasick, running for the head to throw up.

On our third night out, around 2300 hours, an alarm sounded over the ship's intercom. We were given instructions to secure all hatches immediately, as we were going to be encountering heavy seas. Within an hour, our huge 540-foot ship, which weighed thousands of tons, was being tossed around in the angry Atlantic. Everyone in our compartment was fearful, a worried look creasing each brow.

After another hour of being in the storm, curiosity got the best of us, and Louie decided to open the hatch. A few of us gathered around as he spun the wheel on the waterproof steel door. We helped push it open partway and were instantly hit in the face by blowing seawater. The wind was roaring, probably close to seventy miles per hour, and we could dimly make out gigantic waves pounding the ship! Louie slammed the heavy door shut and turned the wheel as fast as he could, making it waterproof. All of us who'd taken a look were even more afraid than we had been! *Boom! Boom!* Every few seconds, we could hear the waves crashing against the steel ship. Many guys started asking experienced sailors if they thought we were going to sink. One of the old-timers, who'd been in the navy for thirty years, said, "I think she'll make it."

None of us could get any sleep because of the horrible crashing sounds and how afraid we were. Finally, after more than seven hours, the noises stopped and the ship was no longer being tossed around. Louie opened the hatch and could see that day was just breaking. The high winds had calmed and the ocean now had small waves. Whew! Thank God our old ship had made it!

As our vessel continued across the Atlantic, we stayed busy during the day by cleaning and painting the decks. Until a person is actually traveling by ship, they just don't realize how big an ocean is. Day after day, Donn and I looked through the binoculars for land; as far as we could see, there was nothing but water, water, and more water.

Finally, we made it to the Mediterranean Sea! I yelled "land!" while looking through the binoculars, and Donn and several of the other guys took turns, doing the same thing. Hell, you'd think we had spotted a naked woman, we were so excited! As it turned out, it was part of Spain's coastline; we pulled into a small port there to take on fuel and other supplies, no liberty allowed. Later that evening, we experienced a beautiful sight: the Mediterranean didn't have a ripple on its surface as far as we could see, even through the binoculars. The only disturbance was created by our huge ship. Another sight that took our breath away was when the sun was going down. The giant, dark-orange ball seemed to be twice its normal size. It was beautiful!

The following day, everyone was surprised to hear "mail call" over the ship's intercom. We all rushed to our compartment, where a third-class petty officer called out the last names of those who received mail. Unknown to us sailors, mail had been picked up while at port in Spain, and when they called my name, I rushed over and took the letter, knowing it was from Mom. My heart went right to my throat when I saw it wasn't from her: it was from Donna! I walked to my rack and nervously opened it. It was a very nice two-page letter and in it, she wanted to know if we could at least remain friends. Oh, God! I could picture her beautiful face as if she were sitting right by me.

Later that night, I sat down and answered her letter. My heart was filled with pain when I wrote, "I'm so sorry, Donna, but we can no longer be friends. You not only ripped my heart apart once while I was in boot camp, but you did it a second time when I went back from leave." I had one hell of a time getting enough courage to actually lick and seal the envelope because of what I had written. Deep down, I still had strong feelings for her, and perhaps I always would, but it hurt too much to have a friendship with her.

Since we were back at sea, we once again watched anxiously through the trusty binoculars for land. Finally—*finally*—I yelled, "Land!" Probably over a hundred miles away, I spotted the coastline of Italy, and once again, all my friends and other sailors took turns looking at it through my binoculars. When we got close enough, the ship slowed down and was carefully guided inside a large sea wall at the mouth of the port. We finally came to a complete stop and the massive anchor was dropped. Yes, the USS *Yosemite* had just safely completed a 4,200-mile cruise that had taken eleven days!

The next morning, we attached steel cables to the boats on the upper deck and the ship's huge crane gently picked them up one at a time, lowering them into the water. Two massive wooden beams attached to the side of the ship were disconnected at one end, swung out, then pinned into place, each extending about eighty feet straight out from the ship. The beams had a twenty-inch flat surface to walk on, and attached at their ends were ropes that extended about twenty feet down to the boats to keep them from drifting away. The boat-coxswains, who would ferry passengers to and from port, used rope ladders to shinny down on. The captain's gig and the officers' gig were tied to one of the beams, and three twenty-six-foot liberty boats were tied to the other.

Once we had all the boats in place, the second-class petty officer in charge told all of the boat-coxswains that he was going to have us take a couple of training runs. He pulled alongside the ship at the loading platform, about ten of us climbed aboard, and we headed towards the dock at Naples. The landing area was about a mile from the ship. After making a few runs and taking turns making landings at the ship and at the dock, the petty officer was satisfied with our performances and told us we'd start taking sailors for liberty at 1630. So around 1600, I put on a clean uniform and headed for the wooden beam the liberty boats were tied to. As I stepped onto it, I glanced at the water below—a long way down! Whew! It'd be a damn wreck if a person fell!

I didn't realize I had an audience until I heard a sailor yell, "Don't look down!" Others said, "Watch your step!" "Easy does it!" "Shall we throw you a towel?" I stayed focused on walking down the narrow beam, thinking, "You ornery bastards!"

My assistant—called a "boat hook"—and I started the boat, untied it, and pulled it alongside the ship at the loading platform, where approximately twenty-five very anxious sailors came aboard. I then took them to the dock at Naples where they got off, whooping, hollering, and heading for the bars. The other two boats were also busy taking sailors from the ship to the dock. Late that night, we started taking sailors back to the ship. Many were extremely drunk, but no one got out of order during the trip back. There was just a lot of loud talking, joke telling, and laughing. I finally made my last run at 0130 and, after unloading the sailors, I parked the boat, climbed the rope ladder, carefully walked down the beam, and headed for my rack.

The following day, it was finally time for the guys and me to go on liberty. Before leaving the ship, a petty officer who'd been in Naples before gave me a heads-up on what to watch out for. He said I'd be approached by very young boys wanting money and pimps offering whores; that certain bars had scantily dressed cocktail waitresses that were nothing more than prick teasers, who would flirt in order to get you to buy them expensive champagne, which was nothing more than colored water. I thanked him for all of the advice.

At 1700 hours, we got into one of the liberty boats and headed for Naples. We were all anxious to slam down some beer and check out the city. After getting out of the boat, we'd only walked a short distance before being confronted by a group of very young Italian boys, ranging in age from seven to ten. They started pulling on our arms, yelling, "Hey, Joe! You give me some money!" Others said, "Follow me—you can fuck my sister for money!"

We finally got rid of them and walked to town, where the sidewalks were crowded with sailors going in and out of bars and restaurants. Besides our ship, there were three destroyers, a submarine, and an aircraft carrier anchored here. It was clear to see that the US Navy had a huge impact on the economy.

As soon as we walked into our first bar, we saw young girls wearing low-cut tops and short skirts that just barely covered their panties. They'd take you by the hand and say, "Hey, Joe—you buy me a drink?" At the same time, they'd gently put one hand on your crotch. Most of them were very pretty and it was tempting, but I'd already been warned about the game they played.

We sat down at a table, ordered beer, and politely told the girls we wouldn't buy them any drinks. We watched them move in on some other sailors who quickly went for their billfolds. While each gal sat on a sailor's lap, she'd down drinks of colored water and charge the sailor $5 for each one. She'd nibble on the sailor's ear, rub his crotch, lean over so he could get a good look at her tits, then order another drink. As soon as a sailor quit buying drinks, she'd go find another sucker. As for us, we did some serious beer drinking. Unable to buy American beer, we drank an Italian brand named Perona. After a few hours watching this carnival-type atmosphere, we walked to a restaurant and ordered a couple of pitchers of beer and some pizza. Boy, was the pizza good!

Louie asked if we wanted to walk up to where there were prostitutes, and we all agreed to check it out. We walked a few blocks up narrow cobblestone alleys to find small groups of women standing around, negotiating prices. We talked to some of them to see how much they charged, and the average-looking gals were $15 to $25. The well-dressed, good-looking gals were charging $50! But by this time it was past midnight, so we decided to wait till another night before parting with our money. I was hoping when we came back that I'd find the one who I'd talked to for a while. She was a beautiful woman!

Over the next few weeks, it was pretty much the same old routine: operate the liberty boats at night and clean them during the day. On nights when we didn't have duty, we went to town, drank a lot of beer, and always went to our favorite pizza place. I received two letters from Mom every week, and on Sundays, I'd write her and Dad a long letter.

Around the tenth of April, I happened to mention that on April 16, I'd be turning twenty-one. Oh, shit! Louie was all over that. He said, "You *will* be getting laid that night!" I started laughing and said, "We'll see."

When the day came, Donn, Louie, Alan, Gary, Bruce, and I all put on clean uniforms after showering and were ready to head to town. While in our compartment on the ship, Louie yelled, "Birthday boy is going to get laid tonight!" Everyone started laughing. Louie was a witty, funny, wild son of a bitch!

To start with, we went to our favorite pizza joint. The bullshit flew while we went through several pitchers of beer and enjoyed our meal. As I returned from the restroom, I noticed that Louie was gone and asked the guys where he was. Donn said, "Don't worry, he'll be back." About thirty minutes later, Louie showed up with a very nice-looking gal hanging on his arm. "Happy birthday!" he said. I stood up, introduced myself, and took the girl's hand. "Goodnight, boys," I waved as I walked out of the restaurant.

We went several blocks to her apartment. Once inside, I was impressed to see that it was very clean and had nice furniture. She offered me a beer and, after talking for a while, the sheets came down on her bed. Needless to say, it felt really good to have sex! I gave her a $10 tip and headed back to the ship. All my buddies were sound asleep, but when reveille sounded off, so did they. I was hit with a barrage of questions: "How was it?" "Was it as good as it looked?" "Did she fuck your headlights out?" Louie walked up with a big grin on his face. "How is that Italian pussy?" "Louie," I laughed, "it was so hot, it'll give me nightmares for months! Now let's go get some coffee and breakfast, 'cause I'm *really* hungry!"

Days turned into weeks; time slowly—but surely—passed. Every night that Donn and I had liberty, we'd head for the bars and do one hell of a lot of drinking. Many times our buddies would go with us, but usually it was just the two of us.

Donn was married, so it was really tough on him, as he really missed his wife, Peggy. It helped that we could talk to one another about missing our loved ones. For me, the worst time was at night when I crawled into my rack, usually around 0200. The berthing compartment would be stone quiet except for the sound of an occasional snore. The god-awful feeling of being homesick would creep into my mind and weigh on my heart. I missed Mom and Dad so much, and the divorce continued to haunt me. I'd lay in my rack, thinking, and it would usually take me an hour or two before I could finally drift off to sleep.

In late June, our division officer informed us that he'd rented a stretch of beach to have a barbeque on July 4. He smiled and said, "There'll also be plenty of beer." His timing was perfect, because it lifted everyone's spirits by giving us something to look forward to.

On the morning of the Fourth, everyone grabbed their swim trunks and a towel and headed out. Once we got to Naples, we were bussed to the private beach that was reserved for US military only. What a beautiful place it was! Over the course of the day, we enjoyed swimming, lying back on the soft sand, bullshitting, and drinking a lot of beer. We were served barbequed hot dogs and hamburgers. We really enjoyed a "day off at the beach!"

I continued getting two letters every week from Mom. She told me that Dad was just lost without me, and that he wasn't even interested in going fishing. It broke my heart to read that, but I knew just how he felt.

The first week of August, our chief got everyone together and told us that our ship would be leaving Naples on September 23, 1969, and that we should arrive at Newport, Rhode Island, on October 4. A huge cheer went up from all of us! Now that we had a target date to circle on our calendars, the days seemed to pass more quickly. The heavy lines were soon unhooked by port personnel and a group of us tugged and pulled them onto the ship, where we wound them around large spools forming a figure eight. Once the two lines from the starboard and port side had been secured, we could hear the gigantic anchor chain rattling against the steel of the ship, coming up from the bottom where it had been resting for seven months.

The deck that we were standing on started vibrating, and we could dimly hear engines starting up. The props were engaged, the water churned, and air bubbles broke the ocean's surface. On every level of the ship, hundreds of sailors were leaning across the handrails on the port side, looking towards Naples. When the *Yosemite* started moving, everyone let out a loud cheer: we were heading home!

Hours later, Italy disappeared from my binoculars, nothing to see now but hundreds of miles of the Mediterranean. Our only stop was Malta, where we took on fuel and supplies, then we continued our long voyage across the Atlantic. During the day, we did a lot of scraping, wire wheeling, priming, and painting of large sections of the deck areas. The month of September passed, and excitement started building among everyone as the distance to the States narrowed.

Our chief called a special meeting to inform us that the ship was going to be changing home ports at the end of October. We would be moving to Mayport, Florida, and we should take that into consideration when making travel arrangements. I'd already had my three-week leave approved: I'd be going home on October 16, 1969, and returning on November 5. I'd be home for opening day of hunting season—October 18—and be able to hunt with Dad until I left.

Around noon on October 4, the *Yosemite* arrived at the Newport, Rhode Island, harbor, where the ship was towed to its docking spot. When we were about a hundred yards from the pier, we could see a large crowd—well over a thousand people—waiting to meet us. We could also see a navy band in place, brass horns once again glistening in the sun.

Minutes later, the tugboats on the port side disconnected their lines and we pulled them on board. Then the starboard side tugs slowly pushed the ship to the pier. By now, there were many sailors yelling and waving at their wives, children, parents, and other friends and relatives on the pier. When the band started playing, tears ran down my cheeks. God, I was happy to be back! Our captain, navigation crew, enginemen, electricians, and a host of others had made sure that we sailed safely to Italy and back, covering over 8,000 miles. It was simply amazing!

In record time, the gangplank was put into place, and what happened next was quite a sight. Many sailors ran down the plank to their wives, wrapping their arms around them and giving them kisses. Some wives handed their husbands a baby—the first time they'd ever held their child. Other sights included moms and dads hugging their sons. I was happy for each and every one of them.

The band stopped playing when the crowd moved away, then they marched down the pier. Donn and I decided to go to the enlisted men's club so he could call his wife and I could call Mom and Dad. It felt so good to have my feet on solid ground—especially because I was on US turf! I talked to Mom and Dad for nearly thirty minutes and told them I'd see them in two weeks. For the next few hours, Donn and I drank several cold Buds—it was great to be drinking American beer! After enjoying a hamburger, we headed back to the ship.

A few days later, I went to the travel agency and purchased all my tickets. I'd be flying home via the same route as I had in November, but because the ship was changing home ports while I was on leave, I'd fly back to Jacksonville, Florida, then take a bus to Mayport.

Shit! Was I ever looking forward to going home! It'd been nearly a year. I'd have three weeks of freedom—being able to do what I wanted to, when I wanted to, not taking orders from anyone. *True freedom!* Until you've had it taken away from you, it's hard to imagine just what it means.

Around 4:00 p.m. on October 16, the jet I was flying on touched down at Walker Field in Grand Junction. Mom, Dad, and I had a joyous reunion: there were lots of hugs and tears of happiness flowed down Mom's and my cheeks. When I walked through the front door of the house, I felt really good: it was such a comforting feeling, being home. A short time later, my sister pulled up in her Mustang, jumped out, and we hugged. She was now seventeen years old, and she'd certainly grown up!

After supper that evening, we kicked back in the living room while I told them of my experiences over the past year. Dad was all wound up about hunting season and showed me his cow elk license that he'd received in a special drawing. He said, "I wanted to surprise you, and it was sure hard keeping it a secret." I started laughing and teased, "Do you think you can get a cow?" "One never knows," he said as he smiled back.

The next day, I purchased my hunting licenses and got all our gear organized, then I visited with everyone—Cal, Larry, Donnie, Erika, and other friends and relatives. Early Saturday morning, Dad and I headed for Big Beaver, and by eight o'clock, he had gotten a cow! He was so pleased with himself and happy—and so was I, just seeing him that way. Our good luck continued, and by Tuesday evening, we had two nice bucks hanging in the barn. Those four days I'd spent hunting with him were so much fun, it was priceless.

On Wednesday, I cleaned the Scout and quartered up the bucks in the barn, and over the next few days, Mom, Cal, and I laughed and joked while we cut and wrapped the meat. On Friday afternoon, Donnie showed up and asked if I wanted to go elk hunting with him on Monday. I said, "Sure, where're we going?" He told me he had permission to hunt on private property owned by Tom Theos, whose land was located about twelve miles east of Meeker.

So early Monday morning, Donnie and I headed out for a day of elk hunting. As usual, he was all wound up and told me the out-of-state hunters he guided had gotten some nice bucks and three bulls off this property, so he was confident that we'd see some elk. From daylight to late afternoon, we tried several different areas, seeing quite a few elk but no bulls.

Around three, Donnie decided to try a place called "Dickerville Ridge." After we drove up a canyon for about a mile, he told me to stop; he wanted to continue on foot. After we walked a short distance, we both put shells in our rifles to be ready. It was a beautiful spot with large oak brush-covered mountains to the north and south; a few miles east of us was the backside of Sawmill Mountain, covered with pine trees.

After another half mile, Donnie tapped me on the shoulder and whispered, "Stop!" He pointed up the canyon about 200 yards to what looked like an elk standing in some oak brush. I put my rifle to my shoulder and found the object in my scope. Oh, shit! It was the biggest bull elk I'd ever seen and had a huge rack—I figured at least a six point. I whispered, "It's a big bull. I'm going to get a rest and take him." Just as I started to walk to a nearby bush, the elk turned and went out of sight. I told Donnie that we'd better run up the hillside located to our north and gain some elevation. If the bull went up the hillside on the south, maybe we could see him. We scrambled up the steep hill and finally got to a place that gave us a good view of the bottom of the canyon, and we could plainly see the steep oak brush-covered hillside south of us.

We both got a rest with our rifles. All of a sudden, at about 350 yards, I spotted the elk headed up the side of the mountain. I whispered, "There he is, Donnie!" *Boom! Boom!* We both shot and missed. *Boom!* Donnie shot and missed. *Boom! Whump!* I shot and hit the bull. He turned and came a short distance down the hill, disappearing into some thick brush and aspens. I watched the area for several minutes in my scope. By now, I was shaking. This would be the biggest bull I'd ever gotten.

Both of us reloaded and started the long walk towards the elk. Several minutes later, we moved with great caution as we neared the area where I'd last seen him. Damn it! The thick brush made it hard to see more than ten or fifteen yards at a time. Finally, I spotted him laying about twenty yards from me. I approached him very slowly, ready to shoot if he moved, but the big bull was dead. Oh, my God! He was perfect—a trophy six point! Chills ran up my spine; my dream of getting a large bull had finally come true! I yelled for Donnie, who was about thirty yards away, and told him I'd found the elk. When he caught up to me, we whooped and hollered and I slapped him on the shoulder. "Thanks for bringing me to this great place!"

We inspected the bull's rack: the six points on each side were perfectly matched, none of them chipped or broken. The tips of many of the points were snow white, showing that the bull had really polished his horns prior to rut in September. The mane hair was long and dark brown. His blonde-colored body was huge! I guessed him to be around six or seven years old. Because of all the hunting pressure in the White River Valley, it was rare now to find a bull elk of this size.

After we both had a cigarette, I cleaned the bull and finished when the sun was nearly down. We agreed we'd have to return the next morning with help to get him off the mountain. We weaved through the thick oak brush, working our way down the steep mountain towards the bottom.

Daylight was dimming fast, and by the time we arrived at the Scout, it was dark. When we got to town, we told everyone about the big bull. Dad was ecstatic and called his boss to get the next day off so he could help us load it. I called my friend, Ken, and he agreed to come with us.

Early Tuesday morning, we headed back to Dickerville Ridge. It had snowed about an inch in town overnight, but because of the elevation change—from 6,200 feet at Meeker to 7,200 where the elk was located—there were eight inches there. We had to chain all four tires before going up the canyon. It was a winter wonderland when we arrived at our parking place, with the trees and brush covered in snow. Once the four of us hiked up to where the elk was, Dad said, "Boy, he is a dandy, Son!" Ken was impressed, too, and because of the deep snow, it was fairly easy to slide the elk down the steep mountain toward the Scout. I took several pictures of the bull while we were doing this, then took more once we got to the road in the bottom of the canyon.

Uncle Donnie, left, with Danny and six-point bull elk near Dickerville Ridge.   PHOTO BY KEN BICKNELL

Chapter Nine: ANCHORS AWAY!

By noon, we had the elk loaded and were headed into town. At the house, a large crowd gathered and flocked around the Scout, looking at the bull. Mom was thrilled, as was Cal. After talking with many of Mom and Dad's neighbors and other hunters, we took the elk to show him off to Erika, then we went on to Purkey's Processing. I told Bryce Purkey that I was going to have the elk shoulder-mounted and wanted him to cape the bull—where the hide from the neck and the head are left intact, minus the horns—and we'd pick up the cape and the horns the next day to take to the taxidermist.

When I took the guys home, Donnie said he'd like to go hunting again on Friday in the same area, and he invited Ken to go along. Ken was excited to go, so it would be the three of us.

Early on Friday morning, we headed out for another elk hunt. By daybreak, we were nearing the canyon where we'd gotten the bull. Because there was still quite a bit of snow, we elected to chain all four tires, then drove very slowly and quietly up the bottom of the canyon, watching the steep hillsides for elk. Just as we got to the spot where we'd loaded the bull, Donnie said, "Stop! Shut it off...I think there's another bull up there." Ken, who was sitting in the middle, leaned forward so he could see what Donnie was looking at, then said, "Bull, my ass! That's a *bear*!" I grabbed my rifle from the gun rack mounted on the dash, threw the door open, and slammed a shell into the chamber. I jumped up on the steep bank by the Scout and rested my rifle on its top. At a distance of about 200 yards, I found the bear in my scope. It was standing on its hind legs and appeared to be looking in our direction. Just as I started to pull the trigger, I heard Donnie open the door on the passenger side. I jumped off the bank and headed for the hood of the Scout to get a better rest. Boom! Ken fired a shot with his 30:06. *Boom!* Donnie shot another round, and I'd lost sight of it by this time. *Boom! Whump!* When Ken shot again, you could hear the bullet hit what I figured was the bear. *Boom!* Donnie again. *Boom!* Ken again. The shooting stopped and it now became quiet. Ken said, "I'm sure I hit him with my second shot, but I can't see him anymore." I thought about a strategy. "I'll walk up the mountain; you guys stay here and give me directions to where you saw him last."

I slowly started up the mountainside with a shell in my rifle's chamber. I was concerned when I started getting into the thick oak brush; there was the possibility that the bear was just wounded, and with visibility so poor, I would never see him coming. I knew the bear was big, because of the brief look I'd had of him in my scope. I guessed him to be around 400 pounds.

Minutes passed, and I saw a bunch of magpies fly up. I knew they'd been pecking away on the guts of the bull elk I'd cleaned on Monday. I walked over to the spot where they'd been, and now everything was beginning to make sense. There were hardly any guts left, and the snow was packed down all around the area; it appeared that the bear had been feeding on what was left for the past day. Just then, Ken yelled, "Go about fifty yards higher!" His voice echoed up the canyon's slopes.

I climbed up, zigging and zagging back and forth, looking for the bear's tracks and blood. I found a lot of elk tracks in the sugary snow, but I couldn't find the bear's. I gave up and walked back down to the Scout. Once there, we decided to drive back down to the main road, head a mile south, then drive up another road that would take us east. Perhaps we'd find the bear's tracks there. By the time we got to the other road, it was nearly ten o'clock, and the bright sun was now causing the snow to melt. With the Scout in four-wheel drive and low gear, the tire chains were flinging mud and snow as we headed up the steep mountain. Minutes later, I spotted something. "Look!" "At what?" Donnie asked. I pointed up the road at a patch of blood-spattered snow.

I stopped and we all got out to investigate. Sure enough, Ken had hit the bear, and his huge tracks were headed south. We all put shells into our rifles and started following the blood trail. After about 200 yards, Ken said, "Stop!" "Why?" I asked. "I want to be in the middle instead of at the end, just in case the bear circles around behind us." Donnie said, "Why do you think *I'm* in the middle?" "Alright, you guys!" I yelled. "We don't have *time* to argue about who's where! The snow's starting to melt, and we could lose his tracks!" We continued to follow the blood trail; a few minutes later, we realized that the bear had made a circle and was now heading back north, nearly in the same direction he had come from. Thirty minutes later, we were just fifty yards from the Scout with the bear still headed north towards Dickerville Ridge canyon. I told Donnie to drive back around to the spot where they'd shot from, and that Ken and I would continue tracking.

Before long, we dropped off the steep mountain where the bear had been to begin with and moved cautiously through the thick oak brush.

Chapter Nine: ANCHORS AWAY! 147

Although it wasn't bleeding hard, the bright red specks on the snow were easy to spot. A few minutes later, we tracked the bear across the old road in the bottom of the canyon, just a hundred yards above where the Scout had been parked earlier. Donnie hadn't made it back around yet, so Ken and I continued heading north, following the trail.

Soon, we crossed over the top of the hill we'd been climbing. Because we were now on a north-facing slope, the snow deepened by about six inches. After another half mile, I stopped. I turned to Ken and whispered, "The tracking is over." He whispered back, "What do you mean?" I pointed down the trail about fifteen yards where the bear's tracks disappeared in the snow. "There must be a hole here somewhere—probably the bear's den." I flipped the safety off my rifle, put my finger on the trigger, then positioned the gun so I could get off a quick round if I needed to. Slowly and carefully, we moved towards the spot where the tracks ended. Sure enough, there was a hole there that the bear had dug in the side of the hill, probably a couple of weeks ago to prepare for hibernation.

Instead of looking in the hole, we turned and quietly walked back down the trail about thirty yards to figure out a plan. I bent over and picked up a handful of snow, putting it in my mouth. The three miles of tracking and a case of nerves had caused me to have cottonmouth. Ken scooped up a handful, too.

While we watched the den, I lit a cigarette. Shit! This had turned out to be one hell of an ordeal, and it still wasn't over. I whispered, "One of us has to stay here and watch the den while the other one goes to the Scout and gets my tarp and some rags. We'll have to dump out some of the gas from the five-gallon can so it won't be so heavy. Then, along with Donnie, everything needs to be brought back here. We'll pour some gas on the rags, light them, throw them in the hole, and cover it with the tarp to try to smoke the bear out."

After hearing my plan, Ken said, "I'm *not* staying here by *myself*." I said, "You have a 30:06, don't you?" He smiled, "That might not be enough." I told him to go get the stuff and I'd see him and Donnie in a little while.

I walked over to a log, sat down with my rifle across my lap—safety off—and stared at the den opening. The forest was eerily quiet. About an hour later, I heard some brush cracking and looked to see Donnie and Ken coming down the trail. After setting everything down, Donnie decided to walk over to the den. I watched as he walked right to it and looked into the hole. All of a sudden, he took off running. As he came by us, he screamed, "He's in there! He's in there!" He ran past us and I yelled, "I *know* he's in there! Come back here!" He finally stopped running and walked back to us. He was panting and puffing, totally out of breath. His face was pale and he looked like he'd seen a ghost. He said, "I…uh…*saw* him, you guys! I *saw* him!" Now I was getting frustrated. "Ken, make sure you have a shell in the chamber and take your gun off safety. Donnie and I will get above the hole and be ready to shoot, then you walk over to it, just like Donnie did, and when you see the bear, shoot." Ken said, "I don't want to do it." "Why not?" I asked. "The bear might come charging out!" he cried. Donnie said, "*I'm* damn sure not stepping in front of that hole again!" So I thought to myself, "Son of a bitch! I guess *I* have to do it!"

I waited till they took up positions above the hole, then I flipped the safety off on my 7mm magnum and slowly started walking towards the hole. My heart was pounding hard: I could feel and hear it in my ears. Before stepping to the front of the den, I put my rifle to my shoulder and my finger on the trigger. Fear was just about to overtake my mind, knowing that I was going to be just a few feet from a powerful animal that had the tools to tear me to shreds. I was going to have to aim down the barrel of my rifle, since the distance would be too close to use my scope.

Finally, I made it to the den and peered inside. All I could see was darkness; then my eyes adjusted. Oh, shit! There he was—only ten feet from me! I could dimly make out his huge head and see his small black beady eyes, staring at me. With my heart right in my throat, I aimed the barrel of my rifle so that I'd hit him in the forehead and squeezed the trigger—*boom!* The instant I shot, I ran to my left, ejected the empty, slammed another live round in the chamber, and turned towards the hole with my rifle on my shoulder, ready to shoot. Damn! I couldn't hear a thing! The loud blast had come right back to me, and my hearing was temporarily dulled. I noticed that Ken and Donnie had run up the hill, but I kept my eyes trained on the area around the den. Smoke was billowing out—the air was filled with the smell of gun powder. I yelled, "Get down here!" When they got to where I was, I said, "Why the hell did you run?" "We thought he was coming out!" they answered. "Well thanks a lot, you guys. You were supposed to shoot him if he *did!*" My hands were trembling, so I lit a cigarette to calm myself down. After a few minutes, the smoke cleared; it was time to take a look to see if I'd hit him. I told Ken and Donnie to get above the den again and added, "Make *damn* sure you don't take off running this time!" They both smiled and said, "Okay...okay." I slowly walked towards the den; it was no different than the first time—one spooky son of a bitch! I made sure the safety was off my rifle and put it to my shoulder, my finger on the trigger. Once my eyes adjusted, I could see the bear's head slumped over. Blood was running out of his forehead, exactly where I'd aimed. I let out a sigh of relief, stepped back, and took the shell from the chamber.

We removed the rope from my tarp. It was about a half inch in diameter and twenty feet in length. I tied a loop in each end, with the idea that we would put a noose over one of the bear's front paws and another around the head.

The den's entrance had a steep incline, so Donnie and Ken said they'd hold onto my ankles and ease me down into it, with the promise that they'd quickly pull me out if something went wrong. The den stunk terribly with the bear's strong, musky odor, and there was barely enough light to see. I slipped one loop over a giant front paw and cinched it down; I placed the other loop over the bear's head and neck and started pulling it tight when I heard, "*Grrrrr!*" I screamed, "He's alive! He's alive! Get me out!"

Donnie and Ken let go of my ankles and took off. I scrambled like hell, desperately trying to back out of the hole. My hands and knees kept slipping as I pushed. I imagined the bear's powerful jaws clamping down on one of my arms and ripping it apart! Finally, I got out of the den, got to my feet, and ran for my rifle. Hands trembling and heart pounding, I slammed a shell into it and stared at the den. My two fair-weather friends then appeared from the brush. I was so damned mad at that point that I said, "*Fuck* you guys! I could've been *killed!*" Both of them could see how mad I was, and they quickly apologized. I yelled, "Both of you have talked me into taking all the risks all day long when it's not even *my* bear! Now *you* guys check out the den! I've had it!"

As they walked towards the den, I told them that I felt it was probably just some exhaled air from the bear's chest that had made the sound. I smoked another cigarette and watched them approach the den, which was great entertainment! They both seemed to be scared enough to piss their pants. Moments later, Donnie said, "I can see the bear; he's not moving." I walked over and grabbed one of the ends of the rope, and Ken and Donnie got hold of the other end. We pulled as hard as we could—grunting, groaning, farting—and we were only able to move the bear a few inches, but—finally—we pulled him from the den. He was very large with coal-black fur, and his claws were over three inches long. I pulled up a lip and looked at his teeth, curious as to how big they were; the eye teeth were easily two inches long! We all agreed that he weighed at least 400 pounds.

Now there was just one minor problem: none of us had a bear license. We decided to head to town to buy one and return tomorrow to get the bear. We made sure our rifles were unloaded and headed down the trail to the Scout. By the time we got there, it was 4:00 p.m., which meant this escapade had started nearly nine hours earlier. I grabbed two Budweisers from the cooler while Ken picked out a Pepsi and Donnie poured himself a cup of coffee. Oh, shit! Did my cold beer ever taste good! After nearly inhaling the first beer, I popped the tab on the second one. We ate a quick sandwich and headed for town, as we needed to get to the hardware store before six to buy the bear license.

We pulled into Gambles just before closing and bought the license, then went on to Mom and Dad's to tell them of the day's events. After that, we walked over to Cal and Larry's, and Larry offered to go with us to help with the bear, so I told him I'd pick him up at seven. I asked Dad if he wanted to go but he declined, saying the Scout was going to be full.

The next morning, we headed for the high country. I was able to get the Scout within three-quarters of a mile of the bear's location, and the four of us arrived at the den in about thirty minutes. The bear was bloated because we hadn't gutted him the day before; no one had been interested in the meat and Ken was planning to take him to the taxidermist, so we had decided to leave him intact. Now its body was breaking down, in effect rotting from the inside out.

Larry got hold of the bear's left front leg and Donnie and Ken grabbed the section of rope that was tied to the right front leg; I grabbed the part that was cinched around the neck. We all started dragging him down the snow-covered trail. We soon came to a small log in the middle of the path, and when we pulled the bear over it, it caused the gas in its abdomen to expel from the rectum. Holy shit! Everyone let go and took off running! It was the worst stink any of us had ever smelled. Several feet from the bear, we were all laughing at each other as we waited for the air to clear. A few minutes later, we took up our positions and began pulling the bear down the trail again. Moments later, the same thing happened and everyone took off again, laughing. I said, "You guys, this isn't going to work. We're going to have to gut him." They all agreed, so I took my hunting knife from its sheath and handed it to Ken. He smiled and said, "I don't want to do it." I replied, "It's *your* bear." We then scooted the bear around to where its head was facing uphill. Donnie and Larry each held a front leg to keep the bear balanced on its back and I pulled the left hind leg back so Ken would have plenty of room. He bent over and gently poked the tip of the knife through the hide near the groin area. *Sssssss!* The gas came spewing out. Donnie ran a few feet away, bent over, and started throwing up. Larry ran the opposite direction and started gagging. Ken and I ran just a few feet away and busted out laughing while we watched Donnie throw up. He raised up and said, "It's *not* funny!" But that just made us laugh even harder, and then Larry started laughing, too.

Finally, things settled down and we regrouped. Ken said, "I can't gut him." I said, "I'll try, but you have to hold my nose while I'm doing it." Then the four-ring circus began! Donnie held the bear's right front leg with his left hand and held his nose with his right; Larry held the other front leg with his right hand and held his nose with his left. Ken squeezed my nose shut with his right hand and squeezed his nose shut with his left. I gutted the bear as fast as I could, taking less than ten minutes. The stink was so bad that I could actually *taste* it! Once I had the guts out, Ken continued holding my nose as I dragged the stinking mess away. When we returned, we threw several handfuls of snow into the body cavity to help clean it out, which rid the bear of much of the smell. Oh...what I wouldn't have given to have someone filming the whole ordeal!

After Ken and I washed our hands off with snow, the four of us dragged the bear to the Scout. We decided not to load him in the back because of the smell, so we put him on the hood. That was another grunting and groaning circus, but we finally got him on and tied down. We drove back to town, showing the bear to Mom and Dad and Cal. I thanked Larry for helping out, then the three of us headed downtown and parked on main street at the Meeker Café, where many people flocked around to see the bear. We decided to go to the bar for a few beers, then went past Donnie's house to show the bear to Erika. Finally, we drove to Ken's and unloaded the bear in his shed. He and his dad were going to take it to the taxidermist in Craig. I told Ken that I'd see him later that night at the Stagecoach Inn, and I took Donnie home, thanking him for one hell of a hunting season. He smiled and said, "If I don't see you before you leave, good luck! Plan on doing some fishing when you get back next summer." I shook his hand, slapped him on the shoulder, and said, "I'm counting on it!"

My last few days of leave passed quickly and, early the morning of November 5, I loaded my suitcase in the trunk, hugged my sister goodbye, and Mom, Dad, and I headed for the airport. We talked a lot during the trip and, after checking in at the airport, I gave both of them a long hug. "I'll see you in June." Once I got to my assigned seat on the plane, I looked out the window and could see them still standing at the terminal. God, what would I do without them!? *Click.* I latched my seatbelt and we were soon airborne. I was dreading the next seven months, but I couldn't have had a better leave—far beyond my wildest imagination! I'd spent a lot of quality time with Mom and Dad, and my longtime dream of getting a big bull elk had come true. As far as the bear went—well, it was truly one for the record book.

Danny tying down "The Bear," near Dickerville Ridge.
PHOTO BY KEN BICKNELL

Chapter Nine: ANCHORS AWAY!

I walked across the gangplank of the USS *Yosemite*, located at Mayport, Florida, at 2330 hours. That was certainly cutting it close, as I was due to check in at 2400.

Over the next few weeks, I enjoyed Florida's November weather as I got to know the area. On the ship, I was usually standing watch or painting; socially, Donn and I would take a bus to Jacksonville on Friday and Saturday nights and hit the bars.

In mid-December, our chief called a special meeting on the boat deck. Everyone was wondering what it might be for; some even thought that he might announce that we were going on another cruise. A large group of us gathered anxiously and at 0800, he came up the stairs and took a position in front of the group. He said, "I have some great news for you sailors. The US Navy is starting to cut back on personnel. This means that most of you will be getting out ninety days prior to your scheduled discharge date."

I yelled "Yahoo!" at this point and everyone started laughing—even the chief! Chills ran up my spine, I was so damned happy! I'd be getting out the first week of March. The rest of the day, I was on cloud nine. That evening, Donn and I went to the enlisted men's club; I called Mom and Dad to tell them the great news and Donn called his wife, Peggy. Afterward, we drank till closing time. He told me he was going to fly home in a few days and move his wife down to Mayport. I was glad for him, 'cause they'd been apart for ten long months.

On Christmas day, Donn invited me over to meet his wife and have dinner with them. It meant the world to me, because around the holidays, homesickness really set in. Peggy was great and made me feel at home. The temperature was in the mid-seventies—a gorgeous day—so we decided to barbeque. Late that evening, Donn took me back to the ship. At night, it had become my habit to color in the day that had passed on what was called a "short-timer" calendar, which was a naked lady with a hundred days; the last one was in her crotch area. God, was I ever looking forward to the day I'd walk across the gangplank for the very last time!

The Vietnam War continued to rage on. With at least 40,000 Americans killed and thousands more returning home as amputees, massive protests were being held by Americans from coast to coast, wanting the war to end immediately. So far, their cries had fallen on what seemed to be the deaf ears of the politicians.

In mid-January, Donn and Peggy insisted I move in with them so I wouldn't have to stay on the ship. At first, I turned down their offer, because I felt as though I'd be imposing. Finally, I agreed to do it, knowing it'd be a breath of fresh air, and that it would give me a home-like atmosphere. Peggy had the spare bedroom in their trailer set up very nicely for me. It certainly felt a lot better to get into a queen-sized bed instead of the rock-hard small rack on the ship! It was also nice to sit down at the supper table with them and enjoy a home-cooked meal. Monday through Friday, Donn and I would leave at 0615 to go to the ship. We rarely had night duty, so at 1630, we'd head home. Usually on the weekends, we'd go to a beautiful beach area and spend the day drinking beer, laughing, and joking.

Soon the month of February showed up and, on the fourteenth, Donn and Peggy gave me a surprise going-away party. Many of my longtime navy buddies were there, including our chief and division officer. Donn and the other guys had gone in together and bought several cases of beer, while Peggy had two large tables set up on the lawn with everything well organized. During the afternoon, we played horseshoes and catch with a football and enjoyed barbequed hamburgers and hot dogs. There was a lot of joking and stories told about the past—including all the pranks that had been pulled on each other—and there was much laughter. Just before sundown, I gave a little speech and thanked everyone for coming. I shook hands with the chief and the division officer, acknowledging all they'd done for me, and gave Donn and Peggy each a huge hug and thanked them for a great day!

I continued to color the days on my short-timer calendar hanging in my locker on the ship. *Tick-tock, tick-tock!* As time passed, the excitement grew. It was now Saturday, February 28, 1970. In just two more days, I'd be headed home! On Sunday, Donn, Peggy, and I drove to our favorite place on the beach for the last time, and that evening, I packed all my things.

Early Monday morning, Donn and I drove to the ship, where I cleaned out my locker, took care of all the needed paperwork, and told many friends goodbye. As I neared the gangplank, chills ran up my spine and I got goose bumps. I'd waited for hundreds of days to walk across this plank for the last time!

Donn got permission to pull his car onto the pier just a few feet from the ship. While loading my sea bag, many of the guys I'd served with

Chapter Nine: ANCHORS AWAY!

were leaning over the handrails on the upper decks. One of them yelled, "You lucky bastard!" Others yelled, "Good luck!" I gave all of them one last wave, then Donn and I pulled away, drove to his trailer to pick up Peggy, and headed for the airport in Jacksonville. I checked in and they waited with me at my designated gate. A few minutes later, it was time for me to board. I gave both of them long hugs, tears streaming as we all cried like babies. Donn and I were as close as brothers after serving together, and Peggy and I had become dear friends. We told each other goodbye and I walked away, knowing that I'd probably never see them again.

I arrived at Stapleton International Airport in Denver too late to catch my scheduled flight to Grand Junction. I quickly called Mom and told her that I wouldn't be there until tomorrow morning. I met a very nice gal from Texas and we had supper at the airport, then drank until the bar closed. We spent the rest of the night visiting, and she walked me to my gate when it was time for me to leave.

Just before the jet arrived at the Grand Junction airport, I looked out the window and recognized the mountain range below called the "Book Cliffs." I thought, "Please, Mr. Pilot…please make a safe landing!" Once my feet touched the ground, I considered myself officially free—minus a gorgeous wife! Not by choice, I'd successfully completed my two-year obligation to the United States military. I started crying when I spotted Mom, Dad, and my sister waiting for me. It's impossible to describe how happy I was at that moment! I gave my sister a hug then held Mom for a solid minute. She whispered, "Thank God it's over!" Dad and I shared a long, warm handshake, then he slapped me on the shoulder. "You *did* it, my boy! Welcome home!" When I walked into the house a few hours later, it felt so good to know that my military days were over.

CHAPTER TEN
Home At Last

I WAS AWAKENED BY TOM, our cat, early the next morning. He jumped up on my bed and purred and purred as I petted him. Gosh, I got to thinking about how old he was—probably around ten or twelve. As I lay there, it felt as though a huge weight had been lifted from my shoulders, knowing that I was, indeed, home for good! I got up and had coffee with Dad before he went to work, then visited with Mom and Cal the rest of the day.

The first week I was home, several relatives stopped by to visit. Later, the taxidermist called to say the six-point elk mount was ready, so Dad and I drove to Craig to pick it up. We hung the big bull in the living room, and it looked so real! Dad enjoyed sitting in his recliner, admiring it.

Before long, I was dating two different gals and doing a lot of partying at the VFW, pool hall, and Stagecoach Inn. After three weeks, I decided to go back to work at the county. The first time I got back into the cab of a dump truck really felt strange; it was as though I'd been gone forever. In mid-April, I drove to Grand Junction to custom-order a 1970 Plymouth Road Runner with a Hurst four-speed and a .383 engine. The dealership called just a few weeks later and said the car was in. My sister took me to get it, and when we arrived, I looked down the street and said, "Donna, I'll bet you that's my car." We walked over to get a closer look. There she was, her dark-blue metallic paint glistening in the sunlight. I looked through the window and saw the wood-grained pistol grip on the gear shift; the vinyl bucket seats and the back seat were snow white, and the carpet was dark blue. I said, "Yeah, this is it!" Donna said, "Oh, God—it's so pretty!" I signed the paperwork and they handed me the keys. My hands were shaking when I started to crank her up. Oh, shit! Did the engine ever sound good! My *first* brand-new car!

Chapter Ten: HOME AT LAST

We headed for Meeker, Donna following me, and when I pulled away from each stoplight in Grand Junction, I wanted to get on it, but I knew I had to wait until she was broken in. At home, I gave everyone a ride, but Mom declined to go, saying, "It's too much of a hot rod for me!"

With my Coleman cooler in the trunk of my Road Runner filled with Bud and ice and the eight-track stereo blasting out tunes from Creedence Clearwater Revival, the Rolling Stones, Elvis, and others, my summer of 1970 began. Many nights found me parked at some secluded area with a gal in the back seat, the car filled with the aroma of her perfume. Wild, wild, wild!

My sister wasn't impressed with the women I was dating or my wild ways. She told me I needed to find a nice girl. I laughed and said, "Do you have someone in mind?" She answered, "As a matter of fact, I do. Her name is Caryl Morgan and she doesn't smoke, drink, or swear." I told her to ask Caryl if she'd like to go to a movie with me. A few days later, Donna said she'd talked to Caryl and that she was interested, so I called her and made a date for a movie. I was nervous when I went to pick her up and she introduced me to her parents. She was very attractive, quite nice, and things went well on our first date. I asked her if she wanted to go to the movie again the next weekend, and she said, "Sure." I was being cautious; I wanted to find the right gal to help me create a home and family.

Towards the end of June, Dad and I loaded our fishing gear, cooler full of beer, and some cold fried chicken and headed for Trappers Lake. We were both so excited, 'cause it'd been three years since we'd been on a fishing trip. At the parking lot, I filled my backpack with beer and chicken. Then, loaded up with our fishing rods, net, and tackle box, we headed up the trail.

There were still some snowdrifts left in the shaded areas of the dark timber, and I walked at a slow pace because of Dad's short stride and limp. While taking some breaks, we joked and teased each other. About an hour later, we arrived at one of the main inlets on the east side of the lake. The ten-foot-wide stream was gushing down the small valley, carrying snowmelt from the distant peaks. We were going to have to wade across it, so Dad picked up a dead tree limb about the circumference of a cane to help him keep his balance. I took his fishing rod and stepped into the nearly knee-deep rushing water. Ai-yi-yi! It was icy cold! I crossed as fast as I could, slipping and sliding on the slick rocks, then I waited for Dad. As soon as he stepped into the water, he said, "Mercy! She's a cold son of a bitch!" I started laughing and replied, "Yes, she is! We should buy some waders!" When he reached dry land, I said, "Is it worth it, Dad?" He smiled, "Depends on whether or not we catch some fish!"

Around eleven o'clock, we finally arrived at our favorite fishing spot. I took the beer from the backpack and buried it in a big snowdrift. Dad was anxious to start fishing and quickly rigged up his rod with a bubble and fly. I decided to start with a cold beer and sat down on a nearby log. I had a perfect view of the amphitheater on the other side of the crystal-clear lake. The majestic mountain's sheer north-facing slope was stacked with several feet of snow. What a beautiful day it was, with not a cloud in the dark-blue sky. A stiff breeze picked up, sending tiny waves across the water's surface. They created a soothing sound as they slapped against the shoreline. The large pine boughs danced in the wind; the air was filled with their sweet scent. I leaned my head back against the tree behind me and enjoyed the beautiful scenery.

It felt so good to be sitting with Dad, knowing that I was free to enjoy myself, done with the service. I often thought about Donna, wondering what she was doing and if we would've made it if not for the military.

"Got him!" Dad yelled. I jumped up, grabbed our net, and waited for him to bring the fish in. Moments later, I scooped the beautiful native trout into the net. "He's a beauty, Dad!" I quickly rigged up and started fishing. Lady luck was with us, as the trout really started hitting, and by two o'clock, we had our limit. Dad was smiling from ear to ear.

After I finished cleaning the fish, I put them in our old trusty canvas bag and placed it in a snowbank. What a catch it had been—beautiful native trout twelve to sixteen inches long! These pink-meated beauties were going to be very tasty!

We kicked back and enjoyed Mom's fried chicken and a few cold beers. We weren't in any hurry to leave this beautiful place, so for the next few hours we sat visiting. Dad smoked his signature Roi-Tans and I smoked my cigarettes. Finally, it was time to go, and we headed down the trail. It was another special day with my dad.

A few weeks later, I was visiting with Donnie and Erika when a good friend of theirs named Carlin stopped by. He asked me if I'd be interested

Chapter Ten: *Home At Last* 159

in going to work at the coal mine where he'd been employed for many years. "Boy, Carlin," I answered thoughtfully, "I don't know if I'd like working underground." He said, "Ah, heck—you'd get used to it in a couple of weeks. It's just as safe as working in this living room. The pay is twice as much as county wages, and because we work under the United Mine Workers union, the medical insurance is the best."

Damn! The idea of making twice as much money kept echoing in my mind. After thinking about it for several minutes, I told him to tell the mine superintendent that I wanted a job. Carlin told me the only drawback would be that I'd be required to work the night shift from 4:00 p.m. till midnight. After he left, Donnie said, "Hell, I think you made a good move. The place has a good safety record, and nobody has been seriously hurt there for many years."

Mom, Dad, my sister, and Caryl were concerned about my working underground and felt that maybe I should stay on at the county. But I made my decision, and on July 27, 1970, I drove to the mine, about twenty-two miles north of Meeker, for an interview. It went well, and I was given papers to fill out and told when to show up for a physical.

On August 3, I drove to the mine for orientation along with some other new hires. My heart started pounding hard when I was handed a belt to strap on that had a battery along with a light that clipped onto my hardhat. We walked down the porthole and, at about fifty yards, got into one of four mining cars connected to what was called "the motor," which pulled the cars down two steel rails designed just like a railroad track. The motor was powered by electricity: a pole went from the motor to a copper band attached to the roof of the mine. Basically, it functioned the same way as a trolley car. The operator of the motor flipped on the power, the cars started moving on the track, and we headed down a tunnel about twenty feet wide with a ten-foot-high roof.

The farther down the track we went, the harder my heart pounded! I knew that we were inside a mountain with millions of tons of earth overhead, traveling at just ten miles per hour. I became more and more apprehensive as the lights shining out from our hardhats danced and skipped off the nearby coal ribs. The bright light from the motor cast its glow down the track as we went deeper into the mountain, and a huge wave of doubt about having taken this job started rattling through my mind.

Finally, after traveling nearly a mile, we came to where coal was being mined. We walked down to what was called "the face," where miners were busy putting up timbers to support the roof, and a crew was operating a roof bolter that added additional support. We were shown the coal seam that was drilled then loaded with explosives and "shot"—blown up. The broken-up coal was then picked up by a machine called a "joyloader" and put into a shuttle car, which was powered by an electrical cable. The car hauled the coal to a bin and dumped it, and then it was scattered onto a conveyer belt and transported to the mining cars sitting on the track. After ten of them were loaded, the motor would take them to what was called "the dump," located about 300 feet from the porthole. Each car would then be dumped, and another conveyer belt would take the coal out of the mine and deposit it into large metal bins, called "the tipple."

We stayed for about an hour, watching the mining operation. The freshly mined coal had a petroleum smell to it, and I was glad when we got into the mine car and headed out towards daylight! The superintendent told us to report to work on August 17.

At the supper table that night, I told everyone about the scary experience. But there was other news during our meal: my sister, who'd just graduated from high school, said that she'd gotten a job with the phone company in Glenwood Springs and would be moving there in a few weeks. The following day, I gave Rio Blanco County my two weeks' notice, so there was no backing out of the mining job now. I would just have to overcome my fear of working in the dark.

A few days later, Cal was admitted to the hospital, and it wasn't the first time. Over the past year, his health had really been going downhill. On Thursday evening, I went to visit with him for a few minutes, and Larry was there, so we chatted, too. On Saturday, I decided to go see him again. When I got there, Larry was just coming out of his room and told me he was gone. Oh, my God! I put my hand on his shoulder and told him how sorry I was. A veil of sadness was cast over the family, as well as other relatives and friends. Cal had always been liked by everyone and didn't have one enemy.

Funeral services were held at a small church, then graveside services were at Highland Cemetery, where I was one of the pallbearers. I stared at the casket after we placed it alongside the grave, tears streaming down my cheeks. Cal had been such a special guy; he'd repaired Donna's and my bikes many times over the years and taught me about trout fishing and how to cut up deer and elk. To me, he would always be a legend!

On August 17, I started my first shift at the coal mine. I was given the job of dump operator; my working station was only a hundred yards from the porthole. The motor operator would bring ten to twelve loaded cars from inside the mine, leave them at the dump, and go get the empty cars about fifty yards below the dump to take back into the mine to be filled. Each car had a hand brake, so I'd uncouple a car and let it roll into the dump, where it would be stopped by hydraulic rams. I'd push a button and the car would roll 360°, dumping the coal onto a conveyer belt. The belt took the coal out of the mine to where the tipple operator controlled a series of screens, separating it into four different grades—mine run, lump, nut, and stoker—which were stored in large metal bins. The majority of the coal was put into the mine-run bin and hauled by semis to Craig, where it was loaded onto rail cars and shipped to coal-fired power plants.

During the eight-hour shift, I'd dump anywhere from seventy to a hundred mining cars, and when the motorman stopped bringing cars, my job was to pick up the large chunks of coal that had fallen on each side of the 250-foot conveyer belt, placing them back on the belt. Many of these weighed seventy-five pounds or more. With all my required duties, the eight-hour shift went by very fast, and I was happy when I saw how much my first paycheck was! I decided to start making two car payments each month so I could get my Road Runner paid off sooner.

Before long, hunting season arrived, and on opening day, Dad and I were rather shocked: there were many, many camps near our hunting country! There were tents, pickup campers, and small pull trailers—way more than we'd ever seen before. The White River Valley had been advertised in several outdoor magazines as being a great deer and elk hunting area, and out-of-state hunters had taken the ads seriously. I couldn't help feeling sorry for the game because of the extreme hunting pressure.

Since we could only hunt on the weekends, we didn't get a bull elk, but we did manage to shoot a cow and a couple of nice bucks. When hunting season was over, I told Dad our old hunting country was just too crowded and we really needed to start looking for some private property to hunt on.

The winter months passed and in May, Caryl—who was in her senior year in high school—graduated with honors. In fact, she had an extremely high grade-point average and had received some scholarships. She'd always planned to attend BYU, but our relationship had become serious, and she was instead leaning towards marriage. I had mixed emotions about that, because I knew she'd have a great career if she went to college. But love is love, and at the end of May, we drove to Grand Junction and purchased her engagement and wedding rings. The date was set for July 10, 1971, and vows would be said at her friend's ranch, eight miles west of Meeker. Caryl told me that every summer, Esther Clark had a beautiful flower garden. I called my longtime friend, Gary Wright, in Yuma and asked him to be my best man.

We rented a small one-bedroom apartment on Park Street and, during the month of June, Caryl and both of our mothers worked very hard, getting it all arranged. When the big day finally arrived, I was extremely nervous. The setting was something like you would see in a magazine! The dark-green lawn had been perfectly groomed and there were rows of many varieties of flowers, along with sculpted hedges. When Caryl walked down the aisle between the flowers, my eyes filled with tears. She was so pretty in her white wedding gown! The bridesmaids, including Caryl's best friend, Kathy, were wearing beautiful dresses. Minutes later, we joined hands, took our wedding vows, and—after saying "I do"—I kissed Caryl. Mom, Dad, and my sister had grown to love Caryl, too, and were so happy that I'd married her.

After a fun-filled reception, Caryl and I got into our Plymouth Road Runner and headed for the Holiday Inn in Grand Junction. With shaving cream, someone had written "Hot night tonight!" on its back windshield and tied a bunch of empty beer cans to the bumper. We were happy and laughing hard as we drove down the highway.

After a couple days in Grand Junction, we came back to Meeker and drove up to the high country to enjoy ourselves for a few more days, then we settled down in our small apartment. Caryl, a tremendous cook and good with arranging and taking care of the place, fell into the roll of "housewife" easily.

Dad had traded in the old Scout to buy a brand-new 1970 Ford Bronco, and at the end of September, Caryl and I borrowed it and went to the high country to watch and listen to the elk bugle. She absolutely loved the trip and was fascinated by the sounds the bulls made. Just weeks later, Dad and I loaded up and headed to Big Beaver for opening day, but when we got there, our hopes were dashed: once again, the area looked like a town, with camps strung throughout the woods everywhere we looked. It was even worse than last year!

We walked to our usual sitting places, and what happened next was unbelievable. Two different hunters showed up just after sunrise. One took a sitting spot not seventy-five yards away from me; the other sat fifty yards away on the other side of me. Son of a bitch! Absolutely no damn hunting ethics at all! Now what the hell would happen if a bull elk *did* show up? It'd be a full-blown range war! I was so damned mad that I gathered my things and started walking to where Dad was. I'd only gone a short distance when I came across a tent set up on our actual hunting ground. By the time I reached Dad, I was so mad that I couldn't see straight, and I told him about the hunters and the camp. *Boom! Zzzzzzzz...Boom! Zzzzzzzz...* Shit! Some dumbass hunter had just fired two rounds south of us, and we actually heard the bullets whizzing over our heads! I said, "That's it, Dad! Let's get the hell out of here before one of us gets shot!"

Oh, God! Was it ever a sad walk down the trail back to the Bronco. We'd used this hunting area for the past fifteen years, since I was eight years old! Thirty minutes later, I started the engine and we drove off Beaver Knob. I was certain that we'd never hunt this beautiful place again; there were just too many hunters now. On the way to town, we decided that some way, somehow, we were going to have to find some private property to hunt elk on.

By the time hunting season ended, we'd gotten two bucks on private property just four miles north of town where we had permission to hunt. Mom, Caryl, and I cut and wrapped the two deer, but it sure was strange not having Cal there to talk to and joke with.

The valley was soon blanketed with snow and bitter cold arrived. Caryl and I enjoyed our first Christmas as husband and wife, but in mid-January, Dad found our old cat, Tom, dead, curled up in the coal shed. Like Cal, that cat had been around since I was a very young boy, and I knew I'd miss him. I had discovered by now that there wasn't anything good about death: the whole thing was a sad event surrounded by sorrow.

CHAPTER ELEVEN

A Chance Encounter

THE WINTER MONTHS PASSED, and on April 16, 1972, I turned twenty-four. Caryl gave me the greatest birthday present when she said, "You're going to be a daddy!" Oh, God—I was thrilled! She said that the baby was due in November. We quickly drove to Mom and Dad's, and I'd never seen Caryl so happy as when she told them the news. She'd always loved kids, and now we were going to have our own.

The first of May, we were able to move into the downstairs apartment at the complex where we lived. Thank God, as it had more room and was much nicer, and Caryl wouldn't have to deal with any more steep stairs. With each passing month, her tummy grew, and so did the excitement. By the first of October, she had a new crib set up along with a cute dresser and everything else she'd need for the baby.

Dad, my uncle Jake, and I had gotten lucky and received permission from Bob and Marge Wilber to elk hunt on Oak Ridge, about twelve miles east of Meeker. I'd hunted the area with Donna's dad when we were married and knew that it was a good place for big game. On opening day, I got a nice three-point bull and Jake, a spike bull; later, all three of us scored with good-sized bucks. It'd been so nice to hunt behind a locked gate with just a handful of hunters who we knew and were friends with!

At around 9:00 p.m. on November 9, I was notified at work that I needed to get to town as soon as possible: Caryl's mom, Gladys, had taken her to the hospital to have the baby! I ran out of the mine, removed my belt and light, and jumped into my Road Runner. I peeled out of the mine's parking lot and drove the twenty-two miles to Meeker like a bat out of hell—sometimes going as fast as eighty or ninety! When I arrived at Pioneers Hospital, I met Gladys, and we both nervously waited for the next few hours. Finally, the doctor came to the lobby and said, "Congratulations! You have a very healthy little girl!" Oh, God, we were so happy! A few minutes later, a nurse told me I could go into the room, and what a sight it was! Caryl was holding our newborn, a very precious little girl. I asked her if she was alright, and she said, "Yes, I'm fine. Just really tired." She handed the baby to me. Oh, shit! I was so nervous when I cradled that little doll in my arms that I only held her for a minute, then I handed her to Gladys. We decided to call her "Kila," a name that I'd thought of a couple years ago.

I told Caryl that, even though it was two in the morning, I was going to call Mom and Dad to tell them the news. I knew I would wake them, but I had to share my excitement! After I talked to them, I went home for a while but was too wound up to sleep. At six, I drove to Mom and Dad's and, after visiting for a while, we came back to the hospital. They were thrilled when they got their first look at Kila, their first grandchild. It was such a special time!

A couple days later, I brought Caryl and Kila home and took tons of photos of Caryl holding our newborn. Over the next few weeks, it was just as I'd always imagined it would be. Caryl was a great mom and took extraordinary care of Kila. It seemed as though she was always giving her a bath and rubbing lotion on her. Mom came by almost every day, proud as a peacock! Needless to say, the holidays that year were a very special time for us: we were finally a family! Weeks turned into months, and as the long winter passed, it was just amazing how fast Kila grew, and she became cuter with each passing day. I nicknamed her "Dolly."

By the first of May, the mine cut back on coal production on the night shift, so I was put on the day shift. Some of us were given the job of building track. After placing timbers on the ground and leveling them, we'd put two sections of rail, properly spaced, on top of them. Then, with the use of a steel-headed sledgehammer, we'd swing away, driving the spikes into the timbers, which attached the rail securely to them. It took a few days for my co-worker, Eddy, and I to get our accuracy down in hitting the head of the spike with precision, but we finally got the hang of it and made great progress.

Chapter Eleven: *A Chance Encounter*

While waiting to get a haircut in the month of June from Hank, who had been a barber in Meeker for many years, a conversation started between him and one of his buddies. Hank, who was around sixty-five, said, "Bill, do you remember all those moonlight fishing trips we used to go on forty years ago?" Bill replied, "Ah, hell—yeah, we caught so many big trout, they just loved that sucker meat!" *Ding-dong!* Instantly I thought, "Son of a bitch! I'd like to try that recipe on a private stretch of the river that's way too risky to slip in on during daylight hours." I never said a word; I just listened to their fishing stories, but I couldn't wait to tell Larry and Donnie. Later that evening, when I told them about my idea, they were excited, too!

Just a few days before the full moon in July, Larry and I caught some suckers, which were considered a "trash" fish, filleted them, and cut them into strips about two inches long by a half inch wide. We placed the meat in pint jars and put them in the fridge. Donnie ended up having out-of-town guests, so he couldn't go, but he said, "Let me know how you do." Caryl informed me that I'd better not get caught. I smiled and asked, "Would you pay my fine?" She smiled coolly and said, "Don't push your luck!"

The stage was set. The following evening, Larry and I loaded our fishing gear, a long-handled net, sucker meat, and a cooler with Pepsi and beer, then headed out. We arrived at our destination just before dark. Moments later I said, "Look!" I pointed towards the mountain peak east of us, and there she was—the gorgeous, pale-orange moon, peering over its apex. Within a few minutes, the entire moon was in sight, Mother Nature's lantern illuminating the entire valley. What a beauty!

We gathered our gear and crossed the barbed-wire fence onto private property, and while walking through the tall grass, my heart pounded with excitement. Both thoughts—getting caught trespassing and catching a record-size trout—were truly adrenalin pumpers!

Hoooo-hoo-hoo-hoo! Hoooo-hoo-hoo-hoo! The sound of an owl broke the silence of the otherwise stone-quiet summer night. Soon, we arrived at the river and found a deep hole. We rigged up, attached a chunk of sucker meat to our hooks, and—standing a few feet from each other—cast the barber's recipe into the hole. In less than a minute, Larry yanked his rod and said, "Got 'im!" The drag on his reel started screaming. *Ka-sploosh! Ka-sploosh!* There was the trout, leaping out of and crashing back into the river. Hell! It sounded like a beaver slapping his tail! I quickly reeled in and grabbed the net. After Larry got the trout played down, he eased him close to shore and I netted him. He was a dandy—we estimated the big rainbow to be around twenty-four inches.

I cast back into the river and, while Larry was putting on some new sucker meat, I said, "Got 'im!" My drag started screaming and the fight was on! Minutes later, Larry netted my fish—the same size as the other one. Over the next couple hours, we fished two other holes and had a ball. After catching a total of nine, we decided to shut it down and not press our luck. I picked up the heavy gunnysack of fish, Larry grabbed our gear, and we headed to the vehicle. Minutes later, we were driving down the dirt road, joking and laughing. We had finished the risky excursion safely and had so much fun!

When we got home, we measured and weighed our catch. Three of the nine were twenty-four inches and weighed five and three-quarter pounds; the other six were between twenty-two and twenty-three inches, weighing five pounds apiece.

After cleaning the trout, we wrapped them individually in foil and placed them in the freezer, finishing up about 3:00 a.m. Later that day, we took the twenty-four inchers to Donnie's to show them to him. He was so excited! "We need to try the sucker meat at 'the pond' some moonlit night!" He was referring to the place where I'd caught a big rainbow when I was in high school. Larry and I thought it was a great idea, and maybe we could plan to do it in August, or even next summer. As things go, everyone got too busy, so the pond trip was postponed till next year.

At work, I had successfully bid on the tipple operator position. The job involved changing screen positions to fill huge bins with stoker, nut, and lump coal and assisting the loading of the semis with mine-run coal. I also operated a huge electric winch to pull the cars out of the mine on the rails; then, with a front-end loader, I filled the cars with roof bolts, timbers for roof support in the mine, bags of rock dust, and other supplies. The winch was then used to slowly lower the cars down the steep incline into the mine; later, the motorman would hook onto each car and pull it to where the coal was being mined. As a tipple operator, I would be working outside, which was much more agreeable to me.

Chapter Eleven: A Chance Encounter

Once again, it was a good hunting season, with two elk and two bucks in our freezers. Then in November, Caryl planned to go to Salt Lake City with her parents on the weekend prior to Thanksgiving. She'd made arrangements with Mom to babysit Kila and told me she was going to take her there on Friday night before leaving on Saturday. The week passed, and on Friday night, the trucks stopped hauling coal at around 9:00 p.m., so by eleven, the bins were full. Because we'd done exceptionally well during the week, our foreman said we could leave an hour early, so I jumped in the shower at the change house, put on some nice clothes, and headed for town. I decided to stop at the VFW and have a couple of beers before going home.

When I walked through the door of the VFW, the first thing I noticed was my first wife, Donna, seated at the far end of the bar. God, she was so pretty! A guy yelled my name and I turned to see Joe, a friend who I'd graduated with. I walked over, shook his hand, and ordered a bottle of Bud. Over the next few minutes, the bullshit was flying; it was sure good to see him again! When I turned around to order another beer, there was already one sitting at my spot. I asked the bartender who bought it, and she nodded at the far end of the bar towards Donna. I occasionally glanced her direction, and I noticed that guy after guy asked her to dance, but so far, she'd declined to get out on the floor with any of them.

My mind started whirling. Hell, I wasn't even paying attention to what Joe was saying! I asked myself, "You're not going to go talk to her, are you?" Within seconds, I picked up the new beer and started walking towards her, and the closer I got, the harder my heart pounded. I tried to appear calm and said, "Long-time no-see. Thanks for the beer." She said, "You're welcome. It's good to see you again, too." I was nearly hypnotized when I looked into her big brown eyes. After a short conversation, she asked, "Would you please take me home?" Oh, shit! My heart went right to my throat! I said, "Sure." She picked up her purse and we headed for the door. I couldn't help noticing several sets of eyes looking at us as we walked out. Even knowing how word traveled so fast in a small town, I found myself in a trance, willing to roll the dice and gamble my marriage.

Once we got to her house, we sat down at the kitchen table and talked nonstop for two hours. It was such a pleasant conversation, both of us laughing and remembering. Then I glanced at my watch and about shit when I saw that it was 3:00 a.m. I told her I had to leave, and as I placed my hand on the door knob, she put her hand on top of mine and softly said, "Do you *really* have to leave?" I turned around and we wrapped our arms around each other, then our lips met. Moments later, we headed for the bedroom.

Clothes came off quickly and we had very passionate sex; hell, it was just as though we'd never been apart! Afterward, we lay in bed, talking for a while. I was scared to look at my watch, but I finally did. Shit! It was now 5:30 a.m., and I knew I was in deep trouble. I tried to remain calm and told her that I *must* leave.

We were both feeling some sadness when we kissed goodbye. I guess it was because we'd experienced such a great night together, and we knew that it would probably never happen again. Reality quickly set in when I opened the door and headed for my car. It had been a cold night, probably around zero. The windshields were covered with heavy frost and I feverishly scraped them off. I decided to drive down to my uncle Jimmy's house to use his phone; I wanted to call Joe and ask him to be my alibi. If Caryl should call him, I wanted him to tell her that I went to his house after the bar closed and that we shot pool, drank, and bullshitted the night away.

Luckily, Jimmy and his wife were up and let me in. I called Joe, and after I hung up, Jimmy said, "Sounds like you're in a little deep." "Oh shit, Jimmy, I'm in *way* over my ass!" He and his wife started laughing. All of a sudden, I couldn't hear the car running anymore. When I opened the front door to look outside, I was shocked to see that it was *gone*! Uh-oh! I knew that Caryl must've had someone driving her around to look for me, and that she'd taken the car.

Jimmy smiled and said, "Now it looks like you need a ride home." A few minutes later, he dropped me off at the house and I walked in. The moment I dreaded was here, and I was greeted by the wrath of hell! Caryl ripped my ass up one side and down the other, and off the end of my tongue came lie after lie. I told her if she didn't believe me to call Joe. Finally, her parents pulled up and she grabbed her suitcase, storming out. Oh, shit! For the time being, I was saved. Later that morning, I drove down to Mom and Dad's to see them and Kila. When Dad left to go check the mail, I told Mom the entire story. "Oh my God, Son. Do you think Caryl believed you?" "Not really," I answered, "but hopefully she'll calm down by Monday and the storm will pass."

Chapter Eleven: A Chance Encounter

That whole day, I replayed what had happened between Donna and me. Damn it! I just *had* to see her one more time! Later that night, I drove to her house, and we talked for nearly two hours. She had been living with a guy, but they had broken up. She said, "Danny, if you weren't married, things would be different, but—you have a little girl now." We decided it would be best not to see each other again, and the tears streamed down our cheeks as we held each other one last time.

I was at work when Caryl got home on Monday, so I didn't see her until quite early Tuesday morning, after I got off work. When we did see each other, there was another heated discussion. We had Thanksgiving at Mom and Dad's on Thursday, and she was still angry with me. Over the next three weeks, our bedroom was like a walk-in cooler, but by the time Christmas showed up, a thaw had finally taken place in our house. Thank God things had gotten back to normal and we enjoyed the holidays together.

The last part of February 1974, the dayshift tipple operator, Jessie, asked me if I'd work his shift; he needed the day off. I told him I would, as it would give me eight hours of overtime pay. Around one in the afternoon on the day I was working for him, I was sixty feet off the ground up in the tipple when I noticed a white car pull in near the office. I saw three guys get out, open the trunk, and put on shiny white hard hats. Moments later, the three of them and the mine superintendent walked over to the porthole with their mining lamps on, and they disappeared into the mine.

I figured it was federal mine inspectors, since that wasn't out of the ordinary. Less than an hour later, they all came back out, and about an hour after that, the white car left. The mine superintendent walked out of the office and signaled for me to come down from the tipple. Once I got to him, he told me there was going to be a special meeting at 4:00 p.m. when all the night shift was present. "What's going on?" I asked. "The mine's been ordered to close," he said. "But why?" He said it was because of the smoldering fire in the old mine north of the one that we were working in. My heart just sank: what a devastating blow! Then anger set in. Hell, that fire had been smoldering for probably ten or fifteen years—maybe longer!

At the meeting, the night shift was told to clean out their lockers. The day shift was told that they could continue working over the summer, bringing out all the mining equipment. Son of a bitch! Just that quick, my high-paying job with good benefits was gone! I loaded all my things into the trunk and headed home, my mind whirling. "What the hell do I do now?" I kept thinking.

When I got home, Caryl came running out to see why I was home early. When I told her the news, she started crying, and I started crying, too. That night, I got no sleep, and the next morning, I drove to the mine, got my lay-off papers, then drove to the Colorado State Unemployment office and applied for benefits. During the next couple of months, I put in several job applications but didn't have any luck. The first of June, I went to work on an oil drilling rig. I didn't like roughnecking—in fact, I hated it—but the pay was good. The first of July, Dad stopped by and told me that he'd heard that Texaco might be hiring a couple of guys. The large energy company had several oil fields north of Meeker. The next day I drove to Craig, where Texaco had its area office, and got a job application; I turned it in two days later, along with my resume. I was praying for a job with them.

In mid-July, Caryl told me she was pregnant again and that the baby was due in February. We were both happy, but now I truly needed a permanent, good-paying job. Just weeks later, on the first of August, the manager from Texaco's Craig office called and told me he wanted to interview me. I was thrilled! At least now I had a chance. The following day I drove to Craig and had a lengthy interview with him. He said that he'd let me know in a few days if I'd been picked. A week later, he called and told me he'd like to see me again, so I made the drive to Craig one more time. During those fifty miles, I continually prayed. Once in the manager's office, he extended his hand and said, "Congratulations! You've been picked for the job," and he gave me directions to the clerk's office, where I needed to get the paperwork to schedule a physical.

When I told Caryl the news, she cried—and so did I! I passed the physical with flying colors, and when I returned the paperwork, the manager told me to report to the Hamilton area crew base, located twenty-five miles north of Meeker, on September 3. I only worked a couple more days on the drilling rig; I was so happy to tell them that I was done!

The manager had told me to call Don Brumback in Meeker, as he and two other guys took turns driving each day to the crew base. Mom knew

Don very well; he'd lived in Meeker all his life and was just a year younger than Dad. She said that when Don was a young man, he'd tried out for Mr. America. He had served four years in the navy during World War II and had been undefeated in the boxing program. She told me that I'd never find a nicer guy to work with, and I felt that was a good sign. He was the head roustabout and would be my immediate supervisor.

Early Tuesday morning, September 3, 1974, Don pulled up at our house and picked me up. He introduced himself and then introduced Al, who held a "pumper" position, and Larry, who was "relief pumper." Once we got to the crew base, I was introduced to Owen, the foreman, and Jack, a pumper who lived in Craig.

A few minutes later, Don and I got into our work vehicle—a one-ton Ford truck equipped with a winch, gin poles, and two large metal tool boxes. After fueling the truck, we drove about fifteen miles west to one of the oil fields that was located at a placed called "Maudlin Gulch." Don showed me a "battery," which was made up of several large metal tanks. Most of the tanks received oil, and others held salt water. There were several horizontal and vertical vessels that were called "treaters," which separated the oil from the water of the sixteen producing wells. He also showed me around inside various metal buildings that housed shipping pumps, recycle pumps, salt water disposal pumps, and a large manifold. He explained that my job was the same as his—a roustabout—and that our duties included changing packing and oil in pumps, changing out leaking pipe fittings, valves, gauges, and meters, keeping all battery and well locations clean, and hauling replacement sucker rods and tubing to well locations when needed.

My first day at work passed quickly, and at 3:30 p.m., we headed for the crew base. I was convinced that I was really going to like my new job, and I already knew that I was working for a nice guy. Don was so knowledgeable, as he'd worked for Texaco for twenty-five years, and he explained everything really well.

When I got home, Caryl asked how my day had gone, and I told her it was great! While sitting at the supper table, I mentioned buying a new pickup. She was all for it, because we'd need two vehicles now. We made plans to look for one the next Saturday. The rest of my workweek went very well, with Don showing me the other oil fields that we were in charge of and the large tanks where the oil was collected from the different oil fields.

On Saturday, Caryl and I shopped for the pickup, and we made a deal on a new 1975 three-quarter-ton Ford 4x4. We were both so happy! Ah, yes—life was sweet! A caring wife, a beautiful little daughter, a great job, a brand-new pickup...and in a few months, we'd be having another baby! Over the next few weeks, I settled in at my job, so thankful that I'd gotten it.

CHAPTER TWELVE
The Temptress

IT WAS FALL 1974, AND DAD, JAKE, AND I had another great hunting season, shooting a cow elk, two bulls, and some nice-sized bucks. Then snow and bitter cold arrived in the valley as winter set in. Kila was now two years old and Caryl was in her eighth month of pregnancy, delivering our second child, Amber, on February 2. We just barely made that one in time! After I got Caryl to the hospital, I sat down for just ten minutes when the doctor walked out and said, "Congratulations. You have a healthy little girl!"

Spring 1975 came and went. I celebrated another birthday as we gradually got used to Amber being the newest member of our family. Mid-June arrived, and Dad and I had a great fishing adventure at Swede Lake. He had permission from Vic Mobley, the manager of the Y-Z property on the South Fork of the White River, to drive through it to the national forest boundary, where the lake was located.

It had been a few years since we'd been to Swede, and as we admired the beauty of the South Fork Rim, Dad said, "Probably all we'll get is a wet ass and a hungry gut." I started laughing hard. He often spoke that phrase, but it never ceased being funny. We arrived at Bailey Lake, where I loaded my backpack, then we headed up the timber-covered hill.

When we got to Swede Lake, I put our beer in a canvas bag in the water so it would stay cold. It was about ten o'clock, and with the temperature around sixty-five, it was a picture-perfect day! I decided to walk down the west side of the lake to where many trees had fallen into the water, while Dad stayed on the south end.

Once I got to my spot, I walked out on one of the fallen logs about forty feet to cast my spinner. *Splat!* It landed on the green algae on the water's surface, and I let it sink a few inches before reeling it in. *Thump!* A wicked strike! As I set the hook, all hell broke loose! It was a challenge to fight the fish, try to keep him from getting tangled up on the log's branches, and keep my balance...all at the same time. I finally got the fish landed—a beautiful fourteen incher. I held him up and hollered at Dad, and he waved back.

After catching a few more fish, I decided to walk out on a log that was much narrower than the others. By the time I got to where I wanted to be, I was standing on about eight inches of dry log. I made a short cast, and my spinner landed in a spot that I'd always wanted to try. Maybe there was a big brook trout hanging out in its old tree limbs.

Thump! There he was, and I yanked! Oh, shit! I lost my balance and almost fell backwards, then I leaned forward and almost fell in face-first, then back again. Shi-i-i-it! *Ka-sploosh!* I landed in the lake, back first! I scrambled to get to the surface and, still holding my rod, grabbed the log. I could feel the fish tugging on my line, so I reached over and hit the release button. Holding on to the log and treading water, I gradually worked my way towards shore. *Sereeee!* Dad let out one of his shrill whistles. I looked over at him and he yelled, "Damn, that was a real circus! I wished I would have had a movie camera!" Embarrassed, I stood up and waved at him. Shit! I wondered if the fish was still on my line. I cranked up the slack and—sure enough—he was. Moments later, I landed him, a nice fifteen-inch trout. Was he worth it? Not even!

Slosh, slosh, slosh! I walked towards Dad, and every step I took, water squished out of my tennis shoes. Once I got to him, he started laughing—I mean, guffawing! "Oh, Son—was that ever a show!" I laughed, too, and sat down to take off my shoes and socks. Dad said, "Remember what I told you?" "What?" I asked. "About the wet ass and hungry gut?" We both busted out laughing and spent the next couple of hours visiting. When my shoes and socks were fairly dry, I put them back on and we headed out. It was another beautiful summer day with Dad that had given me a lifetime memory.

Time flew and by mid-November, Dad and I had filled both freezers with deer and elk. It was so hard to believe that we'd now been hunting together for twenty years! Kila, nearly three, adored her grandma and had taken to calling Dad "Papa." The holidays came and went, and on February 2, 1976, we had a birthday party for Amber, now one year old. Later on, in May, Caryl and I began going to the Sleepy Cat Guest Ranch, eighteen miles east of Meeker. Their restaurant served some of the best rib-eye steak found on the Western Slope and their seafood was delicious. The good food, along with a bar and dance floor, kept the place packed on weekends. We went there every Saturday night while Mom kept Kila and Amber.

The summer months were a carbon copy of the previous year. Dad and I went on several fishing trips and Donnie, Larry, and I gave it hell around the nights of the full moon in June, July, and August, catching gunnysacks full of trout. At the end of August, Caryl and I became friends with a married couple named Daryl and Dee Dee, who were involved in the same church as Caryl. Daryl was twenty-five and Dee Dee, a petite woman with a bubbly personality who was well-built, was twenty-three. From the very beginning of our friendship, all of us really hit it off. We started playing cards together and going out to dinner, and we even went to Sawmill Mountain in the fall to hear the elk bugle—a brand-new experience for Daryl and Dee Dee. I was somewhat the renegade among the four of us, drinking beer, smoking cigarettes, and occasionally throwing in a few cuss words, while they drank sodas and didn't smoke. But I also seemed to be the life of the party, as I frequently caused the three of them to bust up laughing.

In mid-October, Caryl told me she was pregnant again. We were happy about it—we had planned the pregnancy—and were hoping for a son this time. Because the house we were living in was quite small, we decided to rent a bigger one, so we moved to a place on Water Street. Although the move took place right in the middle of hunting season, Dad and I still managed to get our elk and deer.

During the winter months, Daryl and Dee Dee came to our new home many nights to play cards, usually on weekends. On Thursday nights, I usually played poker either in the basement of the Commercial Club, located next to the bank, or at one of the player's homes. Because we only allowed seven players, it was on a first-come basis, and there were many guys who enjoyed playing: Donnie; Jake; Larry; Bryce, who owned the wild game processing plant; Harry, owner of the grocery store; Dick, Harry's brother; Gerald, the postmaster; Clarence, a retired rancher; Gerhard, another rancher; and Chris Halandras, who was one of the best-known sheepmen in the White River Valley. Chris was a well-built, handsome

Greek about thirty-four years old. He was usually one of the last players to show up, and when entering the room, he would yell, "'Deal!' cried the losers!" and everyone would laugh.

Winter passed and by April 1977, the weather was warming up. One evening, Caryl suggested we go for a drive, so I loaded the girls into the pickup and helped Caryl get in, as she was now nearly eight months pregnant. Kila was four and a half and Amber was two. We decided to drive up Coal Creek, just east of Meeker. The girls sat in the middle, jabbering away, while Caryl and I watched for deer. We drove about fifteen miles then turned around to start home, as it was nearing sundown.

Amber told me she had to go to the bathroom, and Kila said, "Me, too!" I asked if they could wait, and they told me no. So I pulled to the side of the gravel road and helped them out. I gave them some toilet paper and asked Kila to help her sister. I pointed them toward the passenger side and said, "Hurry up!" They both started giggling and went to where I'd told them to go.

All of a sudden, Caryl rolled down her window and yelled, *"What are you girls doing? Danny, get over there now!"* I ran around the pickup to see what was going on. Both girls were standing there with their pants and panties down. Kila said, "Amber wanted us to try peeing like you do, standing up." Damn! I could see their panties were soaked. "I should give you girls a spanking!" I said. I reached into the toolbox and grabbed some paper towels to absorb some of the pee.

While bending over to wipe Amber's panties, Kila said, "Here comes a car, Dad." Oh, shit! That's all I needed! I started scrambling around like a wild man, trying to get them cleaned up and get their pants pulled up. Caryl just busted out laughing. I yelled, "It's *not funny!*" Then the girls started laughing. I got their pants pulled up just as the car got to us. I loaded them in the truck and went on to town. What a nice little drive it had turned out to be!

My birthday arrived once again, and this time, Caryl and the girls had gotten me a Chinon 35mm camera along with a set of lenses—standard, wide angle, and telephoto. God, I'd wanted a nice camera since high school, and I was so happy to get this one. I'd taken many pictures over the years, mostly of our fishing and hunting adventures and of family. Friends and relatives had always complimented me on the quality of my photography, and now—thanks to Caryl—I could practice this passion of mine.

Chapter Twelve: *The Temptress*

The morning of May 18, Caryl was starting to have labor pains. I quickly called my boss, Don, to tell him he shouldn't pick me up for work. Then I called Mom and asked if she'd please pick up the girls. She showed up just minutes later and loaded the kids and their suitcases into her car.

By noon, Caryl's pains were coming close together, so I called the hospital and told them we were on our way, then called Caryl's mom so she could meet us there. Five minutes later, we arrived at the hospital, and nearly two hours passed before the doctor walked into the lobby to congratulate me. We had a baby boy! I grabbed Gladys, gave her a bear hug, and yelled, "Yahoo!" I ran to the pay phone and called Mom. This was an especially happy time for her because our son—Christopher—had been born on her birthday!

A few days later, we drove to the hospital to bring Caryl and Christopher home. The entire day, Kila and Amber never let that baby out of their sight! They helped their mom any way they could, including putting messy diapers in the trash, and over the next few weeks, our home gradually returned to normal.

In mid-June, fishing season kicked off, with Dad and I going to Swede and Trappers Lakes and Larry, Donnie, and I making our usual moonlight runs in July and August. The first of September, Dad traded in his Bronco and bought a brand-new half-ton 4x4 Ford pickup. What a beauty! The trucking company he worked for had been sold to a larger company, and he was now bringing home much bigger paychecks. Later that month, Mom babysat the kids while Caryl, Daryl, Dee Dee, and I drove to Bailey Lake to enjoy the fall colors and look for elk. We had so much fun, enjoying a picnic lunch while listening to the many bugling elk.

At work, everything was going great: I really liked my job, Don was the best guy I'd ever worked for, and there was a new-hire, Lou Stevens, who I became friends with. Another plus was getting to see an abundance of wildlife in Maudlin Gulch; it was loaded with elk, and its steep canyon walls echoed with the sounds of bulls bugling during rut.

In October, hunting season opened, and it was another successful year for Dad and me. The good news and happiness continued when my sister and her husband, Dan, had their first baby on November 21—a boy they named Jason.

By December first, the little town of Meeker was buzzing with excitement over the Meeker Cowboys wrestling team. Coach Bill Turner had done an outstanding job, and many of the sports writers had Meeker ranked as one of the top AA teams in the state. Caryl, Daryl, Dee Dee, and I decided to go to the Friday night contests and quickly got hooked, attending every match. In mid-December, Meeker was scheduled to wrestle the Steamboat Sailors at Steamboat Springs, ninety miles away. The Sailors had always been the powerhouse in the Northwestern League, so the four of us decided to make reservations at the Ramada Inn in Steamboat to attend the match and spend the night. Mom, bless her heart, agreed to babysit the kids.

There were a lot of great matches that night, and the Meeker Cowboys ended up posting the best team score. After the last match, we drove to the motel and decided to go to the bar. There was a live band that night, and we wanted to dance, so we sat visiting while the band took a break. Once they returned, they started playing a slow song. Dee Dee extended her hand towards me and said, "Come on—let's dance." We walked to the dance floor and I held her close—but not *too* close. In a low, sexy voice, she said, "I had a dream about you." "Oh?" I said, "What was it about?" She said, "I was wearing a short silky dress while dancing a slow dance with you, and I wasn't wearing any panties."

Whoa! My knees nearly buckled and my feet almost stopped moving! I softly asked, "Then what happened?" She whispered, "You put your hand up under my dress and started playing with me." Oh...son of a bitch! I couldn't believe what she had just said!

The song ended and we walked back to the booth to sit down, thank God. My heart was about to blow out of my chest and my legs felt like rubber. I had to reach way, way back into my mind to pull myself back to reality. I couldn't—as in *could not*—believe what had just happened! Dee Dee laughed and joked with Daryl and Caryl as if everything was perfectly normal. "Come on, honey. I feel like dancing," she said to Daryl. A few minutes later, Caryl and I hit the dance floor, too.

Over the next few hours, I knocked down about six beers and took some long drags off my cigarettes. I was still in shock! Finally, at 1:00 a.m., we called it a night and went to our rooms. Caryl went right to sleep, but lying on my back, eyes wide open, I stared at the ceiling, replaying Dee Dee's words over and over. I didn't close my eyes all night.

The next morning, we met Daryl and Dee Dee at the restaurant and had breakfast. Oh, shit, did my coffee ever taste good! Afterwards, Caryl said she was going to go pay for the room, then Daryl said, "Yeah, I'll go with you and pay for ours." After they left, Dee Dee looked at me and said, "So, how'd you sleep?" I smiled and said, "I *didn't*." She let out a short, teasing-type laugh and started staring at me with her dark-brown eyes, causing a rise in my Levis. No more words were spoken. It was as though the two of us were in a trance...we just kept staring at each other. I glanced down at her sweater, which her big tits certainly filled out. I thought, "You good-looking thing! If you're looking for some wild sex, deal me in!"

I soon spotted Daryl and Caryl coming back, so we got up from the table, got our suitcases, and walked out to the car for the drive back to Meeker. Dee Dee and I acted normally, but I knew it was just a matter of time before we'd head down Cheater's Avenue!

Soon, Christmastime rolled around. I drove to Piceance Creek and cut a beautiful tree, and Kila and Amber helped their mom decorate it. It was so pretty! Christmas morning was special, watching the girls open their presents. A week later, Dee Dee and I had a couple minutes alone—long enough to taste each other's lips and create a deep desire to have sex. We had started calling each other and had had several steamy phone conversations. Whenever we attended wrestling matches, or if the four of us were playing cards, Dee Dee and I would give each other an "I want you" look when Daryl and Caryl weren't paying attention.

In late January, I made reservations for the four of us at the Regency Hotel in Denver so we could attend the state AA wrestling tournament taking place in February. As always, Mom agreed to babysit and, needless to say, we all had a great time. In March, Dee Dee and I had agreed to meet one night on a county road. We had an hour, and during that sixty minutes, the windows on my pickup were really steamed over. Still, we didn't have sex. I was terribly frustrated and said, "It doesn't make any sense to take these chances and not go all the way." She laughed and said, "Maybe next time."

Over the next two weeks, I gave some serious thought to just walking away from Dee Dee and this game playing. I would say to myself, "Hell, you have three beautiful children and a nice wife. Do you want to lose them?" But those thoughts evaporated the next time the four of us sat down at the table to play cards. Dee Dee was seated straight across from me, and soon I would feel her foot running up and down my leg. Son of a bitch!

Between her beauty, build, bedroom eyes, and teasing ways, my willpower didn't stand a chance.

On May 18, 1978, the family celebrated Christopher's and Mom's birthdays by having a dinner at Mom and Dad's. By now, Chris—a cute little boy with a few freckles across the bridge of his nose—was walking and getting into everything. Caryl and the girls took such good care of him—and, yes, he was getting spoiled! We all had a great time, and Chris blew out the one candle on his birthday cake.

Soon, June rolled around, and it was nice to feel the warmth of summer. Don took a couple weeks of vacation, so I was assigned the head roustabout position in his absence. While driving into Maudlin Gulch, I came across the landowner—Dean Gent—who was repairing his fences. I thought, "What the hell—I'm going to stop and ask him if he would allow Dad and me to go hunting in the gulch on a yearly basis." To my surprise, he told me we could, with one stipulation: that we had to hunt in the late season, as he had paying hunters the first two seasons. I shook his hand and thanked him. Oh, shit! I couldn't wait to tell Dad! I knew that even if we hunted the late season, we were almost guaranteed to get our elk every year, and they'd probably be big bulls.

Now that summer was here, I wasn't seeing much of Dee Dee, because we only played cards during the winter, and wrestling wouldn't start up till December. Still, we snuck around and made phone calls to each other, and she damn sure knew how to get me aroused. Some of the things she said almost made *me* blush!

Over the summer, Dad and I went on several fishing trips, and, of course, Donnie, Larry, and I still had a lot of fun moonlight fishing. In September, I thanked Bob and Marge Wilber for allowing us to hunt on Oak Ridge the past several years; a few weeks later, Caryl and I drove to Maudlin Gulch one evening to look and listen to the elk, and we saw nearly 200! There were several bulls, including some five points and a couple of six points.

During the second hunting season in October, Don and I stopped by at the Indiana hunters' camp in Maudlin Gulch to see how they'd been doing. Shit! There were eight hunters and they had seven nice four- and five-point bulls hanging in the trees.

Opening day of the late season—November 4—finally arrived, and Dad and I were so excited that we'd set our alarm clocks for 3:00 a.m. By

4:30, we were in Dad's pickup, headed down the Craig highway towards Maudlin Gulch. I knew exactly where we should go—a place called "Deer Canyon." There was a four-wheel-drive road that went up the bottom of it for about three miles, and I was confident we would find elk there.

Boom! Just as the sun was coming up, Dad fired a round and got a four-point bull. Talk about a happy guy! A couple days later, I shot a big four-point buck and, on Saturday, November 11, I shot a five-point bull. What a great place to hunt!

On Monday, it was back to work. If it was my turn to drive, I left the house at 6:45 a.m.; otherwise, one of my coworkers would pick me up at seven. Morning after morning, I'd just get to my car or their vehicle when I'd hear Caryl yell, "Your daughter wants a kiss goodbye!" Yes, my little Dolly, Kila, who'd just turned six, would be standing at the front door in her pajamas, just out of bed, wanting a kiss before I left. Sweet! Amber and Chris were totally different—they loved sleeping in.

It was now time for our Thursday night poker games to start again. By now, they'd escalated to $100 buy-ins. Oh, yeah—sitting down at a table with six other players, a cold beer by my hand, listening to chips rattling and cards being shuffled, bullshitting, squeezing back cards as I hoped to catch the winning hand. I just loved it! We usually played from seven till midnight. When I came home a winner of two or three hundred dollars, Caryl would be happy. If I dropped a couple hundred bucks, she'd be pissed off. Usually, I managed to win or at least break even.

The first of December, wrestling season kicked off, and the four of us started going to the matches again. I still hadn't had sex with Dee Dee and was beginning to wonder if it would ever happen.

As all of these things called "life" were going on, I virtually treasured the sincere, unconditional love and care that my dear mom was giving to Kila, Amber, and Chris. While babysitting, Mom would run the tub brimful of bubble bath for the girls, and they just loved getting in together. Later, she'd put makeup and lipstick on them, and they'd clog around the house in some of her high heels. She watched over Chris like a hawk, making sure he didn't get into something he shouldn't, and spent hours reading kids' books to them. Her cupboards were always filled with every single kind of breakfast cereal they wanted, and she cooked whatever they desired.

Yes, Mom had her demons—especially her plastic glass full of beer—but the love she gave to our kids set my heart aglow! Dad loved them to pieces, too, and they loved their papa. It was tear-jerkin' special to see all of this in action!

Christmas rolled around again, and Mom and Dad drove to Denver to spend time with my sister's family. Their son, Jason, was now one year old. Soon, 1979 arrived, and in mid-January, there was a nice older log home that came up for sale, located right across the alley from Mom and Dad. Caryl and I met with the owners, who were still living there, and they showed us around. The ground level was nice with a large kitchen, bedroom, a bath, and living room, which had a standing fireplace. The basement was another story. It only had one bedroom, an unfinished utility room, an unfinished bathroom with a toilet that should've been replaced many years ago, and an old gas furnace that had large ductwork hanging from the ceiling. It truly needed a lot of work. There was an unattached garage and a nice big yard with chain link fencing. We decided to buy it anyway and use my VA benefits to mortgage the loan, and by mid-March, it was approved and we moved into the first home we could truly call "ours"—or at least it would be in thirty years! Kila, who had turned six the previous November, and Amber, who was four, were so excited, because now their grandma and papa were just across the alley. And Mom and Dad were thrilled!

Jake stopped by to see the house, and I asked him to take a good look at the basement and tell me what he'd recommend. He was a good carpenter and extremely knowledgeable in the plumbing and electrical fields. After about an hour, he said that if it was his place, he'd strip the entire basement, build two standard-sized bedrooms, a master bedroom, utility room, and a new bathroom. He'd also put in new windows, remove the old gas furnace and duct work, install a new boiler, and put in hot water baseboard heating throughout the entire house. He said, "You'll also have to install a new breaker box and run all new wiring in the basement." Oh, my God! It sounded so daunting!

He told Caryl and me that he'd help us, and we were so thrilled to hear those words. But because he had his own business and I worked five days a week, we were limited to working on our new home on weekends and evenings. So on Saturday, March 31, Jake backed his pickup into the driveway and we unloaded all his tools and started the massive project.

Meanwhile, Dad bought a used camp trailer that looked brand new, both inside and out. He and Mom were so proud of it! Kila and Amber helped Grandma clean and stock it for a camping trip and Mom hung all-new curtains, making it into a little dollhouse. Then Mom and Dad took the girls camping at the North Fork campground near the White River, twenty-six miles east of Meeker. Dad and his friend, Ollie Williams, fished at Lake Avery, just six miles from the campground, and Mom and the girls stayed at the trailer. When Kila and Amber returned a week later, they said that Grandma had fixed them pancakes for breakfast and barbequed hot dogs and hamburgers on the grill; after dark, they'd roast marshmallows on an open fire.

Working on the house chewed up the summer months: we worked every weekend and from 5:30 p.m. till ten during the week. There were no fishing trips with Dad, no moonlighting with Donnie and Larry, and just a few sneaky phone calls to Dee Dee. It was just basement, basement, basement!

By the tenth of August, a friend named Rick Bishop had finished hanging all the sheetrock in the basement, and we were finally getting down to the final stages of the remodeling project. We'd be installing wood paneling in the bedrooms and hallways, painting the bathroom, and putting in light fixtures and outlet covers. Oh, shit! It seemed there was finally some light at the end of the long tunnel!

Caryl informed me that she was going to go to Salt Lake on Friday, August 17, for a church meeting and return on Sunday. She'd made arrangements with Mom to babysit, because I'd be working, covering a pumper's vacation. I didn't think much about it till Daryl and Dee Dee stopped by to see how the project was going. Dee Dee happened to mention to Caryl that, due to his new job, Daryl would be out of town on Friday night. Dee Dee and I had continued our phone calls and had another rendezvous, but—as usual—nothing happened. She had decided she wanted a romantic-type setting to have sex—not do it in a vehicle! So I thought maybe—just *maybe*—it would finally happen!

A couple days later, Jake told me he wouldn't be coming down Friday evening, as he had other plans. The stage was set with everything falling into place. When I got home from work Friday evening, I jumped in the shower. Afterwards, I gave Dee Dee a call and told her I'd be at her house around ten o'clock. She said, "I'll be waiting." Oh, shit! My heart started racing! The thought of going to bed with her after all this time was driving me crazy!

I got to her place around ten and parked my car a long distance away. A few minutes later, I tapped on her door. When she opened it, she was all decked out and I could smell her sweet perfume. There was very little talking, just a lot of passionate kissing. Within a few minutes, we headed for the bedroom. Clothes soon came off and wild sex began! We stayed in bed till 4:00 a.m.; it just didn't seem like we could get enough of each other. Finally, I got up and dressed, kissed her goodbye, and headed for my car.

While walking those few blocks, a horrible thought came to mind: "This night is going to come back to haunt you!" Oh, God! I could only hope and pray that Donnie's theory of first intuition being right 99 percent of the time would be wrong *this* time.

That day at work was a long one: I was tired and worried. God knows how much I enjoyed gambling—sitting down at a poker table, crawling over barbed-wire fence, sneaking into the most private property in the valley to go fishing, poaching deer and elk—because all of it created an adrenalin rush! But the high-stakes cheating game with Dee Dee was going to have to stop. There was just too much to lose! I wasn't sure how I was going to break the news to her, but I'd made up my mind I was walking away.

On Sunday evening, Caryl returned, and on Monday evening, we started work again in the basement. By August 31 it was nearly done, and the next day, my sister, her husband, Dan, and little Jason drove over from Denver with the pickup full of rolls of carpet and carpet pad. Dan worked as a carpet installer, and by late Sunday evening, he'd finished laying the carpet in all three bedrooms, the hallway, and on the stairs. He'd done a fine job, and on Monday, they returned to Denver.

A few days later, we hung the doors on all the bedrooms. Finally—*finally*—the project was completed! Caryl and I commended and thanked Jake for his expertise and hard work. He'd turned a rather dingy-looking basement into a showcase, and our family would have quiet, efficient heat for the coming winter. Kila and Amber were jumping with joy, because they now had their own bedrooms. Chris wasn't sure what to think, as he'd no longer be sleeping in the same room with his sisters.

Days later, Dee Dee and Daryl showed up to look at the basement. The air was filled with awkwardness between Dee Dee and me, and I couldn't help noticing that she was rather reluctant to make eye contact when I was talking to her. There was no doubt we were both feeling remorseful. They told us the basement was beautiful and, after a short visit, said goodbye.

CHAPTER THIRTEEN

The Chickens Come Home to Roost

IT WAS FALL AND THE VALLEY WAS ABLAZE WITH COLOR, so Caryl and I made several trips to Maudlin Gulch to watch and listen to the elk. One evening, we took the kids and saw a trophy six-point bull standing in the middle of the road, not more than thirty yards away! Instead of taking off, the big bull laid his rack over his shoulders, stretched out his neck, and let a big bugle rip, not paying any attention to the pickup. The kids were so excited that their eyes got as big as silver dollars!

The weeks passed, and so did hunting season. Once again, Dad and I were successful, getting two nice bulls and two bucks, both families' freezers full for the winter. Wrestling season soon kicked off, as did the seasonal poker games. Daryl, Caryl, Dee Dee, and I continued to go to the matches together, but things were different: there just seemed to be something missing.

On Saturday morning, December 15, our home was buzzing with excitement. Caryl was busy packing a lunch and filling thermos bottles with hot chocolate. We were going to take the kids to Piceance Creek to cut our Christmas tree. All were dressed for the cold, and the cab was filled with lots of giggling from the girls during the forty-mile trip. They were so excited! In about an hour, we pulled out on top of a timber-covered ridge that was thick with piñon trees. It was a beautiful winter wonderland with six inches of snow on the ground. I helped the girls out, pulled the hoods up on their snowsuits, and tied the drawstrings. After they put their gloves on, I grabbed my bucksaw and gloves and we headed out in search of the perfect tree. Caryl and Chris stayed in the pickup, watching. *Brrrrrr!* It was only about 20°, and there was a slight breeze. "Dad, I want a big bushy tree," Amber said. "Yeah, one that goes clear to the ceiling," said Kila. "Okay, girls," I relented. "We'll find one."

We trudged through the snow looking at tree after tree. By now, the girls' cheeks had turned rosy red from the cold. Finally, we found one they were both satisfied with. I knelt in the snow and started sawing it down. Just as I made the last cut, I yelled, "Timber!" The girls busted out laughing! I told them to grab one side of the tree and I'd grab the other side, and we'd drag it to the pickup. After we got there, I helped them in so they could warm up, then I loaded the tree and stowed the saw. When I got in, everyone was having hot chocolate, so I poured myself some coffee and relaxed. Moments like this were so rare and special! I loved life with my family, and I knew I didn't want to lose them.

By ten o'clock that night, the perfect Christmas tree was standing tall in our living room, beautifully decorated by Caryl and the girls. Its top decoration was one inch from the eight-foot ceiling. After plugging in the lights, the girls ran around and turned out the house lights. The entire family stood for a couple minutes, admiring what we all believed was our perfect tree! By Christmas Eve, the once-empty space beneath it was stacked with presents. We had a family favorite for supper—deep-fried jumbo shrimp—and later, I built a fire in the fireplace, plugged in the lights on the tree, and turned out the lights in the living room. Soon, flames were dancing and the pine was snapping and popping. With all the multi-colored lights on the tree, the living room was aglow with the Christmas spirit.

We finally got the kids into bed at eleven, then the night belonged to Caryl and me. We sat on the couch talking, listening to the stereo, and staring at the flames in the fireplace. It was such a great atmosphere, and the beer I was drinking tasted extra good. We had a very romantic night and didn't get to sleep until 2:00 a.m.

"Dad, Mom—get up! Let's go open presents!" the kids yelled as they jumped on our bed. I looked at my watch in disbelief: it was 5:30! Quickly, Caryl and I got out of bed. We knew how excited they were. And soon—very soon—wrapping paper was flying! It was so much fun watching the three of them open presents. Kila had just turned seven, Amber was five,

Chapter Thirteen: THE CHICKENS COME HOME TO ROOST

and Chris was two and a half. My, if a person could only freeze time... They were all extremely happy, as Santa had been very generous!

The new year of 1980 saw a few changes take place. Caryl decided to become a licensed babysitter. She was well-liked and highly respected in the little town of Meeker, and she was soon having to turn needy parents away because she had all the kids she could handle. She was making darn good money, thank God, because the remodeling job had dealt a severe blow to our finances. Some days she'd have as many as eight or ten kids, many of them very young. Personally, I didn't see how she was able to do it, but she had unlimited patience.

Poker chips rattled every Thursday night, and Daryl, Dee Dee, Caryl, and I attended most all the wrestling matches. The cheating between Dee Dee and me had completely stopped. Although it was extremely awkward, we tried to act as though nothing had happened. In February, the four of us attended the state wrestling tournament once again.

In mid-March, I pulled up in front of the house a little past five o'clock. I'd delivered my coworkers to their homes, as it'd been my turn to drive. I opened the trunk, got my lunch pail, and walked through the front door.

The house was quiet. I walked to the top of the landing and yelled downstairs, "Anybody home?" There was no answer, so I figured Caryl and the kids had walked over to Mom and Dad's. I opened the fridge, pulled out a can of Bud and popped the tab, then walked to the storm door. I stared at the mountains north of town. It was a beautiful sight, and I often looked at it.

Schook! Snap! Damn! That sounded like the slide action on a semi-automatic pistol when a person is putting a shell into the chamber. I turned around. Sure enough, here came Caryl towards me with my .22 caliber semi-automatic pistol in her right hand. Tears were streaming down her cheeks, her eyes badly swollen. She stopped six feet from me, aimed the gun at my chest, and screamed, "You dirty rotten son of a bitch!" I yelled back, "What the hell is wrong with you?! Put the gun down!" "I know *everything*, you bastard! Daryl just left the house. Dee Dee confessed to the bishop and to Daryl about you and her going to bed in August while I was in Salt Lake. He also said he'd seen you walk out of the VFW with Donna back in 1973—the night you claimed you were with Joe. You lying, cheating, no-good son of a bitch!" She was trembling, the pistol shaking, and I could clearly see her finger on the trigger. Oh, shit! *Ka-thump, ka-thump, ka-thump!* I could hear my heart pounding in my ears! I knew the gun was going to go off—if for no other reason because of her shaking. Any second now, I was going to hear the pistol firing; hell, I could even feel the bullet hitting my chest!

"Caryl! Put the damn gun down before it goes off!" "I don't care if it does, you cheating bastard!" "Please, put the gun down!" Sobbing uncontrollably, she said, "Get your stuff and *get out!*" She released her grip on the pistol and it fell to the carpet, then she turned around and headed downstairs. I bent over and picked it up. The red dot on the left side was showing, meaning it was off safety. I pushed the clip release button and it dropped into my left hand. I always kept nine bullets in it and none in the chamber. I pulled the slide back: a long rifle hollow point shell kicked out and landed on the carpet. Yes, with just a very tiny flick of a finger, it would've gone off. I'd taught Caryl many years ago, when I worked nights at the mine, how to operate and shoot the pistol, and she damn sure hadn't forgotten it.

I took the pistol out to my pickup and buried it in the toolbox. Now what? I was feeling horrible for what I'd done to Caryl. She'd idolized me since 1970, when she was only seventeen. I'd failed my precious kids, too. Oh, God—please, please help me!

As I leaned across the bed of the pickup, Caryl walked out towards the car, looked over, and said, "I'm going to Mom's to get the kids. I'll be back in two hours. You'd better be gone when I get back." I walked into the house, grabbed another beer, lit a cigarette, and sat down at the table. My mind was spinning out of control. I called work to say I needed to take the next day off, then I called Don and told him not to pick me up.

Yeah—my selfish, cheating ways had caught up with me, and it looked like I was going to pay a heavy, heavy price. Even though I'd cheated, I still loved Caryl, and of course I loved my three kids as much as any dad would. They meant everything to me.

Over the next two hours, I rushed around, packing my stuff and having one hell of a time. Finally, I had most of my necessities loaded, so I started up the truck and backed out of the driveway. I decided I was going to go apologize to Daryl. Crazy? Maybe so, but I felt it was the right thing to do.

The conversation lasted less than five minutes. He was really angry and extremely hurt. Dee Dee sat at the table and didn't say one word. Just

Chapter Thirteen: THE CHICKENS COME HOME TO ROOST

before walking out the door, I said, "Daryl, I know it's probably not going to change anything—undoubtedly, you'll always hate me—but I *am* truly sorry."

I drove to Mom and Dad's and broke the news to them. Neither were shocked; in fact, Mom confessed that she'd suspected there was something going on between Dee Dee and me for a long time. "I could tell by the way she looked at you," she said. And Dad asked, "Was it worth it, my boy?" "Not even," I said. I unloaded my things and—at the age of thirty-one—was once again back in my old bedroom.

When I returned to work, I told Don what had happened. He put his hand on my shoulder and said, "I'm so sorry, Danny. I sure hope you and Caryl can work things out. I want you to know we all make mistakes—including me." What a good guy he was—a class act!

During the next two weeks, I had some long talks with Caryl's mom and the bishop of her church. I had tried talking to Caryl myself, but she refused to listen and would ask me to leave. I was hoping they could talk her into giving me a second chance. Finally, Caryl and I sat down and talked. She suggested we start seeing a marriage counselor on an individual basis, and I agreed. She also thought it might be a good idea if I started attending church, so I agreed to that. I was desperate and would do anything to put our family back together.

We met with the counselor once a week over the next couple of months. He was very professional and didn't cut me any slack. I attended church every Sunday during the months of April, May, and June. During the services, I felt so out of place, and to make matters worse, I was usually sitting by people that I didn't really know, while Caryl and the kids sat on a bench some distance away.

The first of July, Caryl decided to allow me to move back in. I was so happy and relieved, as were the kids. Believe me, I thanked the man upstairs! But by no means were things great between Caryl and me. She was struggling to forgive me, and I knew there was no way she'd ever forget. I apologized many times, but her heart had been shattered, and I really wondered if our marriage would survive.

But time marched on, and the girls had a fun-filled summer camping with Mom and Dad at the North Fork campground. They loved going with Grandma and Papa but Chris, just three years old, was still too young. I met Dad and his friend, Ollie, on weekends at Lake Avery, where we caught some beautiful trout. During the full moon in August, Donnie, Larry, and I caught many four- and five-pound rainbows.

School began on September 2; Amber would be starting kindergarten and Kila would be in second grade. The previous year, she'd gotten nearly straight A's. At the end of September, Caryl and I drove to Maudlin Gulch several evenings to watch and listen to the elk bugle. Those times brought in a breath of fresh air for us, relieving a lot of tension.

In October, Dad was all wound up, counting the days till we'd be going hunting. At the end of the month, Caryl told me she wanted to go with us on opening day, which was November 1. That made me hopeful; maybe things were going to work out after all.

After the kids went trick or treating on Halloween, we took them to Mom and Dad's to spend the night. The next morning, Dad pulled up in front of the house at 4:30 a.m. and I loaded the cooler along with my hunting gear. Caryl got in and Dad went around to the passenger side. I always drove, because I knew which roads to take when hunting in Maudlin Gulch.

Just after daybreak, we headed up Deer Canyon. We strained our eyes, looking up and down the oak brush-covered hillsides for elk. The road was so badly rutted that I had to put the pickup in four-wheel drive, and we couldn't travel any faster than about five miles per hour. After a few miles, I touched the brakes and asked Caryl to hand me the binoculars. Dad whispered, "Do you see some elk?" "I'm not sure," I said. I peered through the binoculars far up the distant slope. Oh, shit! The blond-colored object that I thought might be a rock was a big bull elk! I estimated him to be a thousand yards away. "There's a big bull," I whispered, and still looking through the binoculars, I told them I figured he was a six point, but that he was too far away to really be sure.

I quietly put the pickup in reverse and backed down the road, putting a ridge between the elk and us. After grabbing my rifle, I headed up the ridge's back side to eliminate any chance of the elk seeing me. What I'd be fighting was the time factor: I knew it was going to take me at least ten minutes to climb the mountainside in order to reach an area that might put me within shooting range, but there was a good chance the elk would be gone.

I slowly neared the top of the ridge, stopping twice on the way to catch my wind. I crouched down and moved very slowly, then leaned my

Chapter Thirteen: *The Chickens Come Home to Roost*

gun up against a bush to crawl on my hands and knees for the last few feet to see if he was still in the same spot. Sure enough, he was there! I estimated the distance to the big bull to be around 500 yards.

I gathered up a couple of flat rocks and slowly moved to the spot I'd be shooting from. I placed one on top of the other then dropped to my knees, pulled off my coat, and laid it across the rocks. After retrieving my rifle, I put a shell in the chamber and lay down on my stomach by the gun rest.

So far, I'd remained calm. I wriggled around, did some adjusting with my jacket on top of the rocks, and felt I had a good rest for the rifle. Placing the dot of my scope a few inches over the top of the bull's front shoulder, I held my breath and squeezed the trigger. *Boom!* The bull dropped, the sound of the shot echoing across the canyon. I yanked the bolt back, slammed another shell into place, and peered through the scope. The bull was lying motionless. "I'll be damned!" I thought. "I just pulled off the shot of my entire hunting career—at 500 yards!"

After watching for nearly ten minutes, I was satisfied he wasn't going to get up. I lit a cigarette, shaking my head in disbelief, then hiked back down the mountain, arriving at the pickup in minutes. I decided not to take my gun back up the steep mountain to retrieve the elk. I was convinced he was dead, and I didn't want it hanging off my shoulder while I was pulling him down the slope. It took the three of us nearly forty minutes to hike up to the bull. Caryl got to him first and yelled, "It's a six point!" Moments later, Dad and I got there. What a dandy! Six perfect points on each antler! I'd hit him at the base of the neck, near the shoulder. Dad slapped me on the back and said, "You did it, my boy! A beautiful shot!" Caryl and Dad each held a front leg, keeping the bull balanced on his back, while I gutted him. I didn't cut through the brisket as I normally would, as I was going to have him mounted and didn't want to damage any part of his cape. When I was finished, we stared at the pickup down in the bottom of the canyon. Hell, it was so far away that it looked like a kid's toy! Although it would be downhill all the way, it was hard to drag a big bull elk when there was no snow on the ground!

It took nearly two hours to get the bull off the mountain. We stopped several times along the way, and after we got within fifty yards of the pickup, I ran to get the camera. It'd been eleven years since I'd gotten the big six point at Dickerville Ridge. This bull wasn't quite as large, but he was certainly worthy of lots of photos. It was hell getting the big boy loaded. At one point, I thought we were going to have to go get some help, but—finally—he was in the truck.

When we got home, everyone was excited, and the neighbors and other hunters soon swarmed the pickup. A photographer from the *Meeker Herald* stopped and took a picture of me with the bull. After all the excitement was over, we took him to Purkey's and I asked Bryce to cape him and remove the horns.

Weeks passed, and on February 2, 1981, we celebrated Amber's sixth birthday, and on the first of April, I picked up the elk bull mount. I'd gotten permission from the Wix family, owners of the Sleepy Cat Guest Ranch, to hang it in the lodge amongst the other trophies.

As far as Caryl and I went, our relationship continued to deteriorate. Arguments were becoming more frequent and more heated. We weren't only hurting each other, but I knew the kids heard them. It was just a bad situation. Caryl had mentioned the word "divorce" more than once, and it terrified me!

On May 18, we celebrated Chris and Mom's birthdays. The little man was now four, and he was very handsome! During the evening, Mom told the kids that she and Papa were going to Aunt Donna's in Denver for a week starting Memorial Day weekend. She told Kila that when she got back, she and Amber could help her clean the camp trailer and get it ready to take to the North Fork campground.

When they returned on June 8, Dad called and told me to bring everyone over to the house—that he had something he wanted to show us. We all hurried over, wondering what it might be. After walking into the living room, the kids started yelling, "Look at the little dog!" My sister had taken Dad down to one of the pounds in Denver and he'd picked out a small, black-and-tan-colored "Heinz 57." "Is it a boy or a girl, Papa?" asked Kila. "It's a girl," he answered. "What's her name, Papa?" "Pepper," Dad replied. Oh, God, the kids were so happy!

Over the next few days, the girls helped Grandma get the camper cleaned and stocked and, on Saturday morning, Dad, Mom, the kids, and Pepper got in and waved goodbye. The North Fork campground was a beautiful place and the other campers there had young kids, so they would all have a good time. Mom had told us she'd bring them home the following Sunday.

The next Saturday before their return, Caryl said, "I'd like to have a talk with you." My heart started racing as fear shot through my body. I swallowed hard and said, "What about?" "I've filed divorce papers, and in two weeks, the kids and I are moving to Provo, Utah. I'm going to go to business school."

Tears started streaming down my cheeks. "Please—please don't, Caryl!" I stammered. "You should've thought about the consequences before crawling into bed with Dee Dee," she said. "Please—can't you forgive me?" I asked. "God knows I've tried," she sighed, then she started crying. I stood and put my hand on her shoulder. "I used to worship the ground you walked on, Danny. You were my everything, even the breath I breathed, but you killed that feeling!" She told me that she'd like me to stay at Mom and Dad's until they moved. Her church friend, Laurie, had lined up a place where they could live in Provo, and her parents and brother were going to help her move. She said, "I thought maybe you could take a load in your pickup and Chris could ride with you, but if you don't want to, that's alright." By now, my body was numb. "Yeah, I'll do that," I agreed. "Please get your things now and get out," she added. "I don't feel like talking anymore."

Two hours later, I was sitting at Mom and Dad's, crying my eyes out. It was like a stick of dynamite had gone off in my chest! I didn't go to bed: I sat up all night, drinking beer and smoking cigarettes. I was so glad I had the weekend off.

The next day, Mom, Dad, and the kids returned from their camping trip. After everything was unloaded and Kila, Amber, and Chris had walked home from Mom and Dad's, I broke the news. They were both very hurt: Mom started crying, and when I told them that Caryl and the kids would be moving soon, I started crying, too.

After I regained my composure, I walked over to the house and talked to the kids. The girls said very little; it seemed as though they were trying to sort it out. But Chris was completely quiet. Bless his little heart, he just really didn't understand what was going on.

I went back to Mom and Dad's and called my boss to tell him I needed the next day off. It was time for me to slow down and catch my breath. Mom stayed up with me till midnight, trying to comfort me. I just couldn't seem to stop crying. When daybreak came, I was in the kitchen, pouring a cup of coffee. I hadn't been able to get any sleep, and while combing my hair, I noticed my eyes were nearly swollen shut. My world had come crashing down, and I didn't know how in hell I was going to make it. I knew I was to blame, and nobody else! But—oh God! Those three precious kids were my everything! After Dad left for work at 7:30, Mom and I spent the day talking. Her heart was shattered, too, because she wouldn't get to spend much time with her grandkids anymore.

The following day, I returned to work. Once Don and I were headed up the road, I told him what was going on. I tried to keep from crying, but I couldn't, and he told me how sorry he was and that he'd pray for me. He said, "Please try to remember that you're not losing your kids forever. They'll always be your kids! You can still have a good relationship with them." I had the utmost admiration for the guy, and I hung on every word he said.

By Thursday, June 25, Caryl, her brother, and parents had nearly everything packed into the pickups and a U-Haul trailer. The girls and Caryl would be leaving on Friday, and Chris and I would take a load of boxes to Provo on Saturday. When I got to town Friday evening, Don dropped me off at my house so I could load all the boxes into the back of my pickup, then I walked over to Mom and Dad's. Chris came running up to me, and I bent down to give him a big hug. Mom and Dad told me that the girls and Caryl had stopped by around 7:30 a.m. to leave Chris and say their goodbyes.

After supper, I gathered up some of my good clothes and grooming needs and grabbed Chris's suitcase, and we headed to the house. It was ghostly there: many things were missing from the walls now, and the kids' bedrooms were completely empty. I tried with all my might to stay in a good mood, because I didn't want to start crying and upset Chris. But—son of a bitch! This was so difficult!

We watched TV till about ten, then I asked Chris if he was ready to go to bed. "Yeah," he answered, "if you are, Dad." Caryl had decided to leave our king-size waterbed, and after undressing, Chris and I crawled in. Within a few minutes, he'd fallen asleep. I gently placed my hand on his shoulder, tears streaming down my cheeks. My stomach was tied up in knots! Finally, around 1:00 a.m., I dozed off.

Around six the next morning, we got up. After Chris slipped on a light-brown pair of denim pants, I stretched a dark-brown polo shirt over

Chapter Thirteen: THE CHICKENS COME HOME TO ROOST

his head and tucked it in. I had him sit on the edge of the bed to get his socks on, followed by his shoes. "C'mon, Son. I need to comb your hair." We walked to the bathroom, where I knelt down and, facing him, carefully parted and combed his hair. "You're looking good, Son!" I said, and he just smiled. We went upstairs, where I fired up the coffeepot and fixed him a bowl of cereal.

By 7:30, I'd finished loading everything into the pickup, including a pillow up front in case Chris got tired. "Are you ready to go, Son?" "Yeah, Dad," he said. We swung around the block and stopped at Mom and Dad's so he could tell them goodbye. And what a scene it was! Mom fought back tears as she gave Chris a long hug, then Dad took his turn. I told them I'd probably be back late that evening. As we headed down the highway, Chris asked, "Is Provo far away, Dad?" "Yeah, Son—it's about 260 miles." "Will we be there before dark?" he asked. "Yeah—we should be there by two o'clock." I pointed out several different scenes as we drove along, including some ducks swimming on the river. I was fighting my emotions every single mile. We stopped in Vernal to use the restroom and made another stop in Roosevelt, where we had a hamburger and gassed up the truck.

A few miles down the highway, I noticed Chris's head bobbing, then his eyes closed. "Here Son, lay down and put your head on the pillow." He stretched across the seat and went sound asleep. Every once in a while, I'd glance down at him: such a sweet, precious little guy! I started crying when I realized that, in just a few hours, I'd have to tell him goodbye!

Just before we arrived in Provo, Chris woke up. "Did you have a good nap, Son?" I asked. "Yeah, Dad. Are we almost there?" "In about thirty minutes." The girls came running out to greet us when we pulled into the parking lot at the apartment complex. They gave both of us hugs and said, "We've been watching for you!" We went inside, where Caryl hugged Chris and the girls showed me around. They were happy and very proud of their two-bedroom apartment.

The girls helped Caryl and me unload the many boxes from my pickup. By now, it was three o'clock, and the dreaded moment had arrived: it was time to tell my children goodbye. I asked Caryl if I could talk to her for a minute, and we walked out to the pickup. "Caryl, will you please, *please* reconsider?" "No, Danny," she was adamant. "You brought all this on yourself." "But this is ripping my guts out," I said. "You know I love you and our kids!" "You should've thought about the consequences before you stepped out on me!" "Yeah, I should've," I replied. "I guess I need to get going." "I'll tell the kids to come say goodbye," she said, then added, "drive careful."

I hugged Kila first and said, "I love you, Dolly. Please watch over your sister and little brother." She told me she would. I gave Amber a long hug and told her I loved her so much, and she replied, "I love you, Dad." Now it was the little man's turn. I had to give him a quick hug, because my eyes were filling with tears. "I love you, Son—so much! Please be a good boy!" "I will, Dad," he said, looking into my eyes. The three of them stood waving as I pulled away, tears gushing down my cheeks.

During the first fifty miles, I had to pull over twice because of how hard I was crying, then dry heaves set in. I was finally able to pull myself together and stop crying. I gassed up in Roosevelt again and wolfed down a hamburger. Then, with the radio playing country-western, I started racking up the miles. My next stop was Rangely, where I bought a case of beer. I now had sixty miles to go before I'd be home.

Finally, I pulled into the driveway at nine. Oh, God, was I relieved that the trip was over! I was mentally and physically exhausted. As soon as I walked into the house, I called Mom and Dad to let them know I was back. While putting my things away, I closed the doors on the kids' bedrooms. Their emptiness was just too hard for me to look at.

For the next several hours, I sat outside in a lawn chair on the patio and drank beer and smoked, staring at the star-filled sky. I was hurting and I just didn't see how I was going to survive. It was 1:00 a.m. when I finally turned in, the king-size waterbed feeling empty and strange.

Early the next morning, I rolled out of bed and went upstairs to brew coffee. The entire house was eerily quiet and had a much different feel to it, so I decided to turn on the stereo to fill the quiet with some sound. Around eleven, I walked over to Mom and Dad's to spend the day with them. Mom fixed fried chicken for supper; afterwards, she packed a work lunch for me. She said she'd try to pack my lunch each day, and I let her know that I appreciated that. Now it was time to head back to my lonely house. Yes, it was nothing but a house now; it was no longer a home filled with love.

The next morning, I returned to work. Thank God for Don! We'd become extremely close and, with his kind words, he tried every way possible to help me with my emotional pain. That evening, when he

Chapter Thirteen: *The Chickens Come Home to Roost*

dropped me off, there were no young kids running around that Caryl was babysitting. Kila, Amber, and Chris weren't there to grab my lunch pail and open it to get the Hostess Twinkies or other treats. Caryl always packed extras so they'd have something from Dad's lunch pail, and it was a ritual. Every single day was a struggle for me now. When I left in the morning, I caught myself looking around for Kila—my Dolly—to come running to the front door, insisting I give her a kiss goodbye. Walking into the stone-quiet house when I got home from work was so painful that some nights, I went to Donnie and Erika's, and other nights, I went to Jake's. I just had to get out of that house! Most evenings I ate supper with Mom and Dad, except on weekends when they were gone camping.

Over the next several months, I spent time with them at their campsite along the White River, fishing with Dad at Lake Avery. At night, my bed in their camper was very comfortable and, with the nearby window open, I could hear the dull flowing sound of the river just fifty yards away, easing its way down the valley. Only a few feet from me were my wonderful, unconditionally loving parents, who were trying their best to help me through this difficult time.

Shortly after our return from camping, Caryl called and invited me down to see the kids before school started. I talked to them on the phone every week, but I missed them so much! I told her I'd take a couple days' vacation and drive down on August 14, and early that morning, I loaded my bags and cooler into the pickup and headed for Provo. My heart raced in excitement, knowing that in just a few hours, I'd be able to see my kids again! I pulled into the parking lot at the apartment complex around one, and the kids came running out to me. "Dad! Dad!" they all yelled as they got to me. I gave each of them a long hug as my eyes filled with tears. What a feeling, to see and hold them again! I asked all of them how they'd been doing and, with smiling faces, they said, "Fine, Dad." I struggled to get words out of my mouth without crying.

The girls grabbed my bags and I picked up Chris to carry him into the apartment. What a feeling, to have my little man in my arms! I just couldn't hold him close enough.

Caryl greeted me at the door. "Hi, Danny. How have you been doing?" "Do you want the truth?" I asked. "Maybe not," she said. I asked her how things were going for her, and she said everything was fine. Once I sat down, the kids told me all about Provo and the many big stores it had, and that their mom had taken them to a drive-in movie. Their excitement and happy little faces lit up the entire room.

That evening, we went to a restaurant for supper and the next day, the girls picked out school clothes and helped Chris pick out some that he liked. It was hard to believe, but he would be starting pre-school this year! He stuck to me like glue the whole time we were shopping; that evening, we went to the drive-in, loading up with popcorn and sodas. Everyone enjoyed the movie except Chris, who fell asleep halfway through.

On Sunday, after taking Caryl and the kids to lunch, it was time to say goodbye. My heart went right to my throat as I gave them each a long hug and a kiss then waved goodbye. My stomach was upset the entire trip home, and finally, at eight, I pulled into the driveway, completing the 520-mile trip.

Time passed and September finally arrived. It was my favorite month because of the beautiful gold, yellow, and orange colors of the trees, especially the aspen. I returned to Provo in mid-October and spent another weekend with the kids, who were doing well in school, and Caryl said she was getting good grades in business college. Saying goodbye certainly wasn't getting any easier, though.

The first of November, Dad and I started hunting. For some unknown reason, the elk weren't in Maudlin Gulch as they usually were, and we only saw a few cows. After seven days of getting up at 3:00 a.m., I asked him if he wanted to take a break. His response? "You can't shoot an elk in your living room!" So the hunt continued, and before the season ended, we got two bucks and a spike bull.

By December, as the snow stacked up and bitter cold caused long icicles to form on the eaves of the house, a lonely, depressed guy had started drinking more than ever. Caryl called and said that she and the kids were going to come to Meeker for Christmas, and that finally brought me out of my depression. We had a great holiday together; the little man spent a few nights with me and the girls spent some nights with Mom and Dad. It was a happy time for us, but they bid everyone goodbye a few days later, and pain filled my heart once again.

Chapter Thirteen: THE CHICKENS COME HOME TO ROOST

"'Deal!' cried the losers!" yelled Chris Halandras when he walked through the door. Six of us were already seated playing poker, and we all laughed as Chris sat down. The Thursday night poker games were now on again. It gave me something to look forward to, and the winter months were finally passing. During spring break, I drove to Provo and spent a couple days with Caryl and the kids, a bright spot in my otherwise bleak existence.

In April, I was telling Don how badly I felt, and he said, "I'd like to give you some friendly advice: I really think you should start dating. You're going to have to start a new life no matter what, and maybe when Caryl hears that you're going out with someone, she might decide to give you another chance." Hmmmm. "Yeah, Don, maybe you're right," I said. He was a blessing in disguise. He'd listened patiently to me and watched me cry several times over the last ten months.

When the month of May came, an economic bomb went off. The oil giant, Exxon, decided to shut down its oil shale venture that had been in operation for the past few years, and thousands of people lost their jobs. The company's worksite nearest us was located about sixty miles southwest of Meeker near the town of Parachute, and the shutdown had a huge impact on Craig, Meeker, Rangely, Glenwood Springs, Rifle, and Grand Junction. Many small businesses were going to have to close their doors. Meeker had grown by several hundred people due to the oil shale boom, and it was now projected that real estate prices that had previously gone through the roof were going to plunge.

That wasn't the only surprise in the month of May: Don, Lou, and I were informed that we were going to be transferred from the Hamilton area oil field to Wilson Creek, which was ten miles south of where we'd been working for the past eight years. Texaco was consolidating its operations, and rumors were flying around that some people in the area were going to be transferred even further away.

Don had worked at the Wilson Creek oil field for over twenty years before taking the head roustabout position in the Hamilton area, and he was very disappointed. Wilson Creek was an old field: most of the wells had been drilled in the 1940s, and it also had a very old gas plant. But since there were no other jobs in the area, we didn't have any choice.

In June, I finally broke down and took Don's advice: I started dating a gal named Linda. She was a few years younger than me and was divorced with two young girls. It was somewhat awkward for the two of us to begin with, just coming off divorces, but we soon relaxed and started having some good times. She was extremely attractive and well-built, and when we started having sex, it was great! Going an entire year without had never been in my playbook!

The summer rolled by and, on August 14, 1982, I got a phone call from Caryl that shocked me. She'd decided to give us another try! I was so excited that I broke down crying on the phone. I didn't know for sure what had made her have a change of heart, and I didn't care. I told her I'd take some vacation days, rent a large U-Haul, and be on my way! She started crying and said, "We'll start packing and be waiting for you." Oh Lord, I was so happy!

Late that night, I drove to Linda's and broke the news to her. It was really tough. Even though we'd only been dating for a few months, she took it very hard and began crying. I spent several hours holding her, telling her I was sorry and that I wished her the very best.

On Monday, August 16, I headed for Provo with a big U-Haul trailer in tow. With the radio blasting out country-western, I was one happy son of a gun! I pulled into the apartment complex around three, and the kids and Caryl came running out to greet me. I wrapped my arms around Caryl and we both started crying. The past couple of years had been so hard for us all. I gave each of the kids a big hug, and they said they were ready to move back to Colorado. I laughed and said, "Well, let's get to packing!"

By the time darkness set in, we'd made a lot of progress, and the bed of my pickup was stacked with boxes. My heart pounded with happiness as I watched my three little gems smile and laugh. We ordered pizza in, and once Caryl and I got the kids tucked in, she asked if there were any vacant company houses at Wilson Creek. She wanted to rent one and rent our house out so we could start brand new, away from family members and friends. I said, "I'm sure I can rent one, and that sounds like a great idea!" Early the next morning, I called the main boss at Wilson Creek, and he said I could rent one of the houses. They only charged $100 a month!

Chapter Thirteen: *The Chickens Come Home to Roost*

At high noon, we headed back to Meeker in our convoy, pulling into our driveway around seven that evening. The kids wanted to go see Mom and Dad, so we walked over to their place. What a joyous reunion it was! Even Dad's little dog, Pepper, got in on the action!

The girls decided to spend the night at Mom and Dad's, so Caryl, Chris, and I stayed at the house. I slept on the couch—Caryl said no sex till we were married again. The following day, we went to Wilson Creek to unload the truck and U-Haul and spent the rest of the week packing up things at the house in town. Dad borrowed one of the company trucks on Saturday and helped us finish moving. By Sunday evening, we had all the beds set up and had unpacked most of the boxes: the family was ready to start anew. Caryl was making plans for us to be married again, and the wedding would take place on September 18 at the home of one of her friends.

No, it's not a trophy bull—just a shot of my hero, my dad, so happy and proud!

PHOTO BY DANNY W. CAMPBELL

I returned to work Monday morning and shared my news with Don, who was nearly as happy as I was. Days later, on September 7, the kids started school and rode the bus to Meeker, about twenty miles away. A few weeks later, our wedding went off without a hitch with family and close friends attending. It was quite a deal, having our kids at our wedding! Don gave us a beautiful wall clock that he had made out of red cedar. Bless his heart! I knew I'd cherish it forever.

Mom kept the kids while Caryl and I went on a three-day honeymoon in Glenwood Springs. We had so much fun together and were very happy. After we returned, our family received some good news: on September 22, my sister had a baby boy who they named Dustin; and we were able to rent our house in Meeker, which paid the mortgage. Just weeks later, Dad and I started hunting season, and he got a beautiful spike bull on opening day. Before the season ended, I got a five-point bull, and the two of us bagged two nice bucks.

Because the elevation at Wilson Creek was about 7,600 feet, the snow and cold showed up much earlier than it had in Meeker, and in December, it really started stacking up. Texaco made sure the roads were plowed every day in order for the school bus to travel safely.

We all loaded up in the pickup a week before Christmas and traveled to Piceance Creek to once again search for the perfect tree. Truly a family affair, I cut down the one that Kila, Amber, and Chris decided was the most beautiful *ever*! The kids had a blast during Christmas break, sledding with the neighbor girls, Casey and Kelley, who were the same age as Kila and Amber. The roadway to the main office was quite steep with huge snowbanks plowed up on each side—the perfect hill for sledding!

Just before New Year's Day, the radio station in Craig, KRAI, started promoting a contest. If a person could pick the #1 song of 1982, they were going to give away a set of records containing the most popular country-western songs ever recorded. Amber said, "Dad, you should enter that contest. As much as you listen to the radio, I'm sure you could pick the #1 song." I laughed and said, "Oh, Amber—I doubt it." "Will you please try, Dad?" she persisted. So the next day, we drove to the radio station in Craig and I filled out the form, picking Willy Nelson's "Always On My Mind." They told me the winner would be announced on January 2, 1983, at 5:00 p.m.

I hurried home from work that day and we all huddled around the radio just before the announcement. At straight-up five, the disc jockey

Chapter Thirteen: *The Chickens Come Home to Roost*

said, "We are now going to play the country-western song voted #1 by radio station DJs throughout the United States. Here's Willy!" "Always On My Mind" started playing! Amber yelled, "You *did* it, Dad!" We all hugged and, as the music continued, I put my arm around Caryl and said, "There's a lot of truth in that song." She didn't say anything as tears ran down her cheeks. She just turned to me and held me until it was over.

As it turned out, there were two more winners. The radio station called and said they had held a drawing, as there could only be one winner—and my name wasn't drawn. Boy, was Amber mad! "That's just not fair, Dad!" she exclaimed. "I know, Amber—I agree."

As the winter passed, we spent our weekends in Craig shopping or drove to Meeker to visit with Mom and Dad. Sometimes the kids would pack their suitcases and stay with them and ride the bus home on Monday. Mom and Dad loved it when they stayed over.

When school was out in May, our renters informed us they were moving out, so we decided it would be best if we moved back home. The kids had had enough of staying at Wilson Creek and were extremely happy to hear the news. Once again, Dad borrowed the company truck, and by June 6, we were resettled. And it wasn't long before the phone was ringing off the hook, parents asking Caryl if she was going to reopen her daycare business. She told them she was, and soon the house was filled with small children again.

June saw Mom, Dad, and the kids camping at the North Fork campground, and Caryl and I began going to Sleepy Cat every Saturday night, where we dined, danced, and enjoyed being together. Almost every Sunday, I'd meet Dad and Ollie at Lake Avery, where we'd usually catch our limits of rainbow trout. Ah, yes—life was back to normal, and I was so happy!

As with all summers, it passed quickly, and at the end of August, the kids were getting ready to go back to school. Chris would be in first grade, Amber in third, and Kila, fifth. On school mornings, Kila always got up on her own around 6:30. Caryl would get Chris up around 6:45 and attempt to wake Amber up at the same time, usually with no success. While Caryl would be getting Chris ready, she'd say, "Would you please go downstairs and get Amber up before the guys pick you up for work?" Down the stairs I'd go and say, "C'mon, Amber—get up! You're going to be late for school, and I have to go." She'd pull the covers up over her head and yell, "Leave me alone!" "C'mon, Amber—now!" Back up the stairs I'd go, have a few sips of coffee, then head back down to see if she was up. Nope, still snoring away. "Amber, get up—*right now!*" "Okay! Okay!" she'd growl. Morning after morning, we went through this ritual, so I nicknamed her "Bear."

My precious mom having a beer at the North Fork campground.
PHOTO BY DANNY W. CAMPBELL

The months rolled by and on May 18, 1984, Chris turned seven, so Caryl invited Mom and Dad over for supper to celebrate Mom's and Chris's birthdays. I bought Chris his first rod and reel and promised him we'd go fishing at Lake of the Woods at the end of June. The time soon rolled around, so I told him that we'd need to catch some night crawlers the night before going. I asked our next-door neighbor if we could get some out of his garden, and he said he'd water it that evening. Around 9:30 that night, we grabbed the flashlight and a small coffee can and walked over to the garden. I had Chris shine the flashlight while I showed him how to catch them. After I got a few, he said, "Okay, Dad—you hold the light. I want to catch some." Oh, God, it was a kick watching him! He found out it wasn't as easy as it looked. Some darted back into their holes before he could grab them; others he pulled in half when trying to get them out of the ground. He'd say "Darn it!" when he missed or pulled one in two. He finally got the hang of it, though, and we got all we needed.

Early Sunday morning, I walked into Chris's bedroom, placed my hand on his shoulder, and whispered, "It's time to get up, Son." After a little moaning, he realized why I was waking him and jumped out of bed to dress. He had his morning cereal and I had my coffee, then I loaded our lunch stuff, fishing gear, and cooler, and we headed up the beautiful White River Valley. "Do you think we'll catch some fish, Dad?" Chris asked. "Yeah, Son, I'm sure we'll get some. Are you feeling lucky?" "Yeah, Dad!"

We arrived at the trailhead around nine and headed down the trail. It was a beautiful summer day, just a few puffy clouds drifting across the dark-blue sky. A raspy chirping sound broke the morning silence. "What is that, Dad?" I stopped and pointed out a fired-up pine squirrel sitting on the limb of a tree above, scolding us.

A few minutes later, we arrived at the river. I said, "Damn it!" "What's wrong, Dad?" Chris asked. "The old tree that we always used to cross the river has been washed away." "Does that mean we're not going to be able to go fishing, Dad?" "I don't know, Son." With the snowmelt now gone, the river wasn't running wild, so I decided to walk along the bank in search of a shallow crossing. Maybe I could piggyback Chris across the river. I knew we had to reach the lake, as my little man's heart was set on going fishing.

After about 200 yards, we came to a promising spot. I took Chris's rod and started wading across. In the middle, it was just below my waist. Once I got to the other side, I sat everything down and unlatched my backpack. I waded back across to Chris, got down on my knees, and said, "Okay, Son—wrap your arms around my neck, and when I stand up, lock your legs around my waist. I'll put my arms under them and we'll cross the river." The rocks were slick, so I took my time. As we neared the middle of the river, Chris really started squeezing his arms tight around my neck. I said, "It's okay, Son—we'll be to the shore in a couple of minutes." Once we made it to solid ground, I bent down and Chris released his tight grip from around my neck. "That wasn't too bad, was it, Son? He gingerly replied, "Not bad."

Minutes later, we arrived at Dad's and my favorite spot. I cut off a couple of willow branches and poked them in the soft ground near the shore so we'd have a place to rest our rods. Soon, I had Chris's rod rigged up, then I threaded on a couple of juicy night crawlers. I said, "I'll cast you out the first time, Son, then you can try it." "Okay, Dad." *Ka-fonk.* His rig landed a long way out in the calm lake. I handed him the rod, told him to reel up some of the slack, and place it in the willow's crotch to wait for a bite.

He'd just set his rod down when I noticed the line move. "Grab your rod, Chris—you're getting a bite!" He picked it up and I said, "Now, wait until you feel him really start biting before you yank." The line started jerking, and I said, "Now!" Chris yanked and his rod started rocking. "You got him, Son! When he starts pulling hard, stop reeling and let him pull line. As soon as he stops, start reeling." Chris excitedly said, "Boy, Dad! I hope he doesn't get away!" Oh, what a thrill to watch him! Finally, he pulled a nice twelve-inch brookie on shore. I yelled, "You *did* it, Son! You landed your first trout!" Smiling from ear to ear, he said, "Boy, Dad—he fought hard!" I laughed and removed the hook, put the trout on our steel stringer, and placed him in the water.

I rebaited his hook and told him to throw it out again, and after several tries, he got the hang of it. I finally got rigged up and cast into the lake. I told Chris if I got a bite, he could yank and reel in the fish. Over the next couple hours, the brookies were really biting and he had a ball. He caught one after another but was very disgusted when the biggest one he'd hooked got away just before he pulled him onshore. I said, "I'm sorry, Son, but that's a fisherman's story: the big one usually gets away!"

We ended up with a total of twelve brookies ranging from ten to thirteen inches in length. Chris watched intently while I cleaned them. "Boy, Dad—you're quick!" I laughed and said, "That comes with many years of practice." I knew that the pink-meated trout were going to be very tasty, since the water temperature was still quite cool.

We kicked back in the shade of a pine tree and had just started having some lunch when Chris pointed towards the lake and said, "Look, Dad—what's that?" I replied, "It's a big old beaver." He was cruising across the lake about thirty yards from us. *Bang!* The beaver slapped his tail on the surface as he dove. "What's that, Dad?" "The beaver slap their tails on the water to warn other members of their family that danger is near. He did that because he spotted us." "Will we see him again?" "Probably—just keep watching." Sure enough, he surfaced about forty yards from where he'd dived and went on his merry way. "Boy, Dad—that was neat!" "Yeah, it was,

Son. Usually, they come out in the late evening or early in the morning, so you don't see them in the middle of the day."

"So, have you got a girlfriend yet?" I changed the subject. Chris's face turned red and he said emphatically, "No, Dad!" "Weren't there some cute girls in your class?" "Yeah, a couple," he admitted. "Maybe next year, huh?" "Ah, Dad..." We visited for a few hours and enjoyed the spectacular scenery. Near us stood purple, yellow, red, and orange wildflowers; off in the distance were beautiful mountain peaks that rose up into the dark-blue sky.

Around three, I said, "Well, Son, I guess we'd better gather things up and head out." "I wish there was a bridge across the river," Chris said. "I do, too, Chris, but we'll make it." Soon, we came to the crossing, and I waded over with all our gear then returned to get Chris. I knelt down as before and said, "Okay, Son—get on your horse!" He didn't say a word; he just wrapped his arms around my neck and legs around my waist. As I neared the middle of the river, he once again started tightening his arms around my neck—so much so that I said, "Don't squeeze too tight, Chris—I can't breathe!" He eased his grip slightly and we made it across to shore. "Not too bad, huh, Son?" He said, "I'm glad we don't have to cross it again, Dad!" I started laughing and we headed up the trail. There are certain days in one's life that you cherish, and this day—with my little man—would always be one of them!

Two weeks later, Caryl suggested that we take the girls on a fishing trip, so plans were made. On July 14, we loaded up in the pickup like sardines: Kila, Amber, Tara—a girl the same age as Chris who Caryl had babysat for years—and Caryl, with Chris on her lap. We were headed for Native Lake, which was a couple miles on the other side of Lake of the Woods. About an hour later, we arrived at the trailhead, where I loaded my backpack to the brim with soft drinks, beer, and a big bag of fried chicken. Caryl had a large bag filled with chips, cookies, and candy bars. I handed all the kids their fishing rods, picked up my gear and the can of crawlers, and we began the two-mile hike.

It was a beautiful walk in. We had to cross two rushing creeks, and the girls whooped, hollered, and giggled while wading them. Caryl took everything in stride, and I could tell she was happy that we were going on an outing together.

Just before we got to the lake, Kila started complaining that her head hurt; minutes later, it had developed into a migraine. Caryl gave her some

Tylenol and Kila lay on a blanket we had spread under a small grove of pine trees near the lake's shore.

"Oh, it's so pretty here," said Amber. I took her, Chris's, and Tara's rods and rigged them up. Amber watched me thread part of a night crawler on Tara's and Chris's hooks and said, "I want to put mine on." I smiled and said, "Are you sure?" "Yeah, Dad." I cast all their rigs into the lake and told them to keep a close watch on their bobbers. If they saw them moving around or go under, they needed to tell me.

I'd just turned around and started walking towards Caryl and Kila when Amber yelled, "Dad, my bobber just went out of sight!" I rushed over and her bobber resurfaced, but then started moving again and went under. "Yank, Bear!" I mean to tell you, she reared back on that rod! A brookie jumped into the air, and I could see line coming from his mouth. "You got him, Bear!" There was no playing the fish; she just started cranking the handle. When she got him close to shore, I told her to gently pull up on her rod and ease him onto the grassy bank. She did as I told her and landed a fat eleven-inch brookie. "Way to go, Bear!" Chris and Tara ran over excitedly to see Amber's catch then went back to tending their rigs.

I unhooked the fish and put it on the stringer as Bear quickly threaded on another night crawler. This time, she wanted to do her own casting. I said, "Okay, but I'd better give you a few lessons first." She watched me make three or four casts then tried herself. The first few times were misfires but then, by golly, she got the hang of it and actually did quite well. Her line hadn't been in the water two minutes when she got another bite. "Shall I yank, Dad?" "No—wait until the bobber goes under." Soon, the bobber disappeared. "*Now*, Bear!" She yanked, and the tip of her rod started jerking. "I got him, Dad!" "Okay, just reel him in slow." She did, but when she got him close to shore, she gave the fish a hell of a ride, and it landed behind us. I started laughing, put my hand on her shoulder, and said, "Good show, Bear!"

Caryl came down to watch and, a short time later, Chris hooked and landed one. Then Tara told me she was getting a bite. I coached her, and she landed one. Thank God the fish were biting! Over the next two hours, the kids kept me busy, running back and forth to unhook fish, help one or the other cast, and bait hooks. After the fish finally stopped biting, the grand total was Amber, seven; Chris, four; and Tara, three. They ranged in size from nine to twelve inches. I told them they could go get something to eat and I'd come join them after cleaning the fish.

Chapter Thirteen: THE CHICKENS COME HOME TO ROOST

When I walked up to where Kila and Caryl were, Kila said she still had a bad headache. She was resting on the blanket with her head on Caryl's leg. The rest of us sat down, relaxed, and had lunch; at about four, we gathered all our things and headed down the trail towards the pickup. Amber, Chris, and Tara just loved wading across the foot-deep, crystal-clear creeks! Except for poor Dolly not feeling well, we all had a good day together, and Amber and Tara had gone on their first fishing trip.

School started on September 4, and the kids enjoyed getting back together with their friends. Then the weeks quickly passed and hunting season was knocking on the door. As usual, Dad was wound up and counting the days. Now that Chris was seven, I'd talked Caryl into letting me take him on his first hunt. She wasn't crazy about the idea and thought I should wait another year, but he was so excited that she relented.

On the morning of November 3, I got up at 3:00 a.m. After a cup of coffee, I tiptoed into Chris's room, laid my hand on his shoulder, and said, "Are you ready to go elk hunting?" He moaned and said, "I guess, Dad." After he dressed, I fixed him some hot chocolate and toast and filled his thermos bottle with hot chocolate.

Around 4:30, Dad pulled up in front and I loaded all our gear so we could head for Maudlin Gulch. Dad said, "Do you think you can spot some elk, Levi?" "Yeah, Papa." For unknown reasons, Dad had nicknamed Chris "Levi." It wasn't long before Chris had laid his head on Dad's shoulder and fallen asleep.

At six, we arrived at the mouth of Deer Canyon and woke Chris. Dad and I poured our usual cups of coffee and Chris had a cup of hot chocolate as we waited for daybreak. Finally, the sky started to lighten, and when we could just make out shapes, we drove slowly up the bottom of the massive canyon. "Watch close on both sides, Chris," I said. "I am, Dad." We'd driven about a mile when I gently tapped the brakes, shut the engine off, and whispered, "There's an elk." "Where?" both Dad and Chris asked. I pointed to a steep oak brush-covered hillside about 200 yards away. "There," I pointed again, and both of them spotted the elk.

I quietly opened the door, eased my gun out and put a shell in the chamber, then found a rest. Once I got the elk in my scope, I could clearly see it was a nice bull. *Boom!* The elk went down. I kicked out the empty, slammed another round in, and waited to make sure he didn't get up. After five minutes, I was satisfied he was down for the count and took the live round out of the chamber. When I opened the pickup door, Chris said, "You got him, Dad!" "Yeah, Chris." "How big is he, Son?" Dad asked me. "I think he's probably a five point," I guessed.

We started walking up the steep slope. Chris was so excited that he quickly got ahead of Dad and me. "Son, when we get close to the elk, you have to stay back till I make sure he's dead." "Okay, Dad!" I soon reached the elk, and it was obvious he was dead. I said, "Okay, Chris—come on up." Chris and Dad walked up the hill to where I was. "Dad, the bull is so *big*!" Chris announced. "He's a good one, Son," I replied. Chris then started counting the points. "Five on each side, Dad." Dad slapped me on the shoulder and said, "Old dead-eye did it again!" I started laughing. "Just shithouse luck, my boy!" I mimicked Dad's saying. Chris busted out laughing then, too.

Dad and Chris each held the elk's legs while I gutted him. When I finished, I told Chris to stay behind a safe distance while Dad and I dragged him down the hillside. We were fortunate, as I was able to back the pickup into a small ditch so the tailgate was nearly touching the ground, making it easy to slide the bull in.

We drove to the end of the canyon in search of more elk or a buck, but we didn't see anything. By now it was nearly noon, so we had lunch—Mom's fried chicken! We laughed and joked and, around two, we decided we'd better get the elk to Purkey's. The next day, I shot a four-point buck, so for Chris's first season on a hunt, he'd certainly been in on a lot of action! It was a special time that the three of us—Dad, Chris, and I—happily shared.

The next week, Dad and I continued hunting and ran into Dean Gent, the owner of Maudlin Gulch, who was driving around, checking on things. He told us that he was sorry, but this would be the last year we could hunt there; he'd been offered a large sum of money to lease his property during hunting season. I told him I didn't blame him, and we both thanked him for allowing us to hunt there over the past several years.

On the last weekend of hunting season, Dad and I talked about where to go next year. "Well, Dad, I don't know what we're going to do. I do know that I'm not going to hunt on public land. There's just too many

Chapter Thirteen: THE CHICKENS COME HOME TO ROOST

hunters." "Well, by God," Dad said, "I'm not going to quit elk hunting! I'll tell you *that* for sure!" "All the good private places are charging at least $1,000 a gun," I replied. "I'll find us someplace to hunt, Son," he said. "We're *not* going to give it up!"

The first of December, Caryl said she'd heard the Gofer Food convenience store wanted to hire a clerk. Because I knew the owner, Bob, very well, she asked if I'd please talk to him about hiring her. I did, and after Caryl had an interview and explained to him that she'd attended one year of business college, he hired her. I was happy for her, because she was burnt out on babysitting.

In January, Dad stopped by one day, all fired up. He'd talked to George and Bud Rienau and asked them if there was a chance of us hunting on their property next season, and they had said we were more than welcome. George, who was just two years ahead of me in school, owned a cattle ranch with his dad, Bud, eight miles north of town. Dad said that George commented that we should apply for a cow elk license for that area, saying that it was almost a guarantee of getting a cow. Leave it to Dad—he'd come through and found a place for us to hunt!

Summer came, and the first part of June, shock waves rippled through Wilson Creek: a group of coworkers were called in and told they were being transferred out of state. Our good friend, Bonnie—the mother of Casey and Kelley—was included. Lou and I were worried, because we'd be next, due to seniority.

The summer months were great: the kids camped with Mom and Dad, Caryl and I dined at Sleepy Cat several times, and I took Chris fishing on the White River. On one occasion, he landed two beautiful trout—one fifteen inches and one seventeen. But he was happier when he landed a nineteen-inch sucker! "Son, that's nothing but a trash fish," I said. "I don't care, Dad—I like him! And I want to take him home and show him to Mom, Kila, and Amber." So I put him on the stringer, alongside the two nice trout.

When we got home, he showed his mom and sisters his big catch. Kila and Amber teased him and laughed about the sucker that he was so proud of. Chris insisted that I take some pictures of him holding his catch, so I did. It was a great day, and seeing him so happy and excited touched my heart.

By the end of July, Caryl had been promoted to manager at the Gofer; and in late August, Don was offered a retirement package that he just couldn't turn down, and a big party was held in his honor at Sleepy Cat. The place was packed with longtime coworkers, retirees, Texaco bosses from Denver, and many friends. Don had worked for the company for over thirty-five years and was a legend in the oil field. I was extremely happy for him, but—oh, God—how I was going to miss him! He had been just like a second dad to me. Back at work, it just wasn't the same without him, plus there was a lot of worry. It was expected that there would be more layoffs and transfers soon.

On September 3, 1985, the kids started school, and soon the leaves were turning colors. As hunting season neared, Dad became more and more excited because he'd drawn a cow elk license. He loved elk hunting so much! On October 19, the three of us loaded up in Dad's '77 Ford pickup and headed for the Rienau Ranch at six in the morning. George and his two young sons—Austin, nine, and Ross, eight—met us at the gate. We followed them about a half mile and, after going through another gate, stopped and had coffee while we waited for daybreak. When it was just barely light, we slowly drove towards the hunting country. After a few miles, we came to a spot that George called "the picnic grounds" and pulled both vehicles into some thick brush. George pointed to a nearby area and whispered to Dad, "That'd be a good place for you to sit." Then he pointed to a ridge about a mile away and told Chris and me that that was where he wanted us to sit. I grabbed our snack bag, binoculars, and rifle and we started down the trail.

When Chris and I got to the sitting place, the sun was just coming up over the distant mountains. From where we were, you could see a large area of terrain covered with thick oak brush. "Hand me the binoculars—I think I see some elk," I whispered to Chris. "Where, Dad?" I pointed a long way off on a steep mountainside north of us. I counted eight with one young bull in the herd, but it was too far to shoot. I handed the glasses back to Chris, and he watched them until they went out of sight. "Darn it, Dad—I wish they'd been closer." "Yeah, Son—maybe we'll see some more." A few minutes later, Chris said, "I can see Papa in the binoculars, Dad." "What's he doing?" "Just sitting. I wish a big bull would come close to Papa." "I do, too, Chris."

Over the next few hours, we saw a lot of deer—does and fawns—but no more elk. At eleven o'clock, we spotted George and his boys near Dad, so we walked to the picnic grounds. George said they'd seen quite

Chapter Thirteen: THE CHICKENS COME HOME TO ROOST

a few elk, but none within shooting range. Dad saw several deer and the same elk Chris and I had seen. We visited for nearly two hours, having some of Mom's great fried chicken, then hunted again, but we didn't see any more elk.

At about four, we told the Rienaus we'd see them the next morning. When we got into Dad's pickup, Chris said, "Can I drive on the way out, Dad?" "Oh, I don't know, Son." "*Please*, Dad?" "Alright." I pushed the seat all the way back and Chris slid over, got on my lap, grabbed the steering wheel with both hands, and we headed out. I kept the pickup in second, so we were going very slowly. When we started down a rather steep hill, Chris said, "Are you nervous, Papa?" Dad, puffing away on his cigar, said, "Nope." "Yes you are, Papa. You're eatin' coal and shittin' diamonds." The cab of the pickup erupted with laughter! Dad and I couldn't believe that Chris had said that. Finally Dad asked, "Where did you come up with that, Levi?" Chris replied, "At school." "Chris, Chris," I laughed, "I don't know about you!" He just smiled and kept on steering.

Over the next week, Dad and I went back to the Rienau Ranch and got two bucks and a cow. Although we didn't get a bull elk this time, we really enjoyed George and his boys. The Rienaus were good people and it was a great place to hunt, and what made it doubly sweet was that it was so close to town.

The next month, on November 9, Kila turned thirteen. Yes, my Dolly was now a teenager! It was hard to believe that the kids were growing up so fast.

CHAPTER FOURTEEN

The Transfer to Hell

I WAS AT WORK ON DECEMBER 13 when a call came over the two-way radio of the one-ton truck that Mike and I were in, requesting that I report to the pumper's shack located next to the mechanic shop. I looked at Mike and said, "Something bad is about to happen." "Why do you say that?" he asked. "I've just got a bad feeling." "Ah, hell, I wouldn't worry about it," he replied. "I'm telling you, Mike, something's up." Mike stayed there and I drove to the pumper's shack. Before walking into the small 10x10 building, my heart was in my throat. When I opened the door, three Texaco bosses and the regional manager from Casper, Wyoming, were standing there. The manager said, "You've been transferred to Cleveland, Oklahoma, and you'll need to report to work there on January 6. Do you have any questions?" "Isn't there anyplace closer?" I asked. "That's it—take it or leave it. I don't really care!" he replied tersely. My stomach was tied in knots; hurt and anger ripped through my mind. He said, "I'll need an answer within five days." I didn't say another word; I just turned and walked out. I drove back to where Mike was and told him what had happened. He was as shocked as I was.

At 4:00 p.m., I drove home and broke the news to Caryl and the kids. Kila and Amber instantly said, "We don't want to move to Oklahoma!" Chris was quiet, but Caryl said, "What're we going to do?" "Shit, I don't know," I said. "There are no jobs to be found around here, especially one that pays as well as this one." I was scared and my mind was spinning out of control.

At six, I walked over to Mom and Dad's to talk to them. They were both upset and asked what I was going to do, but I had no answers. Mom started crying, "Hell, we'll be lucky if we see the kids more than once a year if you move to Oklahoma!" "I know, Mom, I just don't know what else to do!" Over the weekend, I got very little sleep and couldn't eat, but by Monday I had made a decision. I drove to Wilson Creek and had a long talk with the boss, telling him I was going to take the transfer. He gave me directions and the phone number of the office in Oklahoma. The town of Cleveland was about thirty-five miles from Tulsa and about 900 miles from Meeker.

On December 16, Caryl and I loaded our luggage and headed for Oklahoma while the kids stayed with Mom and Dad. Oh, what a long drive! We stopped several times and finally decided to spend the night at Salina, Kansas. Neither of us was in a good mood and there hadn't been a lot of talking. The next day, we checked into a motel in Cleveland, both of us physically and mentally exhausted. The following morning, we drove to Texaco's office where I met the boss and the crew. A young guy named Mike was extremely nice and gave me his phone number, saying that when we moved down to give him a call and he'd help us unload everything. I thanked him, as it sure was a nice gesture.

The rest of the day was spent with realtors, looking at houses. By three in the afternoon, Caryl said, "Maybe it'd be best if you just rented an apartment for now and stayed down here by yourself until school is out. Then you'll see if you really want to stay here permanently." Those words hurt: I didn't want to be alone, but I could see that it made sense. By five, we'd found a nice apartment and I gave the owner a check, telling her I'd be down the first week of January. That night, Caryl and I got into a huge argument. I said that if we ended up buying a house in Cleveland, there was no way we could afford to pay two mortgages. Renting or selling the Meeker house was out of the question because of the economic climate, so those options were out. I felt the only solution was to file bankruptcy. She hit tilt and told me I was wrong! The following day, we started the long drive back to Meeker. Hundreds of miles passed, and neither of us spoke a word. What a goddamned mess!

On December 22, I drove to Wilson Creek and told the boss I wanted to take some vacation time to prepare for the transfer. At home, there was a Christmas tree standing in its usual spot, presents beneath it, but the house was filled with nothing but sadness. Our family was in such disarray because of this transfer.

On January 2, 1986, I rented a U-Haul and Caryl and I packed all my things. Mom had us over for supper and fixed my favorite—chicken-fried elk steak—and around eight, it was time to tell them goodbye. As Mom and I hugged, we both cried. I gave Dad a big hug and could see a lot of hurt in his eyes. "Keep your chin up, Son," he said.

Early the next morning, I finished loading everything. It was bitter cold, around ten below zero. When I got into the pickup to start it, the seat was as hard as a board. While it was warming up, I went inside to say goodbye. Still in their pajamas, I gave Dolly, Bear, and the little man— my three precious gems, the greatest treasure a man could or would ever have—long hugs. I tried hard not to cry, but tears poured down my cheeks.

Caryl walked me to the pickup and we kissed goodbye. It was hard to say anything. "Please drive careful," was her admonition. "I will," I replied, then got into the pickup and pulled away. It reminded me of the tearful goodbye at the bus stop in Rifle when I went into the military, and the other heart-wrenching goodbye in Provo when Caryl and I had divorced.

The drive was uneventful and I arrived in Cleveland the next afternoon, questioning myself and wondering if I was doing the right thing. I called Mike and he came over to help me unload everything. What a guy! I told him how much I appreciated all his hard work and he said, "Not a problem! I'll see you Monday morning." Later that night, I called Caryl to tell her I'd made it safely and asked her to let Mom and Dad know. On Sunday I went grocery shopping; that evening, I cooked deer steak for supper and packed my lunch for work.

Early the next morning, I loaded my coveralls, gloves, and lunch and headed out. The guys I'd be working with gave me a warm welcome— including Lou, who'd also been transferred from Wilson Creek. During my first day, Mike drove me around to many of the scattered oil fields. Most all of the equipment, including the pump jacks, were very old, and the majority of the wells had been drilled in the 1940s and '50s. The terrain was not at all pretty—it was very flat!—and I missed seeing the mountains.

And so the grind began: I worked and came home to a lonely apartment, 900 miles from all my loved ones. It was a struggle each and every day. Thank God for Mike! He invited me over to his house a few nights for supper. His wife, Cindy, was very nice, and they had a young boy— Michael, Jr.—who was Chris's age. They took me rabbit and quail hunting with them a few times.

Chapter Fourteen: THE TRANSFER TO HELL

The phone calls home didn't help me much, as hearing everyone's voices just made me miss them even more. Bless Mom—she once again wrote me two letters every week. In mid-March, I was called into the office by the main boss. He said, "Have you purchased a house yet?" "No, I was going to wait until I moved my family down the first of June." "Well... uh...I'd suggest you don't buy one." "Why?" "Uh...it appears that you're going to be transferred again." My heart began to beat faster. "To where?" I asked. "Uh...either Texas or Louisiana." At this, I exploded. "Me and my family have been turned upside down by *this* transfer! Now you're saying I'm going to be transferred *again*? Tell me something: how many fucking groceries should I buy?" No other words were spoken. I got up and walked out.

Later that night, I called Caryl and told her what was going on. She said, "The kids and I are *not* going to get tangled up in those transfers!" "What am I supposed to do, Caryl?" "I don't know, Danny," she said. "Shall I throw in the towel?" "I don't know!" "Just where in hell does that leave me?" "I don't know!" "Goodbye, Caryl!" *Click*. I hung up on her.

At work the next day, I became light-headed and somewhat disoriented, so I asked Mike if he knew a good doctor. He gave me a name and number, so the following day, I went to see him. The nurse couldn't believe her first reading on my blood pressure, so she took a second reading, which was the same. The doctor then came in and gave me a thorough examination. He said, "Your blood pressure is extremely high. In fact, if it stayed at this level for an extended period of time, you'd be at risk of having a stroke or heart attack. Are you under a lot of stress?" I told him what was going on. "There's no job worth having a stroke or heart attack over. I'm going to give you a prescription to see if we can get your blood pressure down. It might be best if you return to Colorado. If you do, make sure you see your family doctor there immediately." I thanked him for his advice, filled the prescription, and called the boss to tell him I was having some medical problems and didn't know when I'd be back to work. Then I called Caryl. I told her what had happened and that I was going to fly home on March 22; she'd need to pick me up at the airport in Grand Junction. She asked how I was feeling and I said, "Horrible." I notified the apartment manager and told her that I would be gone for at least a month, then on Saturday, Mike took me to the airport in Tulsa. I thanked him for all he'd done for me and, just minutes after boarding the plane, it lifted off. Oh, God! My mind was about to spin out of control. I was half nauseated and didn't know what the hell I was going to do.

Caryl and the kids were waiting for me at the airport in Junction. I was so happy to see them and, during the drive home, I caught up on how the kids had been doing in school and everything going on with our family, friends, and around town. Once Caryl and I were alone at home, we had a long talk about the situation. Neither one of us had any answers, and she continued to say that she and the kids weren't getting involved in transfer games. I was feeling so frustrated; I wanted the income from the job, but I sure didn't want to live alone in Oklahoma! Later, when we went to Mom and Dad's, it was so good to see them! They always made me feel so solid and grounded, even when I was having a hard time getting my bearings.

On Monday, I made an appointment to see our primary physician. My blood pressure was still extremely high and, after a long discussion with the doctor, he prescribed nerve medication in addition to the blood pressure drugs. He wanted me to come in every few days so his nurse could monitor my blood pressure, and over the next several weeks, it stayed high, so the doctor prescribed a different dosage. I asked him if he felt it was safe for me to go get my things in Oklahoma. He said that I could, but to try to avoid any stressful situations. Caryl was upset that I was going to move back, but I told her that the stress of living alone in Oklahoma—and the probability of having to go through yet another transfer—just wasn't worth the health risk.

In mid-May, I flew back to Oklahoma. Mike picked me up in Tulsa and helped me load my things into a U-Haul trailer. "I'm sure sorry things didn't work out for you here, Danny," he said. "Thanks, Mike. I'm not really sure what I'm going to do now." We said goodbye and around one o'clock in the afternoon, I pulled out of Cleveland and arrived in Meeker the following day, mentally and physically exhausted.

"Now what?" I asked myself, then answered, "Good question." I really didn't know what the hell I was going to do. I was still receiving full benefits from Texaco because I was under a doctor's care, and the Oklahoma doctor's words kept ringing in my ears: "There's no job worth having a stroke or heart attack over." My health problems continued to plague me. The first of June, my doctor in Meeker suggested that I see a good psychiatrist. He felt I needed help managing the emotional issues surrounding the transfer. He recommended a doctor in Glenwood Springs who he thought

Chapter Fourteen: THE TRANSFER TO HELL

was the best on the Western Slope. At first, I was offended by this idea, but I decided that he knew what was best for me. So I called the office in Glenwood and set up an appointment for the following week.

My first appointment was for two hours, and besides interviewing with the psychiatrist, I also had to take a battery of written tests. Afterward, he concluded that the transfer, then the subsequent threat of another transfer, had created extreme depression and high anxiety. He consulted with my primary care physician, and I was put on additional medication.

On my next visit with the psychiatrist, I asked if I could have documentation of the test results and his diagnosis typed up so I could sue Texaco. He told me that I just might have a valid case. But when I told Caryl what I was going to do, she shook her head in disbelief and said, "Do you really think you stand a chance of winning?" I said, "I'll find a lawyer who'll take the case on a percentage basis, so I won't have anything to lose by trying." "I think you're wasting your time," she said. "We'll see, Caryl." Mom thought it was a good idea, but Dad didn't have much to say one way or the other. Just like when a poker player pushes his entire stack of chips into the middle of the pot and says, "All in!", that's where I was—only with a lot higher stakes! I found a highly recommended attorney in Glenwood Springs and, after a long conversation and looking over the documents, he said that he thought I had a very strong case: he'd file suit against Texaco for being the cause of my existing health problems.

As legal wrangling over the case began, I got back into the groove of old routines. Dad, Chris, and I went fishing a few times at Lake Avery; fall soon arrived, along with the start of school; and I drove to the Rienau Ranch and began another hunting season with Dad and Chris. Our conversations generally followed the same lines: "Papa, do you think you'll get your cow today?" "Yeah, Levi, I just feel lucky." And I'd say, "You say that every year on opening day, Dad!" and we'd all laugh. We had fun over the weekend and saw a lot of elk, but none were within shooting range. As usual, George and his two boys treated us very nicely.

On Wednesday, I had a doctor's appointment in Glenwood, so I didn't go hunting with Dad. At nine that morning, he came roaring into the driveway, yelling, "I got my cow, and I need you to go with me to get it gutted and loaded!" I said, "Okay, Dad, but let's stop at the grade school and get Chris."

My uncle Jake pulled up at that time—he was going to drive with me to Glenwood—so we picked up Chris and drove to the ranch. I was so darned happy and proud of Dad; he'd just turned sixty-two on September 23, and it more than made his day to get this elk. After gutting and loading the animal, Chris said, "Today was your lucky day, Papa!" Smiling from ear to ear, Dad said, "Yes it was, Levi!" We returned to town, dropped Chris at school, and Dad let Jake and me out at the house so we could start our drive to Glenwood. By the time hunting season ended, I had shot a young bull and Dad and I both got a buck. At least the time hunting had helped me feel less stressed out.

In November, I was notified by Texaco that I needed to go to Denver and meet with one of their doctors for an exam and testing. So Jake drove me over, and I spent nearly four hours going through their testing process and being interviewed. I was told that my attorney would get the results in a few months.

The holidays were upon us, so I tried to stay in a good mood. The kids certainly didn't need to worry about our future: that was my job. Soon after, bitter cold gripped the valley, and Caryl and I began arguing more—mostly about my drinking and spending time at Jake's instead of with the kids. It was the new year of 1987, and I felt my life was really starting to unravel!

In February, my attorney called and told me he'd received the results from the testing in Denver. He said they showed the same results as those I'd taken with my doctor, and he figured that increased my odds of getting some type of settlement. Oh, God! Did that ever make me feel good! Maybe—just *maybe*—I'd get lucky and get a nice settlement. But several months down the road, on the first of July, my attorney called again and wanted to meet with me. Once seated in his office, he said, "I'm afraid I have some bad news. A judge in Denver has ruled that a company has the right to transfer an employee anywhere in the continental United States. He based his ruling on a similar case from 1982." My heart sank when he handed me the letter from the judge. He reminded me that I had the right to appeal the ruling, but he didn't think it would be worth it. "I'm really sorry, Danny," he said. "I thought for sure you'd get a substantial settlement." "I did, too," I replied.

The drive back to Meeker seemed to take forever. Damn, I was disappointed! Later that evening, when Caryl got home from work, I showed

Chapter Fourteen: THE TRANSFER TO HELL

her the judge's ruling. She said, "I *told* you that you wouldn't win." "Thanks a lot, Caryl!" I said. "At least I tried!" "Yeah? Where'd it get you?" she responded angrily. "You know, Caryl, through this entire mess, I got very little support from you. Of the many, many trips to Glenwood, you went with me *one time*! As far as the transfer, I don't think you ever had any intention of moving to Oklahoma." "It's your story," she replied, then walked off.

Over the next few weeks, things went from bad to worse between Caryl and me. The first of August, she said she wanted to talk to me, so we walked out of the house to the front gate so the kids wouldn't hear the conversation. Before she even spoke a word, I knew what was coming. "Danny, the kids and I are moving out and I'm filing for a divorce." Instead of begging or pleading with her, I said, "Okay, Caryl." The look in her eyes truly spoke volumes: she was tired—*very* tired. She'd asked me several times to stop drinking and spend more quality time with the kids—especially Kila and Amber. An aggravating factor was that she'd never really gotten over my infidelity.

When I told Mom and Dad, Mom said, "It doesn't surprise me a bit. I never did think you and Caryl were meant for one another." Dad said, "I just wished you'd stay together for the kids' sake." "We've tried, Dad," I reasoned, "but we're both tired of trying." The kids didn't have much to say about the divorce or moving to a different house. I was glad that they would at least be staying in Meeker.

By the first of September, the walls in the house were bare, the kids' bedrooms were empty, and I'd shut all their doors. Once again, the place was stone quiet. Here I sat, lonely, a can of beer in one hand and a cigarette in the other—no job, getting a divorce, preparing to file bankruptcy. Due to the real estate market in Meeker, I knew that we wouldn't be able to sell the house—not even for what we'd paid for it. I just shook my head in disbelief; I didn't have a clue as to what I was going to do. There were flat-ass no jobs to be had anywhere in or around Meeker.

On top of everything I was facing, I now no longer had medical insurance, so I couldn't see my psychiatrist any longer. When I spoke with him, he advised that I continue to see my primary physician and stay on my present medications.

I put the house on the market and found out that I could stay in it at least a year without making payments. Then I brought my resume up to date and started applying for jobs. I went everywhere—the county, state highway department, the coal mine north of Meeker, the mines in Craig, and so many other places. I knew I had enough money to make it through the winter, but then I would be broke.

Hunting season came, and Dad, Chris, and I had another successful year. As usual, Chris teased his papa and Dad teased him back. It was one of the few bright spots of the entire year for me. More time passed, and soon snow covered the yard, then Christmas arrived. I made sure the kids had a beautiful tree for the house where they were living and a few nice presents. For me, it was quite depressing—so much so that I didn't put up a tree. Where it usually sat was just a bare, carpeted floor.

The long cold winter was nearly over. I played poker now and then and, thank God, I actually won some money! I desperately needed it. The first part of March, Mom had to have back surgery at St. Mary's Hospital in Grand Junction. For the past couple years, osteoporosis had weakened her spine so badly that surgery became the only option for pain relief. After nearly a week, she returned home, and I was hoping and praying that she would feel better.

From mid-March through April, I went to Piceance Creek to cut cedar posts to sell to a local fence supplier. In May and June, I worked at odd jobs—yard work and painting outbuildings. With no one interested in buying the house, I became more and more depressed every week. I'd received many letters from the mortgage company and was now getting threatening phone calls every few days. Finally, I'd had enough and went off on the guy who kept calling. "Mister, I've gotten a divorce, filed for bankruptcy, I don't have a job, I can't sell the house, so don't waste your fuckin' time—or mine, either—with your two-bit fuckin' threats!" *Bang!* I slammed the phone down.

On the first of August, I moved out of the house. After the final load was on the truck, I did a walk-through, making sure I hadn't missed anything. I could hear the kids' voices as I went by their bedrooms. "Dad, come give me a kiss goodnight." Tears streamed down my cheeks when I closed the front door for the last time.

Like adding a big dose of salt to an open wound, I was moving just 120 feet east into a very tiny one-bedroom house. Everytime I pulled into

Chapter Fourteen: THE TRANSFER TO HELL

its driveway, I looked through the windshield at the house that was once a happy home. At night, my headlights would reflect off Amber's and Kila's bedroom windows. I soon started shutting off the headlights as soon as I turned into the driveway. I just couldn't stand to see them shine on the house of shattered dreams.

In mid-September, Dad told me the power plant—American Atlas, located in Rifle—was looking for some temporary workers for their annual fall outage, and he gave me their phone number. They told me to come over and fill out an application, and if I knew of anyone else that needed work, to bring them along. One of my uncles, Harold, and I drove over and were hired. Although the job only lasted three weeks, they paid very well, and it was money I desperately needed. The first of November, I got lucky and went to work at a resort located about twenty-five miles east of Meeker. The job included snow removal, maintenance on the cabins, and being a snowmobile guide for the guests. It was nice to get a steady paycheck, if only for a season.

The weekend before Christmas, Amber called and wanted to go with me to cut a Christmas tree, so "Bear" and I trudged through the snow for nearly an hour before finding one that satisfied her. Shit! It was the biggest, most bushy piñon we'd ever cut down! But it made her happy, and it truly was a special day. The holidays came and went, and the only thing I really enjoyed was when the kids invited me up on Christmas Eve to watch a movie.

The new year of 1989 arrived and I started dating a couple of women. I was really starting to hammer booze now, and not just beer. A tall glass filled with ice, a couple shots of Bacardi rum, and topped off with Pepsi was my favorite, and there wasn't a day that went by when I didn't drink—not one!

The job at the resort ended at the end of April. I quickly applied for unemployment benefits, but I wasn't going to be able to draw much. In mid-June, Uncle Harold and I obtained some permits from the forest service to cut lodge pole pine for corral poles in the high country, and we sold them locally. On the first of September, we began cutting and splitting firewood and stockpiling it a few miles west of town at Ollie's—Dad's fishing buddy's—place in Lion's Canyon. I was hoping to sell enough during the winter to get by.

On September 23, Dad turned sixty-five and decided to retire. He shocked the entire family when he said, "I'm giving up my beer drinking.

It's just getting too expensive." We couldn't believe it! Soon after, hunting season arrived, and by its end, we'd gotten our elk and deer. I gave Caryl and the kids half of all the meat, and of course Mom was happy with their full freezer.

During November, I put flyers in the windows of businesses to advertise firewood for sale. I had cut and split all of the wood earlier in the fall, and I was amazed at how fast it sold. But I really didn't know if I had enough money to make it through the winter. Why? Because of my booze bill at the liquor store! I was spending close to $400 a month on beer, rum, and Pepsi.

The holidays passed, and I hunkered down in the tiny house where I was living and watched the snow start to pile up. Most days, I'd just listen to the stereo and drink, drink, drink! I usually drove to Mom and Dad's each evening and had supper. Some evenings I would go to the home of a gal I was dating to have supper and spend the night. Neither of us was interested in getting seriously attached. My only highlight was when Bear and I went to Lion's Canyon to cut a Christmas tree. Even though the entire trip only took three hours, it filled my depressed heart with joy!

During the winter months, I could count on Dad showing up nearly every morning around 10:30 after he drove to the post office to check their mail. He wasn't just stopping to visit: no, he was checking to see if I was alright and would beg me to slow down on my drinking. My quills would come up. "I know you mean well, Dad, but it's *my* life!" "Please, Son—please slow down. I don't want something bad to happen to you." After he'd leave, I'd feel guilty for a few minutes, but then—in spite of the hell—I'd walk over to the fridge and pull out a Bud.

At the end of February 1990, Kila stopped by. I'd certainly given her the right nickname, as she was now seventeen and a "doll." Her slender build, along with her big brown eyes...she was so pretty! It seemed as though she'd grown up overnight. We talked about everything, from school to my mom. She told me she'd just come from Mom and Dad's and she'd had a long visit with her grandma. She was concerned about Mom's back problem and the osteoporosis, as the surgery earlier in the year hadn't been helpful. We talked for nearly two hours, and it really lifted my spirits.

The first of March, I began cutting cedar posts again. Dad went with me every day to help me load them, now that he was retired. He didn't want me going by myself in case I had an accident with the chainsaw. In reality, I was just pissing in the wind, trying to make a living by cutting fence posts, corral poles, and firewood. By the time a person figured up all the expenses—gas, parts for the chainsaw, and wear and tear on the pickup—I wasn't making much money.

By the first of May, the low country was filled with gnats and the heat became unbearable, so I gave up cutting any more posts. Now what? I just didn't know what to do. God knows I'd been trying to find a job, and Dad was also asking around for me. I pounded booze more than ever, drinking twelve to sixteen beers and a fifth of Bacardi every day in order to maintain my high. Pitiful!

In mid-June, I was standing in front of the mirror, shaving, when I actually stopped and took a long look at myself. My eyes were nothing more than slits; my face was swollen and puffy. I was staring at a stranger, someone that I no longer knew. I didn't have a shirt on, and I looked at my large beer belly. I finished shaving and stepped on the bathroom scales: I now weighed 215 pounds. I'd gained twenty-five pounds over the past three years! I yelled out loud, "You're a goddamned mess. The drinkin' *has* to stop!" Both anger and fear started rippling through my mind. I was convinced if I didn't do something soon, I was going to be taken to "Boot Hill." I'd heard that the Veteran's Medical Center in Grand Junction had a drug-alcohol rehabilitation program, so I started giving serious thought to checking myself in.

The last week of June, I drove to the North Fork campground to see Mom and Dad and tell them what I was going to do. Dad wasn't at the camp trailer—he had gone fishing with his friend, Ollie—so Mom and I had a long talk. She was happy about the idea. "Son, I really think you should do it." I gave her a hug goodbye so I could get back to town to call the VA. The lady there was extremely nice and told me they had a five-week program that would be starting July 2. I had to be there at 8:00 a.m. I thanked her and said I'd see her then.

The kids and Caryl were all very happy when I told them what I was going to do. Caryl had tears in her eyes. "God, I wish you would've made that decision years ago." "Yeah—me, too," I replied.

CHAPTER FIFTEEN

An Angel Named Mary

I CONTINUED TO DRINK FOR THE NEXT FEW DAYS and nights, having several mixed drinks on Sunday, July 1, the day before I was to check in at the VA. My alarm clock went off at 4:30 a.m. the next morning, and I quickly got out of bed and brewed some coffee. After a few cups, I made sure I hadn't forgotten anything, loaded my suitcases into the pickup, and rolled out of Meeker at 5:30.

I arrived at the Veterans Administration Medical Center around 7:30 and waited in the parking lot till they opened at eight. I filled out all the required paperwork and was escorted to Building 6 a few minutes later, where the lady in charge, Becky, introduced me to the counselors who would be giving the classes. She showed me the entire facility, including the berthing area, shower room, and a small kitchen. I was happy to see some coffeepots there! Becky informed me that we'd eat at the cafeteria located in the hospital; in time, we'd be able to do some barbequing ourselves in back of Building 6. She said there would be a total of twenty-five guys enrolled in the program, and we'd have access to a primary care nurse, a medical doctor, and a dietician. She was such a nice young lady, and she did a remarkable job explaining everything to me.

After lunch at the cafeteria, we had our first class and were given a lot of literature to read. The afternoon passed quickly; after supper, I met and visited with some of the other guys that were in the program. One guy, Paul, was extremely witty and told a lot of jokes. He was a certified electrician and we soon nicknamed him "Sparky."

I crawled into my bed at ten o'clock, my skin crawling. I wanted a drink so bad! I tossed and turned all night and only got a few hours of

Chapter Fifteen: An Angel Named Mary

sleep. Up at five, I went to our kitchen to brew coffee. A guy named Bob soon walked in and poured himself a cup, then we went outside to the patio to visit so we wouldn't wake anyone.

By seven, everyone was up, so we walked to the cafeteria and had breakfast. At eight, our classes began, and each of us was required to stand up and give our name and a brief summary of our problem, whether drug or alcohol related. Some of the guys told horrible stories about alcohol literally destroying their lives!

During the rest of the day, we were shown movies and slide presentations that pertained to alcohol and drugs. Many segments showed the effects that heavy drinking had on a person's health over a long period of time. There were graphic pictures of damaged livers that had caused death. I actually got queasy during that presentation, and I wondered if my liver was damaged.

Since the Fourth was a holiday, the counselors and instructors had the day off, so most of us sat around, visiting and reading some of the literature we'd been given. When we went to the cafeteria at noon, I felt as though I was going to fall down. As soon as we got inside the building, I quickly went to the wall so I could periodically touch it while walking down the hallway. It seemed to take away the fear of falling, and I attributed the feeling to withdrawal symptoms.

Later, just before dark, Bob and I walked to an area on the VAMC grounds where we were told we could watch the city's fireworks display. *Boom! Bang! Boom!* Soon, the quiet evening was filled with the sounds of fireworks going off. The dark sky was full of explosions of brilliant red, white, blue, green, and orange cascading outward.

I shook my head in disbelief as I thought about my situation. Here I sat, forty-two years old and a hundred miles from my loved ones, watching the Fourth of July fireworks with a total stranger. I was uncertain of what the future was going to bring, and I wondered if I'd win my battle against alcohol addiction.

After nearly thirty minutes, the fireworks concluded. Bob and I walked back to Building 6 and I went to bed, fighting—with all my might—the desire to have a drink! I quietly whispered a prayer and asked God to please, please help me!

The next few days were nothing short of hell. I'd get up at five always wanting a drink and go to bed at ten always wanting a drink. The class time certainly helped me stop dwelling on alcohol, but when there was no class, my mind and body both seemed to torture me.

Friday night, July 6, I decided I was going to do something about my personal appearance and lose some weight—especially my ugly beer gut! So the next morning, I got up at five, drank coffee with Bob till six, then laced up my tennis shoes and headed out, walking a large perimeter around the VAMC grounds. I continued walking until I figured I'd gone three miles. That evening, just before sundown, I made the same walk, and on Sunday, I did the same thing. It damn sure helped me get my mind off booze, and I was now determined to follow through on my exercise every day in order to drop the pounds. The next day—Monday, the ninth—I had an appointment with the dietician and explained to her that I wanted to be put on a strict diet. She gave me some menus to follow that I could take with me to study.

The next two weeks passed by slowly. We spent many, many hours in classrooms and I walked many, many miles around the campus. By now, it was no longer a casual walk—it was a very fast-paced walk! My energy level was gradually improving and—best of all—I was able to punch some new holes in my belt! After my evening walk, I took some time to look around for golf balls. The VAMC was located next to a golf course and many balls were hit over the fence. I carried a small bucket with me and, on a good night, I'd find ten to fifteen balls, many of them nearly brand new. Hell, I'd hunt them until dark! As I went through this exercise, the horrible craving for alcohol was finally starting to subside. I was impressed by the VA's instructors and counselors, who went all-out to help us understand that there *is* a life—a *better* life—without drugs or alcohol.

On Saturday, the twenty-first, Caryl brought the kids down for a visit. Oh God, was I ever happy to see them! They stayed for nearly two hours, and I explained much of what had been going on in the classrooms and showed them my five-gallon bucket, now full of golf balls. It made me feel good that all of them, including Caryl, noticed that I'd lost some weight. Just before they left, I gave each of the kids a long hug and told them how much I loved them.

Our group had been informed earlier in the week that we could have a one-day pass on Sunday, July 22, from 8:00 a.m. till 6:00 p.m., and that we'd be required to take a Breathalyzer test when we returned. They explained that if you failed the test, you'd be kicked out of the program.

Chapter Fifteen: An Angel Named Mary

Mom and Dad decided to drive down to take me out to dinner. It was so good to see them, and after we finished eating, Dad drove to a nearby park and we sat on the lawn in the shade, visiting till about four. They were both happy that I'd checked myself into the program, and we talked about how much better I was feeling. I hugged them goodbye when they took me back just before six, and I told them I should be home August 6.

During the following week, we took an arts and crafts class and had a choice of several projects we could do. I decided to hand-tool a new belt with a polished agate stone mounted on the buckle. My old belt had several new holes punched in it, as the pounds had been nearly falling off. On Friday, I decided to walk over to the hospital and weigh myself. It was hard to believe it when I stepped on the scales! I now weighed 195 pounds. Yes, in the twenty days since I'd started walking and hunting golf balls, I'd lost twenty pounds! I figured I'd walked close to 150 miles.

Saturday evening, we barbequed hamburgers and hot dogs. After I finished eating, I glanced over at a nearby picnic table and noticed that Sparky was seated with two women and a guy. I wasn't sure who they were, as he hadn't mentioned anyone coming to visit him. Close to sundown, I sat in a lawn chair near Building 6, dropping and catching a golf ball as it bounced off the concrete. One of the women who'd been visiting with Sparky stopped and said, "Hi, my name's Mary. I'm Paul's sister." I looked up and had one hell of a time finding the words to introduce myself. She was so beautiful! "Uh...my name's Danny," I finally managed. She had big beautiful green eyes, by far the prettiest I'd ever seen, and gorgeous blonde hair! She was around 5'2" and I guessed her to weigh about 110. She was extremely well-dressed—lots of jewelry, tight designer jeans, and high heels. I mean to tell you, she looked like a movie star! She asked me where I was from, and I told her. She said she lived in Delta, about forty miles south of Grand Junction. I tried to stop myself, but I couldn't keep from staring at this gorgeous gal. Those green eyes were nearly hypnotizing.

The people she was with walked up and were ready to leave, so I told her it was nice to meet her and said goodbye. Oh, shit! When she walked away, I couldn't help staring at her cute little bubble butt in those tight jeans! What a beauty!

Sparky walked up to me and said, "So what'd you think of my sister, Mary?" "My God, Sparky," I gushed, "she's *beautiful*!" He started laughing and said, "Do you want a date with her?" "Wasn't that her husband with her?" I asked. He laughed again and said that the guy was their brother, Leonard, and the other lady was their sister, Carolyn. He said, "Mary is married, but her husband is in extremely poor health. He has an incurable disease called 'Huntington's,' and he probably won't live much longer." "I'm sorry to hear that," I said, "but you tell Mary that I'd do anything for a date with her, including washing and waxing her car!" He really started laughing at this, and he told me he'd call her on Sunday and tell her what I'd said. Later that night, when I went to bed, I couldn't get her off my mind. Yes, I *did* want a date with that stunning beauty!

Late afternoon on the following Sunday, Sparky walked up and handed me Mary's phone number. He said she got quite a kick out of what I'd said about washing and waxing her car, and that I could call her. Yipee! I slapped him on the shoulder and thanked him twice.

The following week passed by quickly, and I finished making my new belt. For some reason, it was very special to me, maybe because I looked at it as a symbol of completing something I'd started—the VA rehabilitation program. That Friday, I weighed myself one more time after walking another thirty miles during the week: 190 pounds! Simply amazing! Then the weekend passed and on Monday, August 6, it was time to check out of the VA's rehabilitation center. I told the friends I'd made goodbye and wished all of them luck. Sparky and I had a brief conversation and I asked him to tell Mary that I'd be giving her a call. As we shook hands, he said he'd let her know.

I walked over to Becky's office to say goodbye to her. She told me to always remember that alcoholics cannot drink moderately; even one or two would cause them to go right back to their previous habits. The old saying that sticking to beer and not drinking the hard stuff would be okay was also an absolute farce. Alcohol is alcohol, whether it's 3.2 beer or a shot of 100-proof whiskey. She went on to say that the success ratio of those who completed the five-week program was quite low, statistics showing that only three out of twenty-five would stay off booze or drugs. Most of the group would go back to drinking or drugging within weeks, or they might stay clean for just a few months or maybe a year. I found these statistics very discouraging to hear.

As I drove back to Meeker, a twinge of fear entered my mind. I asked myself, "Do you think you'll be able to make it in the real world without alcohol?" Damn! Could I? For the past five weeks, I'd been insulated from

Chapter Fifteen: An Angel Named Mary

the outside: I hadn't had access to alcohol and wasn't faced with the everyday problems of no job, bills, etc. Then my mind drifted back to Sparky's sister, Mary. Oh, God! Those big green eyes were mesmerizing, and then there was her petite little figure! I knew it was probably a long shot of having a chance with her, but what the heck—I'd made up my mind that I was going to call her.

I got home around noon and, after unloading everything, just kicked back and replayed the past five weeks. I hoped and prayed that I'd be able to stay away from the liquor stores. Soon, one of my neighbors came over to visit, and he told me he'd heard that a construction company named TIC, based out of Steamboat Springs, was hiring people to do a job on Piceance Creek and had set up an office in Meeker. What great news! I decided to go down the next day and fill out an application.

The following morning, I drove to their office and turned in a resume, filling out all the necessary paperwork. The lady said that if I was hired, the job would start at the end of August. I decided to drive up to Caryl's and visit with the kids for a while. Mom and Dad were staying at the North Fork campground, and I had decided to go see them the next day. The girls couldn't get over how much weight I'd lost! I asked Chris if he wanted to go fishing the next day, and he said, "Are we going to go to Lake Avery with Papa?" I told him that's what I'd planned. So over the next few days, we fished with Dad and Ollie. We caught several trout, spent time at the campground visiting with Mom, and Chris played with Dad's dog, Pepper, who Dad always took with them. Mom was in a great mood—she just loved camping.

I finally decided to call Mary on Friday night. Shit! I was so nervous when I dialed her number, just like a teenager asking a girl for a date! When she answered, I managed to tell her who I was and asked if there was a chance of taking her out to dinner sometime. She said, "Perhaps for the first time, it'd be best to meet at Target's cafeteria at Mesa Mall in Grand Junction and have a sandwich or coffee." I said, "Anywhere is fine with me." "I'll meet you there at noon on Saturday, August 18, then." "Thanks so much, Mary. I'll see you then. Goodbye!" I was shaking with excitement when I hung up the phone! Oh, God! I was going to get to see that beauty again!

The following day, Mom called and told me they'd come to town to get supplies, so I said I'd come over. I'd already told them about meeting

Mary, and when I got there, I told Mom I had a date with her in Grand Junction for next Saturday. "Mom, she's beautiful! I mean, a *doll*!" Mom said, "Why don't you take our car instead of your old pickup?" "Thanks, Mom—that's a great idea." Mom and Dad had a pretty, light-yellow 1984 Thunderbird they'd bought a few years before. When Friday rolled around, I drove to Mom and Dad's and picked up the T-Bird, took it to the car wash, and cleaned the interior. I made sure it was perfectly clean.

I got up early Saturday morning and put on some nice clothes, doing a little extra primping. I wanted to look my very best for Mary. I arrived at the Target cafeteria at 11:30, ordered a Pepsi, and sat down at a small table, positioning myself where I could watch the main entrance. Noon came and went, and no Mary! Minutes ticked by; soon it was 12:30—and still no Mary! I knew in my heart that she wouldn't stand me up, so I figured maybe she'd had car problems.

At 12:45, she came rushing through the front door and came to my table. "I'm so sorry I'm late! My mom fell at the nursing home and they think she probably broke her hip. She's enroute to St. Mary's Hospital right now in an ambulance!" Well, it wasn't car trouble! "Gosh, I'm sorry to hear that, Mary." "I'm sorry about our date, Danny," she said. I could see she was really shook up, so I answered, "Don't even worry about it. I'd be glad to go with you to the hospital." She seemed receptive, so I followed up with, "Let's go."

I spent the afternoon with her at St. Mary's, where the doctors confirmed that her mom had broken her hip. Mary and I walked to a nearby motel around four and she reserved a room for the night. She asked me if I had to go back to Meeker, or could I stay the night? I told her I didn't have to go back, so I rented a room, too. I wanted to spend as much time with her as I could.

Later that evening, we went out for supper with her brother, Leonard, and his friend, Jamie. Finally, at nine, Mary and I were alone at her motel room. We talked nonstop for several hours, getting to know one another. She told me that she and her husband, Maynard, had been together for nearly thirty years, but it had been a rocky relationship. They had gotten divorced once then remarried each other. They had one child—a daughter named Sheri—who was living in Farmington, New Mexico.

Maynard had been employed by the US Bureau of Reclamation for twenty-five years and had been a supervisor for the surveying department until 1985, when he was diagnosed with Huntington's disease, which was incurable and fatal. They'd lived in Farmington during the time of his employment, but they decided to move to Delta in 1987 after he had to retire because of his illness. Mary had wanted to be closer to her family for support, and all of them lived in the area. She'd like to start a new life but felt obligated to do her best to take care of Maynard. She said, "This disease is a slow death. Sometimes people live for fifteen or twenty years after being diagnosed. When Maynard's two cousins were diagnosed with it, their spouses left them. I can't, and I won't, abandon him." She then got tears in her eyes and said, "Believe me—it's hard, *very* hard, being a caregiver day in and day out, especially with him yelling at me a lot of the time for no reason." I put my arm around her and told her how sorry I was. By now, it was three in the morning. We were both tired and decided to call it a night. She gave me a very sweet kiss and I told her I'd see her in a few hours. When I got into bed, I felt so good. The day and night had gone well, considering everything. There was no doubt in my mind that not only was Mary a gorgeous lady, but that she also had a lot of class!

I spent most of Sunday with her at the hospital while she visited with her mom. At around four in the afternoon, she told me that she had to get back to Delta to take care of Maynard. "I'm glad we got to spend some time together. I'd like to see you again," she said. Oh, those words sent me to Cloud Nine! I suggested that maybe, later on in the week, I could bring Mom down to Delta for a visit. I wanted the two of them to meet. She told me that sounded good and gave me directions on how to get to her place. After a goodbye kiss, she wished me a safe trip home.

The following Friday, Mom and I drove to Mary's home in Delta. She came out to greet us and, after the introductions, took us inside to introduce us to Maynard. I felt a little uncomfortable, but Mary did her best to make Mom and me feel at home. It was quite evident that Maynard was in bad shape, his body jerking and twisting during our brief conversation.

Mary showed us around their nearly new 14x80-foot mobile home, followed by a tour of her yard. What beauty! It had sculptured bushes, a well-groomed lawn, and a variety of colorful flowers. She pointed out lilies, snapdragons, and four o'clocks then showed us her beautiful rose garden. The yard looked like something you'd see in a *Better Homes & Gardens* magazine. She also had a vegetable garden full of onions, radishes, squash, and some huge tomato plants that were loaded with fruit. She got a plastic sack, picked several, and gave them to Mom.

We stayed for about two hours then told her and Maynard goodbye. When she walked us to the car, I asked if I could call her again. She smiled and said, "Sure." On the way home, Mom commented, "Gosh, Son, she certainly is pretty and so nice. I sure hope things work out between the two of you!" I thought for a moment then said, "You know, Mom, even though I haven't spent much time with her, I can tell that she's a very special lady."

Early Monday morning, August 27, I drove to Piceance Creek for my first day of work. Shit, it was a long, hot day! I had to carry concrete forms and help put them in place. The hourly pay was only $8.50, but I needed the money. Within a few days, I became friends with some guys that told me I could ride with them to the job site. That was good news, because it was about eighty miles round trip each day, and my old pickup really slurped up the gas.

During September, I called Mary several times and we had lengthy conversations. I made a date with her for Saturday evening, September 29, and reserved a room at the Hilton in Grand Junction. She had agreed to spend the night and, if we were going to be intimate, it should be at a nice place.

She met me at the Hilton at three, all decked out in a gorgeous lavender dress, jewelry, and high heels. What a beautiful lady! We checked into the room, where the view overlooked the nearby golf course. But my mind was spinning out of control: I was picturing her lying on the big king-size bed with no clothes on. I knew that petite little body would be something special to see.

We drove to a nice restaurant where we enjoyed a candlelight dinner. She had crab legs and I had steak and shrimp. We laughed and joked, and I kept staring at her big, beautiful green eyes. When we arrived back at our room around ten, my heart started racing with anticipation. Mary disappeared into the bathroom and when she came out, she was wearing an extremely sexy nighty. She nearly took my breath away! The room was filled with the smell of her perfume.

I dimmed the lights, leaving just one lamp on, and lay beside her. We started kissing passionately; it wasn't long before we were both naked, and then we made love. It was beyond special to hold her close to me. Later, I put my arm around her and we drifted off to sleep.

Chapter Fifteen: An Angel Named Mary

The next morning after breakfast, we checked out of the room and I walked her to her car. After giving her a goodbye kiss, I told her I'd be calling her, and perhaps we could have a repeat of last night. She smiled and said, "Maybe so. You never know for sure." During the drive home, I replayed what had happened over and over.

Then it was back to work on Monday. Mary and I called each other almost every evening now, and it may sound strange, but she'd told Maynard that she and I had become good friends. She said that Maynard was very understanding because of his condition, not knowing how much longer he was going to live. He realized that she was going to need someone to lean on during the rough times to come, and he seemed to have taken a liking to me.

The first weekend of November, Mary and I met again in Grand Junction and stayed at the Ramada Inn. We had so much fun, and by now, we were falling in love. Shortly after that, at the end of November, my job ended, and I was now back to looking for another one. In December, Mary and I met twice in Grand Junction and stayed at the Holiday Inn. We went to the mall and out for dinner, then stayed in our room, making love. We nicknamed Horizon Drive, where all the motels were located, "Honeymoon Avenue."

The holidays finally passed and on Saturday, January 5, 1991, I heard the fire whistle echo across Meeker. I stepped outside, as most residents do when it goes off, but I didn't see any smoke. About an hour later, I decided to drive down to Mom and Dad's to visit. When I opened the door, Mom said, "Did you hear where the fire was?" "No, I didn't, Mom." She said, "I heard on our scanner that it was the Sleepy Cat Lodge." "Oh, no! I have both of my six-point bulls hanging up there!" "I forgot about that, Son!" "Where's Dad?" I asked. "He drove out to Lion's Canyon to visit Ollie." After talking with Mom for a while, I told her I was going to drive up to Sleepy Cat to look at the damage. When I got there, I was shocked to see that there was nothing left but smoldering ashes, the two fireplaces still standing on each end. I felt so sorry for the Wix family, who'd owned and operated the lodge for years. I drove back to Mom and Dad's and told them the grim news. They were both sorry for me, as my trophy bulls were gone forever.

On Monday, a friend of mine named Ben stopped by and told me he'd heard that a company bought the old Gary Refinery, located three miles west of Fruita, Colorado, which was thirteen miles west of Grand Junction. The new company had plans to restore it and put it back into production. He asked me if I wanted to ride down with him and put in an application, and I said, "Hell, yes!"

The following day, we drove to the office of the new company, Landmark Petroleum, and filled out applications and gave them resumes. Two days later, a foreman from Landmark called and asked me to come in for an interview on Friday, and it went very well. The foreman said, "Why don't you come back in a couple of hours, and I'll have a decision." Oh, God! I said a long prayer during the two-hour wait. I needed this job so badly!

I returned at three and the foreman told me I was hired; I would need to report for work on Monday, January 21. We shook hands, and my heart was pounding with excitement as I drove to a gas station to call Mary from a pay phone. Heck, she was just as happy as I was! I asked her if she'd meet me the next Monday at the Holiday Inn to help me find an apartment, and she said she would. We spent most of that day looking and finally found one on Bookcliff Avenue, just east of Mesa State College. We celebrated by going out for supper at a nice restaurant, and I begged her to allow me to have a couple glasses of wine. She reluctantly agreed but reminded me that she didn't want me to start drinking again. The next morning, I kissed her goodbye and she said she'd meet me at the apartment Thursday morning around eleven.

With a lot of help and two loaded pickups, I headed west on Thursday and met Mary at the apartment. By three o'clock, we had both pickups unloaded, and the next day, Mary and I got the place set up and stocked with all the necessities. My precious little angel worked her tail off! It was now a cozy-looking little home, thanks to her. And now we'd only be forty miles away from one another instead of 140! She spent the night, and it was a very romantic evening as we ate by candlelight.

Mary stayed till Sunday then wished me good luck at my new job. The next day, I drove to the refinery and went through orientation. My first week, filled with safety training and other classes, passed by quickly. I was so darned happy to have a job!

Mary couldn't come down the following weekend due to Maynard not feeling well. I was disappointed, but I understood. But what happened Saturday afternoon was simply shocking! I started thinking about having a cold beer. My heart began racing with that very thought, and Lord knows I tried to get it out of my mind, but I couldn't. What I did next was drive to the liquor store, where I bought a twelve pack of Budweiser.

My hands were trembling when I got back to the apartment and popped the tab on the can. As I put it to my lips, Becky's words from the VA ran through my mind: "An alcoholic cannot drink in moderation!" During the next few minutes, I drank the beer and felt guilty. Damn it! I'd worked so hard over the past seven months to stay away from booze, and here I sat—drinking beer! I drank three more during the afternoon, then I decided to shut it down. Dirty rotten son of a bitch!

On Sunday, I drank another four beers. I just couldn't make myself stay away from it. "Remember, Danny—alcohol is alcohol, whether it's 3.2 beer or a shot of 100-proof whiskey," Becky had said, and her words echoed through my mind. I felt so bad that I finally called Mary and told her what I'd done. She was so disappointed. "How *could* you, Danny?" "I don't know, honey, but I did." "I'll tell you for sure," she said, "I will not *put* up with you if you start drinking a lot. Do I make myself clear?" "Yes." During the workweek, I limited myself to just three beers per night, but once I'd gone through the first twelve pack, I bought another one. I was flirting with disaster.

When Mary came down on Saturday, we had a long talk about my drinking. She said, "I love you with all my heart, but if your drinking becomes a problem, as bad as it will hurt me, I'll walk away from our relationship." I told her that I understood, and that I wouldn't go back to heavy drinking. Who was I trying to bullshit? Her or me?

The months of February and March passed. At work, we repaired and replaced many worn-out valves and piping in the rundown refinery. Mary came down every weekend and always spent Saturday night with me. She started cooking at the apartment, and what a cook she was! Never in my life had I tasted such delicious beef roasts, and her fried chicken was beyond belief. She was just a very special lady, and I loved her with every ounce of my heart.

In late April, the refinery started producing three grades of gasoline, two grades of diesel, and jet fuel. My job involved unloading large metal rail tank cars filled with a thick, gooey product called "pitch." It required crawling under the rail cars and connecting a four-inch line to a fitting, then opening a valve and turning on a pump that transferred the pitch to the refinery. I also had to go on top of the car and unbolt a hatch in order to vent the car while the pitch was unloading. Some of the rail cars leaked the pitch onto the ground, and it was a mess crawling underneath them to hook up the fitting.

I was now on shift work: two weeks from 6:00 a.m. till 6:00 p.m. and two weeks from 6:00 p.m. till 6:00 a.m. The night shifts were horrible, because I got very little sleep in the daytime with all the noise around the apartment complex—doors slamming, vehicles starting up, traffic going by. I didn't drink any beer, either, because I got home at 6:30 a.m., and I couldn't drink in the evening before going in to work. The only way working these shifts was good was that I would get twenty hours of overtime, so I was making some damned good money.

On Friday, May 24, Mary and I drove to Meeker to attend Kila's high school graduation. At the school, Mom, Dad, Mary, and I walked up to the stands at the football field and took our seats. The band started playing and, off in the distance, we spotted the seniors marching towards us. I watched closely; I had my camera ready to start taking pictures. Finally, I saw Kila and started clicking away. She was wearing a pair of dark sunglasses and, of course, her cap and gown. I noticed she was carrying three long-stemmed roses.

She walked up to where Caryl was seated, handed her a rose, and gave her a big hug, then gave her grandma Gladys a rose and a hug. After Mom received her rose, she started crying, and tears started running down my cheeks, too! From Mom changing Kila's diapers when she was just a baby to this day, they'd formed a bond of love that went far beyond special.

The ceremony began and, after a few speeches, the handing out of diplomas started. When Kila's name was announced, my heart was filled with pride: she had graduated with honors and was presented with two scholarships. In closing remarks, the speaker announced that Kila had selected Mesa State College in Grand Junction to further her education.

When the ceremony was over, Mary and I made our way over to Caryl and I introduced them to each other. I then wrapped my arms around Caryl and whispered in her ear, "Thanks so much for doing such an outstanding job of raising Kila and making sure she got good grades." Her eyes filled with tears as she looked at me and said, "You're welcome." Dad, Mom, Mary, and I caught up with Kila and I gave her a long hug and congratulated her. "Dolly, I'm so glad you're going to Mesa State. You'll be able to come over and visit me!" "Yeah, Dad—I know!" she smiled.

We had a great time with my family that day, and I was glad that they had all met Mary.

Week after week, Mary and I continued our same schedule, where she came down nearly every weekend unless Maynard was having problems. Kila had gotten a job with the US Forest Service for the summer, and she was working on many of the trails in the high country around Meeker. She told me that she stopped at the North Fork campground at least a couple times a week to visit with Mom.

In late July, I called Mary and told her I was going to have to work on Saturday, so I wouldn't be home till about 6:30. She said she'd probably come down around four and do some cleaning in my apartment. When I pulled into the driveway that evening, I was disappointed that her car wasn't parked out front. I figured something had come up and she wouldn't be coming down after all.

After I got into the apartment, I quickly set my lunch pail down and hauled ass for the bathroom. I really had to pee! I had a full stream going when a voice just two feet from me said, "Need a hand?" Jesus Christ! I whipped around, pee flying everywhere! The shower curtain came back and there stood Mary in the tub, laughing so hard she could hardly stand up. I got myself zipped up. "You could've given me a heart attack!" "Once you started peeing, I just barely eased the shower curtain back before I said a word. I wanted to see your reaction. It was *priceless*, Danny!" she laughed. "Yeah, Mary—get your little butt out of the tub!" She'd hidden her car in the garage; it belonged to the apartment and I never used it. Yes, along with Mary's many talents, she was also a prankster!

Fall arrived, and in mid-September, Mary had to put Maynard in a nursing home. His health had gotten so bad that it was just too much for her to take care of him at home. I felt so sorry for him, and I knew it was a difficult time for both of them.

Hunting season opened shortly afterward, on Saturday, October 19, and I came from Grand Junction to spend the weekends with Mom and Dad till we filled our licenses. Dad, Chris, and I loaded up in Dad's pickup and headed for the Rienau Ranch at 5:30 a.m. Chris was fourteen now and was going to try to get his first deer. I'd borrowed a 25-06 for him to use because it didn't kick very hard. At 6:30, George, Austin, and Ross pulled through the wire gate where we were having coffee, waiting for daybreak. Soon, it was just barely light enough to see, and we drove back to our hunting country and walked to our usual sitting spots. Chris was so excited, and I was praying we'd see a buck within good shooting distance.

Just after sunup, we started seeing some deer—one beautiful four-point buck in the binoculars too far away to shoot. As usual, Chris checked out his papa many times in the binoculars. At eleven, we walked back to the picnic grounds and enjoyed Mom's fried chicken. George had seen a couple different herds of elk, but nothing was within shooting range. He said, "So, Chris—where's your buck?" He told George about seeing the four point and wished he'd been closer. George smiled and said, "Well, I'm certain you'll get one."

Late that afternoon, George pointed out an area where he'd been seeing quite a few deer in September and the first part of October, telling us we should sit there for the evening hunt. So Dad, Chris, and I hunkered down in some brush and waited. Just as the sun was going down, a doe and two-point buck walked out into a meadow about 100 yards from us. I whispered to Chris to get a good rest on a nearby tree limb. He moved very slowly, did as I told him, and I heard him flip the safety off. *Boom!* The buck went down. I whispered, "Put another shell in the chamber and let's wait a few minutes." I watched the downed buck in the binoculars and he wasn't moving. I said, "Put your rifle on safety, Chris, and we'll walk down to him." Moments later, we arrived at the buck. Chris had hit him behind the front shoulder and the deer was dead. As he took the shell out of the chamber, Dad patted him on the back and said, "You *did* it, Levi!" Chris smiled from ear to ear. I said, "That was a good shot, Son!" I was so proud of him! It was dark when we got to town and hung the buck in the shed where Caryl and the kids were living. Caryl and Amber came out and congratulated Chris while I skinned the deer. The next morning, I got a four-point buck, and the next weekend, we got Dad's cow. We thanked George for another great year and told him we'd see him and his boys again next year.

During the winter months, Kila stopped by the apartment several times and visited. She was really enjoying college and had decided to get

Chapter Fifteen: An Angel Named Mary

a degree in nursing, a profession that would be fortunate to have her. Maynard continued to go downhill; even though he was in a nursing home, he'd call Mary many times every day, insisting that she come to the facility four miles away. She'd drop whatever she was doing and go spend some time with him. Often, she'd just get home from being there and he'd call again, telling her to come back out. It wasn't unusual for her to make four trips back and forth a day.

Because of the physical limitations of Maynard's illness, he'd sometimes drop his electric razor when shaving and it would break. Mary had bought a total of three razors and usually had one at the repair shop in Grand Junction every week. One of his peculiarities was that he insisted that only Mary could do his laundry, and since their daughter, Sheri, lived in Farmington, Mary was the only one nearby to help with that and his care. It was all very difficult and sad, but—bless Mary's heart—even though it was often very hectic for her, she always tried to come down and spend time with me on the weekends.

In February, rumors started flying around the refinery that there was going to be a layoff. I'd been down that path before, so I figured it was just a matter of time before I was called in. Sure enough, at the end of March, I was laid off along with many others. Damn it! Now what? I got all my things from my locker, drove to my apartment, and called Mary to tell her what had happened. When she asked what I was going to do, I said, "I don't know, Mary. The way the economy is, there are no jobs to be found, especially one that will pay enough for me to stay in this apartment." She told me that Sparky, her brother, had a trailer in the same park where she lived. Since he was usually gone for long periods of time working at jobsites, she thought maybe he'd rent it out to me. It turned out that he was glad to rent the trailer—all I had to pay was the space rent and utilities. So over the next few days, Mary and I moved all my things there, and I'd now be living just 150 feet from her! That made me feel good, but I was so disappointed that I didn't have a job.

I filled out all the necessary paperwork at the Colorado State Unemployment Office so I could start getting my benefits, which I could draw at the maximum for six months. I knew that it was going to be next to

...d a job that paid what I'd been making. Over the next few ...illed out job applications time and again and turned in my resume where I could, but as time passed, I became more and more depressed. At the end of May, Mary insisted I plant a garden at my place and help her plant hers. She said it would help get my mind off not having a job, so I took her advice and planted potatoes, corn, and three tomato plants. I'd never had a garden in my life, and by June, I was so excited to see that things were starting to sprout! I watered it regularly and kept all the weeds pulled, and it was actually a lot of fun!

Danny and his children at Mary's home in Delta, Colorado. Kila, left, age nineteen; Amber, seventeen; and Chris, fifteen.
PHOTO BY MARY HARTWIG

About once a week, Mary would bring Maynard home for supper, and he always insisted that I come over and eat with them. We became good friends, and I'd drive out to the nursing home at least two mornings every week so we could sit outside and drink coffee, smoke, and visit. Another weekly routine was going to the job service center and checking the bulletin board for work: always nothing! The economy was in turmoil nationwide and was so bad that President Clinton had gotten a bill passed

Chapter Fifteen: An Angel Named Mary

that extended unemployment benefits for six months. God, was that ever great news for me!

The first of August, the kids came for a visit, and Mary and I showed them around both of our gardens. By now, the corn was tall, so I took several pictures of them standing in my little cornfield and some of them in Mary's flower garden. Later that month, Mom and Dad made the trip down to spend the night, and Mary went all-out for supper, with fried chicken, potatoes and gravy, salad, and corn on the cob—plus an apple pie! Everyone was too full to have dessert except for Dad, and he had a large piece. Since I only had one bed at Sparky's trailer, Mom and Dad stayed in Mary's spare bedroom and I spent the night with Mary.

Around ten, we hit the hay. About midnight, I woke up and started thinking about that apple pie and a glass of milk. I got out of bed, slipped on my Levis, and tiptoed down the hallway to the kitchen. I didn't need to turn on any lights, because Mary had left the light on above the stove.

I walked over to the counter where the pie had been sitting, but I saw that it was gone. I quietly opened the microwave door to look inside—Mary sometimes put leftover pie in there—but...no pie. Well, where in the hell was it? I just happened to glance in the sink and saw an empty Pyrex dish. Had Mary cut the pie in pieces and put them somewhere? I tiptoed back down the hallway to her bedroom, gently touched her on the shoulder, and whispered, "Where did you put the pie?" "It's sitting on the counter," she answered sleepily. "No, it isn't. The Pyrex plate is in the sink." "Are you sure?" she asked, not so sleepy now. "Yes." She got up, tiptoed to the kitchen, then returned in a few seconds. "Do you think your dad ate the entire rest of the pie?" she wondered. A little smile played over my lips as I answered, "Yes!" "Are you serious, Danny?" "Yes, honey. He said earlier that it was *really* good!" We chuckled to ourselves as we settled back into bed, quickly dropping off to sleep.

Early the next morning, it was time to settle the case of the missing pie. "Dad, did you get up last night and eat all of Mary's pie?" I asked. "Yip," he answered quickly. Mom said, "Oh my God, Don! You didn't!" "So you enjoyed my apple pie, Don?" Mary teased. "Yip, it was good to the very last crumb," he smiled, and we all had a good laugh. They stayed until noon, and we loaded them up with garden vegetables before they left. That evening, I called the kids to tell them about the apple pie. Kila couldn't stop laughing apa ate the whole pie?" Laughing back, I said, "He sure

Mid-October, I loaded my hunting and fishing gear, kissed Mary goodbye, and drove to Meeker to spend time with Mom and Dad. He and I had a ball fishing, and the next day, we started elk hunting, leaving the house at 5:30 a.m. Chris had decided to go with his good friend, Tim, whose dad had permission to hunt on private property. We were disappointed that he wouldn't be with us, but Dad and I were happy to make our traditional, first-day-of-the-season hunt together on the Rienau Ranch. As usual, we met George and his boys just before daybreak; by 7:30, Dad had gotten his cow and the Rienaus helped us load it.

By now, Dad and I had become very close friends with George, and he was a great guy. He stood about 5'9" and I guessed him to weigh around 155 pounds—just as tough as a boot and in tremendous shape. He'd served in a special forces unit during the Vietnam War and was extremely intelligent. A certified welder and mechanic, he could damn near disassemble a carburetor and put it back together blindfolded! He'd been raised on the ranch—he started driving a tractor when he was ten years old and shot his first buck the same year. There were many times when Dad and I would watch him as he loaded his hay wagon. He tossed around eighty-pound bales as if they were pillows from a bed! He put up several tons of hay on the ranch and also did contract haying for other ranchers in the valley.

I thought I was pretty handy with a hunting knife until I watched George. Hell, he could gut an elk in less than ten minutes and a deer in less than five! Seeing him in operation put Dad and me in a rare position: we were speechless! Yes, George Rienau was a special guy, and better yet, he treated both of us extremely well.

In November, the City of Delta called to interview me for a job I'd applied for, so I went down to their office. It went well and I had high hopes of being hired, but they called a few days later and said I didn't get the job. Damn!

Chapter Fifteen: An Angel Named Mary

During December, my depression worsened and I started drinking more. Mary quickly set some ground rules and told me she wouldn't allow any beer in her house. So one day, I decided to pour beer into a Pepsi can and took it with me to Mary's. We'd only talked a few minutes while sitting at her table when she said, "What's in the Pepsi can, Danny?" I could feel my face turning red. "Pepsi." "It doesn't smell like Pepsi," she replied. Then she reached over, picked up the can, and took a sniff. "Pepsi, my ass! You can take your beer and head back to your trailer! Don't try playing games with me, Danny. I'll bust you every time!" With my tail between my legs, I walked back to my trailer. My great plan had gone over like a snowball in hell!

Just before Christmas, Mary and I drove northeast of Delta to find a tree for her house. She spent hours decorating it, and it was beautiful. Sheri, her daughter, came up from Farmington, and Mary brought Maynard home for a Christmas dinner. I felt somewhat out of place, but I darn sure enjoyed the delicious meal—turkey with all the trimmings.

The new year of 1993 rolled in and late in January, I got a call from my uncle Harold, who'd gotten a job at a power plant located just south of Brush, Colorado, a town approximately eighty miles east of Denver. He'd worked on the construction phase of installing two gas turbines and a steam turbine, and he'd ended up getting a permanent job with the same company we'd worked for in Rifle during some outages. He told me the company was going to start construction on Unit II in March, and he thought he could get me a job with the construction contractor, Raytheon. He said, "If things go well for you on the construction phase, you might end up getting hired permanently in operations and maintenance." I thanked him for calling and told him I'd think it over. I walked over to Mary's to tell her about it. "I really don't want to move to eastern Colorado. We'd be hundreds of miles apart." "Danny, you might not have any choice," she said. "Your unemployment is going to run out soon, and then what?" "Yeah, I know...but I really don't want to move down there."

After thinking about it for a few days, I called Harold and told him I'd decided to try it out and asked if he could find a rental for me. He said that he and his wife were living in Fort Morgan, ten miles from Brush, and suggested it might be better if I lived there, too. I told him that it sounded like a good idea and that I'd talk to him about it again in February.

Damn, damn, damn! What a gut-wrenching decision! The old saying came into play: "Desperate people do desperate things." Mom and Dad felt it was the right decision; the kids didn't really have any opinion one way or the other, and I already knew how Mary felt.

By the third week of February, Harold had found a trailer house for me to rent and said I needed to report to Raytheon's office on March 8. I told him I'd arrive on Saturday, the sixth, and call him when I got there. The timing was right down to the wire, as I'd be getting my last unemployment check on Friday, the fifth. It wouldn't be enough to cover the first month's rent, damage deposit, and utility hookups, though, so I called Mom to borrow $350 from her.

Mary overheard the conversation and the next day, she walked up and handed me an envelope that had five $100 bills in it. "I know you'll pay me back," she said, "but I don't want you running short. I've decided to go down with you and spend two weeks helping you get set up." Tears streamed down my cheeks as I wrapped my arms around her. "Thanks so much, Mary!" What a precious lady she was! And so, just shy of forty-five years old, I was going to be moving a long way away from the woman I loved and starting off financially from less than zero!

We spent the next several days packing my stuff and loading it into my pickup. On Saturday morning, we pulled onto Highway 50 headed for Grand Junction. There was just one place for Mary to sit, which was right up against me. The rest of the seat had so much stuff sitting on it, from floor to ceiling, that there was no more room!

We soon hit I-70 heading east, and we talked as I sipped on a cup of coffee and Mary sipped on her iced tea. We passed by the towns of DeBeque, Parachute, Rifle, Silt, New Castle, Glenwood Springs, and No Name, then wound our way through quite a marvel: Glenwood Canyon. Sheer rock cliffs, seeming to touch the blue sky above, towered over us on both sides of the roadway. Between the cliffs ran the Colorado River, slicing its way alongside the interstate. The canyon was a thing of extreme beauty, and the highway built through it was an incredible engineering feat, with the westbound lanes built high over those of the eastbound.

Just east of the canyon's mouth was the small village of Eagle; miles later, we drove through Vail, where we saw skiers coming down the snow-covered slopes. Soon we started up Vail Pass; the highway was bare, but several feet of snow had been piled along the shoulder. The nearby mountains were covered in it—definitely a winter wonderland. After going over the pass, we went by the town of Dillon and Dillon Reservoir, a huge lake still frozen solid, pine trees all around. The next town was Silverthorne, and then on up another incline to Eisenhower Tunnel at 11,000 feet. Down the other side, we passed Georgetown and Idaho Springs; a few miles later, we rounded a corner to see the city of Denver. God, I was dreading driving through the heavy traffic.

Once in Denver, we started watching road signs, looking for I-76 East. There was a constant roar of traffic on both sides of us, idiots driving like bats out of hell, darting in and out, changing lanes. Mary and I knew we had to be getting close to the place to turn off of I-70, but—shit! I missed the turn! Nearly in a panic, I yelled, "Son of a bitch!" Mary said, "Calm down, Danny. Just take the next exit and we'll circle around." "Oh, shit, Mary! It'll probably take us thirty minutes to get back around in this goddamned traffic!" "Just calm down!" she demanded. Following her directions, we were on I-76 in about five minutes. "You shouldn't get so upset, Danny. You're going to give yourself a heart attack!" "Yeah," I muttered. She put a music cassette in the tape player as a distraction.

As we continued northeast on I-76, the landscape was nothing but flat ground. There were a few—just a very few—hills covered with low-growth sagebrush. The farmland was brown because it was March, so it made for a very desolate-looking area! Mile markers zipped by as we passed the towns of Hudson, Keenesburg, Roggen, and Wiggins till—finally—we pulled into the Safeway parking lot in Fort Morgan at 3:00 p.m. I looked down at my odometer and told Mary it had been a 350-mile trip, then called Harold from a nearby payphone. A few minutes later, we were following him to the trailer he'd found for me, located at 401 East Riverview Avenue.

Just after we got into the trailer, the owners showed up and introduced themselves. They were Arlan and Lisa Forbes, a young couple who owned some of the trailers in the park. Lisa's parents, Lou and Grace Davis, owned the park. I paid them the deposit and first month's rent, and they both said that if we needed any help to just ask. They lived in a house just a few hundred feet from the trailer.

By dark, we had the pickup unloaded, and Harold picked up some pizza while we unpacked. After we ate, he reminded me that he'd drop by the next morning to pick me up—we were going to his storage shed to get tools he was loaning me so I could work the construction job—then he said goodbye.

At eleven that night, Mary and I crawled into bed, exhausted. On Sunday, I got Harold's tools, then he, Mary, and I drove to the job site just south of Brush to look at it from a distance. I could see the masts of two large cranes sticking up. The power plant that was in operation was just a little bit south of where the new one was to be built.

We got up early Monday morning and I drove to Raytheon's office in Brush to fill out the necessary paperwork. I was assigned to the millwright division, and the lady at the office in downtown Brush gave me instructions on how to get to the construction trailer at the job site. After I arrived, I was given a short safety class then taken to what was called a "hooch," a small metal building where I could put my three tool boxes. I was introduced to the general foreman—Miles Slape—who took me around to introduce me to the guys I'd be working with. What a friendly bunch! Miles told me that by May 1, there'd be close to 100 employees on location: iron workers, pipe fitters, electricians, two groups of millwrights, and laborers. He also told me that we'd be working from 7:00 a.m. to 5:00 p.m., sometimes six days a week and sometimes five. The target date for completing the construction of the new power plant was October. I thanked him for all the information and got to work. Our group was going to be putting the gas turbine in place, along with all the support equipment, and helping to set a huge boiler.

The days quickly passed, and Mary did everything she could to make the trailer a nice home. While I was at work, she'd walk three blocks to KMart to buy supplies, including new curtains. She had fixed up some dinners for me and put them in the freezer so all I had to do was put them in the microwave when I got home from work. She also taught me how to make goulash, spaghetti, roasts, and lemon cakes.

On Saturday, March 20, the dreaded day had come for me to take her back to Delta. At 9:00 a.m., we pulled onto I-76 and began the long journey. I wasn't sure how many trips my old pickup would be able to make, as "Old Blue" would be nineteen years old come September. She had nearly 200,000 miles on her! I could only hope and pray that Old Blue would get me by for a couple more years, 'cause I damn sure couldn't afford to buy another vehicle!

We pulled into Mary's driveway around four that evening, both of us glad to get out of the truck. Damn, it was a long drive! The following morning, we held each other for nearly a solid minute then kissed goodbye. I tried to hold back the tears, but I couldn't. I wouldn't be seeing her again until May when Amber would be graduating. My precious little Mary said, "Please drive careful, Danny. You know how much I love you. Somehow, things will work out." Weakly, I replied, "I hope so."

At 5:00 Monday morning, the alarm clock went off. After drinking coffee and smoking a few cigarettes, I grabbed my lunch pail and headed for work, arriving at the job site at 6:30. I'd made up my mind: I was going to be the first one in our group to be at work each day and try as hard as I could to make an impression on the foreman, hoping he'd put in a good word for me at the power plant for a permanent job.

Days turned into weeks. Either I called Mary or she called me most every evening, and I called Mom and Dad every Sunday. I really looked forward to checking my mail, as my dear mom continued to write me two letters every week.

I talked to Miles the first part of May and got some days off—from the twentieth through the twenty-third—to go to Amber's graduation in Meeker. As the twentieth neared, my heart raced with excitement! I'd soon be holding Mary, going to Meeker to see Mom, Dad, and the kids, and get to see Amber graduate from high school!

The day I was leaving for Delta, I must have looked at my watch a hundred times while at work. At three o'clock, Miles walked up to me and said, "Why don't you get your ass out of here? I'll pay you as though you'd worked till five." I said, "Thanks, Miles!" and ran to the hooch, grabbed my lunch pail, and nearly ran all the way to my pickup.

By 4:30, I'd showered and shaved and was driving down I-76. I was so happy! I arrived at Mary's at eleven that night, and what a reunion we had! We were like a couple of high school kids, loving and kissing each other. She was all decked out in a beautiful short silk dress with high heels—so sexy! "Red," the brand of perfume she was wearing, had sent me into a frenzy!

Within a few minutes, we'd made our way to the bedroom, where Mary lit two large candles then turned out the light. I quickly got undressed and lay back on the king-size bed. I watched as she took off her dress and slip, and my heart started racing when she unsnapped and slung her bra at me! Teasingly, she very slowly started easing down her pink bikini panties. Once she wiggled out of them, she slipped off her high heels.

The combination of her stunning beauty, petite figure, and the fragrance of Red was almost too much! Striking a sexy pose, she whispered, "Did you miss me?" Fumbling for words, I muttered, "You *know* I did!" Taking her time, she crawled towards me. Finally, I was able to hold her in my arms. To taste her lips and caress her soft, warm body nearly set me on fire! With the candle flames flickering in the darkness, we made passionate love.

The next morning, we loaded our luggage in the pickup and headed for Meeker. My mind once again raced with excitement: it'd been several months since I'd seen my parents and the kids, and tomorrow would be a very special day—not only because my precious Bear was graduating, but also because she was valedictorian of the Class of '93.

We arrived at Mom and Dad's around noon and gave them big hugs. For me, it sort of felt like coming home on leave from the military. I was so glad to see them! At six that evening, Kila, Amber, and Chris arrived to have supper with us. While sitting at the table, I couldn't help noticing how quickly my kids had grown up. Kila, now twenty, and Amber, eighteen, were both such young ladies, and so pretty! Chris, now sixteen, stood 5'10" and was quite a handsome young man. His voice was becoming much deeper, too!

There were many stories told at the table. The kids teased their papa and the room was filled with laughter. I hated to see such a great time end, but it did around eight o'clock when the kids said to everyone, "See you tomorrow."

The following morning, we took our seats in the bleachers at the Meeker High School football field, and moments later the band started playing. In the distance, we could see the senior class marching towards us, and once they were close enough, I started snapping pictures of Amber. She walked into the stands and handed long-stemmed roses to Caryl, her grandma Gladys, Mom, and Mary. When Amber gave her speech, my heart was overflowing with pride! To add icing to the cake, she received three

Chapter Fifteen: An Angel Named Mary 253

scholarships, and it was announced that she would attend the University of Utah in the fall, seeking a degree in nursing.

When the ceremony was over, we caught up with Amber and congratulated her; later that afternoon, Mary and I told everyone goodbye and drove back to Delta. We'd both had a great time being with the entire family—so many memories made. That night, candles were lit, soft music was turned on, and we shared another romantic evening. We were two people so much in love who knew that, in just a few hours, we'd have to say goodbye.

Sunday morning, I started the pickup and pulled out of the driveway, dreading the long trip. At work the next morning, the job site was bustling with workers. Electricians installed thousands of feet of conduit and wiring and large cranes flew steel beams to iron workers where the steam turbine building was being constructed. Impact guns could be heard rattling as bolts were being tightened. Arcs and sparks flew beneath welders' helmets as they joined steel lines together. The constant sound of four-inch grinders beveling steel pipe could be heard.

Our group continued working on the gas turbine, which required a lot of precision work: installing the generator, load gear, turbine, rotor, lube oil pumps, cooling water pumps, valves, and other support equipment. I was shocked to find out that Miles' home was in Grand Junction, and that he and his wife, Judy, drove home every other weekend. I told him I'd be glad to pay for his fuel if he'd allow me to ride with them, and he agreed to it. Mary was ecstatic when I told her about this arrangement; Lady Luck seemed to be with us!

The summer months slowly passed. Every other Friday evening, Miles, Judy, and I would leave Fort Morgan around 5:30 and arrive at the City Market parking lot just off Highway 50 on the southeast side of Grand Junction around 11:00 p.m. Waiting for me in her classic 1977 Olds Cutlass would be my precious Mary, always sharply dressed and so pretty! Our time together was very short, as we'd have to meet Miles and Judy at 2:00 p.m. on Sunday afternoon, but we made the best of every single minute we had!

By the end of September, construction of Unit II's sixty-eight-megawatt power plant was nearly complete. September 28, Colorado Cogeneration, which operated and did the maintenance work on Unit I, called me in for an interview and gave me a written exam. I felt I'd done well, but it was still a long shot of getting the permanent job. They'd only be hiring seven guys.

The evening of September 30, Al, the maintenance supervisor, called and said, "How'd you like to go to work for our company?" "I can be there in fifteen minutes!" I exclaimed. Laughing, he replied, "Monday, October 4 at 8:00 a.m., will be fine." "Thanks so much, Al," I said. "The job means everything to me." "You're welcome, Danny. See you Monday!"

I quickly ran to the fridge and grabbed another beer; with trembling hands, I dialed Mary's number. "Hello?" "Honey, I got the job at the power plant!" I declared. "Really?!" "Yes, the maintenance supervisor just called. I got it!" "I'm so proud of you, Danny! Congratulations! When do you start?" "On Monday," I said, calming down a bit now. "I'm supposed to be at the plant at 8:00 a.m." We talked for nearly thirty minutes, and after we hung up, I called Mom and Dad. They were glad to hear the good news and congratulated me.

The following day, I informed Miles that I'd gotten the job and thanked him for all he'd done for me. I told my coworkers and said, "Tonight, the beer is on me!" At five, I loaded my toolboxes and drove to the bar. The sound of beer bottles clinking along with our chatter and laughter filled the place. After two hours I told everyone goodbye and headed for home.

The first several days at my new job, I was introduced to the guys I would be working with and welcomed by Jim Nolan, the plant manager. One of the employees, Sam Moots, gave me a walk-through of Unit I, which had two gas turbines and one steam turbine. He explained that Units I and II were classified as "peaking units": Public Service called to have the units started, and when demand dropped, they called to have them shut down. The units' function depended on when power need was at its greatest.

The plant was usually started up and shut down on a daily basis. It would be online by 7:30 a.m. and shut down around 10:00 p.m. The control room operators and field operators rotated shifts. The day shift worked 4:30 a.m. to 2:30 p.m.; the night shift worked 2:00 p.m. till midnight. The maintenance crew worked from six in the morning till two in the afternoon. Sam was extremely nice and went out of his way to show me how the plant was operated. My God, it was nearly overwhelming! There were pumps, motors, valves, and piping everywhere I looked. It was darn sure going to take some time to learn everything. Over the first week,

Chapter Fifteen: An Angel Named Mary 255

Jim Nolan gave several hours of classroom training on Unit II. He had an engineering degree and was very sharp and a great instructor! I found out that I would continue working with the maintenance crew till the first of November, then I would be trained to become a field operator. That would require me to be at work at 4:30 a.m. to learn start-up for a few weeks, then I would come in at 2:00 p.m. and work until midnight to learn the shutdown procedures.

On Saturday, October 9, I called Dad and told him I wouldn't be able to come elk hunting the following weekend—a huge disappointment for us both! "It just won't seem like hunting season without you, Son," he said. "I know, Dad," I replied sadly. After talking for several minutes, I told him and Mom goodbye. Tears flowed down my cheeks; this would be the first time we hadn't hunted together since 1956! Damn!

He ended up calling me on Saturday to let me know he'd gotten his cow elk. "Oh, Dad, I'm so happy for you!" "Just shithouse luck, my boy," was his reply. "I wish you would've been there, Son. I saw lots of nice bulls!" "I wish I would've been there, too, Dad. I'll be there next year, 'cause I'll have vacation time coming." I talked to him and Mom for several minutes and told them how much I loved them before saying goodbye.

Zzzzzz! What the hell is that awful noise? Oh....my alarm clock. It was 3:00 a.m. Damn, it was time to get up and go to work for my first day of training. It would take me a while to get used to this routine. Hello, coffeepot! I arrived at the plant a little past four to start my shift.

Weeks passed, and I gave it my best shot to learn all of the procedures needed to start up the units. I even studied them when I got home. In fact, I'd still be starting them up when I was lying in bed, trying to sleep!

When I was informed that I'd have four days off at Thanksgiving, I decided to make the long drive to Delta. I just had to see Mary. We spent the holiday with Maynard at the nursing home. His health continued to slip, but we managed to get him to laugh many times when I told him some funny stories. My three-day stay was filled with making love and treasuring every minute we had together. When I kissed her goodbye Sunday morning, it was a sad time; we had no idea when we'd see each other again.

Over Christmas, I decided not to go to Delta because of poor road conditions. I knew the two mountain passes would be treacherous, and there would be many accidents, as there always are that time of year. Phone conversations with Mary, Mom, Dad, and the kids were nice, but it was so depressing being alone on Christmas day.

CHAPTER SIXTEEN

Riding the Rails

BY FEBRUARY 1, 1994, I'd been promoted to field operator. Using a two-way radio, I communicated back and forth with the control room operator, opening and closing valves in the required sequence. Once the gas turbine and steam turbine were online, I was required to monitor temperatures, pressure levels, etc., and write down the readings. After a couple of hours of running time, it was scorching hot around the turbines—and even using earplugs, they were extremely loud!

Sitting at home one evening in mid-February, I saw a TV ad about Amtrak. Shit! You might say the proverbial light came on! I called the toll-free number and an agent informed me that eastbound train #6 ran on a daily basis from California to Chicago. Amongst its many stops was Fort Morgan! Westbound train #5 also ran on a daily basis and made the same stops. If on schedule, train #6 departed Grand Junction at 11:30 a.m. and arrived in Fort Morgan at 9:20 p.m.; train #5 departed Fort Morgan at 5:00 a.m. and arrived in Grand Junction at 4:00 p.m.

After I hung up with Amtrak, I called Mary. Was she ever happy to hear about the train schedules! Both of us had missed it somehow. We decided to make reservations for March 4 so she could be here for two weeks. Yipee! She left her car with good friends in Grand Junction—an old classmate, Bobbie, and her husband, Ben Bennett—who would take it back to the train station on the day Mary was to return.

The next two weeks passed at a snail's pace. Finally, March 4 arrived. I picked up a dozen red roses to give to Mary when she got off the train, and at 8:30, I drove to the unmanned depot and waited. A grain elevator, towering over 100 feet, stood nearby; it had been abandoned long ago. There were no other vehicles around, which created an eerie feeling. I went inside the train station. It was probably built in the thirties; old, but very well taken care of. The heels of my boots echoed as I walked across the smooth tile. Dark wooden benches were mounted on the walls in the waiting area. It appeared they were original, and their varnished oak still had a nice shine to it.

The ticket window was shut with an old sign that read, "Closed." I imagined that in its day, this train station had been bustling with travelers—especially during the time of World War II. I yelled, "Hey!" My voice echoed back to me.

I decided to move my pickup to the west side of the building to make it easier to watch for Amtrak's light. It was starting to get cold now, so I turned on the truck's heater, then turned on the radio. Time ticked away as I stared into the darkness down the tracks to the west. Ten o'clock, no train; eleven o'clock, no train. It'd been three long months since I'd seen Mary, and I yearned to hold her in my arms again.

Finally, at 11:30, I thought I could see a bright light that appeared to have a bobbing motion many miles away. I got out of the pickup when the light got a little closer. *Honk! Honk!* The train's horn blasted when it was about a mile away. I grabbed the roses and walked near the track. Just before the train got to me, the engineer sounded the horn again, and its loud blast made me jump! The brakes were put on and it came to a stop. I spotted where a conductor was stepping off one of the cars and rushed toward him as he placed a stepstool on the ground. I watched my Mary step off the train, beautiful in her pantsuit, jewelry, and high heels—hair coiffed just perfectly! I handed her the roses and with tears in her eyes, she whispered, "Thanks so much." We wrapped our arms around each other. Oh, my God—it felt so good to hold her! The conductor quickly put Mary's luggage and cooler on the concrete and, with a couple of blasts from the train's horn, Amtrak slowly chugged away.

Standing in the dim light, we held each other tight and shared a long, passionate kiss. Her Red perfume smelled so good; her lips sweet. What had been a lonely heart was now overflowing with love and happiness.

After we arrived at the trailer, Mary talked about the trip. She said it was very scenic, especially the Gore mountain range where the train ran parallel with the Colorado River. She saw many bald eagles perched in the tops of the lofty pines along the river, looking for a meal out of a trout or two. The rugged canyon just below Granby was beautiful with its towering, sheer cliffs; and many times, they had to pull over on the siding to allow coal trains to pass. We talked till nearly one then turned in. She was exhausted from the nearly twelve-hour trip.

During Mary's stay, I cut back on my beer drinking. I didn't want our relationship to end, and I knew that drinking was a sore spot! But—my, oh my—it was heaven coming home from work and having her greet me at the door! A kiss, delicious home-cooked meals, and a beautiful woman who would lie next to me in bed at night! I couldn't ask for more...

The days passed quickly, and on March 19, we drove to the train station for Mary's return to Grand Junction. After a long kiss goodbye, the train's horn sounded two long blasts, then it started moving. It was a sad time, as I wouldn't see her again for over two months.

I began to question if being in Fort Morgan was worth it, but I knew I couldn't find a job on the Western Slope that paid as well, or that had even close to the same benefits I was receiving. I was forty-six years old, so I resigned myself to the fact that I had to keep this job till I could find something comparable in the Junction area.

Time marched on, and at the end of April, Caryl called to say that Chris had a track meet in Colorado Springs on May 7, the same day that Kila was graduating with a nursing degree from Mesa State. She wanted to know if I would go to Chris's track meet, then she would attend Kila's graduation, and I agreed.

Gosh, how Chris had grown! I hadn't seen him for nearly a year, since Amber's graduation last May. Standing six feet, he was long and lean, weighing around 160 pounds. He was a muscular kid and ran a 1600-meter race effortlessly, those legs moving in long, smooth strides. He was a junior in high school now and placed fourth in his event, even though he had competed against more experienced athletes from bigger schools.

I had four days off over the Fourth of July, so I picked Mary up in Delta to drive to Meeker that Saturday. I had seen Chris just a few months earlier, but it had been a long time since I'd seen everyone else! Later, we had a family gathering at the Sleepy Cat Lodge. The Wixes, who still owned the lodge, had replaced the burned-out structure with a beautiful new establishment, and we enjoyed ourselves into the evening with good food and lots of jokes!

Danny and Mary at Wix's newly built Sleepy Cat Lodge.
PHOTO BY PHILLIP MORLAN

We returned to Delta on Sunday and attended the holiday parade in Paonia Monday morning, then Mary rode back with me to Fort Morgan to spend a week. The trip and Mary's stay with me did wonders to mend the loneliness that had been building.

October soon rolled around, and I was winding my way through Glenwood Canyon in Old Blue, who had just turned twenty! She still drove well and was dependable. I was on my way to Mary's, and she would return to Meeker with me to spend some time with Mom while Dad and I went elk hunting; later, she'd come back to Fort Morgan with me for a few weeks. I had paid vacation, and I didn't have to be back at work till the twenty-fourth of October! Damn, I was happy!

Friday morning, I decided to go fishing with a good friend of Dad's, Ferrell Lieber. Dad was going for his annual physical with the VA in Grand Junction, so he couldn't come with us. Ferrell and I had a great time, catching our limits of trout as we worked our way up the White River. We decided to have lunch around two, and after a sandwich, Ferrell reached into a cupboard and pulled out a half-gallon of Wild Turkey. "We'd better have a few drinks to celebrate!" he declared. I told him I'd rather not. "I'm really not that crazy about whiskey," I said. "Ah, hell—I'll mix you a tall one with ice and coke, and you'll enjoy it." I reluctantly agreed, and four tall ones later, we were driving down the road back to Meeker.

As I unloaded my gear, Mary and Mom came out to see if we'd caught any trout. "You'd better believe it!" I said, and I dumped the trout out on the grass. Mary knelt down by me as I arranged the fish and told her about my day. We divided the fish and Ferrell got ready to leave, wishing me luck on the next day's hunt.

While I rinsed the fish in the sink, Mary whispered, "When you're finished, I want to talk to you in the bedroom." I had no idea what it was about, and moments later, we met in the bedroom and she closed the door. "Danny, our relationship is over!" "Why?" I was bewildered. "Because I can smell whiskey on your breath!" she declared. "God, Mary—I only had a few drinks!" I said defensively. "I've warned you for years about your drinking," she continued, "and I've *had* it! We're *done*. I won't, and I can't, live this way. Go get help—find some AA meetings! I'll stay here till you and your Dad are done hunting, then you can take me home." Mary was finished, and I was stunned. But she was right: she *had* warned me over and over about my drinking. But I was still shocked.

Dad arrived just minutes later from Grand Junction, and he and I sat and visited for a long while about how the day had gone for both of us. Mary and Mom fried chicken in the kitchen. It was as though everything was normal—but it *wasn't*! After we all turned in around ten, there were no words spoken between Mary and me. We were both so upset that neither of us really got any sleep.

In the morning, Dad and I sat and drank coffee. Dad was Dad, and he was just thrilled that it was opening day of elk season! We hunted on the Rienau Ranch again, where I shot a four-point bull, and George and Austin helped us load it. Driving back to Meeker, I reached over and slapped him on the shoulder, saying, "I love you, Dad!" "I love you, too, Son, and I don't know what I'd do without you. It was just the physical *shits* not having you here last year!" Good ol' Dad.

Back home, my stomach was tied in knots. That night, I begged Mary for one last chance, but she was adamant. "You've run out of chances, Danny! Now go to sleep!" I tossed and turned the entire night: I felt so shattered. I got up at 3:30 to brew coffee, and Dad came in the kitchen about four. At 5:30 we drove to the ranch, where Dad shot a cow elk. At least it had been a successful hunting season!

Monday morning arrived all too soon, and we said goodbye to Mom and Dad and began the long drive to Delta. Not a word was spoken. Mary told me I could stay the night, so I did, and in the morning, she walked me to my pickup. "I'll always love you, Mary." Tears streamed down her cheeks as she replied, "Drive careful, Danny, and go to an AA meeting in Fort Morgan."

By the time I stopped for gas near Dillon Reservoir, I had cried all I could and dry heaves had set in. I was just a fucking zombie, so much so that I was concerned that I couldn't make the trip safely at this point. I still had to drive over the Divide, through the pounding Denver traffic, and another seventy-five miles to Fort Morgan!

I pulled a cold beer from the cooler and lit a cigarette. I leaned across the hood, staring at the lake and the beautiful mountains around me. If I no longer had Mary in my life, maybe it would be best if I moved back to Meeker. I mean, I hated shift work, I rarely saw my kids, and I only saw Mom and Dad a few times a year. I managed to get back in the pickup and continue the long, agonizing drive, and I was so relieved to pull into my driveway—physically and emotionally drained!

The next day, I kept thinking about getting boxes to begin packing. "But then what?" I thought. "No job, and you'll be flat-ass broke again! Use your head, Danny! You *can't* quit your job!" On Thursday, I drank beer, listened to the radio, and dwelled on losing Mary. While I tossed and turned in my bed that night, half drunk, I decided that the next day, I would check around town to find out where AA meetings were held. By noon the next day, I found the meeting place. There were several cars in the parking lot, so I stopped to get a schedule. A nice gentleman got up from the meeting that was being held and greeted me. After we stepped outside, he gave me the meeting times and I left for home to drink beer the rest of the day.

Chapter Sixteen: RIDING THE RAILS

Saturday came, and I continued drinking. I was desperate. I tried to talk myself into giving it up and going to the meetings, but by midnight, I'd probably consumed eighteen beers; the trash was overflowing with empties! Booze virtually owned my soul! Could I—would I—give it up?

Sunday morning I got up around seven, my head throbbing. I got the coffeepot going and poured myself a tall glass of tomato juice, hoping it would help. While drinking coffee and sipping on my second glass of tomato juice, I thought about no longer having Mary in my life. The phone didn't ring, and it wasn't going to, and I had nobody to blame but myself. "Damn it!" I said to no one in particular. "I'm going to try one more time to give it up!" I went to the fridge, took out nearly a case of Budweiser, and walked out the front door to the dumpster. *Boom!* It echoed when it hit.

Monday morning, my alarm clock went off at three and it was time to go back to work. After mulling it over all day, I was determined to go to my first AA meeting that evening. I was welcomed there by twelve members, and when it was my turn to speak, I gave them a brief summary of my problem. The person who chaired the meeting gave me an AA book and some other literature after the meeting and suggested I get a sponsor as soon as possible—someone who I could call and talk to when I found myself wanting a drink. He gave me the number of a guy who lived in Brush.

The next evening, I called the sponsor. He said, "I no longer consider sponsoring anyone till they've shown they're really serious about quitting. I want you to go to ninety meetings in the next ninety days—even if that means going to two meetings a day—and during that ninety days, not one sip of alcohol! Good luck and goodnight!" *Click!* The phone went dead. I thought, "Boy, that was a nice howdy-do!" But those words of his—"ninety days, ninety meetings, no alcohol"—kept ringing in my ears. Shit, I'd only gone two days without booze, and I wanted a beer so damn bad I could hardly stand it!

Over the next two weeks, I attended meetings every evening except on Saturday nights, when they didn't have one. In my free time at home, I started reading the AA book, committing to memory the twelve steps and repeating them to myself over and over.

Although Mom, Dad, and the kids knew why Mary and I had broken up, I decided not to tell them I was trying to give up alcohol again, because I didn't want them to be disappointed if I failed. I didn't share what was going on with any of my coworkers, either; I just didn't want it known that I was an alcoholic.

Going through thirty days without alcohol was a pure, living hell! I came so close to pulling into the liquor store on the way home from work—but I didn't. The withdrawals were terrible, way worse than I'd experienced when I went through the VA's program. Why? I really didn't know. What I *did* know was that coming home to a lonely trailer every afternoon and not being able to at least talk to Mary on the phone was taking a huge toll on me. I began to doubt if I could stay off alcohol, entertaining once again the idea of packing up and moving to Meeker.

Back on night shift, I now attended AA meetings at noon. By now, I'd become friends with the chair of the meeting and another guy, Louie, who agreed to be my sponsor. The god-awful craving for a drink continued to haunt and taunt me; I even had dreams about drinking and was so relieved when I woke up, realizing it was just a dream! I missed Mary more than I could possibly put into words. Just to hold her in my arms again, or to hear her voice on the phone, would be heaven.

The next several weeks passed. I felt terrible, both physically and mentally, and I was barely functional. Every night I'd kneel at my bedside and pray: "Please God, give me the strength, knowledge, wisdom, and will power to make it through another day without drinking!"

Just before Christmas, I sent Mary a card, hoping I'd get one back. On the twenty-third, I opened the mailbox, and there was a card from Mom and Dad *and* one from Mary! She wrote quite a lot in her note, mostly about things going on in her life, but there was no mention of us getting back together. I finally decided to call her, unsure of how the conversation would go. But it was so nice to hear her voice! We talked for nearly thirty minutes, then I told her about my progress with AA and that it had been over sixty days since I'd had a drink. "I'm proud of you, Danny. At least that's a good start," she said. "I love you, Mary," I continued. "Is there any chance we could get back together?" After a long pause, she said, "I'll always care about you, Danny, but please don't count on us getting back together. Take care of yourself. I hope you continue going to AA meetings." My eyes filled as I said goodbye and hung up the phone. Damn, that hurt!

January 1995 came. It was bitter cold now and it snowed frequently. I continued going to AA meetings every day, and if my days off fell on weekdays, I went to both the noon and evening meetings. It helped to hear the stories other members told of their struggles. In so many cases, alcohol had ruined their lives; some had been fired from their jobs, many had gotten divorces. As one guy put it, "Booze shows no mercy. It'll take your wife, kids, home, job, money, and put you six feet under at a young age!" At the evening meeting on January 23, my sponsor presented me with a small medallion engraved with "Ninety Days." With God's help, I'd achieved ninety days of sobriety!

"Speech! Speech!" some of the members yelled. I gave a short talk, telling them that making it ninety days without a drink was extremely gratifying, but I'd been down the same road in 1990 and failed. At the end, I said, "Maybe this time I *won't* fail."

At home, I stared at the medallion, replaying the past three months where I didn't think I could make it another minute without a drink. The question still loomed: Who would win? Me, or my buddy Mr. Alcohol?

Weeks passed and every day, every night, every conscious thought was a struggle. How I managed to function at work—starting up or shutting down the units—baffled me. Most mornings when the alarm clock went off, I stumbled towards the coffeepot, so tired from lack of sleep. Sweet memories of Mary wafted in and out of my mind. I knew I'd never find another like her, and I didn't want to settle for second best. Somehow, some way, I had to get her back. On the night of March 4, and with hands trembling, I picked up the phone and called her one more time, just to ask if she'd consider giving me one last chance.

"Hello?" Just hearing her voice gave me butterflies! "Hi, Mary. It's Danny!" We traded a few pleasantries then I launched into my reason for calling. "I just wanted to let you know I'm still attending AA meetings, and I haven't had one drink since October twenty-second!" "I'm really proud of you, Danny," she encouraged. "It's so good to hear your voice, Mary," I said. "It's good to hear yours, too," she returned. With a huge lump in my throat, heart pounding, I asked, "Is there any way you'd consider giving me one last chance?" There was only silence, then I could hear her crying. Tears streamed from my eyes—it just hurt so much to hear her sobbing. "Please don't cry, Mary," I pleaded. "I've always loved you, Danny, and I always will. I'm just not sure you'll stay away from alcohol." "I promise I'll never let you down if you give me one more chance to prove it." A long pause, then, "Okay, honey. I'll give you one final chance. But you'd better not let me down." "I won't, Mary, I promise!" My heart exploded, I was so happy! We talked for nearly an hour, and she agreed to come on the train for a visit March twenty-fourth. After we hung up, I said, over and over, "Thank you! Thank you!"

The day soon came, and I made a stop at the flower shop to pick up a dozen "Fire and Ice" roses. In just a few hours, I'd be giving them to my Mary! I arrived at the train station at nine and stared into the darkness. At ten, I spotted the light miles away. My heart began racing and my hands started shaking. Five long months of no Mary, battling alcoholism, and she was almost here!

The train arrived and Mary stepped off—a beautiful angel. We hugged and cried, then kissed. Amtrak blasted its horn, but we kept on kissing; holding each other after so many months was just such pure heaven!

We left the depot and arrived at my trailer. "My, my," Mary said softly. "Do I see rose petals on the sidewalk and steps?" "Yes, and they don't end there!" I said. The petals led to the bedroom, where we kissed lustily and enjoyed each other over the next several hours. It was a virtual wave of love so powerful that it was as though we'd never been apart.

Over the next few weeks, things couldn't have been better between us. Mary attended three AA meetings with me and I introduced her to several of the members and my sponsor, Louie. But her departure time soon arrived and, on April 14, she boarded the train. This time, while waving goodbye, I had a big smile on my face.

Over the winter, Chris trained heavily for track, running nearly every day, and the payoff was that he often placed first in the 1600-meter run. Some newspapers reported him as being one of the premier runners in the Class AAA division, and some had him ranked in the top five in the state. I was so proud of him!

I'd scheduled time off to attend the district track meet in Rifle on May 6. Since most of the immediate family was attending, it would be a little bit of a reunion, too. On the fifth, I drove to Delta, then the next day, Mary and I drove to Rifle's track and field venue. I soon spotted Mom and

Dad pulling up and went to greet them.

When I got to their car, Dad rolled down his window. He looked distraught and said, "I've got bad news, Son." My heart sank: what could it be? "My little partner is gone," he continued. I immediately knew he was talking about his dog, Pepper. "Oh no, Dad! What happened?" "She hadn't been feeling well the past couple of days, and when I was lacing up my boots this morning, she curled up just inches from my feet and passed away." Putting my hand on his shoulder, I said, "Oh, Dad—I'm so sorry!" He removed his sunglasses to wipe away the tears, then Mom cried, "We had Pepper for thirteen years!" It was a sad moment, as everyone knew what a special bond there was between Dad and his dog. "Where is Pepper now?" I asked. "I wrapped her in a towel and put her in a box to take to Ollie's place in Lion's Canyon. I'll bury her tomorrow." "You guys should've stayed home," I asserted. "Oh, we wanted to support Levi. This'll be the last time we'll ever see him run!" Since Chris was in his senior year, it would be his last high school competition in track.

After a long wait, the time neared for the 1600-meter run. I grabbed my camera and headed down trackside, watching Chris as he warmed up. He now stood at 6'1" and had a healthy muscle weight of 165 pounds. The calf muscles in his legs bulged from all the training he had done.

The runners took their positions and I started snapping pictures. *Pow!* The gun went off and about halfway, I could see that Chris was in third place. When they rounded the three-quarter point, he started gaining on the guys in front of him. He blew by the guy in second place and narrowly missed passing the guy in first before crossing the finish line. He waited just a little too long before making his move, but placing second meant that he qualified for the state meet.

Mary and I soon bid everyone goodbye to start our journey back to Delta. We'd return to Meeker in just a few weeks for Chris's graduation, so we would visit more with the family then. The next morning, I drove back to Fort Morgan, and the following Saturday, I drove to Jeffco Field in Denver to watch Chris in the state track meet. I found Caryl, Amber, and Kila in the stands and said hello to them, then left to go down trackside so I could take pictures.

After opening ceremonies and many other competitions, the "best of the best" in the 1600-meter run walked onto the track, shook hands, then took their positions. *Pow!* The runners were on their way, but there was an immediate log jam and Chris was hung up in it, costing him valuable seconds. When they rounded the final turn, he made a move and passed the guy who had beaten him in Rifle. Then, with a hundred meters to go, he was closing in on the leaders but fell short by just a few seconds, placing sixth. It was still one hell of an achievement that garnered a medal, and we were all very proud of him!

Five days later, Mary and I drove from Delta to attend Chris's graduation. We picked up Mom and Dad and went to the high school football field, and as we walked up its steep stairs, I held Mom's hand. She stopped about halfway and said, "I need to get my breath, Son." "That's fine, Mom," I said. "I don't want you to overdo it!" She'd had her share of problems: two endoscopy procedures done over the past two years plus dealing with osteoporosis. She was just sixty-six, and her health wasn't very good.

At ten, the ceremony began. Chris gave roses to Caryl, his grandmothers, and Mary. When he received his diploma, they announced that he was graduating with honors and was being awarded three scholarships. His plan was to attend Colorado State University and get a doctorate in psychology.

After the ceremony, Dad greeted Chris with "You did it, Levi!" Laughing, Chris replied, "Yeah, Papa. They decided to send me on my way!" "Son, when you become a psychiatrist, can I come lay on your couch and discuss my problems?" I asked. He busted out laughing as he replied, "Sure!" After an evening celebrating Chris's achievements, Mary and I drove back to Fort Morgan the next morning, and she spent the week with me before returning to Grand Junction.

In July, Dad and I went on our first fishing trip in three years on private land by the White River. The bank along this area was covered in cottonwoods and willows, and the only sound heard was that of slow-moving water. The best of it was that the landowner, Veryl Cleverley, was a friend of Dad's, and we had his blessings in fishing the private stretch.

Dad was feeling pretty sassy; he was up and down the steep riverbank with little problem. "Not bad for a guy that's nearly seventy-one, eh?" he said proudly. I was panting hard and replied, "Hell no, Dad—I seriously doubt if I'll be walking up a hill like this when I'm seventy-one!" We had a great afternoon, talking and laughing, with Dad proudly telling me about his new dog—Spud—that he'd gotten from the pound.

In the fall, I drove to Kila's outdoor wedding just west of Grand Junction, where she was marrying Dan Settles. A month later, in October, I spent time with Mom and Dad for our annual elk hunt, where we garnered plenty of meat for their freezer. Back in Fort Morgan, Louie called to say he'd scheduled a meeting for the twenty-first to celebrate my one year of sobriety. "You *are* still sober, aren't you?" he asked. "I'd *better* be," I laughed. "Mary's sitting here, right on my couch!" "Bring her with you," he said.

When we got to the meeting on Saturday, there was a big cake with my name on it and one candle. During the meeting, I was called to the front of the room and given a one-year medallion. Chills ran up my spine, as there was no doubt in my mind that this year of sobriety was one of the greatest achievements of my life!

Everyone called for a speech, so I pointed towards Mary and said, "*She's* the one who convinced me to quit, by putting a size five-and-a-half shoe on my butt!" Everyone laughed. "That's why—along with the grace of God, Louie, and reaching for will power that I didn't think I had—I've been able to stay away from booze for the past year." Then I added, "In reality, it's just *one* year. I know I must *never* let my guard down, because alcohol is a sneaky son of a gun!" I started to get choked up then. "I'd like to tell all of you this: it's only because of an angel named Mary that I finally decided to give up booze."

CHAPTER SEVENTEEN

Passages

ON SUNDAY, MARY'S SISTER, CAROLYN, called to say that their mom was very ill and probably wouldn't live much longer. Mary told her she'd call Amtrak and board the train the next day. On Wednesday, Mary called me to say that her mom had passed away. "And at least she won't have to suffer the indignity any longer!" Her mom had lived with Alzheimer's for several years.

It was November, and cold weather was now the norm. I'd become good friends with a few of the guys at work—Gary Arneson and Sam Moots, who were control room operators, in particular. But I would call Rob Lassiter, another guy I worked with, my very best friend. He and his wife, Carla, lived in Brush with their two kids, and we got together twice a month to play cards. They helped me get through the hard times of living in Fort Morgan, when boredom and loneliness nearly got the best of me.

Now 1996, Mary continued to visit via Amtrak over the next several months and stayed as long as she could. Then April finally arrived, and while I was at work on the night shift, I got notice from the control room operator that I had a phone call. My heart sank: I knew something bad had happened.

It was Dad. He said that he'd found Mom at 9:30 that night, lying unconscious on the bedroom floor. He'd called the ambulance, and she was being airlifted by Flight for Life to Grand Junction. "I'm really worried that she's not going to make it, Son," he said. "Oh God, Dad! Let's pray that she'll be alright. I'll meet you at St. Mary's tomorrow, okay?"

At the end of my shift, with zero sleep, I pulled onto I-76 at daybreak, praying that Mom would make it. Mary met me at the hospital and told me that Mom was in intensive care: she was still alive! We met Dad, Donna, Kila, and Caryl in a waiting area. "How's Mom?" I hurriedly asked. "She's in pretty bad shape," Dad replied. He and I were allowed to go into her room; she was hooked up to various tubes and sensors and was on oxygen. She was awake and greeted me. My eyes welled up with tears as I gently squeezed her hand. "Hi, Mom. How're you feeling?" "Not so good," she answered.

Over the next few days, we literally lived at the hospital. Gradually, Mom got better and better—good enough that the doctors planned to release her. They said she had several problems, and the biggest one was her breathing. She had to use oxygen from now on, plus take several prescriptions. We loaded her into the car and Dad took her home. She was okay for the time being, as long as she took her medications and used oxygen.

Shortly afterward, in May, Kila called to say that she'd had a baby boy! His name was Jayce, and a week later, Mary and I went to Grand Junction to see him. What a precious little guy! My time was short, as I'd already used up my vacation days, so Mary and I drove back to Fort Morgan the next day. She was spending two weeks with me!

The summer passed. I no longer went to AA meetings and I stopped having such a craving for alcohol. I felt as though I had enough will power to never have a drink again! "If the temptation ever arises," I told myself, "I'll immediately go back to AA meetings."

The first of September Mary called, crying. She had been visiting with Maynard in the nursing home, and he told her he no longer wanted to live. He said he'd been thinking about a way to end his life, but any scenario he came up with made him afraid the staff there would find him too soon and bring him back to life. His solution was to ask Mary to bring him a pistol so he could shoot himself. She told him she couldn't do that; she'd be sent to jail if she did! But he was determined to find a way.

He had a good case: he was tired of lying in his own shit, waiting for someone to come help him out of bed and into the shower, to change his clothes and bedding. He said, "Mary, you *have* to help me end it—you just have to!" I felt so bad for her and Maynard, but what could we do? "There's really nothing I *can* do except go spend more time with him," Mary decided. After an hour of discussion, we said goodbye.

What a terrible time! Besides countless trips to the nursing home over the years and taking care of Maynard's clothes and various other needs, Mary visited there every other Sunday to play the piano and sing for him and the other residents. During that time, she'd watched him wither away. He was now just a skeleton because of Huntington's disease.

A few weeks later, Mary called again, crying so hard that she could barely talk. She had just come from a meeting with Maynard and his doctor, and Maynard was now determined to end his life by starving to death! "Oh, my God, Mary!" I responded. "He can't take it anymore, Danny!" she said. "He's tired of fighting. The doctor said he understood and would keep him as comfortable as possible."

The days dragged by. All I could think of was Mary and their daughter, Sheri, waiting by Maynard's bed. She called each evening to give me an update. The doctors had prescribed liquid morphine for Maynard, administered on his tongue by the drop. The nurses didn't agree with Maynard's decision to end his life and balked at helping him in any way.

Nine days after Maynard had made his decision, Mary called to say that he had passed. Interment was a few days later in Paonia, Colorado, where he was buried next to Mary's mom. Because many of their friends and relatives were unaware of our relationship, we both thought that it would be best if I didn't attend the funeral.

Weeks later, on October 16, I drove to Meeker for hunting season. When I walked through Mom and Dad's front door, Mom was lying on the couch, oxygen attached to her face. With her spirits high, she was happy to see me. Dad was wound up about hunting season and this year, there were new hunting regulations that I completely agreed with: a bull elk had to have at least four points on one antler to be considered "legal." Over time, this would help the elk repopulate, as they had suffered tremendously from being over-hunted.

Dad and I took advantage of our time together, going fishing and hunting. We hunted on Rienau's land again and bagged a five-point bull and a cow. I spent time with Mom, too, watching her write letters on a clipboard that she rested on drawn-up legs as she'd lie on the couch. She also insisted on cooking meals while I was there, even though I was sure she didn't feel like it. When I left the following Wednesday, I knelt down near the couch and gave her a kiss goodbye, then hugged Dad.

I drove to Delta to spend some quiet time with Mary, as she was still recuperating from Maynard's passing. A few days later, when I drove back to Fort Morgan, Old Blue began losing power up the long passes. I made

Chapter Seventeen: PASSAGES

it home, but when I pulled into my driveway, I knew it was the last trip for the old pickup! I drove to the local dealership the following weekend and bought a new V-6 Pontiac Grand Prix. It was dependable, got good gas mileage—*and* it smelled like "new car"! I was happy!

Mary made several trips to visit after Maynard passed. Even though she wasn't tied to Delta any longer, her home was paid for and she didn't want to rent it, nor did she want to leave it vacant for a long period of time. Our long-distance relationship was hard, but we loved each other and wanted to continue to make it work. And so it was decided that she would still visit me via Amtrak when she could.

We were into 1997 now, and April soon rolled around. Late on the twenty-third, at eleven, the control room operator called me to say I had a phone call. It was ironic to me that I was in the very same place I'd been a year ago when I received bad news! I ran down the two flights of stairs to the phone, fearing the worst. "Son, the ambulance just picked up your mom and took her to the hospital," Dad said. "She's in bad shape again. You'd better come as soon as you can." "Are you alright, Dad?" I asked. "Yeah, I'm fine, Son." "I'll leave at daybreak," I said.

The control room operator told me to go on: he'd have the other field operator handle things. I was a nervous wreck as I drove the ten miles home to pack a bag and call Mary. She'd meet me in Rifle at the Rusty Cannon Motel the next morning and then we'd drive to Meeker. I brewed coffee, sat down, and started chain smoking. Then the tears came: the thought of losing Mom was overwhelming!

I stayed up all night, loaded the car, then left at daybreak. I felt as though I was in a trance during the long drive. Before I knew it, I pulled into the motel's parking lot—and there was Mary, waiting for me! We got to Pioneers Hospital at noon and met with Dad, Kila, Caryl, and a few of Mom's relatives. Dad said Mom wasn't doing well, so Mary and I walked to her room. She looked weak, lying there with so many things hooked up to her, but she recognized us and said hi. I held her hand and told her I loved her. "I love you, too, Son. I'm glad you're here." She asked if my new car was in the parking lot! I told her it was, and she wanted me to pull it up near her window so she could see it. I smiled and said, "Sure, Mom," then ran out to bring the car closer. When I went back to her room, she said, "Son, it's a beautiful car!" We continued to talk. Mary told Mom that she loved her, and Mom closed her eyes to drift off to sleep.

Mary and I left to check into a room at the White River Inn, then we went back to the hospital. By evening, more of the immediate family had arrived, including my sister and Amber, Chris, and one of Mom's brothers, Fenton.

The following morning we met with Mom's doctor, and he said that Mom's body was shutting down: it was just a matter of time before she passed. This was news that we took extremely hard. It was just so difficult to accept that the family's matriarch would no longer be here! A long day of waiting was ahead of us as Mom slipped in and out of consciousness. At two in the afternoon, I went to her room by myself. She appeared to be sleeping, so I slid a chair close to her bed, sat down, and held her hand, looking at this woman who had reared me. Tears streamed down my cheeks as I softly said, "I love you, Mom." To my surprise, she replied, "I love you, too, Son," without opening her eyes. She never spoke another word after that.

While walking back to the lobby, I thought I was going to faint. I told the rest of the family what had happened, wiping the tears as they came. We had supper at a nearby restaurant, then Dad announced that he was going home. "I'm just pooped," he said. I told him we'd see him the next day, and we left shortly afterward to go to our motel. Donna spent the night with Mom.

The next morning, I was sitting outside the motel room, smoking and drinking coffee, when I heard the phone ring. A moment later, Mary came out, placed her hand on my shoulder, and said, "Donna just called: your mom passed away." I slumped over and started crying, but I soon regained my composure and we decided to drive to Dad's. He told me that Mom had been in quite a bit of pain over the past year. "She's better off, Son," he comforted. "You just don't know how much she's suffered." Mary and I went back to the hospital to see Mom; it would be my last time, as she was going to be cremated.

When we arrived, everyone was still there. We went to Mom's room, where I placed my hands on hers. "Tomorrow would've been Mom and Dad's fiftieth wedding anniversary," I said, choking up. I kissed Mom on the forehead and said goodbye. "I'll always love you, Mom."

Chapter Seventeen: PASSAGES

The funeral services were held on the twenty-ninth, and the little church was nearly full. Mom had many friends! Mary played the piano and sang some hymns. After the funeral, the immediate family drove to the North Fork campground, where Mom and Dad had spent so much time, and buried some of Mom's ashes near their campsite. The only sound was that of the White River, flowing down the valley.

I could see it all: the camp trailer, Mom sitting outside in her lawn chair with her faithful plastic glass filled with beer. She visited with fellow campers while Dad and his friend, Ollie, were fishing. There were so many good times experienced here by the kids with their grandma! Damn! It was so hard to believe she was gone!

That night, Donna's son, Jason—who was about twenty—gave a stand-up skit that was the "roasting" of Dad. He told of the many pranks the grandkids, Donna, and Caryl had pulled on Dad over the years, and retold the stories that Mom had shared about him.

Dad had purchased an old '62 Cadillac that had given him lots of trouble, and the kids, Donna, and Caryl drew big lemons on posterboard and taped them to the doors. When Dad spotted them, he said, "*Up* ya!" Jason then gave a complete demonstration of Dad getting one of his shirts off a clothes hanger. Mom always buttoned the shirts on the hangers, and Dad had failed to unbutton the shirt completely to get it off. For several seconds, he fought the hanger, trying to get it through the neck hole of the shirt. When he finally got the shirt free, he threw the hanger on the floor and yelled, "Take that, you son of a bitch!" Everyone cracked up, laughing!

Jason also reenacted the story that Grandma had told them about what Dad did when Meeker first got TV. People either had rabbit ears or an outside antenna, and the picture was usually so snowy that they taped red or green cellophane across the screen to make it more watchable. Time after time, there would be problems receiving the signal from the tower on Black Diamond Mountain north of town, and we frequently just had static on the screen. Dad would jump out of his chair, walk over to the TV, and pound the top of it with his left hand. At the same time, he'd turn the channel selector knob with the other hand—back and forth, left and right—yelling, "You no-good Japan-made son of a bitch!" "Don, knock that shit off!" Mom would yell at him. "You're going to *ruin* our TV!" Sometimes, the TV would actually start receiving the signal again when Dad did this, so that just encouraged him. "Got it, Betty Marie!" he'd declare. "*You* didn't fix it, Don," she'd shake her head, "the signal just came back in!" But Dad was always convinced that his crude repairman actions had taken care of the problem!

Jason brought down the house with this story, and he continued with the skit, giving a list of Dad's favorite sayings—"Tough shitski," "Drier than a popcorn fart," "Columbus took a chance," "If you think that, your ass is sucking swamp water"—and went on to remind us of what Dad would say when the grandkids were cutting up—"Quit! Quit! Quit! Quit!"—over and over, as fast as he could!

The skit lifted my mood, so I decided to give a demo of a story that Mom had never allowed Dad—or me—to live down. It happened when Dad and I were alone, as Mom had gone to visit relatives over the weekend and Donna went with her. I was probably around fourteen. "What's that smell, Dad?" I had asked. "I'm not sure, Son, but it smells like shit." We both started searching for the source of the smell. Finally, we found a spot where Tom, our cat, had crawled in behind the TV and left a big dump. Damn! You talk about stink!

We slid the TV out and got a roll of paper towels. "I don't think I can clean it up, Dad—it just stinks too bad!" "Here, Son, I'll do it," he said. *Uh, uh, uh*...Dad started gagging and quickly retreated. I volunteered to try: *uh, uh!* I had the same result, and I quickly backed out from behind the TV. "I'll try it again, Son." *Uh, uh!* Same thing again. "To hell with it!" Dad declared. "We'll leave it for your mom!" We slid the TV back into place, looked at one another, and busted out laughing.

The following day, when Mom got back from her visit, I told her what had happened. "You guys get that TV slid out, *now*!" she demanded. While she cleaned it up, she said, "I can't believe you guys! I just *can't* believe you didn't clean this up!" "It stunk too bad, Betty Marie!" Dad said, defending us.

While I told this story, Dad laughed hard, as did everyone else. For a while, anyway, we remembered all the things we loved about Mom and shared them with each other, and that made losing her a little more bearable.

Before we left Meeker, Dad and I had a long talk. He insisted he was fine and that he'd be okay. I was glad he had his dog, Spud, there by his side, and that Ollie, his old fishing buddy, stopped by nearly every day to check on him. They'd be spending a lot more time at Lake Avery now.

Chapter Seventeen: *PASSAGES*

A few days later, Mary returned with me to Fort Morgan to spend three weeks. I was so glad she was there, as I knew it would take time to get over losing Mom. No more phone calls from her, no more letters!

I spoke with Dad at least twice a week. There were several people helping him out; a friend, Kathy Warren, picked up his laundry every week and changed his bedding as needed, and Linda Bishop cleaned and prepared meals for him. In mid-July, I spent some time with him. We fished and I cooked for him, which Dad loved, and he reminded me that hunting season was closing in. "Hell, Dad—it's three months away!" I declared. "It'll be here before you know it, Son!" he replied. Hunting season did soon arrive, and it was a successful time for us, with a bull and a cow elk in Dad's freezer. Yes, we did have a good time hunting, but it hurt not having Mom around. I missed hearing her voice coming from the bedroom in early morning when she said, "Good luck!"

Late that fall, Dad frequently called, all fired up over football season. He was an avid Broncos fan, and when they won, he declared what great ball they had played; when they lost, he'd say, "If they'd been playing for shit, they wouldn't have gotten a smell!" No one knew where he came up with those sayings!

Time passed; Amber married her longtime boyfriend, Kaifah Detoles, and continued taking classes in nursing at the University of Utah. She was quite content, and that made me happy for her. My job at the power plant went on like clockwork, and the years seemed to slide by. Dad did well, living on his own, and Mary visited as often as she could via Amtrak. She and I had taken a trip to Estes Park, Colorado, staying at the Travelodge. We just loved it there and made reservations to visit again the next year. Dad and I continued our annual elk hunts on the Rienau Ranch and were always successful. I often thought about packing a U-Haul trailer and moving back to the Western Slope, but I knew I was still stuck in this good-paying job for the time being.

It was now 1999, and Mary and I decided to go to Salt Lake City for Amber's graduation in nursing. It was the first time I'd been on a college campus, and I was blown away by the size of it! We went from one complex to another, in and out of classrooms. I met many of her professors and a few of her friends. It was a special time with my Bear!

Several months later, in September, Mary and I returned to Estes Park for a three-day getaway. On our visit the year before, we had explored Rocky Mountain National Park from every angle, investigating all the roads and where they led. It was so beautiful! There were many towering, jagged peaks, most well over 11,000 feet. Pine trees blanketed the rugged slopes that were dotted with aspen ablaze in their fall colors. Crystal-clear streams rushed down the steep mountainsides. At the Travelodge, where we had stayed previously, we were awakened around midnight by the sounds of a bull elk bugling. We stepped out onto our patio and below us, less than fifty yards away, were picnic tables, chairs, and a large meadow. With the moon nearly full, we could see a herd and glassed them with the binoculars.

There was a large bull in the herd, trying to keep his harem together. Close by in the timber, another big bull was bugling, and the herd bull would answer him. Finally, here came the bull from the forest, trotting across the meadow towards the herd. The herd bull started running towards him: *crack*! They crashed head-on! In the moonlight, we watched them pushing each other, twisting their racks back and forth. They ended up near the picnic tables and knocked over some of the chairs. Finally, the herd bull won out and the challenger trotted away. The entire herd gradually left the meadow, and we crawled back into bed, listening to the bugles go on into the night.

The following morning, our alarm clock went off at 4:30. We'd hardly slept! We loaded our gear and headed for the park: we wanted to be there at daybreak so we could see the elk. We drove from one pretty spot to another, watching herd after herd. At noon, we picnicked and continued exploring, then we headed back to our room at dusk.

The next day, we arrived in the park at the crack of dawn. I took pictures with my 35mm camera and Mary was operating the camcorder. By eleven, the elk had bedded down in the timber and we'd gotten some great pictures of them. Later, about two in the afternoon, Mary said, "Listen—I just heard a bugle!" We sat quietly and, sure enough—*ooooeeee, uh-uh-uh*—we heard him just up the canyon from us. Seconds later, another bull answered him. "Let's go up there and see if we can get close to them," she suggested. "Maybe you can get your dream picture." "Okay," I agreed, "let's see how far we can drive up the dirt road."

After a half mile, we pulled off and got out to listen. The sound of the bulls bugling was about another half mile from us. We got the cameras and started walking towards them on a trail that we'd found. Minutes later, one of the bulls bugled, the sound echoing off the canyon walls. I thought we were very close now—within seventy-five yards. We moved slowly on the path and, after another fifty yards, passed beneath some pines and through thick brush, stepping carefully to avoid the twigs. I stopped and whispered, "I can smell them." Mary nodded and whispered back, "So can I." The trickling sound of a nearby creek was all that could be heard. I figured that the elk were very close to the creek.

Snap...crack! We could hear an elk coming through the brush, straight towards us. Oh, shit! A big bull came crashing out of the undergrowth, right on the same trail that we were on! He stopped about fifteen yards from me, his eyes bloodshot and glazed, slobber dripping off his chin. Under his gaze, my legs turned to rubber. I glanced over my shoulder to motion to Mary to get back. Hell, she wasn't behind *me*—she was behind a big pine tree about fifteen yards away!

I slowly turned my head back to see what the bull was going to do. The white tips of his antlers glistened in the sun. I saw his huge shoulder muscles tighten up and I knew he was going to charge! He was either going to put some of those sharp antler points through my body or knock me down and trample me! Damn! I'd heard about elk charging people during the rut—I just never thought it would happen to *me*! For the longest minute of my life, the elk and I stood frozen, staring at each other.

All of a sudden, he swung his massive rack around and walked away, disappearing into the thick brush. Oh...my...God! I let out a long sigh of relief and walked back to where Mary was hiding. "Damn, that was close!" "I really thought he was going to take you!" she said. "So did I!" I laughed nervously. Hell, my hands were still shaking!

We talked for a few minutes, then the two bulls started bugling again. We really wanted to get some pictures of them, so—perhaps against good judgment—we moved slowly down the trail toward them. We came to a small clearing in the willows near the creek where we had a perfect view of a large herd. I sat down and rested my elbows on my knees so the camcorder would be perfectly still. The bull that almost charged me—a perfect six point—stepped out on the other side of a beaver pond not thirty yards away, stretched out his neck, and let a bugle rip. Instantly, another bull answered. Some young bulls, mainly spikes and two points, came out of the willows and headed for the herd of cows standing knee deep in the beaver pond. The camcorder caught the action as the herd bull jumped off the bank, lowered his head, and charged the young bulls! Mud and water flying, he chased them for several yards, then returned to the herd and let out a long, loud bugle followed by several grunts.

Soon, a big five-point bull showed up, and I knew he was the one that had been bugling. All hell broke loose then! The six point charged the five point, and although the five point was big, he was no match for the herd bull. He turned and ran back into the brush. I continued to film the cows and calves for another fifteen minutes before they moved on. They moved around in the beaver pond and along the creek's banks, talking back and forth—a very unique sound.

That evening, we headed for the motel, talking excitedly about the encounter we'd had. We spent one more day in the park, getting more great pictures and movies, then had a romantic dinner that evening. A fitting end of a great getaway!

At home again, I spent time looking for a quality place to develop my film. I found a professional photographer in Fort Morgan who recommended I use the same business he did—ProLab in Denver—to process my film. He supplied me with order forms and envelopes and I got to work. When I received the pictures from ProLab, I was astonished! Such high-quality processing! I selected the best and had 11x14 prints made; they were so beautiful that I decided to have them custom-framed, and that really added to their beauty. When Mary arrived in December, I had five framed pictures lined up on the couch. "Oh, my word, Danny," she said. "The pictures are spectacular! You have a special eye, and I think you should get more material, set up your own business, and start selling them." "Really?" I asked. "Sure, honey—why not? They're so good!" Smiling, I said, "I might just do that."

New Year's 2000 rolled in and in February, Dad called. He would soon be in the hospital, getting hip replacement surgery. Mary and I got to the hospital just hours after Dad was admitted. "I'll tell you what," he said, "I'm not going to be in this damned hospital very long!" I started laughing. "Dad, you have to stay here until the doctor releases you." He hated hospitals and hadn't been treated in one for thirty-six years, since the accident with his foot.

The surgery went well, but he ended up with an infection and had to stay for nearly two weeks. I called him every day and got to hear his rants, which were always on the order of "It'll be a cold day in hell when I ever go to the hospital again!" Once he was home, he bounced back quickly and was soon into his normal routine.

In late spring, on May 6, Chris graduated from Colorado State University with a bachelor's in psychology. He'd decided to take some time off from college and then go back to pursue his doctorate.

I was proud of Chris, and even though we were on friendly terms, we'd never had the same sort of relationship that Dad and I did, and that made me sad at times. The divorce and not being around him full-time had taken its toll, and I knew there was no way to recoup what was lost. Still, I tried to make the best of it.

In June, Kila had another child—a girl named Aleise. All was well with the family, and Mary and I went to Junction to see them just days later. Another doll! Her brother, Jayce, seemed to be happy to have a little sister.

During the summer, Dad called to say he was using a cane now. "I took one spill, Son, so I thought it might be best." Months later, he and I were on our way to hunt on Rienau's land. At daybreak, we parked at our same spot, and George and Austin met us then went on to their hunting spots. I got my gear together and started walking toward where I normally waited to watch for elk, then stopped to load my rifle. I turned around to see what Dad was doing and tears filled my eyes: there he was, now seventy-six years old, walking across the meadow, cane in his right hand and rifle in his left! I admired him so, my hero! His love and passion for elk hunting went far beyond belief, and our day once again ended in success. Dad's freezer was full of meat that would sustain him through another winter.

In February 2001, the company gave out bonus checks, which were always substantial. I banked every one of my bonuses and, over time, had a large sum of money in my 401K. I was constantly running numbers and accounted for everything I spent. The name of the game was *save, save, save*! If I could put aside enough, I would be able to pack up that U-Haul and get out of town!

Later, in May, I decided to follow Mary's advice and open up my photography business, "Danny's Shutter." Immediately, I sold some pictures. No, I wasn't going to get rich! But I loved photography and it would help cover some of my expenses.

The next few years passed quickly. Dad and I continued our annual fishing and hunting trips and Mary continued to visit me via Amtrak. In January 2003, she called to say that she'd found the cutest little dog—a poodle-Chihuahua mix—and that she wanted to adopt it. I told her I didn't think she'd be able to come visit me on Amtrak then, but she called me back the following day, saying that it was fine with Amtrak as long as she caged the dog for the trip. So in mid-March, I waited at the train station for Mary and Taffy. When they arrived, I grabbed the cage and Mary's suitcases and knelt down to check out this little dog. What a cutie! Taffy came to me and I picked her up; in the dim light I could see her bobbed tail, wagging back and forth. She was so light that she felt like a feather, and her fur was soft. She licked me on the cheek, and it melted my heart! I could see now why Mary just had to adopt her!

Taffy, eight weeks old.
PHOTO BY MARY HARTWIG

Chapter Seventeen: PASSAGES

When we got home, we were both beat from a long day. Mary had just spent eleven hours on the train and I'd been up since 3:00 a.m., working the day shift. Mary put Taffy in the middle of the bed and we crawled in. I gently placed my hand on Taffy and she snuggled right in. She knew she belonged there! Each afternoon when I got home from work, Mary would be waiting for me, holding Taffy. During their two-week stay, I fell in love with that dog! It was a sad day when they left, as I knew I wouldn't see them again till the end of May.

Mid-April, I got a package from Dad just a few days before my fifty-fifth birthday. It was two Motorola walkie-talkies! I called him and said, "Dad, you didn't need to get me anything!" "Son," he said, "I thought they might come in handy when we're elk hunting, and that maybe you and Mary could use them when you go to Rocky Mountain National Park." "What a great idea, Dad... Thanks!" We talked for several minutes—he was doing fine—then said goodbye.

In October, on the seventeenth, I was at Dad's, getting ready for opening season the next morning. George and Austin Rienau came by to visit, and George said, "You guys will have the place to yourself tomorrow morning, as I have to help my neighbor with the hunters who are coming on his land, and Austin has a new job. I'll swing over to the ranch sometime around eleven to see how you're doing." "Sounds like a plan, George," I said. "Oh, by the way," he added, "the hunters on my land during first season saw a big six-point bull two different times, but no one could get a shot at him. I'm sure it's the same one I saw in September during rut. He's really a dandy!" Piqued about the idea of seeing the six point, I said, "I hope we see him tomorrow, George." "You just might," he replied.

The next morning, Dad and I were really wound up. We had high hopes that maybe we'd get a chance at that six-point bull. We pulled up to our parking place and I grabbed my gear, along with a walkie-talkie, and whispered, "Good luck, Dad." "And good luck to you, Son!" he replied. At my sitting spot, I watched a beautiful sunrise, not a cloud to be seen in the dark-blue sky. The heavy frost that covered the grass and shrubbery sparkled like diamonds in the bright sunshine. What a gorgeous October morning!

"Son, can you hear me?" I heard Dad say. I pulled out the walkie-talkie, keyed in the mike, and quietly said, "Yeah, Dad." "There's a herd of elk just west of me, going through some thick oak brush, and they're headed your direction. I think it might be best if you walked over the ridge from where you are so you can watch the valley towards the south." Dad was seventy-nine now and still as sharp as could be, so I heeded his advice. "Okay, Dad. Will do," I responded.

I walked over the ridge and found a good spot to see the valley and oak brush-covered hill south of me. About 350 yards away, I saw an elk walk through a small clearing. I put my rifle to my shoulder to scope the area, watching several pass through the same clearing. I guessed there were about ten in the herd. Suddenly, I got a split-second view of an elk that was trailing about twenty yards behind the herd. I couldn't swear to it, but I thought I saw a big rack on it.

I made my way to a big oak brush bush and rested my rifle across one of its limbs, taking my gun off safety. Had I just seen the six-point bull? "Buck fever" was setting in! Minutes later, I spotted the lead cow walking out into a meadow about 200 yards below me. Soon, the rest of the herd followed, coming out of the oak brush in single file. I counted ten cows and calves, but no bull! I began to wonder if my eyes were playing tricks on me, when out of the brush came a large bull. He was facing me, so I couldn't shoot him. I needed to wait till he turned broadside.

Snap! Damn it! Of all the things that could happen, the branch that I had my rifle resting on broke! I scrambled to find another rest, and when the bull turned, I sighted him in and boom! Rotten son of a bitch! I missed him, just barely shooting over his back. The bull started trotting then and I quickly yanked the bolt back and slammed another round in. *Boom!* The bull went down, but I was disgusted with myself because I knew I'd hit him too high. I could see that he was about to get up, so I put in yet another round and ran to an oak bush that was closer; this time I had a perfect rest. Just as he got to his feet, I shot and he went down again.

I only had one more round in my rifle, so I decided to reload, just in case he got up again. My hand trembled as I fumbled around for it in my pocket. I reloaded and walked down the ridge, keeping an eye on the elk. When I was about a hundred yards away, I sat down and lit a cigarette, hoping it would calm me down. After a few minutes, I continued across the meadow to where the elk was lying. It was the six-point bull! He wasn't a record, but he was definitely a trophy that I'd have mounted!

I called Dad on the walkie-talkie. "Dad, can you hear me?" "Yeah, Son. What'd you get?" "A big six point!" "Are you shittin' me?" "No, Dad—I'm serious!" I told him where I was and he said he'd bring the pickup to me. He arrived in just minutes, and when he got a good look at the bull, he slapped me on the shoulder and said, "You did it, my boy! Mercy, he's a big bull!"

I took several pictures of the elk, and once I'd finished gutting him, we sat down and enjoyed our coffee while listening to the radio. About eleven, George drove in, and when he got to us, he smiled. "Looks like you had good luck! We'll winch the elk into the bed of my truck, then slide him into yours." In less than ten minutes, we had the bull in the back of Dad's pickup—a vast improvement over the grunting and groaning we normally did! We told George we'd see him the next morning, then wound our way down the road towards the highway. At Dad's age, I was grateful that'd we'd gotten the trophy bull, because it would probably be one of the last hunts when we'd bag one that size. We went out the next two mornings, but we never saw another elk.

Another year, 2004, arrived. Kila brought a third child into the world—this one with her new husband, Jesse Watkins—and they named her Jasmine. That fall, in September, I wanted to do a special celebration for Dad's eightieth birthday, but everyone was too busy to get together. Donna and Caryl ended up taking him to Sleepy Cat for a rib-eye steak dinner, which he really enjoyed. The next month, Dad and I hunted on Rienau's land once again, getting a cow elk for his freezer.

Later that October, on the twenty-third, was my ten-year anniversary without alcohol. It was hard to believe it had been that long! Mary was proud of me, and I was so glad to have her in my life; letting go of alcohol was worth it! She and Taffy continued to visit as often as possible, and when I got my bonus in February 2005, I finally had the "magic number" I'd been waiting for! Gratifying? Hell yes, it was! But I'd gone through so much mental anguish over the years that I really wondered if it was worth it.

I was emotionally exhausted. Physically, my lower back was killing me; having to be on my feet on concrete or steel ten to twelve hours a day had caused severe back pain. Basically, I was just flat-ass burnt out. I started having trouble sleeping, and I constantly thought about moving back to the Western Slope and looking for a part-time job.

At the end of July in 2005, Dad and I went fishing on Veryl's land. There was one spot where he could sit on the edge of the bank and cast without it being a tremendous effort. We yelled, laughed, and had a ball, each landing three beautiful rainbows. We decided that was enough and sat back in our lawn chairs in the shade of the cottonwood trees. "I've decided I'm going to leave Fort Morgan," I said. "You know, Son, I can't say that I blame you," Dad replied. "Have you told Mary?" "Not yet. I've been thinking about it for a long, long time, and I want to tell her in person." A few days later, I left Meeker and drove to Delta to talk to Mary about my decision. "You know how much I love you, Danny. I'll gladly support whatever you want to do," she said. My eyes filled as I wrapped my arms around her. "It's time, honey! It's time!"

Monday morning, I called the plant to put in my resignation, and on Tuesday afternoon, Mary, Taffy, and I arrived at my trailer. By Sunday evening, we'd packed up most of the trailer, boxes stacked and labeled. My friend Jim Nolan, who was now CEO of Colorado Energy Management, made sure I received a sweet financial package. All of my friends, and everyone I knew in Fort Morgan, were so kind and helpful, making the move much easier.

The following Monday, Sam Moots took me to pick up the U-Haul. When I put the key in the ignition, I laughed as I said, "You beautiful son of a gun! I've been waiting forever to crank you up!" When I got to the trailer, Mary and Taffy came out to greet me. "Yahoo!" I yelled, and Mary started laughing.

That evening, we said our goodbyes to the many friends we'd both made while I'd lived in Fort Morgan, and the next morning, we loaded up the last of my things. Mary and I made one last pass through the place, and when we walked across the kitchen floor, our footsteps echoed with the trailer's emptiness. We stopped and put our arms around each other, crying. Mary said, "We had so many great times within these walls over the past twelve-and-a-half years!" "I know, doll," I said.

She picked up Taffy and we walked out the front door, locking it for the last time. A few minutes later, we were on I-76, heading west. As I

Chapter Seventeen: Passages

watched Fort Morgan disappear in the rearview mirror, I knew I was leaving as a winner! With Mary's help, the grace of God, and sheer determination, I'd won the battle against booze and was now fulfilling my dream. And bless my dear Mary—I'll bet she'd ridden Amtrak sixty times over the past eleven years!

The following day, we unloaded most of my things in a storage unit and, over the next few weeks, I settled in and helped with the yard work around Mary's place. We drove to Grand Junction, getting together with Kila and her family. I was happier than I'd been in years!

In September, it was time to visit with Dad, so I kissed Mary goodbye and drove to Meeker to spend a week with him. When I walked through the front door, he said, "There's the fisherman!" I laughed and walked over to give him a hug. "So how's it feel to be back on the Western Slope, Son?" he asked. "It's pure heaven, Dad, and it's so darn nice not to have to get up at three in the morning, or not get home till one in the morning. I'm happy—really happy!" "Good," he said, "I'm glad to hear that. I know it's been rough."

The next day, we were off early, driving to our favorite fishing spot at Lake Avery. We sat in our lawn chairs and I rigged up the fishing rods. "I'm getting to be an old bastard, Son," Dad said. For a few seconds, I was at a loss for words. "Ah, Dad—it happens to all of us." "Remember the good ol' days at Big Beaver?" he asked. I looked towards the mountain range to the north where Big Beaver was and said, "Yeah, Dad...that place was special!"

We lapsed back into silence and, while watching my fishing line, I thought about what he had said. Yes, he was getting old—tomorrow he'd be eighty-one! Mentally, he was very sharp, but physically, Father Time was catching up. He was now shuffling along with his cane instead of walking, and it was getting hard for him to get out of his recliner. But what really bothered me most was that there wasn't a damn thing I could do about it! Yet he was still willing to get up early to go fishing and hunting. He was an amazing guy!

The next day, I handed him a birthday card with a little bit of money in it. We decided to take the day off and just go sightseeing up South Fork, taking in the fall colors. We didn't see any elk, but we heard bugling a long way off. We celebrated his birthday that evening at the Meeker Café with a couple of rib-eye steaks. It'd been a great day together.

With the arrival of mid-October came a new child: Amber had her first baby, a girl named Celeste. Amber and Kaifah had moved to Phoenix, so I wasn't sure when I'd see my new grandchild.

Just a few weeks later, I was back at Dad's, ready for our annual hunt. "Are you ready, Son?" he asked. "I sure am, Dad!" I exclaimed. "I think we're going to fill up on opening day," he said. Laughing, I replied, "I don't think we'll get *both* elk in one day, Dad!" "I just feel lucky this year, my boy!" The next morning we were up at four, and I started loading the pickup when I heard Dad call to me from the living room. "Son, would you please help me?" I came bustling in to see what he needed. "I'm having trouble getting my boot laces around these darned grommets." I could see that he couldn't bend over far enough to easily lace them, so—kneeling on the floor—I laced and tied them for him.

While loading our gear, I had started the pickup to warm it. Damn, it was cold! Dad had made sure Spud had plenty of food and water, telling him he'd be back after a while, "Partner." Once we were outside, Dad asked me to get a stepstool from the bed of the pickup to make it easier for him to get in. As I held his right arm so he would be better balanced, he got in then said, "Boy, that made it a lot easier! Thank you, Son." I loaded the stool in the back and we got on the road. This was our forty-ninth year of big game hunting together!

On Rienau's ranch, I was getting ready to pull into our spot when Dad said, "Would you please park where I can sit and watch? I don't think I'm going to walk to my sitting place this year." That shook me up a little bit, but I said, "Sure, Dad," and found a place that would give him a great view. I grabbed my things and headed on to my sitting area, but the only elk I saw were too far away to shoot. I returned to the truck about eleven, and Dad said he'd seen some cows on a distant mountain while glassing through the binoculars. We decided to give it up for the day and just have lunch and go home.

The next morning was the same: a few cows a long way away. We had lunch and then Dad said, "I don't know how much longer I'm going to be able to hunt." A wave of fear rippled through me and I choked up; tears began trickling down my cheeks, but I managed to say, "When you're done, Dad, so am I." "No, Son...I don't want you to give it up. Hell, you're still a

Chapter Seventeen: PASSAGES

young man!" I got my handkerchief and wiped away the tears. "You know, Dad, it just wouldn't be the same if you weren't here with me." For several minutes, there wasn't a word spoken; we just listened to the radio. "Shall we call it a day and try again tomorrow, Dad?" "Yeah, Son, that sounds like a plan." I could see that he was really tired.

The following day saw a change in our luck. I shot a five-point bull, and just after cleaning it, George showed up to help with loading. I told him that I thought we'd settle for one this year. He said that we were welcome to keep hunting, but I assured him that Dad wouldn't need more, and that we appreciated being able to hunt on his land.

Minutes later, we drove through Rienau's gate; I closed it, wrapped the chain around it, and hooked the latch. Pausing, I stared up the canyon, looking at the oak brush-covered mountains. It'd been one hell of a run, but I knew that Dad and I would never go elk hunting again!

The following morning, I told Dad that Mary and I would be back for Thanksgiving and gave him a hug goodbye. The month passed quickly, and we were soon back at Dad's with two apple pies that Mary had baked. After everyone greeted each other, I showed the pies to Dad. "You know I *love* your apple pie, Mary," he said. That night we had an elk steak supper and chatted the evening away. Dad said that Uncle Fenton and Donna were driving over from Denver in late December to take him to stay at Donna's till after New Year's. "Donna is going to take me to Blackhawk so we can do some gambling," he announced. "Do you feel lucky, Dad?" I asked. "You'd better believe it, Son!" We all laughed at this, because most of the time, Dad felt lucky! Two days later, we were ready to go back to Delta. Dad and I hugged and said how much we loved each other, then he stood outside, waving goodbye as we left.

By mid-December, Mary's place was adorned with Christmas decorations. With lights inside and out, I'd plug everything in every evening, just before dark. It had been so many years since I'd really enjoyed the holidays!

Kila had invited us to Grand Junction for Christmas, and Mary had agreed to fry a big batch of chicken for dinner, along with making two apple pies and two cherry pies. Chris and Caryl would be visiting, and Amber and her family would also be there. It had been a long time since I'd spent Christmas with my kids! And most special of all, I was going to see my new granddaughter—Celeste—for the first time!

We arrived at noon, and Amber came rushing towards me holding Celeste. "What a little doll!" I declared. Amber's face was glowing with pride. We brought in all the presents and passed them out to the kids. It was a perfect day and that evening, my heart was filled with joy when we said goodbye. I wish it had lasted longer!

Just after Christmas, Dad called. He said, "I hit a lick, Son!" "Really?" I asked. "I sure did," he said. "I won $370 on a nickel slot machine at Blackhawk!" "Wow! Good for you, Dad!" I laughed. "Just shithouse luck, my boy!" he affirmed, using his usual off-the-cuff explanation. I laughed again, then he passed the phone to Donna. She said they'd take him back to Meeker January 2. "He's been having a great time," she said, "but he wants to get back home to see his little partner!"

A few months later, in February 2006, Dad called, very excited: he'd gotten his cow elk application in the mail. "If I send it to you, will you fill it out for me?" "Of course, Dad," I said. He was afraid he might mess it up. I got it a few days later, filled it out, put a money order in with it, and sent it back to Dad to sign. He called me when he sent it in: he was looking forward to hunting again so much! Maybe—just maybe—we *would* go on one more hunt!

Mid-March, winter finally released its stranglehold and warmer weather became the norm. Now I had spring fever! We drove to Grand Junction and bought two new lawn chairs and Power Bait for Dad and me. In just one more month, the ice would be off Lake Avery, and we had to be ready to go fishing!

Days later, on March twentieth, Mary and I got home from shopping in the afternoon, and there were two messages on the answering machine. She pushed the Play button: "Danny, this is Fenton. You need to call the Meeker Police Department." My legs buckled as he left the phone number, and I grabbed the counter to keep from falling. I knew something had happened to Dad. "No! No!" I cried.

The next message was from Donna, screaming and bawling: "Call me! It's about Dad!" Fear ripped through my body as I dialed her number. She picked up the phone and started crying, "Dad's gone, Danny! Dad's gone!" "No! No! No!" I yelled. I slowly calmed down enough to get out, "Where'd they find him, Donna?" "I don't know! Fenton told me that when he tried calling Dad, a police officer answered the phone. They'd just driven his car home and were leaving his keys on the table. He said Dad had passed away and was at the hospital."

Chapter Seventeen: *Passages*

We both started crying again, so much so that we could hardly talk. I finally said I'd call the hospital to get the details. When I hung up, Mary held me and whispered, "I'm so sorry, Danny." I started crying hard again, and I thought I was going to pass out! Mary helped me sit down at the kitchen table, rubbing my shoulders. Gradually, I could start thinking again, and a few minutes later, I called the hospital. A lady told me it would be best if I talked to Mike Washburn, one of the paramedics who had brought Dad in. She gave me his number and I called him. When he answered, I told him who I was, and he related what had happened. He said someone had called in about 12:30 and told dispatch they'd found Dad outside the senior center, slumped over the steering wheel of his car. Mike said, "We arrived at your dad's car at 12:40 and tried to revive him, then took him to the hospital. The doctor worked on him for several more minutes, but he was pronounced dead at 1:40 p.m. I'm so sorry." I thanked him for his effort and for talking to me, then I called Donna back to tell her what I'd learned. We talked and cried. Then, suddenly, I remembered Dad's little partner. "Where's Spud?" I asked. Donna said she'd called one of our friends, Kathy Warren, and asked her to pick him up. She said that she and Caryl would leave Denver at five for Meeker, and I told her that we'd get there Wednesday morning.

It was time to call the kids. Amber was the only one who didn't already know, and she fell to pieces. They all worshipped the ground their papa walked on, and it was a sad and difficult time for all of us.

I brewed coffee and went outside to smoke while Mary started supper. "I don't feel like eating," I said. "Well, you really need to eat *something*," she insisted. "Probably so, but I'm just not hungry." We talked till nearly eleven, and she held me when I broke down again. I was so lucky to have her—such a caring, special lady! Taffy sensed that there was something wrong, and she kept wanting to get up on my lap to comfort me.

I stayed up that night, as there was no way I could go to sleep. I wanted to go outside, but the temperature had dropped like a rock, so I put on my insulated coveralls. Did it ever feel good to be outdoors! Minutes turned to hours: the image of Dad slumped over his steering wheel kept flashing through my mind as tears streamed down my cheeks.

At 3:00 a.m., Mary came out to check on me. "Are you alright?" I could hear the concern in her voice. "Not really, honey," I said. "I'm just doing a lot of thinking." "I wish you'd come to bed." "I'm just not sleepy, honey. I'll see you when you get up in the morning." With that, she went back in the house.

Daybreak found me still sitting at the table outside, sipping coffee. I'd gone through three pots during the night, and I had no idea how many cigarettes I'd smoked. I felt like someone had put a blowtorch to my eyes, they burned so badly from crying! My heart felt as though there was a big piece of it missing now. Odds were that it would feel that way the rest of my life. Over the past fifty-plus years, Dad and I had gone on hundreds and hundreds of trips together. But no more! The excruciating pain I felt at losing him was nearly paralyzing.

At seven, Mary told me she was going to fix breakfast. She reminded me that I needed to eat something, and this time I didn't argue with her; it had been a long time since I'd had any food.

After I managed to get down some breakfast, I made a list of things that I knew had to be done over the next few days. I called friends of Dad's and asked if they would be pallbearers at his funeral. They were all glad to accept, expressing their condolences at his passing. I talked to Chris, and he was going to be one of the pallbearers.

The day went by more quickly than I would've thought. My tired, hurting body found the bed at nine o'clock and Mary tucked me in, saying, "I love you, honey. Get some rest now, because you're going to need it." Moments after my head hit the pillow, I drifted off.

Early the next morning, we dropped Taffy off with a friend then drove to Meeker, where we checked in at the White River Inn. From there, we went on to Dad's. When I spotted his pickup, tears welled up and streamed down my cheeks.

Donna, Caryl, and Kila were there. Lots of hugs and tears went around and around, and I held Donna for a long time. Not many words were spoken. Caryl said, "Chris will be here this afternoon, and Amber and some of the other kids will get in tomorrow." I saw George Rienau pull in so I went out to meet him. We had a long talk out by Dad's pickup. "If you need *anything*," he said, "I'm just a phone call away. I mean anything." I told him how much I appreciated the offer then said, "You know, I'll probably need some help moving the furniture out of the house." "Well, call me when you're ready," he reminded, then he said he'd see me later. What a good friend!

The rest of the day, the girls packed boxes. Mary insisted on fixing supper for everyone. I didn't do much, just spent a lot of time leaning across the hood of Dad's pickup—thinking and greeting neighbors, friends, and relatives who stopped in to give their condolences or bring food. I was dreading going through Dad's things and avoided it like crazy—especially the hunting rifles, fishing rods, and his clothing. There was just no way I could do it—not right now!

At around seven, we all sat down at the supper table to enjoy elk steak, potatoes and gravy, corn, and salad. Mary had chosen the meal to honor Dad, and she even baked an apple pie! Here's to you, Dad!

By noon on Friday, the place was bare. I gave Dad's pickup to George. He told me anytime I wanted to use it, to feel welcome. I was relieved we'd found Spud a nice home, too.

Everything seemed to be falling into place. Donna, Mary, Caryl, and I met with the funeral director three times and the pastor twice, and flowers had been ordered. Dad would have a nice funeral held in the Methodist Church on March 25, 2006.

Mary and I went to the funeral home that evening to see Dad. As we neared the casket, my heart started pounding. Here was my hero, the greatest guy I'd ever known! He was wearing his favorite brown Pendleton shirt and Levis and had his Denver Bronco ball cap on. I put my hand on his folded hands; I could barely breathe. There was just no way to describe how emotionally desolate I felt at that moment. "I love you, Dad. I'll love you forever." Mary handed me one of Dad's and my favorite framed elk hunting pictures, and I placed it beside him. Bending over, I kissed him on the forehead and said goodbye.

The following day at 1:30, services began. There was a large crowd—Dad had touched many lives in Meeker over the years. I held up reasonably well till the funeral director started singing a song that he thought would be appropriate, Merle Haggard's "Someday We'll Look Back." It was like turning on a faucet when the tears gushed from my eyes. Mary rubbed my arm, trying to comfort me. When the song was over, it was time to go to the cemetery for graveside services. As we crossed the town bridge, I glanced down and saw a fishing hole where Dad and I had spent time when I was a young boy. More tears!

At the cemetery, the pallbearers placed the casket on a stand alongside the grave. The sun glistened off its pine wood as the pastor started speaking. I really didn't hear the words; I just stared up the White River Valley, picking out landmarks where Dad and I had spent so much time over nearly fifty years.

In a few minutes, services concluded and the crowd slowly dispersed. Mary and I walked to the casket and I put my right hand on top of it, said a silent prayer, and whispered, "Goodbye, Dad." My sister did the same.

The next morning, Mary and I said goodbye to everyone and checked out of the motel. We drove by Dad's one last time then headed for Delta. My mind was numb, the past six days nothing more than a jumbled hell! For me, the beautiful White River Valley would never be the same.

Just a few months later, more tragedy struck our family. Donna called, screaming and crying, "Jason's gone, Danny! He's gone!" As if losing Dad earlier in the year wasn't enough, my sister's oldest son had now been found dead. The humorous skit-giver at Dad's roasting, Jason was only twenty-eight years old and would have had a promising career as a lawyer if he had lived.

In September, Mom and Dad's headstone was finished and had been placed on their grave. I called Donna to let her know, and we decided to make reservations at the White River Inn for September 23, which would've been Dad's eighty-second birthday. She said she'd meet us at the motel around two.

When Mary and I arrived in Meeker, I decided to go on to the cemetery instead of checking in at the motel. I was anxious to see the headstone. At its top was CAMPBELL in bold black letters. Just below, on the left side, was a simulation of the North Fork campground and Dad and Mom's camp trailer, tall pines all around. The two of them were sitting in lawn chairs and Spud was lying by Dad's feet; a plume of smoke rose from the barbeque. On the right side of the stone was Dad and me fishing, and just a short distance away was a big six-point bull and a cow, mountain peaks rising in the background.

We stepped around to look at the other side of the stone. At the top were the words, "Thanks for the precious memories." In the center was CAMPBELL, and below that was Mom's name on the left with her birth date and the date she passed away. Dad's was on the right with the same information. Just above Mom's name was "Mom—Grandma"; above Dad's was "Dad—Papa."

Tears streamed again as I stared at their names etched in stone. "Son, always love and respect your parents, because once they're gone, they're gone forever." I was only eleven when Dad said that to me. Now those words were pounding in my mind! I knelt down on my knees and started sobbing. Mary rubbed my shoulders and, after I regained my composure, I decided we should go to the motel to check in and wait for Donna, who arrived mid-afternoon. We went back out to the cemetery then so she could see the headstone. We were all very pleased with how it had turned out and took several pictures of it. After we visited at the gravesite for a while, we returned to the motel and went out for supper.

It was a sleepless night for me, the image of the headstone flashing in my mind like a neon sign. It had been six months, but I was still in tremendous pain. For reasons I couldn't explain, I started thinking about Big Beaver. I thought maybe—just *maybe*—if I drove up there, it might help me achieve some kind of closure with Dad's passing.

The next morning, I told Mary about my thoughts and asked her if she'd mind taking me up to George's after Donna left so I could get Dad's pickup. I wanted to drive up to Big Beaver by myself. "Honey, if you think it'll help you, I'm all for it," she said. "I'll just wait at the motel." "I should be back by four o'clock," I said, not really knowing how long it would take.

Donna, Mary, and I had a nice visit, and around 10:30, Donna left for Denver and Mary took me to George's. It felt strange not having Dad with me sitting in the cab as I drove up the White River Valley. I passed by many of the places where we had fished the river over the years.

I turned off onto a dirt road at Lake Avery and started driving north. It would take about thirty minutes to find out if the old road still existed that would take me back to East Big Beaver. My heart pounded when I got to the old trail, still there after all these years! I turned onto it and headed east, only a few miles to go. Minutes later, I drove through a thick grove of aspens and spotted Beaver Knob. What a moment! I parked exactly where we always had and slowly got out. It was stone quiet, not a sound to be heard. Chills ran up my spine, and I felt as though I was standing on hallowed ground. It had been thirty-five years since I'd been here.

The fall colors were abundant, and I took it all in. Yellows, golds, oranges. The same towering dark-green pines covered the distant hillside.

The place was just as beautiful as it had always been. I walked to the edge of the Knob and looked down at the valley below. Tall yellow grasses and young aspen stood where the beaver ponds had once been, and it looked as though the beavers had been gone for many years.

A flood of memories rushed through my mind; tears trickled down my cheeks. My legs started to give way, so I sat down. I remembered the very first time I'd been here, fifty years ago next month...the day Larry and I watched Dad shoot the huge timber buck. The following year he shot a spike bull—I was so proud of him! I heard my first bull elk bugle here, and Dad explained the elk's annual rut to me.

And the time we heard the two bulls challenging each other, then saw them slam their racks together and fight! What a sight! I could see and hear the two of us, yelling and laughing as we chased the brook trout up and down the small creek not far from here. Trying to catch them with bare hands, we ended up soaking wet!

As clear as could be, I could see my hero, me following in his every footstep down the hill off this knob where I now sat. Dad was wearing his red-and-black checkered wool jacket and carrying his rifle. When we got to the beaver dam that we had to cross, he'd whisper, "Be careful, Son. There's lots of frost on the logs and they're slippery."

I started crying hard then. My hero was gone—gone forever! Minutes later the crying slowed, then I had a sudden thought: I should take pictures of this special place where Dad and I had spent so much time together. I knew I'd probably never be back here again, and I wanted to be able to look at the pictures to remember it. After I had taken several shots, I felt more at peace and decided it was time to leave.

As I sat in Dad's truck, I remembered many pitch-black mornings we had sat right here in his old '49 flatbed Chevy, waiting for daybreak—me sipping hot chocolate while he drank coffee. I'd stare at the twinkling stars in the dark sky, hoping and praying Dad would get a big bull elk. I could hear him saying, "I just feel lucky today, Son." "Really?" I'd answer. "Yeah. I think today is going to be our lucky day, my boy." Click! His Zippo lighter sounded out as he flipped open the cover. I could see the flame dancing in the darkness while he lit his Roi-Tan. Hell—for a brief moment, I could even *smell* the smoke!

I crossed my arms on the steering wheel and laid my head on them, sobbing. Oh, God—the pain I still felt! I cried and cried, emptying myself

Chapter Seventeen: *Passages* 297

of that vast reservoir of sadness. After several minutes, I raised my head and wiped the tears away. Looking over at the empty passenger seat, I said, "I miss ya, Dad!" I knew that wherever he was, he was missing me, too.

Dad's old pickup parked on Beaver Knob, September 24, 2006.
PHOTO BY DANNY W. CAMPBELL